Prose for Borges

*edited by
Charles Newman &
Mary Kinzie*

*consulting editor
Norman Thomas
di Giovanni*

a TriQuarterly book

*Northwestern
University Press*
EVANSTON 1974

Contents

Key to abbreviations

A   *The Aleph and Other Stories 1933-1969,* trans. Norman Thomas di Giovanni (New York: E. P. Dutton, 1970)

DT   *Dreamtigers,* trans. Mildred Boyer and Harold Morland (Austin: University of Texas Press, 1964)

DBR   *Doctor Brodie's Report,* trans. Norman Thomas di Giovanni (New York: E. P. Dutton, 1972)

F   *Ficciones,* ed. Anthony Kerrigan (New York: Grove Press, 1962)

L   *Labyrinths,* ed. Donald A. Yates and James E. Irby (New York: New Directions, 1962)

OI   *Other Inquisitions 1937-1952,* trans. Ruth L. C. Simms (New York: Simon and Schuster, 1968)

SP   *Selected Poems 1923-1967,* ed. Norman Thomas di Giovanni (New York: Delacorte, 1972)

Acknowledgments

Grateful acknowledgment is made for permission to reprint the following material:

Excerpts from "An Autobiographical Essay," from the book *The Aleph and Other Stories 1933-1969* by Jorge Luis Borges. Copyright © 1970 by Jorge Luis Borges and Norman Thomas di Giovanni. Published by E. P. Dutton & Co., Inc., and used with their permission.
"Sepulchral Inscription," "Jonathan Edwards 1703-1758," "Camden 1892," "To Leopoldo Lugones," and excerpts from "Matthew XXV:30," "Allusion to the Death of Colonel Francisco Borges 1833-1874," "Chess," "The Golem," "Isidoro Acevedo," "Conjectural Poem," "Rosas," "Ars Poetica," "The Other Tiger," "Everness," "Spinoza," "Compass," "The Cyclical Night," and "A Page To Commemorate Colonel Suarez, Victor at Junin," from *Jorge Luis Borges: Selected Poems 1923-1967*, edited by Norman Thomas di Giovanni. English translations copyright © 1968, 1969, 1970, 1971, 1972 by Emece Editores, S.A., and Norman Thomas di Giovanni. Reprinted by permission of Seymour Lawrence/Delacorte Press.
Excerpts from "Pierre Menard, Author of the *Quixote*," "The Garden of Forking Paths," "The God's Script," "The Secret of the Phoenix," and smaller selections from Jorge Luis Borges, *Labyrinths*. Copyright © 1962, 1964 by New Directions Publishing Corporation. Reprinted by permission of New Directions Publishing Corporation.
Excerpts from Jorge Luis Borges, *Other Inquisitions*, translated by Ruth L. C. Simms (University of Texas Press, 1964), reprinted by permission.
Excerpt from "Canto CXXXX," from Ezra Pound, *The Cantos*. Copyright © 1966 by Ezra Pound. Reprinted by permission of New Directions Publishing Corporation.
Excerpts from "Final Soliloquy of the Interior Paramour," "Angel Surrounded by Paysons," and "Metaphors of a Magnifico," from *The Collected Poems of Wallace Stevens*, copyright © 1923, 1931, 1935, 1936, 1937, 1942, 1943, 1944, 1945, 1946, 1947, 1948, 1949, 1950, 1951, 1952, 1953, 1954 by Wallace Stevens, all rights reserved; and excerpt from "Someone Puts a Pineapple Together," from *Poems by Wallace Stevens*, edited by Samuel French Morse, copyright © 1959 by Wallace Stevens, reprinted by permission of Alfred A. Knopf, Inc.
We would also like to thank the Center for Inter-American Relations for its assistance in the preparation of this book.

Preface for Americans

One of the most remarkable things about Borges' popularity in this country is that we have had so little trouble absorbing him. We have, if anything, absorbed him so readily that his work has become spent and repetitive on our behalf. It is as if, in adopting Borges as familiar, we dispensed with him as muse, and our feeling for him deteriorates into another of our restless loyalties. We honor Borges as we honor American writers like Emerson—generously in passing but impatiently in points of fact. What's more, the careless yet grudging enthusiasm shown to such different writers, one at the periphery and the other at the origin of our national culture, has a common source in our ambivalence toward ideas. We are nostalgic for erudition, but we mistrust it.

While he is probably our closest approximation to the certified devotee of random learning, Emerson, unlike Borges, could not shoulder, balance, then properly deliver some finished form for his endless avocations. They floated about him in the brilliant, rhythmic, absorbent paragraphs which he rammed together into the addresses. Even their shape betrays the limited units of his thought. The Emersonian essay is a parody of Adorno's definition of the form as that which is begun wherever it seems likely, and ended whenever one gets tired. In his lectures, Emerson merely interrupts into sound, raising the pitch on the apparently ceaseless argument through which he dreamed the North American continent.

Borges' work is often no less patchy than Emerson's. He, too, delights more in digression than in exposition; he, too, is attracted by backwaters of emotion and side effects of experience; he, too, seems to live solitary among a few ideas. But the quality of the utterance is entirely different. Borges seems not only to have *mastered* the Kabbalah, Böhme, and Plato, but also to have gathered himself, as he begins to write, from the plane of cognition into an act of speech. Rather than easing a continuous rhetoric into audibility, Borges prepares his intuition for the exercise of language. His modes of imagination are separable—he can exist elsewhere than in actual discourse. In other words, his mind is sufficient to occupy him. Not only does Borges understand what he has read, he knows what such understanding has meant to him, thus giving us the comfort of his credibility. More elastic than Emerson, more pliant and more quiet, Borges is finally less at odds with the life of the intellect.

But Emerson remains, in more ways than we wish to imagine, our representative and our accuser. He spoke of those poets and leaders whom he wished to praise as men who created something from nothing, eliciting belief and fathering myth where there was nothing before. He spoke of his important figures as "originals"— so that even Lincoln, John Brown, and Napoleon Bonaparte carried the artistic signature of a Shakespeare or Carlyle. He loyally refused to distinguish poetry from history. He abashedly confessed his affinity with Jesus (both were preachers). He desired, above all, a language he called "vascular," words so organic to the natural round that you could cut them and they would bleed. Finding no symbolic apparatus commensurate with the Oversoul he divined in his countrymen, Emerson apotheosized the railroad

viii

and spiritualized the magnetic fields in his search for an image which would *bind*. Having dedicated a long life to becoming our mentor, he entitled one of his last works "The Natural History of Intellect," the finest and, on one view, most pathetic record of the breadth of his aspirations and the strain of his failure. Although Emerson approved of singularity, recommending immersion in the buried and remote as long as one still deeply lived *oneself,* he never achieved such concentration. In the attempt to recognize himself as intellectual leader, moral father, mythmaker, creator *ex nihilo,* and transcendental Red Indian, he could not help but mistrust those same 'buried' lives, that same intense self-exploration, which made men unique but uncivil. He found he had no barriers to understanding; perhaps this is why his assertiveness seems to have had no props. He wanted to close us in an image, exalt us with a word, but he so continually diffused his energy into a democracy of roles that his images are tumultuous, and his voice, on edge.

We have not lost the suspicion of selfhood which we inherit from Emerson. Neither have we outgrown our unreasonable agitation when confronted with fully integral discipline. Those of us to whom Borges appears systematic in his meditations, embrace him all the more unsystematically for the stability he promises, while those to whom he seems ornamental, precious, and circular, methodically empty him of meaning. In the one case, we admire his education as a profoundly foreign quality, and then, with epigonal inconsequence, search out the esoteric context in which he creates. In the other case (a reaction against the first), we resent the difference described by his Argentine, European, and English strains, and so deprecate the cosmopolite until he becomes mere recondite librarian. Borges must either be abstruse enough to worship, or transparent enough to disdain, and our critical valuations have reflected the dreary swing from an emotional love of paradox to a passionless exposure of tautology.

It is the intention of this volume to correct, or at least increase, the alternatives, and the intention of this note to suggest that the play between overenthusiasm and underestimation may reflect as much on our own preoccupations as on Borges'. Upon our reflexive return to the aura of the unformed, the unpopulated, and the unassimilated in our image of ourselves, Borges intrudes a greater demand. Through a combination of accident, temperament, and rigor, he has come intact to us from the nineteenth century. Whatever else his arrival holds, it at least encourages us to reassemble our sense of tradition and our critical means. Emerson spoke for the Union as well when he said, "It is very unfortunate, but too late to be helped: the discovery we have made that we exist."

Mary Kinzie

Baltimore, 1972

Prose for Borges

Prose for Borges

*Prose: a poem so called because not in any regular
meter, introduced on a special occasion and
recited after others; hence also called a* sequence.

The cancellings, the negations are never
    ultimate, are never one last wipe
        that clears the lens, a farewell
to supersession, finale of ruin.

Is it because spirit is not strong enough
    to forgive flesh? The pardon that comes
        must come (if it comes) because
flesh forgives spirit. That is the work of prose:

to pardon, to perish. In other words—and
    prose is always other words—to be
        understood. Even pausing
in passing, the utterance must persevere

in its dismantlement, the vagabond turn
    moribund, till what had sought in us
        to assume a face, though one
of fragments, is discountenanced, disfigured.

Page after page, the old man goes on with it,
    making way for the everlasting
        Next, which exerts its power
by withholding its presence. Goes on with it,

his diabolic labor, to leave nothing
    fixed in the mind, obliterating
        one damned thing after the next—
all the same, all damned. For what matters to us,

the only equality that matters, and
    the only one we can manage, is
        an equality in hell.
Yet ever and again, especially now

when the darkness closes in for good, closes
    out the likelihood of replacements,
        the impulse comes upon him,
the afflatus of unflinching. The old man

remembers a promise made by a parent
    before speech, a premise enduring
        the indignities of change:
what if the things which came out of time

and were changed could be made over, made over
    so as to be thought of without time?
        A language not out to
eliminate itself, resolute rather

to make a stay, creating the boundaries
    it strikes against! That would be the speech
        of angels. The old man smiles
at angels. Time and again he will try it,

the speech that stands against the spirit that moves.
    But he is not an angel, the names
        he listens for are the ones
omitted, rejected, unnamed. The old man

returns (a passion imitating an action)
    to failure, to the new occasion
        for failure, faithful to failure.
The task of his mind is never to begin

and never to end in the moment. Success
    repudiates the words it does not
        use. The old man uses up
what comes to mind. He repudiates nothing

except nothing. There is always more to be
    used up, to cancel, to erase. And more
        to perish. More prose. Because
there is the world, and because the world is prose.

RICHARD HOWARD

4

Recursive prose
MARY KINZIE

> *Consciousness is not lucidity.*
> —*E. M. Cioran*

It is obvious that Borges is not a philosopher. But to call him by a lesser name fails to reproduce the cautious anachronism of a prose *oeuvre* devoted almost entirely to a few metaphysical states. It is the state, however, rather than the metaphysic which should be emphasized, for Borges' concern with the process of thought is restricted to pathology—the study of error within a portentous but limited region. It is a region seldom marked by pain, resentment, or failure, nor is there success or pleasure—not even anomie. In a body of work where even the subtleties of boredom are suppressed, character patently has never fully functioned: character, that is, which involves cupidity and doubt, devotion and revulsion, character which must be capable of breaks and jumps—discontinuities—in order to reflect the anomalous surface against which it balances itself, grounding its consistency. Borges' parallelisms, by contrast, claim nothing for character but its own permeability. There are neither civic nor private complexities in the lives of Borges' figures. Not even the antinomy has meaning. There are only further lateral displacements within selves which are initially isolated, inscrutably limited, and, above all, forgetful.

5

Memory and the epiphenomena to its lapses, nostalgia and dis-embodied regret, are the salient features in Borges' emotional landscape. That his fictional figures labor in different sectors of experience serves to distinguish the ambience of recollection within which it is available for them to forget. That they all fall prey to oblivion of identical structure and mood tends to make one of such disparate actors as the immortal Joseph Cartaphilus, dispensing his incarnations among the authors of *Sindbad* and the *Iliad,* a Roman tribune, a warrior at Hastings, and a hoary bookseller, and, on the other hand, an actor like Emma Zunz, rehearsing a more stunted heritage emanating from her father's suicide to the murder of his tormentor by way of ritual promiscuity. To be an Emma Zunz instead of an Immortal, or a gaucho rather than a *littérateur,* only decides one's accidental point of origin along a changeless continuum; whether one dreams from the balcony of bloody Latin lives, or handles a dagger in a bar, the same veil is rent and the same communion sealed—one becomes the poet-killer, the melancholy but autistic demiurge.

Nor are there sufficient reportorial markers to differentiate Borges' Homer from his Shakespeare, to render the particularity of Dante's death distinct from Colonel Francisco Borges' or Tzini-cán's, or to locate the contributions of Shih Huang Ti and Franz Kafka in such a way that the neurosis of the Chinese emperor can reflect upon the diabolism of the author of "The Great Wall of China"; needless to say, the relation of identity obviates not only history but dialectic. (It is hardly accidental that, despite the fatal pressure of Kafka throughout Borges' work, not one of Kafka's stories, not even a sentence or phrase, is ever discussed. "Kafka and His Precursors" is an additive portrait via Browning, Bloy, Lord Dunsany, and Kierkegaard.)

Borges' literary pantheon, undifferentiate as it is, can yet depend on our stake in the cumulative, extrinsic tradition—part familiarity, part historical presence—to solidify what is not in the text; Borges' essays on Keats, Whitman, and John Wilkins, for example, insinuate their surprises against an edifice of greater or lesser foreknowledge. Since this is not the case with invented figures like Jaromir Hladik and John Vincent Moon, Nils Rune-berg and Ireneo Funes (since for these personae the frame is not historicism but the credulous disinterest of art), we would not ex-pect that vagueness in the midst of detail, that kernel of vacuity, to play itself out in the same way in the fiction as in the essays. Yet Borges seems uniformly to have followed the judgment of Aristole in the *Poetics* that true poetry has only one enemy to prevail against, namely history, and only one weapon, the "universal," as opposed to history's "singular." Borges echoes his avatar, who said that "the end for which we live is a certain kind of activity, not a quality," by admitting that his stories have no characters, and by disparaging the claims of selfhood, even when acting as agent for Judas and Pascal. Further, what Borges wrote to qualify his conjecture in "Story of the Warrior and the Captive" has become the model attitude: "if it is not true as fact it will be so as symbol" (*L,* 129). What we have yet to realize is the proscriptive force of that conditional: without character there can literally be no fact, and what remains are truths symbolic of no realm but that of disremembrance.

Borges' fiction is thus devotedly Aristotelian in its reticent generality; but, unlike Aristotle's exemplary tragedians, who favored thought ("the power to say what can be said") over contingencies of character, Borges retracts the peripatetic dictum from its full generality in the *Poetics* into the latency of the world of Averroes. Here thought, rather than the power of saying what there is to be said and hence limited only by minimal guides such as diction and publicity, ceases to be an implement with Borges and becomes an enigma, a force, a grail. It is as if the idea of thought had been lost or culturally vitiated, while the recollection of its value still persisted in some genetic trace. The apparent responsi-bility Borges still feels toward first philosophy is retained in the pathos of this circular rebuff.

The void

Averroes might be said to exemplify the dangers of partial knowl-edge which it is beyond his competence to increase. His world is primitive, surprisingly sparse, but nevertheless rich with poetry and enormous intellectual energy. The source of this somewhat melancholy contrast between spiritual wealth and its opposite is announced by Averroes' study of Aristotle:

> **This Greek, fountainhead of all philosophy, had been bestowed upon men to teach them all that could be known; to interpret his works as the ulema interpret the Koran was Averroes' arduous purpose. Few things more beautiful and more pathetic are recorded in history than this Arab physician's dedication to the thoughts of a man separated from him by fourteen centuries.... (L, 149)**

The distance which separates Averroes from the object of his exegesis stretches not only across fourteen centuries, but also, and more importantly, across the irrefutable, still irreparable chasm between the existence of abstractions and the existence of individuals; according to Aristotle, the two cannot exist in relation to each other. This is a dialectic which its antagonists can only modify by their belief in the absolute primacy of the one over the other. In the case of Borges' Averroes (and of his other, more diligent representatives of idealism), the abstractions, the universals form the substance of mind and of all truth. (It will be found that Ireneo Funes' belief in the absolute reality of the minute and the singular places him on the other precipice, but facing the same abyss.) The form of "Averroes' Search" takes guidance from this coexistence of mutually ignorant, reciprocally suspending standpoints, which exclude one another to the extent that the one might 'choose' [1] to be unsympathetic to the claims of the other.

At the beginning of "Averroes' Search," the study of Aristotle is momentarily interrupted by a reply to a contemporary entitled "The Destruction of Destruction," [2] in which Averroes maintains "that the divinity knows only the general laws of the universe, those pertaining to the species, not to the individual" (L, 148). Although Averroes anticipates a reverence toward Aristotle similar to that of the ulema approaching the Koran (a book described as

---

1. Single quotes will be used for defined terms and for metaphorical expressions. Double quotes indicate direct citation.

2. It is worth noting that *Tahāfut al-Tahāfut* can not only be translated "The Destruction of Destruction," but also "Vanity of Vanities" and even "The Incoherence of the Incoherence."

8

"irrevocable and eternal," *L,* 151), Aristotle is nonetheless the philosopher for whom there were no plans or theories or good intentions relevant to the unending variety of individual cases. When he himself becomes the individual case, the text which (because for certain reasons it presents barriers to its own interpretation) must be deciphered, then no amount of foresight or reverence will rescue Aristotle from the dilemma that he, ironically, also explicates *within* that text. This is why Averroes' task is "more beautiful and more pathetic" than any Borges can imagine. The first notes of an unrequited desire have been sounded; they are to echo in contradictions and incorrigible misunderstandings throughout Averroes' day.

The first probe of failure into Averroes' mind is his inability to understand the Aristotelian terms 'tragedy' and 'comedy,' words so unyielding that "no one in the whole world of Islam could conjecture what they meant" (*L,* 149). Their intractable referents are poignantly glimpsed, then repulsed, in a number of episodes like the following:

He looked through the lattice-work balcony; below, in the narrow earthen patio, some half-naked children were playing. One, standing on another's shoulders, was obviously playing the part of a muezzin; with his eyes tightly closed, he chanted "There is no god but the God." The one who held him motionlessly played the part of the minaret; another, abject in the dust and on his knees, the part of the faithful worshipers. The game did not last long; all wanted to be the muezzin, none the congregation or the tower. Averroes heard them dispute in the *vulgar* dialect.... (*L,* 149)

Borges has inserted this scene because it is a minor drama which has absolutely no effect on Averroes' understanding of the concepts Aristotle had used for the form. One also notices in the anecdote of the children that the 'part' most coveted, the voice which they all consider primary, forces the attendant roles to become mere stopgaps for a superfluity of voices—postponements of the central custom of prayer rather than accompanying necessities for its enactment. The only favored voice belongs to him who can declare "There is no god but the God." Transliterated, the Islamic saying would variously read: "There is no man but Man," or "There is no individual, but the Species," or, finally, "There are no examples, only the Law which extends to terrestrial objects gratuitously, and not as a rule"—and here we have a perfect image of the form of "Averroes' Search." If there does not exist any universally recognized diversion called theater, then plays and the more diffuse kinds of playacting may as well not exist. Averroes' unwitting recalcitrance thus becomes an almost precise inversion of Berkeley's dictum, cited often by Borges in essays and parables, that one cannot imagine a room which can satisfy the condition that no one perceive it, for as soon as one imagines it, he has, practically speaking, made *himself* imaginatively present in that room. Here, however, Averroes is presented with realities which he can perceive well enough (he observes the children from his balcony), but which he cannot *imagine*. As Borges explains in "The Modesty of History," "Our eyes see what they are accustomed to seeing. Tacitus did not perceive the Crucifixion, although his book recorded it" (*OI*, 167).

Despite the ironic reflection of the children's little drama upon Averroes' lexical blind spot (he had even put down his pen with the desultory notion "that what we seek is often nearby"), the vignette is not a fair example of the play-within-a-play. It carries too little of the story within it, hence understating the suspicion of the larger story's content, and also, being slight as it is and severed from Averroes' agency as surely as from his awareness, the scene does not lead us, by association, to frame ourselves among events in the implied 'larger play'—to act the audience to Averroes' actor. This is not to say, however, that muezzin-versus-minaret is not the kernel of the theme, nor that the little play fails to magnetize the echoes of paradox which succeed it. Its two central implications—(1) that Averroes is strapped to a vantage from which he (2) is forced to view cases contradictory to his beliefs as merely tangential or extraneous to them—resound again and again in different registers, until we can understand what the entire combination will imply for Borges' cosmology.

We learn that Averroes is to meet with friends that evening, one of whom is a Koran scholar named Farach and the other a traveler named Abulcasim. From the outset, before we have any reason to like, dislike, or form any opinions whatever about their characters, we already understand that Farach will be compatible with, if not a parody of, Averroes and that Abulcasim has nonbookish, nonintellectual knowledge of the world's routes and mazes. That Abulcasim turns out to be a coward and a dolt in no way detracts from our original notion of him as a caricature of individuality, with a wealth of particularist knowledge, in the company of giant, spiritually volatile men.

He confirms our suspicions by repeating Averroes' errors in a stupid, entangled way. Of Abulcasim his enemies say that "he had never set foot in China and that in the temples of that land he had blasphemed the name of Allah" (*L,* 150). Borges notes that these judgments were delivered "with that peculiar logic of hatred," and the claims *are* peculiarly alogical—a juxtaposition of derogations from two different quarters. But such logic ultimately encircles orthodoxy as well as spite. Averroes himself can be shown to operate religiously within such a pattern. There is (he might say) no such thing as a *drama of persons speaking lines,* and, moreover, the children *playing parts* disputed in the vulgar tongue. The common terms in each set of statements are those which the speakers thought tangential and, as it happens, also those which create the 'invisible' contradiction. One's predilections will, however, always arrange to obliterate the unwanted articles in one's speech, until such common terms of inhering logical friction are eclipsed by beliefs already held. The two independent and logically acceptable judgments for which the traveler Abulcasim is to be despised automatically exclude the visit to China: (1) he lies about everything, and (2) he is a defiler of God. In a similar way, two different opinions mingle without touching in Averroes' mind: (1) drama does not exist—"tragedy" and "comedy" must be poetic genres; and (2) the children spoke a vulgar dialect. One could also substitute the syllogistic alphabet for the contextual statement: (1) there is no d because there is no D (and there is no g but the G); (2) there is a, there is b, there is c, but these are contingent and ephemeral; a has red hair; b has no concept of theology; *c* speaks in the "incipient Spanish of the peninsula's Moslem populace" (*L,* 149). All that has been affirmed, as far as Averroes is concerned, is the hidden premise which guards his sanity: there is no *g* but the *G.*

Abulcasim is a useful foil for this group of learned men, not only because his weaknesses repeat on their petty level the complication of the others' strengths, but also because the information he brings about the performance of a play in a Chinese theater aggravates Averroes' noncomprehension on the very subject which now eludes him so painfully. In his ingenuous, halting recount of the play, Abulcasim defends himself sanely and well; yet the confirmation we can so easily supply as to his accuracy—our ready accessibility to the drama as an idea and to tragedy as a formal mood—puts us at a disadvantage equal to poor Abulcasim's. Again and again in Borges' work, we find ourselves in league with the similarly initiated against some group, some blank individual, some shiftless force whose counter-knowledge may be nonexistent or whose powers of refutation indeed slack, yet whose unassailable supremacy, lodged with apparent benignity in his (or its) inability to understand our world and our thought, tends to make us feel humble and foolish.[3] We find ourselves, like Abul-

3. It is not only figures such as Averroes, Funes, or Asterion who seduce us into their exaggerated and singular worlds, but whole peoples. The Yahoos of "Doctor Brodie's Report," for example, reach for the narrator's cutlass "not by the hilt but by the blade, seeing it, undoubtedly, in their own way, which causes me to wonder to what degree they would be able to perceive a chair. A house of several rooms would strike them as a maze, though perhaps they might find their way inside it in the manner of a cat, *though the cat does not imagine the house*" (*DBR,* 114–15, my emphasis).

Although the echoes of Swift may largely override his interest in the Yahoos' nearly ungraspable ways of thinking, in another tale about a wearied and degenerate race, Borges subordinates savagery to madness, with none of the terror lost. Investigating the lost City of the Immortals, the narrator explains that "[a] labyrinth is a structure compounded to confuse men; its architecture, rich in symmetries, is subordinated to that end. In the palace . . . the architecture lacked any such finality. It abounded in dead-end corridors, high unattainable windows, portentous doors which led to a cell or pit, incredible inverted stairways whose steps and balustrades hung downwards. Other stairways, clinging airily to the side of a monumental wall, would die without leading anywhere, after making two or three turns in the lofty darkness of the cupolas. I do not know if all the examples I have enumerated are literal" . . . (*L,* 110–11).

The narrator's doubt as to the literal truth of the examples he has given not only suggests that these stairways and cupolas are themselves allegorical expressions, but

casim, unable to do more than what begins to seem minimal—namely, unload our lore, empty our minds of the patent and the proven. And, having emptied ourselves of the admirable self-evidence of our reality, we find the monumental pressure of Averroes' and Farach's inability to understand to be not only more dignified but less backward.

This is how Abulcasim reports what he has seen on his travels:

"The persons...were playing the drum and the lute, save for some fifteen or twenty (with crimson-colored masks) who were praying, singing and conversing. They suffered prison, but no one could see the jail; they traveled on horseback, but no one could see the horse; they fought, but the swords were of reed; they died and then stood up again." (*L*, 152)

Farach's response is representative: " 'The acts of madmen exceed the previsions of the sane.' " Abulcasim is hard put. " 'Let us imagine,' " he urges, " 'that someone performs a story instead of telling it.' " But Abulcasim's lurches toward simplicity are met by Farach's interior poise. Farach asks Abulcasim whether these people spoke and, finding that they did, remarks that " 'twenty persons are unnecessary. One single speaker can tell anything, no matter how complicated it might be' " (*L*, 153).

Farach's reply reduces the frivolity of many actors to the sufficiency of one. Oddly enough, the reduction, instead of singularizing the experience otherwise dispersed among twenty persons, has in

---

also leads him to postulate a more elaborate metaphor in order to represent details which are already partially metaphoric: "I do not want to describe it; a chaos of heterogeneous words, the body of a tiger or a bull in which teeth, organs and heads monstrously pullulate in mutual conjunction and hatred can (perhaps) be approximate images" (*L*, 111).

In the case of the Yahoos and the Immortals, a race has *chosen* to degenerate from what we would call a higher stage to a lower one; the Yahoos left inscriptions on the hills when they descended to the swamps, but they have forgotten how to decipher them; the Immortals built a beautiful city, and then razed it to erect their unruly one, while they live in caves without speaking. Borges adds, however, that such signs of degeneracy only conceal the life of speculation: "Absorbed in thought, they hardly perceived the physical world" (*L*, 113). The claims made for the inhabitants of Tlön, on the other hand, are all the more congenial to philosophic explication: "... they do not conceive that the spatial persists in time. The perception of a cloud of smoke on the horizon and then of the burning field and then of the half-extinguished cigarette that produced the blaze is considered an example of association of ideas" (*L*, 9).

In all three of these worlds, Borges' focus is rather exploratory than normative; rather than wanting to correct the aberrant, he is intrigued by the paradox of trying to explain it in a modern tongue whose presuppositions are alien to it.

13

effect *generalized* the tale which Abulcasim's actors had appropriated to their several, compartmentalized roles. The truth to which Farach alludes, " 'no matter how complicated,' " is an impersonal stream of eternals. The number one stands in a less dangerous, more decorous relation to infinity than do the numbers fifteen or twenty, which spoil that symmetry with their appreciable randomness. One speaker can be self-effacing, whereas twenty are bulky and disparate to that amount. Beyond one, the only number of persons who could speak as Farach would wish, and with the same authority, would be the indefinite number n. Adding anything at all to what someone like Averroes might say could only mean arraying the indeterminate population of Cordova behind him. Since the weight implicitly shifts between one and everything, with no mediation, in Averroes' philosophy and that of his friends, the city of Cordova *is* in back of each. The disadvantage to such instantaneous communion is that 'city' is no less indefinite than they.

Although the figures in "Averroes' Search"—Farach, Averroes, the poet Abdalmalik, Abulcasim—can be said to exist for us, the quality of their presence is not personal. It is rather like that of the "few things," hard without form, unitary without interrelation, which appear in Borges' description of Averroes' realm:

> ...and all around (this Averroes felt also) stretched out to the limits of the earth the Spanish land, *where there are few things, but where each seems to exist in a substantive and eternal way.* (L, 148, my emphasis) [4]

The visual suggestiveness of these lines resonates of those forms of surrealist painting whose intention is to distort an otherwise amply represented object by means of imperfect distances between it and its background. It is tempting to translate these "few things" into actual items—a comb, a basket, a fountain—standing solitary and askew in a desert of Averroes' perception. But his perception is neither so special nor surreal. By leaving the "few things" unspoken, Borges has encouraged the superposition of cognitive

4. So that the translation cannot be faulted with intruding words more suggestive than those Borges actually used, the italicized words are given in the original: "... *en la que hay pocas cosas, pero donde cada una parece estar de un modo sustantivo y eterno.*" El Aleph (Buenos Aires, 1957; 1970), p. 92.

14

indefiniteness upon the particular world. Rather than seeing something which has been described, we reconstruct from examples of nearly barren scenes a fleeting image of their erasure. Instead of recalling the objects which may exist in such 'reference works,' we indulge in studied forgetfulness. The lines about the Spanish land induce in us an indirectly visual appreciation of such a psychological state. Rather than evoking a fountain and comb, the phrases "few things" existing "in a substantive and eternal way" double back and forth across the deliberate indistinction of that limitless and hardly populated space, in order to retrieve the peculiar kind of primivitism which characterizes Averroes' mind.

'Primitive' mentality, in the precise sense of Averroes' ignorance, has been amply described by Maurice Merleau-Ponty:

It is true that we discover the unreflected. But the unreflected we go back to is not that which is prior to philosophy or prior to reflection. It is the unreflected which is understood and conquered by reflection. Left to itself, perception forgets itself and is ignorant of its own accomplishments.[5]

Merleau-Ponty continues the sentences just quoted by asserting that "[f]ar from thinking that philosophy is a useless repetition of life, I think, on the contrary, that without reflection life would probably dissipate itself in ignorance of itself or chaos." The "unreflected" is therefore *not* a prelogical state, either phylogenetically or developmentally in the life of the individual. It is instead a state of ignorance, incurred by passing out of meditation, which recurs in each life, or to which our life periodically, and precipitously, returns.

Averroes' is, then, a consciousness left historically and temperamentally to itself—a consciousness categorically ignorant of its own accomplishments. His thoughts are not backward for being simple-minded, nor is their number pitiful as if vacuity were implied in the small sum. They are, rather, primitive in the same way in which Freud's extrapolated network of drives and balances can be claimed to knit a man's observable beliefs and affinities to-

5. M. Merleau-Ponty, "The Primacy of Perception and Its Philosophical Consequences," in J. A. Edie, ed., *The Primacy of Perception and Other Essays on Phenomenological Psychology, The Philosophy of Art, History and Politics* (Evanston, 1964), p. 19.

gether, until adding to the latter only increases the *unity* (in both senses of the term) of the former. The 'things' in Averroes' world have that responsive density which we measure with respect to our own beliefs as apodictic. These things (articles of belief and states of being) also have that intransigence to change, that inelasticity, which characterizes conservatism, fascism, psychological biases like neurosis, or generally any entrenched repudiation of reflection.

The dissipations of prejudice are naturally one of the dangers involved in the "unreflected," for when invocation is made to some unformed stabilizer or to some ineffable, and hence irrefutable, force (as Averroes, as well as Hitler, has had recourse to do), there is nothing but self-interest or -disinterest to distinguish the zealot from the saint. While the zealot will invoke the ineffable to justify an act or prejudice, the saint disinterestedly refines his acts and prejudices so that the ineffable is, as it were, repeated, re-hearsed, returned to. Averroes' well-cultivated reluctance to change thus preserves for him in our eyes the wonder of an arcane, essentially unknowable steadfastness. His repudiation is in some way nourishing, and the "unreflected" to which he returns, profound.

Borges has indirectly argued the worth of Averroes' primitive loyalty in a little scholastic exercise from *Dreamtigers* called "Argumentum Ornithologicum," given here in its entirety:

> **I close my eyes and see a flock of birds. The vision lasts a second or perhaps less; I don't know how many birds I saw. Were they a definite or an indefinite number? This problem involves the question of the existence of God. If God exists, the number is definite, because how many birds I saw is known to God. If God does not exist, the number is indefinite, because nobody was able to take count. In this case, I saw fewer than ten birds (let's say) and more than one; but I did not see nine, eight, seven, six, five, four, three, or two birds. I saw a number between ten and one, but not nine, eight, seven, six, five, etc. That number, as a whole number, is inconceivable; *ergo*, God exists.   (DT, 29)**

The slight definitional nudge Borges has given to the concept of indefiniteness by substituting the word "inconceivable" adds density and contour to the idea without making "indefinite" (the term it both displaces and further explains) a simple paraphrase of a known integer. Without being a 'concrete particular' like seven or eight, the entity described as "inconceivable" still is not a universal form for mathematical language as, for example, 'quantity' would be. Instead, "inconceivable" provides, in a twist of negative prefix onto its somewhat more spiritual root, the dreamlike ambiguity of a fixed remembrance ("I . . . see a flock of birds. . . . I don't know how many . . .") which is peculiar not to mathematical description but to the state of the envisioning. And if the problem should, as Borges supposes, involve the existence or nonexistence of God, that problem too must be answered from a premise commensurate in subtlety with the mingled clarity-and-unfixedness of the flock of birds observed. As in the number of things which exist in Averroes' Spanish land, both conviction and uncertainty combine in the conundrum of the birds; "fewness" is both "substantive" *and* "eternal"—both sharp and hazy, hard and formless, axiomatic and illusory.[6] To say, therefore, that Averroes' loyalty to the Koran, to Aristotle, and to the poetry of Zuhair are the 'things' of primitive "fewness" which support him while blinding him to their own limitations—to say that these are loyalties durable yet inelastic, palpable and yet not subject to reformation, is a means of rescuing Averroes from the charge of dullness or mental paralysis.

To further counteract the impression that his are nothing more than the qualities of elevated prejudice, there is the indisputable creativity of Averroes' reasoning; as is shown by his response to the conjecture that the blood-red petals of certain roses bear the inscription "There is no god but the God," Averroes' mind is far from atrophied or credulous:

"It is less difficult for me to admit an error in the learned Ibn Qutaiba [who made the conjecture], or in the copyists, than to admit that the earth has roses with the profession of the faith." (L, 150)

While professions of the faith may dictate the form of Averroes' mornings and the moods of his sleeplessness, the changeless Truth

6. "I have glimpsed or foreseen a refutation of time, in which I myself do not believe, but which regularly visits me at night and in the weary twilight with the illusory force of an axiom" (L, 218). Here again, in his essay "A New Refutation of Time," Borges confesses his interest in that border country of reflection (where thought is intimated) which forms the 'pathetic' center of so much of his work. That such glimpses of a refutation involve Borges in emotions as well as theories is evident from his attempt in this piece to probe the matrix of nostalgia and happiness in order to explain the temporal sense; his effort becomes a history of time lived and time glimpsed—its spiritual autobiography.

is *not* an aimless fantast in the back garden. Thus, however completely Averroes agrees with Farach about the superiority of one speaker to fifteen or twenty, it is not he who speaks that compact judgment, commenting instead on the proposition of the blood-red roses in such a way as to leave room for doubt on any point of contention. As a secondary effect of Averroes' reserve in given instances, the closure on his universe (which still remains closed) admits considerably more mobility. When the poet Abdalmalik deprecates the metaphors of the poet Zuhair, saying that "five centuries of admiration have rendered . . . valueless" his comparison of destiny with a blind camel, Averroes raises the one dissenting voice:

"... if the purpose of the poem is to surprise us, its life span would not be measured in centuries, but in days and hours and perhaps minutes ... a famous poet is less of an inventor than he is a discoverer. In praise of Ibn-Sharaf of Berja it has been repeated that only he could imagine that the stars at dawn fall slowly, like leaves from a tree; if this were so, it would be evidence that the image is banal. The image one man can form is an image that touches no one. There are infinite things on earth; any one of them may be likened to any other. . . . However, there is no one who has not at some time felt that destiny is clumsy and powerful, that it is innocent and also inhuman. For that conviction, which may be passing or continuous, but which no one may elude, Zuhair's verse was written." (*L*, 153–54)

If the suspension of his belief in the inscribed roses in some way suggests that Averroes' thought is not hidebound, this defense of the image which accommodates a feeling "no one may elude" is proof that his thought is not ancillary, either. We come to believe, in fact, that Averroes is a noble man—ignorant insofar as circumstance imposes on him to select and discard from within the slender allowance of his era, and nevertheless compelling admiration for the subtlety his choices reveal. This stature is (sadly, for Borges) mitigated by a wisdom which becomes, against the context of unreachable other worlds, an inverse wisdom. Because he never sat through performances of Aeschylus and Sophocles in the amphitheater of Herodutus, Averroes can never grasp the world of dramatic form. Because he and Aristotle have equally denied the flow of causation from generic to specific, the one will never understand the other. The similarity in their mental constitutions

18

prevents the identical transfer. It is in this light that we must view Averroes' ingenuous formulation of the immutable Law that "to be free of an error, it is well to have professed it" (L, 153).[7] Like all eternal verities in his spare, uncluttered realm, the very phrasing of his plight admits of no application, no corrective, no 'profession.'

Averroes, the man who doesn't know what he knows, returns the next morning to his library to make his last mistake. He returns "as the muezzins were calling the faithful to their early morning prayers." He seems too accustomed to the sound to do more than dimly listen—which reminds Borges, reminds us, that we hear something more in the sound. We hear the three children in the patio; we hear the players in Abulcasim's theater clanking their swords of reed; we hear the multitude of stilled reminders that Averroes is somehow lost to us: "he felt aged, useless, unreal"; "The fear of the crassly infinite, of mere space, of mere matter, touched Averroes for an instant" (L, 152); the Spanish land "stretch[ing] out to the limits of the earth." All this we recall, straining to hear from the page what the protagonist hears but cannot recognize, as Averroes completes the circle, writes his definition, prolonging an error he cannot profess:

"Aristu (Aristotle) gives the names of tragedy to panegyrics and that of comedy to satires and anathemas. Admirable tragedies and comedies abound in the pages of the Koran...." (L, 155)

By certifying the false monologous forms, Averroes insures his ignorance even after the timid suggestion of Abulcasim that one

7. Professing an error should allow one to achieve a distance from his act. Borges returns to this idea in his "Autobiographical Essay," where he speaks with considerable hindsight about his early habit of writing "to be un-understood": "The Gnostics claimed that the only way to avoid a sin was to commit it and be rid of it. In my books of these years, I seem to have committed most of the major literary sins. ... Today, I no longer feel guilty over these excesses; those books were written by somebody else" (A, 232). The attitude of the autobiographical Borges differs from that in "Averroes' Search" as patter is different from pathos. The attitude in his other fiction, however, reinstates the 'anachronistic potential' of the idea of propitiating an error: ". . . to confess to a thing is to leave off being an actor in it and to become the onlooker—to become somebody who has seen it and tells it and is no longer the doer" (DBR, 99). The narrator of "Guayaquil" writes this sentence in hopes that such preparation will enable him to understand what he is about to narrate. Like Averroes, he believes in a truth which has yet to be put into practice.

19

might perform rather than tell a story. He returns to the convention of the singular speaker, before the second actor was introduced— a choice which, lagging more than fourteen centuries behind the drama's progress from unity to duality, produces an effect of useless ingenuousness similar to Pierre Menard's.[8] Borges appears to believe that anachronism, by itself, is one of the truly profound paradoxes—a supposition borne out in the intra-reflecting destinies of Aristotle-Averroes, Averroes-Zuhair.

Sheer contiguity serves the storyteller as it could never serve Averroes, "closed within the orb of Islam," to illuminate every inch of his path of mistakes. Averroes can see four terms in verse

8. One should also compare Borges' 'ingenuous' invention of Pierre Menard with his interpretation of nazism. In his unnerving sketch of Hitler and Argentine sympathy with him, Borges recalls the visit from an acquaintance on June 14, 1940: "Standing in the doorway, he announced the dreadful news: the Nazi armies had occupied Paris. I felt a mixture of sadness, disgust, malaise. And then it occurred to me that his insolent joy did not explain the stentorian voice or the abrupt proclamation. He added that the German troops would soon be in London. Any opposition was useless, nothing could prevent their victory. That was when I knew that he too was terrified.

"... for Europeans and Americans, one order—and only one—is possible: it used to be called Rome and now it is called Western Culture. To be a Nazi (to play the game of energetic barbarism, to play at being a Viking, a Tartar, a sixteenth-century conquistador, a gaucho, a redskin) is, after all, a mental and moral impossibility. Nazism suffers from unreality, like Erigena's hells.... I shall hazard this conjecture: *Hitler wants to be defeated*. Hitler is collaborating blindly with the inevitable armies that will annihilate him, as the metal vultures and the dragon (which must not have been unaware that they were monsters) collaborated, mysteriously, with Hercules" (*OI*, 135–36).

As for Pierre Menard (who cultivated himself as an anachronism, repeating in the 1920's the inspiration of the man Miguel de Cervantes), so for Hitler, too, there must have been (Borges imagines) a suspension of their endeavor midway between belief and doubt—belief, sufficient to the magnitude of the repetition; doubt, sufficient to make disbelief a constant temptation and so enrich the "collaboration." In Menard's case, disbelief took the form of placing a distance between himself and Cervantes: "To be, in some way, Cervantes and reach the *Quixote* seemed less arduous to him—and, consequently, less interesting—than to go on being Pierre Menard and reach the *Quixote* through the experiences of Pierre Menard" (*L*, 40). In Hitler's case, disbelief took the form of enhancing his likelihood of victory. The certainty of taking London, for example, made his barbarism all the more "energetic."

One might also wonder what form Menard's belief in contingency would impose on our understanding of Hitler: "I cannot imagine the universe ... without the *Bateau ivre* or the *Ancient Mariner*, but I am quite capable of imagining it without the *Quixote*.... The *Quixote* is a contingent book; the *Quixote* is unnecessary. I can premeditate writing it, I can write it, without falling into a tautology" (*L*, 41). One wonders what effect the non-necessity of the savagery Hitler emulated might have contributed to his sense of uniqueness.

20

which, for its author Zuhair, had two: " 'he has seen destiny suddenly trample men into the dust, like a blind camel' " (L, 153). Averroes notes that " 'when we repeat it now, it serves to evoke the memory of Zuhair and to fuse our misfortune with that dead Arab's' " (L, 154). If Averroes can see these four terms, then Borges can see not only the first two terms (Zuhair's), Averroes' additional two terms, but also the following four: the evocation of Averroes in the blindness of the camel; the destiny which relegates the philosopher to failure; Borges' own feeling for the 'memory' of Averroes; and finally, the "fusing of [his] misfortune with that dead Arab's [sc. Averroes]." Eight terms appear as Borges tells the story—a geometric progression which the reader can suddenly find that he, too, extends, multiplying the terms of old Zuhair's metaphor through each stage of its tradition, as it is carried from Zuhair through Averroes, to Borges, to present readers, to their successors, and so on. There is, ideally, nothing which can force the series to a close. There is no man who caps the well of all experience gone before him, just as there is necessarily no heart which will *not* potentially be moved by us, finally understand us. The implication is, of course, that there is no possible mistake we will not commit in *someone's* eyes. Averroes seems to understand this despite himself: " 'Time broadens the scope of verses,' " he explains, " 'and I know of some which, like music, are everything for all men' " (L, 154). Thus he partially answers the question, posed in alternate terms during the gathering with Farach and Abulcasim, concerning the private versus the universal image: what can *one* thing mean, for *one* man? It is a question Averroes answers in full when he 'solves' the interpretation of the two troublesome words in Aristotle—there is no individual thing whose definition is not equivocal.

Averroes cites the verse which has given him, in exile, a measure of comfort—words "composed by a king who longed for the Orient [which] served me, exiled in Africa, to express my nostalgia for Spain":

> **"You too, oh palm!, are**
> **Foreign to this soil . . ."** (L, 154)

Averroes (not knowing what he knows) has already placed this verse well along the road to becoming "everything for all men"; for the time being, the verse provides at least more for our comprehension than for his. Not only is Averroes foreign to his foreign soil, he is also foreign to his homeland, which is not only "the Spanish land, where there are few things," but in addition a land comprising extraneous acts and their meaning. A variety of clues, however, is 'foreign' to him who does not look for clues. The relation is foreign to nominalism. Tragedy and comedy are foreign to the Moslem. The exception is foreign to a Law which neither proves by evidence nor is disproved by contraries. (Once again, the irony is that Averroes should be hindered by these rules of alienation in light of a puzzlement stemming from Aristotle, principal author of mutual exclusion.) Each allusion compounds its meaning in unforeseeable points of contact, while eluding its progenitor; and this holds true for Averroes, but no less true for the temporarily final author, the capstone of the written series before us. Borges must let Averroes disappear. Averroes, who wanted "to imagine what a drama is without ever having suspected what a theater is, was no more absurd than I, wanting to imagine Averroes with no other sources than a few fragments from Renan, Lane and Asín Palacios" (L, 155). Borges and his narrative echo their reciprocal foreignness. Author exposes philosopher to witnessed but discounted contradiction; narrative ultimately exposes author to his own ignorance. Set against the sullen, "substantive" paucity of Borges' emblematic Spain, Averroes, his narrative frame, and their author revolve inevitably, circling ignorance, and falling to partial knowledge as though it were absolute.

The garbage heap

In contrast to the ominous wastes of "Averroes' Search," Borges' short story "Funes the Memorious" is stubbornly detailed. Borges begins the story with the words "I remember," and ends it with Funes' demise "of congestion of the lungs." Between the two, memory is elongated and then flooded with its own accumulations. The story's thesis is that the exaggeration of one talent to the exclusion of others produces not grotesques, but wonders. Funes' memory is so highly developed that every element in his 'vision' becomes a distinct and integral world. His power to concentrate is like a stop-motion camera which breaks down the fluidity of motion to its constituents; the single frame then becomes as coherent and various—in other words, as *flowing*—as is the flow of normal sight. " 'I alone,' " says Funes, " 'have more memories than all mankind has probably had since the world has been the world. . . . My dreams are like you people's waking hours. . . . My memory, sir, is like a garbage heap' " (*L*, 64).

Because each memory he has also comprises the somatic responses which accompanied it (as well as each time he has recalled that memory with its accompanying sensations), Funes considers that each of these memories—being different—should exist under a different name. The names given these singular memories are absurd, barren of connotation, and thus entirely self-referring. And Funes has no desire to fit these names into some kind of system—genus to species or species to subspecies. He also considers that, to correspond to the vividness with which he perceives it, each number should be unique and irregular (in place of the set of numbering systems with two indices of quantity, placement or digitation, and denotative symbols, of which the binary system has the fewest). Funes' system contains an unending series of one-quantity/one-word equivalences, yielding numbers like "Maximo Pérez" (7,013), "The Railroad" (7,014), and others like "Olimar," "sulphur," "the reins," "the whale," "the gas," "the maté kettle," "the Negro Timoteo," "meat blanket," and "Napoleon." That his names entirely lack the connotations of common usage makes Funes' discipline nonsensical. He is forced into an extreme solipsism, unable to communicate in the vocabulary of names he has given to his impressions. The use of a word is as unique to Funes as is its referent, and to communicate, it is necessary to abstract from the individual experience to others'.

Indeed, when dealing with one of Borges' peremptory and polar realms, it is next to impossible to allow oneself in good conscience to use words which would not have currency in that particular realm, or which nurture concepts foreign to it. But if the reader will persist in using vocabulary which grates against the very semantic framework of one or another kingdom, he will at least be taught the measure of friction his omniscience can generate. Here, for example, 'communication' is an extraneous consideration. A private, dissociated world is only cultivated, not relayed. That is the failure of any strict nominalism; if unalloyed, it is without tangents or relations, and its closure is inadvertent. Borges actually calls Funes "a vernacular and rustic Zarathustra," and of course "vernacular" has less to do with rural diphthongs than with the spirit's distortions in solitude.

Funes is clearly the man who knows too much, as Averroes was the man who knew too little. At opposite poles, they enact the disadvantages of the Aristotelian view. If Averroes cannot descend from the profession of the Koran to embrace Abulcasim's bizarre evidence, Funes, at the other edge of the abyss, cannot afford to yield up the treasure of his sensations to the vulgarization of the common noun. As Borges writes of Funes, "He was, let us not forget, almost incapable of ideas of a general, Platonic sort"; "I suspect . . . that he was not very capable of thought. To think is to forget differences, generalize, make abstractions. In the teeming world of Funes, there were only details, almost immediate in their presence" (*L*, 65, 66).

Contiguous or unmediated detail likewise fights its way to the surface of that secondhand story, the narrator's. The very shape of the story compels the complementary world of the author to proliferate. The small town of Fray Bentos vibrates with the presence of the scholarly narrator; everyone soon knows which Latin books he has brought with him, and, by a forcible inversion of the minuscule, Borges seems to have drawn up the town's curiosity into an obsession with his own uniqueness. He is more than eager to publicize the news of his father's grave illness, enhancing the melodrama of having received a telegram to that effect. "May God forgive me," says Borges, ". . . the desire to communicate to all Fray Bentos the contradiction between the negative form of the message ["my father was 'not at all well' "] and the peremptory adverb . . .

perhaps distracted me from all possibility of real sorrow" (*L*, 62).

It is fitting that Borges terms his first recollection of Funes "perspicuous," because his prose has been made to *comprehend* the afternoon on which Funes was first glimpsed as a hierarchy of exactitudes—a mood of increasing sensuous precision which flatters the intentness of his title character as much as it seems to have been born from it:

> I was returning from the San Francisco ranch [on horseback] with my cousin Bernardo Haedo.... After a sultry day, an enormous slate-colored storm had hidden the sky. It was urged on by a southern wind, the trees were already going wild; I was afraid (I was hopeful) that the elemental rain would take us by surprise in the open. We were running a kind of race with the storm. We entered an alleyway that sank down between two very high brick sidewalks. It had suddenly got dark; I heard some rapid and almost secret footsteps up above; I raised my eyes and saw a boy running along the narrow and broken path as if it were a narrow and broken wall. I remember his baggy gaucho trousers, his rope-soled shoes, I remember the cigarette in his hard face, against the now limitless storm cloud. (*L*, 60)

Violent motion whips the sky and trees; excited by the elemental display, the cousins spur their horses; they seek the refuge of blocks and bricks. Before the riders have entirely checked the momentum of competing against the storm, the "secret steps" of the stranger pick up that velocity Bernardo and Borges had borrowed from the sky, and this boy in gaucho pants then channels it along the narrow walk. The two actors now have a measure of omniscience, inasmuch as Funes has taken their self-involved action from them. Now *he* holds the stage.

In this paragraph one catches a visual reflection of the tension created when the enormity of abstractions impinges on a man who knows too much to reconcile information with an order larger than his memory—the place where it is stored. The focal point of vision is increasingly curtailed, coextensive with its calendar of ever shorter segments of time. The temporal sense contracts relative to the shrinkage of space and to the diminution of a broad and restless sky into this least of the landscape's 'creations'—the minute scuffing of Funes' steps. The footfall of the stranger reverberates like the ticking of a stopwatch, which was set at an indeterminate moment long ago but which now dwindles into the disappearing slice of

25

seconds which remain before a deadline, or a bell: " 'What time is it, Ireneo?' " Cousin Bernardo asks. Funes replies without breaking stride (he is to dam and flood the passages which follow, but at his own relative velocity), and informs them to the very second, fishing the knowledge from the immediate array of his information: " 'Four minutes to eight. . . .' "

The storm cloud now fills the place—in context—of that indeterminate time long ago. It covers all, darkening the sky, impersonal, enormous, and, if you will, 'universal.' Against such a sky, the only silhouette in the universe would be the brown face of Funes with the cigarette in his mouth. He seems to resemble the rough, burnt rodeo drifters of the Far West, or the tireless Okie farmers who similarly look, at age nineteen, as if they had come wiry and septuagenarian from the womb. There are few Borges characters whose faces come before us with the incipient clarity of Funes'—unless, perhaps, it is John Vincent Moon, the scar-faced Englishman in "The Shape of the Sword." While Moon has his past engraved in his cheek, Funes has each fractional perception engraved in his memory, and, for portraying the 'allegorical concreteness' of each, Borges resorts to an uncharacteristic overplay of descriptive detail.

It is doubly fitting that Borges has called his first memory of Funes "perspicuous," especially as his recollection of Funes' *Doppelgänger,* Averroes, is opaque. While Funes immerses himself, schools himself for the surprise of each variant reading of memory, Averroes holds himself back with saturnine constancy from the temptations of singularity, whether in the form of living too selfishly or, on a deeper level, of remembering what only one man could remember and what would then be peculiar to him alone. Funes' "own face in the mirror, his own hands, surprised him every time he saw them" (*L,* 65); they are brand new acquisitions; he dotes on them. Averroes, by contrast, "looked at himself in a metal mirror. I do not know what his eyes saw, because no historian has ever described the forms of his face. I do know," Borges continues, "that he disappeared suddenly, as if fulminated by an invisible fire, and with him disappeared the house and the

26

unseen fountain . . ." (*L*, 155). Borges' complaint about the lack of historical bases for an account of Averroes' appearance is a circumlocution designed to slip his character out of sight—historians naturally don't record the Elijah-like fulmination, either. The point is that Borges' inability to imagine Averroes' face is structurally cognate with the fiction of fiery dissolution; in each case, Borges excuses his narration from the onus of detail on the grounds of Averroes' own incompatibility with minutiae. Funes, on the other hand, is eminently 'imaginable'; his face and hands more nearly approach actual presence. Thus, if the culmination of the one story is the obliteration of Averroes when Borges presses his own conception onto ground where his partial knowledge will not support him, then the inception of the other is the blossoming of Funes' secret discipline beneath the slow sweep of the author's gaze across his protagonist's curious and afflicted details.

Not only does Borges vary his narrative participation in the two tales relative to the distance each figure maintains between himself and his circumstances, but he also adopts a subtly different narrative tone. In the Averroes story, after reporting in the opening paragraph the various names under which the protagonist has been known, Borges creates the setting within which the philosopher's increasing burden of noncomprehension is to grow:

He wrote with slow sureness, from right to left; the effort of forming syllogisms and linking vast paragraphs did not keep him from feeling, like a state of well-being, the cool and deep house surrounding him. In the depths of the siesta amorous doves called huskily; from some unseen patio arose the murmur of a fountain; something in Averroes, whose ancestors came from the Arabian deserts, was thankful for the constancy of the water. Down below were the gardens, the orchard; down below, the busy Guadalquivir and then the beloved city of Cordova, no less eminent than Bagdad or Cairo, like a complex and delicate instrument, and all around (this Averroes felt also) stretched out to the limits of the earth the Spanish land, where there are few things, but where each seems to exist in a substantive and eternal way. (*L*, 148)

There is, for all the exoticism of this paragraph, a strange sense of familiarity in the way the philosopher's posture and his fleeting perceptions of a sleeping world are given to us. Despite the *vastness* of the paragraphs, the *depths* of the somnolence at this time of day, the *unseen* courtyard, and the indeterminable *something* in him

27

which is responsive to the constancy of water, Averroes is presented from a perspective nearly within the character. It is not as though Averroes were disappearing into the vague, ancestral "something," but rather as though we were with him, trying to identify it. It is not as though we lost Averroes to the vast paragraphs, but rather as though we were turning back from those sparing glimpses to courtyard and city, and renewing the effort of the syllogism with the same delicious abstinence Averroes himself maintains. In other words, the point of view is interior. Borges is not methodically estranging us from Averroes, but attempting to make us proximate and sympathetic to the limitations of his knowability.

His presentation of Funes, on the other hand, involves the quality of remoteness as an integral part of the protagonist's identity. The effort seems to be to extract the quintessential vagueness from the morass of indubitable fact:

> I remember him, with his face taciturn and Indian-like and singularly *remote*, behind the cigarette. I remember (I think) his angular, leather-braiding hands. I remember near those hands a maté gourd bearing the Uruguayan coat of arms; I remember a yellow screen with a vague lake landscape in the window of his house. (*L*, 59)

The details—Funes' "Indian-like" face, his narrow, competent hands, the maté cup resting near them, the yellowness of the screen —seem correct and complete until the word *"remote"* is introduced. The italicized *remote*ness serves, like the vague, homogeneous landscape on the yellowed shade, to make us uncomfortable with naturalism by reducing it to a limited foreground. Just behind and to the side of the immediate foreground of Funes' hands and meek possessions, something else begins to occur. Perhaps in a shiver of oblivion, or perhaps in a premonition of their covertness, details have begun to blur into somber uncertainty.

Although Borges' intellectual and temperamental impatience with the novel is well known (as we can gather not only from remarks in the essays but also from the compressed form of his own stories and from his favorite gambit of supposing a prose work of major length in order to give his précis of it), there are other ways in which he makes his discontent felt. In the case of his treatment

28

of detail in "Funes the Memorious," Borges implies the further objection against the naturalistic accretion of descriptive information, that even the most tiresomely particular character, living solely on the meat of his own impressions and failing to fashion even the low-level anecdotes associated with simple types, has the kind of philosophic roundness that novelistic treatment would betray and trivialize. Even such a 'common' character can create a world as intricate and endless as God's. Perhaps we can begin to see that Borges' method in holding us back from Funes is simply a variation of the pedagogic in the opening paragraph of "Averroes' Search"—to familiarize us with the Arab philosopher's primal emptiness is ultimately equivalent to estranging us from the surface of Funes. Toward the end of the story, Borges certifies the notion of profundity in the smallest scale:

> The two projects I have indicated (an infinite vocabulary for the natural series of numbers, a useless mental catalogue of all the images of his memory) are senseless, but they betray a certain stammering grandeur. They permit us to glimpse or infer the nature of Funes' vertiginous world. . . . He was the solitary and lucid spectator of a multiform, instantaneous and almost intolerably precise world. (*L*, 65)

The rising arc of Latinisms in this passage, culminating in that last sentence (where all the words except "almost" and "world" have direct Latin derivations), raises the problem of narrative voice even more forcefully than before, since it is a problem which occurs identically in the paragraphs from the two stories discussed above. In the opening paragraph of "Averroes' Search," words like "ancestors" (*antepasados*), "constancy" (*constancia*), "limits," (*confín*), "complex," "delicate," and "instrument" (*complejo y delicado instrumento*) seem to flow gracefully enough through the prose, until we come to that dizzying knot in the last sentence. In the paragraph just excerpted from "Funes the Memorious," the 'knot' is all the more striking since the story as a whole is so laden with Roman allusions, starting with Borges' traveling library of Pliny and Julius Caesar, to Funes' learning of the language. And of course the first paragraph, beginning with "I remember," charts the disappearance of Funes behind the word *"remote."*

Since the narratives themselves are so concerned with memory,

29

singularity, durability, and hence with Latin, it seems appropriate to ask some questions about the author's language. If Borges is saying something genuinely rich about Funes' powers and their implication, in what way does his tone of voice invite us further into Funes' "intolerably precise world," and in what way does the invitation call too much attention to itself? If there is pretension or excess in the tone, to what extent do their insights excuse the words' slight turbidity? Borges' fondness for the Latin tone, specifically for its consonantal pressures, must make us wonder what value he attaches to it, for if we are aware of it at all, we perceive it as a somewhat dogged cacophony softened by a philosophic aura. We could put it another way and say that the suspicion of elusive meanings restrains us from suspecting frivolity behind the rough-hewn mode.

There is frequent use throughout Borges' prose of this two-toned (half metaphysical, half ridiculous) Latinate style. Although the following examples were taken at random, the pattern seems to be that of attaching a heavy (Latin) adjective onto a looser, simpler, more understandable noun: "enormous dialogue," "rancorous scar," "populous towers," "populous dogma," "arduous schools," "unanimous night," "copious interjections," "inextricable pages," "portentous doors," "intimate ignorance," "remote pages," "sordid nightmares," "notorious proof," "abundant Hydra"—and the list continues.[9] Beneath all this adjectival enthusiasm, there *is* a sense of humor, but of an unusual kind. It is humor with all the insistent nonchalance of *opera buffa*—the humor of willing participation in an admittedly extreme world, be it the world of passionate comic reversal, or of an equally passionate meditative vanity. The effect of humor, to continue the parallel with light opera, is unconscious

9. In other Borgesian patterns, like the series, his tendency is also adjectival to the extent that accumulation takes place among attributes, so that the act or person modified remains stationary, while the secondary qualities glide and shift: "With frightening love, with anxiety, with admiration, with envy, Dante must have formed that line" (*OI,* 100). "In relief, in humiliation, in terror, he understood that he, too, was an appearance . . ." (*A,* 62). And the proudest, most Roman list of all is probably that describing the Library of Babel, which "will endure: illuminated, solitary, infinite, perfectly motionless, equipped with precious volumes, useless, incorruptible, secret" (*L,* 58).

on the part of those involved in the action, or (what puts the realization on a higher plane) simply unimportant to them. The librettist's exaggeration of interests, his invention of tests which endanger a given passion, creates a world in which the contrivance may indeed be hypothetical, but the response to it quite real. Because the comic undertow does not prevent the protagonists from deep and credible displays, parody, when it occurs, is after the fact. The comic heroes' focus upon the 'hypothesis' (of the plot) is so intense that its absurdity is irrelevant next to its possibility—its suggestive stress on their possible strength to meet it.

Similarly, one cannot argue the proportion of earnestness as against playfulness in Borges' style without disrupting its spirit. And the prime characteristic of his tone is, I would suggest, to *burrow* itself in verbal nodes whose weight of prefix and suffix, of negativity (in the use of "in-" words), and of inverted expressions of understanding, serve to alert his expository energy but without explaining anything. The "infallible," "incorruptible," "incomprehensible," "interminable" lists are like river soundings, clumsy but deep, for a vocabulary which would capture, not echo, its referents —soundings for a more precise language of mystery. As it stands, Borges' language nestles near the border of a little comic world full of apologies, postures, and plaints, stiff with longings and regrets— and all subject to this frame of prickly Latinisms which constitutes the genre, the decorum to which he has so often chosen to restrict himself.

If we accept the notion of Latin influence as Borges' gentle version of *opera buffa*—his willing participation in a linguistic world which paradoxically precipitates, intensifies, *and* cloaks those kernels of mystery—then there is no need to try to measure the degree of self-consciousness or -oblivion. From the outset, Borges' very adoption of the voice in question accounts for its own interpretation. It is not sufficient that the tone parody itself, reflect, rebound, or ultimately collapse upon itself; the voice must exceed its absurdity in such a way that its intense preoccupations can pull the burden of mockery in negative trace. It must parody its imprecisions, while allowing them room to acquire edges. It is this sharpness that we perceive—a tentative dimensionality. This is the quality which must now be explored.

> Turn on my tongue, O Spanish verse; confirm
> Once more what Spanish verse has always said
> Since Seneca's black Latin . . .
> —Borges, "Ewigkeit"

Latency

In describing Borges' language in the introduction to *Other Inquisitions,* James Irby compares the aspect of its witting/unwitting subjugation to the frame, with self-perpetuation: "Taut and effortless, transparent and mannered, deeply true to the genius of the Spanish language yet heterodox, his rhetoric is also a silent parody and extension of itself" (*OI*, xv). To be "a silent parody *and* extension of itself" is Irby's delicate oxymoron for the symbiosis between Borges' tone of voice and the kinds of investigations he conducts in the volume. Those investigations ("inquisitions") nearly always pertain to one of two ideas.

The first we might call the collation, whereby Borges desires to unearth a hidden history, as in "Avatars of the Tortoise":

> One concept corrupts and confuses the others. I am not speaking of the Evil whose limited sphere is ethics; I am speaking of the infinite. Once I wanted to compile its changeable history. . . .
> These pages belong to that illusory *Biography of the Infinite.* Their purpose is to record certain avatars of Zeno's second Paradox. (*OI*, 109)

And in "Kafka and His Precursors," Borges further extends the notion of history as the extraction and collation of buried resemblances, by implying the changeability of the past under the magnetic effect of a present (or recent) writer:

> If I am not mistaken, the heterogeneous selections I have mentioned resemble Kafka's work: if I am not mistaken, not all of them resemble each other. . . . His work modifies our conception of the past, as it will modify the future. In this correlation the identity or plurality of men matters not at all. (*OI*, 108)

The second idea motivating the inquisitions is that of closure, whereby Borges traces the synchronic history of one 'life' among a man's innumerable 'lives.' In "About William Beckford's *Vathek,*" Borges describes the project:

> Reality is so complex, history is so fragmentary and so simplified, that an omniscient observer could write an indefinite, and almost infinite, number of biog-

32

raphies of a man, each of which would emphasize different facts; we would have to read many of them before we realized that the protagonist was the same man. . . . A history of a man's dreams is not inconceivable; or of the organs of his body; or of the mistakes he has made; or of all the moments when he imagined the Pyramids; or of his traffic with night and with dawn. (*OI*, 137)

Borges' fondness for such whimsical partitions on the life of one man is equivalent to Funes' habit of comparing "the forms of southern clouds at dawn" with the "mottled streaks on a book in Spanish binding he had seen only once and with the outlines of the foam raised by an oar in the Río Negro the night before the Quebracho uprising" (*L, 63*). The point is not so much that Funes indulges in the particular to an extent that it becomes poetic, but rather that his microscopy duplicates Borges' vision of the biography of a man's mistakes, or of his dreams, but on the level of objects and perceptions; Funes' assumption is that they have 'lives' as complex and poorly annotated as do humans. Instead of partitioning a life, Funes places similarly private, whimsical partitions on a day, a moment, a pain behind the eyes, or on "the forms of southern clouds at dawn on the 30th of April, 1882." Since Funes can also discern in the speechless world about him "the tranquil advances of corruption, of decay, [and] of fatigue" (*L, 65*), it is just as likely that, instead of sculptural form, he will see in those clouds the history of their changes in hue, or the history of their dilation and dispersal, and that he will subsequently examine his memory of the clouds for their morphology.

The second important point about Funes' microcosm is that it reenacts not only the pattern of closure, the placing of partitions on a single thing (a memory or a life), but also that of the collation. (His unique manipulations of memory further imply that the two forms of 'hidden history' intersect.) Those southern clouds, for example, function with respect to the past as held in Funes' memory in the same way Kafka functions with respect to Kierkegaard's parable of the North Pole expedition and to the unknown friend in Browning's "Fears and Scruples"—that is, the cloud's forms create *precursors* in the shape of a remembered book binding and of a palimpsest, the foam from a certain oar created upon the water —and another unique 'history' emerges.

33

In Borges' fiction, the form of 'hidden history' I have called the collation is apparent as a kind of specious, instant union between a figure and his archetype; the term 'specious' is used both because it pairs reason with fatuity and because the primarily cerebral origin of the theme produces unlikely intuitions. A good example of the 'specious union' occurs in Borges' page-long set of hypotheses about Don Quixote's reaction to the murder of someone. The intentionally laconic proposals are, I think, meant to echo Kafka's even shorter "Prometheus," and end, as does the model's, with proposal number four:

> **There remains another conjecture, alien to the Spanish world. . . . Don Quixote, who is no longer Don Quixote but rather a king of the Hindustani cycles, intuitively knows as he stands before his enemy's cadaver that to kill and to beget are divine or magical acts which manifestly transcend humanity. He knows that the dead man is an illusion, as is the bloody sword that weighs down his hand, as is he himself, and all his past life, and the vast gods, and the universe. (DT, 37) [10]**

Since the figure of Cervantes' Don Quixote is already a magical one, who evokes, if he does not always control, the themes of irony and illusion, to make him a murderer in a parable where more modern ethical sentiments are easily brought to bear is to

10. One notes an immediate similarity between the Borges and Kafka parables in the use of an iteration with cosmic proportions:
"According to the third [legend, Prometheus'] treachery was forgotten in the course of thousands of years, the gods forgotten, the eagles, he himself forgotten.
"According to the fourth, everyone grew weary of the meaningless affair. The gods grew weary, the eagles grew weary, the wound closed wearily." Franz Kafka, *Parables and Paradoxes* (New York, 1961), p. 83.
The link with Kafka is also apparent in Quixote's immediate assumption that the most offensive of objects—the man he has just murdered—is an allusion. Kafka is master of the suddenly vanished fact, whether it is the song of the sirens (which is, in reality, silence), or the message which disappears when it comes time to deliver it, or the Messiah who comes only when he is no longer necessary, or the disclosure that *Don Quixote* could only have been written by the one who stood to be best entertained by it—Sancho Panza.
That the form of Borges' fourth conjecture is probably indebted to Kafka (although not necessarily to this particular example) can be seen by comparing it with the closing paragraph of "The Silence of the Sirens": "A codicil to the foregoing has also been handed down. Ulysses, it is said, was so full of guile, was such a fox, that not even the goddess of fate could pierce his armor. Perhaps he had really noticed . . . that the Sirens were silent, and opposed the aforementioned pretense [stopping his ears with wax] to them and to the gods merely as a sort of shield." *Ibid.*, p. 91. Both Borges and Kafka descend to a kind of epilogue for their most vivid conjectures, which are then delivered offhandedly; as if to soothe our incredulity, they pretend to neither believe nor care.

introduce an element of banality. And it is this banal danger of actual murder which Borges then rescues him from. Balancing Quixote's fate as a sympathetic character over the alternatives of sanity and madness, Borges then prepares for the ultimate elevation to divine and cyclic knowledge. It is a knowledge unavailable to the Don Quixote we know—it even makes him ludicrous—but it illustrates Borges' attempt to parabolize an established character, if only by re-forming him into that figure with which he is best able to deal: the vacant, dreaming priest, the murderer, the dying god, the pantheistic clerk. It is a measure of how deeply habitual Borges' favored personae are that he can only rescue Don Quixote from the tightfisted pages of Cervantes by reducing his quest to an act whose consequences cannot fail to involve our judgment, and that, against these odds, the only Don Quixote to come to consciousness is one who steps entirely outside the tradition which makes him what he is.

The same could be said of the man in "The Waiting" who spends his days watching detective movies and waiting for Alejandro Villari to kill him. He has taken the name Villari, "not as a secret challenge, not to mitigate the humiliation which actually he did not feel, but because that name troubled him, because it was impossible for him to think of any other" (L, 166). Drugged by single-mindedness, "Villari" is thus dressed with all the details which would ally him with an underworld of small and not very smart hoods, fluent in the arts of waiting, keeping still, hiding. He has an approximate range of background detail which appears to 'situate' him culturally and socially; but for all that, his most remarkable trait is his improbable enthusiasm for the ritual he is enacting— propitiating his own death as he takes on the obsessions of his opponent. "He would," Borges writes, "submissively try to like the [gangster movies]; he wanted to anticipate the intention with which they were shown. Unlike people who read novels, he never saw himself as a character in a work of art" (L, 166). Ingenuous in his desire to fathom others' motives, "Villari" becomes forgetful of his own; being unfamiliar with literature therefore makes him a pure specimen for an experiment with identity. The experiment includes a dream in which his murderer does not recognize him, also an inability to decide whether the real Villari's death would be "a relief or a misfortune," and, finally, his philosophic observation about the immediate disappearance of time into the past, juxtaposed with Borges' remark that "in moments like this, he was not much more complex than [a] dog" (*L,* 167). The final incongruity is, of course, that he reads Dante while waiting for the other gangster to catch up with him.

It is obvious that the portrait of "Villari" does not hold together, but its seams are visible in ways that seem intentional. As for Don Quixote, so for "Alejandro Villari," the assumption of banality or criminality forms the potential abyss (whether of book-length commentary on the *Quixote* or of a novel about the underworld) from which Borges can then stylistically redeem his representative men. It is the exhaustive—which is to say, psychological—platitude from which Borges persistently recoils.

Even when his subject is the commonplace, the particular, and the tawdry, Borges sustains the subterfuge of mystery. The two constants of "The Waiting" are banality and magic. Funes' miniaturist vision is boring as well as dizzying; and even such tales as Borges has proudly labeled "straightforward," [11] like "Guayaquil," are grounded in historical epiphany, reincarnation, or gnostic communion. In fact, Borges' second recurring gesture, that of yielding to the complexity of reality and choosing only one of its many possible truths (the biography of a man's mistakes or of his "traffic" with twilight and dawn), is merely a different way of getting at the same thing. By probing into smaller and smaller realms of existence, placing ever more refined partitions on those deepening, multiplying worlds, distortion slowly gives way to structure, and the bland closure of singlemindedness to a circular universality.

Although the descent into the particular stands in marked contrast to the ascent to the 'logical epiphany,' the former's exclusiveness often occurs as an interior layering within the global, expansive tendency of the latter. Juan Dahlmann in "The South," for

---

11. See the second paragraph of the preface to *Doctor Brodie's Report.*

example, views the landscape of that magic, nearly prehistoric region as an ageless, indifferent voice which shelters a personal call:

> ...he saw gullies and lagoons and ranches; he saw great luminous clouds that resembled marble; and all these things were accidental, casual, like dreams of the plain.... The elemental earth was not perturbed either by settlements or other signs of humanity. *The country was vast but at the same time intimate and, in some measure, secret.* The limitless country sometimes contained only a solitary bull. (*F*, 170–71, my emphasis)

In the series of attributes in the italicized sentence, "vast" and "intimate" are really exaggerations addressed to the country itself. Like the Spain in "Averroes' Search," however, the South is a surrealist duality, alienating the few marks (like the bull) which signal its tremendous expanse, but at the same time smothering them. "Intimate" is the fulcrum, equalizing the balance between the landscape's alien mood and Dahlmann's intuition of a personal tie. Vastness gives way to intimacy and finally secrecy, as the invitation to infinitude is met by Dahlmann's sympathetic projection and retention of boundaries, the systole and diastole of personal identity. The country's vastness is only periphrasis for its retentiveness—its intimacy with itself, its dialogue with consciousness—and hence reveals itself as the very germ of privacy.

Since both involve the subtle blur between the self's boundaries and the infinite, the subtle passage of forms through their own alterations, Borges' interest in 'hidden histories' is analogous to his interest in language and the making of metaphors. What complicates the study of his work is that he can also hear the philosophical nuances in such an analogy. This invariably leads him to include in his histories and lifelong metaphors the question of sameness. How much can something change and still remain the same? How great a distance must one travel before an oddity will, by repeating itself (or simply by evidential growth), lose its singularity? And, by the same token, he wonders whether the tangential and minute might not empty as rich a stream into this ocean of resemblances as does the River of Heraclitus.

Although Borges' dual interest in the esoteric history and the making of a metaphor is present in nearly every piece he has written, there is one essay in *Other Inquisitions* which sets both

37

under the aegis of philosophy, in such a way as to lead us gradually back to Funes and his Latin. I am speaking of "From Someone to Nobody," in which Borges inspects the fabric of Western thought under the guise of showing the collapse of plurals and superlatives into the simple negative, *nihilum*.

The essay is not so much the exploration of a concept as it is the convocation of its rhetorical variants. It begins with the various intensive expressions for God: *Elohim* ("the gods," which occurs with a singular verb); *Yahweh* ("I Am That I Am"); King of Kings ("a superlative of king in the original text"); and then the use of the prefix *omni-* (*omnipotent, omnipresent, omniscient*— words "which make of God a respectful chaos of unimaginable superlatives," *OI,* 147).[12] Then Borges transfers his attention to Erigena, who in the ninth century A.D. wrote that God " 'does not know what He is, because He is not a what, and is incomprehensible to Himself and to all intelligence.' " Erigena was the first to use the Latin word *nihilum* (nothing) to describe the Divinity.

This was a shift which, whatever its effect on subsequent thought, at least gives Borges an origin for an important trend among his own historical gallery. In this case, the gallery is represented solely (and perhaps sufficiently) by the figure of Shakespeare; the process of which his double-jointed elusiveness partakes Borges calls the "[m]agnification to nothingness." The subtle association of Shakespeare with gods and buddhas is perhaps the closest Borges ever comes to acknowledging that the cult of genius has been substituted for theology.

In "Everything and Nothing," Borges redeems the analogy between God and Shakespeare by recording the Lord's remark to the Bard, " 'I too have no self' " (*SP,* 260), and by magnifying the idea of nothingness until it becomes a positive, if shadowy, value:

In him there was no one. Behind his face ... and his words (which were swarming, fanciful, and excited), there was only a touch of coldness, a dream undreamed by anyone. (*SP,* 259)

12. He has elsewhere called them "a clutter of insipid superlatives." See "The Approach to al-Mu'tasim" (*A,* 49).

By comparing the two essays, we have a means of reading between the genial scholia in which Borges appears to deride the logical frailty of the celestial *nihilum:*

[God] is not sapient, He is more than sapient; He is not good, He is more than good; inscrutably He exceeds and rejects all attributes.... He is Nothing and Nobody; those who imagined Him thus did so in the belief that it was more than being a Who, more than being a What. **(OI, 147)**

Similarly, the Lord's declaration to Shakespeare in "Everything and Nothing" that both of them are " 'many men and no one' " forms its own corrective commentary on Borges' imputation of inconsequence to those who think that

To be one thing is inexorably not to be all the other things. The confused intuition of that truth has induced men to imagine that not being is more than being something and that, somehow, not to be is to be everything. **(OI, 148)**

Despite Borges' derogation of the idea that "somehow, not to be is to be everything," this is so constant a premise in his fiction that it not only supports the obvious jump from the single to the Divine, but just as forcefully grounds the descent into an Other which is *smaller* than the self.

The dual potential of Otherness may seem more manageable if we think of it not merely as a possible addition of being, but also as a possibility of being elsewhere. If you are one thing, you are nothing Other; isolation, the alien which begins where one ends, a solitude of wholeness—these are the characteristics of being one thing as Borges sees it. Consequently, there is not one of his figures who could be called 'one thing'; all his people are, with respect to Otherness, entirely porous. They are nothing, they are everywhere Other, and, within the uniformity of being every-where else but *there*—of being always Other—they are, through-out that Elsewhere, the Same. Being purely one thing, one can never become Same to himself. The cosmic Sameness to which Borges recurs, however, is a comparative mode and requires dis-tance—an absorption in an Elsewhere. What remains to be seen is that stepping beyond oneself into an Other can also take the form of interior reduction.

We would ordinarily think that Funes' sensuous preferences are precisely the opposite of Averroes'—that they are, in effect, 'positive' rather than 'negative'; that they deal with a minutely partitioned but still solid reality; and that the mottled binding on that Spanish book, the maté cup, and the dog, seen at three fourteen from the side, may have a strange place in an even stranger hierarchy; but that at least they are not *mistakes*. It is equally true, however, that Borges carefully underscores the mysterious, protean tendency of exaggerations to decompose. In his role as narrator of Funes' tale, he is continually made to feel the purpose within a system which the character invents but cannot control, nor use for his own development. Funes' memory is, in addition, not the first among his talents to cause the narrator uneasiness; beyond the refined mnemonics which enables Funes to call each thing he has seen, each time he has seen it, by a different name, there is his far more disconcerting ability to see *slowly* the intricate form of an object we can only see *quickly*. Borges labels this perception "immediate"—but this is an extrinsic description, operating by analogy with our own vision. Intrinsically, Funes' time has been differently geared, so that what we call immediacy of perception is actually a tireless staring over time—an Other time.

Averroes' perception is agnostic to time because he remains above it, unhurried by it, impervious to its surprises; Funes' perception is agnostic to time because he moves *beneath* it. In each case, being originates in a set of temporal rhythms which meet a schedule Elsewhere. In his deliberate externality, everything escapes Averroes, while nothing escapes Funes in his, not even the most ephemeral impressions. They have this in common, however: that Funes' 'intimacy' is estrangement, too. His categories and terms are, in principle, esoteric. His knowledge becomes similar to Averroes' in all important respects: internally manipulable yet unable to influence the real world; tending to reduce itself to structures, but structures which appear to describe the creators' mental processes —a knowledge, in each case, which will not let itself be pinned down.

Just as there is no Borges figure who can claim selfhood as 'one thing,' so there is no knowledge on the part of any of them which can claim a field of mastery. All knowledge is, in this sense, alchemical; it has only spurious referents, and, as a result, its premises and theories take on equivocal meanings. There remain only different ways of stating the equivocality. "Averroes' Search" suggests the fruitlessness of forms confined in the ideal; the maxim of the equivocal in this tale would be that there is no one thing whose definition is either important or ascertainable. "Funes the Memorious" suggests the replication of superfluity in the particular; the variant reading of the maxim also comes forth. If there is no one thing whose definition is not equivocal, there is, just as defensibly, no one thing whose definition does not imply the whole of creation. The reciprocating gloss of the one story on the other repeats the dynamic of the shift from someone to nobody, the last stage of which opens the field from nobody to everything.

"[S]omehow," Borges wrote, "not to be is to be everything." He marked that sentence as the result of a "confused intuition" of the "truth" that being one thing is to be nothing else. Now the irony has become twofold. Not only does Borges find the first part of this wobbly syllogism uninteresting, and the conclusion highly provocative; he also proves his greater affection for the change from nothing to everything in the very tale in which he concentrated so much 'singularity.' "Funes the Memorious," which purports to be an investigation into the singular, in fact reveals that being one thing may be universal (as it is for Averroes), but it is not additive, divisional, or multiplicative. In other words, Funes has not been able to 'possess' so large a number of his moments without in some way dispersing himself among them. The paradigm of this compromise is (to paraphrase Auden) the retention of the I against a simultaneous loss of the self.

Because Funes' overdetermined mental order allows him to keep the I but lose the self—because he, too, is incapable of becoming a *character*—Borges resorts to the 'approximate style' with which we have become so familiar. It is a way of saving his special literary genre from becoming sheer silliness or sheer condescension. It reserves for the scholastic duality of nothing-and-everything the possibility of a secret order within the merely facile—merely verbal

41

—formulas. It is in this way that Latinisms find their true place in Borges' vocabulary. By alerting us to the intensities in Borges' thought, they partially absolve their own haziness; they secure the simple noun from exhaustiveness, painting a corona of uncertainty about the factitious; and they also induce quality and texture in the abstract, making nothingness rhythmic, recursive. The Latinate style mirrors the state of mind—the "unreflected"—to which Borges' figures have returned.

> **His voice was speaking in Latin; his voice (which came from the darkness) was articulating with morose delight a speech or prayer or incantation. The Roman syllables resounded in the earthen patio; my fear took them to be indecipherable, interminable; afterwards, in the enormous dialogue of that night, I learned they formed the first paragraph of the twenty-fourth chapter of the seventh book of the *Naturalis historia*. The subject of that chapter is memory; the last words were** *ut nihil non iisdem verbis redderetur auditum.* **(L, 62)**

The Latin in this passage refers to Simonides' art of memory, which had been brought to such a pitch of perfection that he could repeat exactly what he had heard only once (lit., that nothing once heard be not repeated in the very same words).[13] The paragraph as a whole works in much the same way as the earlier description of the meeting in the storm does—shrinking from the realm of the abstract to that of the ironclad—from vastness, infinite possibility, and infinite portent to the tightened capsule of particularity. Here, instead of a storm and blowing trees, we have the

13. The story of Funes, which Borges has called "a long metaphor of insomnia," owes much to the chapter on memory in the crabbed and questionably accurate *Naturalis historia,* where Pliny describes as follows the wanderings of the spirit during sleep: "... let sleep creep at any time upon us, [memory] seemeth to be vanquished, so as our poor spirit wandereth up and down to seek where it is, and to recover it again" (Philemon Holland's translation, 1601).

Funes, however, has trouble sleeping, and turns his head toward a block of new houses he has never seen in order to induce forgetfulness; he also imagines himself "at the bottom of the river, rocked and annihilated by the current" (*L,* 66)—descriptions which are only enhanced by Pliny's image of the aimless spirit trying to recover its identity (memory) during sleep.

In the same chapter (VII, 24), Pliny also records pathological cases, among them the fate of a man who fell from a roof and was stricken with amnesia. Between Borges' first meeting with Funes in the storm, and the "enormous dialogue" of the second meeting, Funes has meantime been paralyzed by a fall from a horse. The spirit of Pliny's pathology is retained, except that Funes suffers the opposite of amnesia: "Somewhat later he learned that he was paralyzed. The fact scarcely interested him. He reasoned (he felt) that his immobility was a minimum price to pay. Now his perception and his memory were infallible" (*L,* 63).

42

expanse of a rhetorical void. And instead of Funes' gaucho pants and the high brick walls, there is the aggressive symmetry of the double negative, *nihil non.*

In the descent to closure in the two paragraphs, however, the visual and rhetorical narrowing is a movement toward anagogic rather than spatial simplification. Just as Borges unexpectedly distances Funes' face by using the word *"remote,"* here he super-imposes upon Funes' retentive chaos the idea of an interior, reflex order within the things, the impressions themselves. By belliger-ently rejecting descriptions, Funes mirrors Borges' fascination with the *nihilum* which exceeds attributes; even the word "dog" is too general a term for the multitude of canine images he slowly as-sembles. This is why he desires a language which can be used only once—an endless tongue of absolute reference. (The in-habitants of Tlön are less demanding; they settle for nouns com-prised of adjectives.) By renouncing the adjective along with the noun, and hence denying that linguistic attribution of any kind is possible, Funes has become as refractory to formulation as Erigena's God. Rather than remaining a mere Nietzschean hermit, Funes has exceeded the bondage of words (or imposed 'types') through the intensity of his desire to be free of them. Borges respects this purity, granting it whatever substance he is able. His use of the Latin tone in the first part of the Pliny paragraph is his effort to qualify a system which, like Averroes', admits neither content nor correction.

It must further be argued that the negatives "interminable" and "indecipherable" are imprecise, not merely abstract. Their pretense is to withhold more than the simple, slack ambiguousness which they might reveal on the pages of someone else's work. These negatives are more on the order of the inconceivable, as opposed to the indefinite, number. It is not sufficient that Funes be a parody of retention, he must also exceed the attribution of memory in such a way that he not only steps beyond it but trails its insuffi-ciency along behind him. Funes is not memorious; he is more than memorious. Incapable of ordering the trivia that come his way, he does more than order them—he perceives things so in-

43

tensely that they become vast. As the second excerpt below will make clear, Funes' mind is, given the negligible transforming of scale, identical with God's:

A circle drawn on a blackboard, a right triangle, a lozenge—all these are forms we can fully and intuitively grasp; Ireneo [Funes] could do the same with the stormy mane of a pony, with a herd of cattle on a hill, with the changing fire and its innumerable ashes, with the many faces of a dead man throughout a long wake. (*L*, 64)

What is a divine mind? the reader will perhaps inquire. There is not a theologian who does not define it; I prefer an example. The steps a man takes from the day of his birth until that of his death trace in time an inconceivable figure. The Divine Mind intuitively grasps that form immediately, as men do a triangle. This figure (perhaps) has its given function in the economy of the universe. (*L*, 212)

According to Borges' note to "The Mirror of Enigmas," there exists a 'form' to describe the lurching, random 'path' our days have traced. This form has an 'immediacy' of reference in the Divine Mind—an 'immediacy' of apprehension which is incommunicable except through the allegorical use of concepts like 'path' and 'form.' [14] This does not prevent the human reference, the human totality subsumed by such words from being a fixed reality in the mind of God. Similarly, Funes' apprehension of the 'forms' taken by an unmoving dead man's face or by a horse's mane may be verifiable to him alone. This does not prevent his 'immediate' grasp from being apodictic. To convey both the monumental weight and the immediate familiarity which contribute to this elevated act of perception, Borges allows analogues to the way we recognize chalk circles or achieve familiarity with the right triangle. What must be borne in mind is that all such familiarity is a concession—an allegorization. It is only the "instantaneous and almost intolerably precise world"—the economy of Otherness —which is perennial.

14. Borges may have been struck by a similar idea in Keats's poem "The Fall of Hyperion" (1819):

> ... there grew
> A power within me of enormous ken,
> To see as a god sees, and take the depth
> Of things as nimbly as the outward eye
> Can size and shape pervade.
> (ll. 302–5)

In the closing paragraph of "Funes the Memorious," Borges describes how the light of dawn permits him his second and final view of Funes' face:

> ... Then I saw the face belonging to the voice that had spoken all night long. Ireneo was nineteen years old; ... he seemed to me as monumental as bronze, more ancient than Egypt, older than the prophecies and the pyramids. (*L*, 66)

It should no longer be surprising that we hear in Borges' account of the most trivial and unique creature on earth echoes of Averroes' deafness to fact, of Quixote's Oriental weariness, and of the colorless voice which speaks to Dahlmann out of his vast and mythic South. In writing the phrases "as monumental as bronze, more ancient than Egypt, older than the prophecies and the pyramids," Borges incants not only the specious generations to which Funes is heir; not only the link with a Divine Mind of such indiscriminant breadth; not only the narrator's fear of prolonging an interview which Funes will never allow to be forgotten. Borges is also drawing an echo from the Roman poet who desired, in stating a hope, to create a reality, asserting simply that he "will not entirely die," that he had made something as indestructible as bronze out of mere words:

> *Exegi monumentum aere perennius*
> *regalique situ pyramidum altius ...*
> (Horace, *Odes*, III, 30)

> I have built a monument more enduring than bronze,
> Loftier than the royal pile of the Pyramids.

To discover a verse from Horace beneath the prose of Borges is a little like being told that one author (who was Dante, Shakespeare, Homer, etc.) wrote all the books. Whether Borges believes this or not is unimportant. What is important is that Borges' voice coincides with such belief.

Borges justified:
notes and texts toward
stations of a theme
RONALD CHRIST

*A man proposes to himself the task of sketching
the world. Through the years he populates a
space with images of provinces, kingdoms, bays,
ships, islands, fish, rooms, instruments, stars,
horses, and people. A little before his death,
he discovers that this patient labyrinth
of lines traces the image of his face.*
—*Epilogue to* The Maker (El hacedor)

I want to imagine the image in that paragraph—to try to see it. Not the face itself; *that* vision belongs to others and, besides, it really doesn't interest me. Instead, I want to contemplate the person Borges presents (remembering of course that "person" means "mask"), because I have tended to watch the images of those provinces, stars, horses, and people, without reading their hieroglyphic. In other words, I want to concentrate on the impression Borges gives off rather than the impression he gives—borrowing that useful distinction from Erving Goffman. I want to witness the performance of his self—regretting, though, that the word "performance" is stiffening into cant determined partly by Borges' own fiction: the film *Performance* [1] proceeds from his story "The South."

Perhaps it will seem that I'm playing with (and failing at)

1. *Performance* is the crucial locus, but some other contemporary indications of the pervasive metaphor are Erving Goffman's *The Presentation of Self in Everyday Life*—the opening chapter is entitled "Performances"; Richard Poirier's *The Performing Self*, which actually treats Borges; and Harold Rosenberg's *Act and the Actor: Making the Self*. None of these writers, however, and not even Borges himself, makes much or enough of Pirandello, who surely gave the most feelingful expression to the figure, just as none attends to Bergman's *Persona*, the most perfect expression.

46

biography, thematics, or, worse still, psychology. That's a risk I'll have to take, relying all the while on you to keep in mind that the image, the *persona,* the "naked mask" is what I want to see, what I think needs to be seen, and not the man or the mind or the spirit behind the mask, if indeed we can still believe in such things.

C'est un assez grand miracle de se doubler, et n'en
cognoissent pas la hauteur ceux qui parlent de se tripler.
—*Montaigne*

1

Two anecdotes about Borges, one centrifugal, one centripetal:

On an evening when he was going to give a lecture at the School of Visual Arts in New York, Borges, his entourage, and a number of the audience were waiting for an elevator to take them up to the lecture hall. The elevator doors opened and the crowd broke like a wave, separating the nearly blind Borges from the man guiding him; the doors closed and the man called out: "Is Borges here?" "No," a voice responded. "It's the other Borges." It was Borges who spoke.

A critic interviewed Borges and then published the conversation with a note explaining, in part, how significant it was that the entire dialogue had taken place in English. Later the critic translated someone else's interview with a Latin American poet for the same magazine in which the Borges interview appeared. But the editor, who had spent hours working over the Borges interview and its introductory note, was dissatisfied with the way the second poet spoke and complained to the interviewer: "You'd better have the translator go over this again. I just don't understand. He did such a good job translating Borges."

Trivial and *therefore* meaningful, these anecdotes reveal at their intersection two forms of an attitude toward a single character, the writer Borges—an attitude which is dependent on a sense of foreignness, of otherness. On the one hand Borges trifles with the splendid invention of "Borges y yo" and jokingly distinguishes between his personal, physical presence, and his authorial, professional presence without specifying, notice, which or who the other Borges is. He is putting on his audience by putting on his work. His joke is made for the amusement of the others in the elevator, and therefore, to establish the distance and objectification of the performer before his audience, Borges subverts the communication of a direct address by an abbreviated monologue. While pretending to answer his questioner, Borges in fact ignores the presence of that questioner by indirectly addressing his monologue

47

to the crowd, who have *not* asked the question. But then, his inter-locutor also has oddly ignored Borges' presence—the "subject" of his question—by asking "Is Borges here?", not "Are you here, Borges?"

Borges often fools in this way, and his joking is no less an expression of his relation to self than of his relation to others; in order for Borges to be Borges to Borges, he must imagine an other against whose background he can stand out—the one literally the foil for the other. In order to be one, he doubles himself. On the other hand, for Borges to be Borges to us—native readers of English, to that editor—we think of him as remote, as Argentine, as a writer of strange fictions in a *foreign* language. Both strategies produce a sense of self by defining the other; but whereas Borges' maneuver has been the efficient method and enticing substance of his art for years, our conception is snobbish and debilitating, keep-ing us on the outside of Borges' art while it only apparently recognizes his true otherness. For Borges, the maneuver has been a justifying game and proof of self; for us, it has been a means of keeping him at a distance, for resisting an awareness of just how close he has come to the center of our lives. Finally, Borges will be justified, will be Borges, when we recognize how he has doubled himself by becoming a major author in *that* language, Spanish, and then, *with the same works,* a major author in *our* language, English. Borges will be justified from within and with-out when his intimacy—that is, his Englishness—is known to us. Borges' translation of Borges is therefore that justification.

2

It's all there in that essay Borges published in 1926, in a collection
entitled *The Extent of My Hope*—one of those early works he
now completely rejects, refuses to reissue, and buys up whenever
he can in order to burn. His reaction seems excessive; but maybe
that is because we are not so much aware of the posturing in his
early prose (the imperial assertion of those three paratactic clauses,
supported by that immodest, almost Johnsonian "perhaps," to
transmit an egoism at odds with the cautious, gentle tentativeness
of that writer we know), as we are impressed by our glimpse of a
young man defining his destiny, his plan for being someone, for
being Borges.

In the "Profession of Literary Faith," a writer lays his life on the
lines of the page he is writing; the affirmed hope of the volume's
title conjoins with the eschatological imagery and the occasion of
credo in this essay to establish what can only be called a context
of formulated crisis. Borges may now reject such tense postures,
but there is no doubting the earnestness, the deliberateness, the
cleverness with which he has indeed devoted himself to a justification through literature, nor is there any point in ignoring the way
he subsequently developed the myth of his not-so-much-having-
lived-as-written. In fact, as the wording of that last clause suggests, *to have written* is *to have lived*. Here, really, is a literary
Calvinism, a justification through good works.

When one removes the ultimate perspective of the Last Judgment, however, as Borges intends in the brief paragraph following
the sentences quoted above, the proof of good works is not in a
post-mortem reward but in their seeming continuity with life and
living things:

49

> Simply: that page, which in the dusk—before the resolved truth of day's end, of sunset, of vague new breeze, of girls who stand clear against the street—I would dare to read to a friend.[2]

That shift, delicately hinged on the egregious "simply," is not a shift to simpler language; if anything, this paragraph is more idiosyncratically plotted than any other passage in the essay. No, Borges shifts here to a feeling whose chronological perspective is not eschatalogical in the way of the Last Judgment scene in the preceding paragraph, but whose syntax is nevertheless a postponement: literally, a periodic *post-pone-ment*. The indefinite structure of that sentence, locating a terminal pathos, is all the more expressive for placing Borges' timid passion more in the context of things and people (dusk, breeze, girls), by delivering it last, and thus fulfilling a spurious contemporaneity of scene and agent. Sequence, after all, is not simultaneity.

A discredited *theory* of time is everywhere evident in Borges; but what about this *syntax* of time which expresses saddening delay? Eschatology is the theology of last things; similarly, periodicity is the syntax of last things. Both, in Borges, yield little cause for exultation.

Periodicity is pathos in Borges. (Periodicity is *the* pathos in Borges?)

Passion, then, in the fullest sense, is the informing emotion of these two linked passages which stand like a prose diptych displaying a religious tableau and a (literary) genre subject. While our rejoicing in the mastery of the confrontation can hardly match the arrogance of the master, we can still observe the structure exhibited: namely, in each panel, the image of one who reads, speaks his justification to a silent audience whose reaction is implied but unspoken. The relation in each case is through the page and that relation is projected or anticipated while the response is withheld.

2. Here as elsewhere, except when noted or indicated by parenthetical reference, I am responsible for the translation of Borges' prose. While I would not defend this rendition on most points, I think it does suggest a measure of the real difficulty in Borges, which is always rhetorical.

I have extorted the translation on my own, but I am grateful to Carter Wheelock for, among other things, helping to elucidate this passage for me.

To demand the muse is commonplace, inspiration is commonplace; to rely upon the audience by virtue of one's act is daring: expiration is literature.

That is, Borges' writing demands the other, not in the sense of readers or publishers or critics or students (although it wishes for them too), but the other as measure and guarantee of his existence, worth. His prose is grounded as speech in an other, it is imaged forth in such speech and it discovers his value in such speech; yet that prose issues into a world of monologous singleness, where the "I" is all and therefore unsure of its very being because the "You" who might ransom that being is remote, perhaps imaginary.

The justification engraved upon the medallion scenes in this early essay is iconographically clear, but its constitutive relation, as the Spanish testifies, is subjunctive, is conditional.

The urge to extend hope finds both expression and justification in writing, but at the boundary of that hope there must be the other, if not supplied and available, then manufactured and sustained: the other, in hypostatic procession, must then emanate from the self.

"All living is meeting," writes Martin Buber in *I and Thou*—but a question is *how?* In this diptych, Buber has proposed an answer: through the written page. He presents himself to the angels in the page which is vindication, and he communicates with his friend by means of the page which is expression. In both cases, he is in, he lives through the page; and thus the central issue of his writing—Do I exist? Can a man exist?—is located early in his work and a possible solution is offered: yes, by relation (with friends, with angels) through the writing. But, as Buber also writes, "Relation is mutual"; and in each of the scenes Borges evokes there is no direct response to his gesture of existence: we do not hear the judgment or see the echoing faces. In fact, the counter-implication is possible: the angels, having heard, will condemn; the friend, too, to whom he dares read the page, will not respond. What we are left with in that case is the cause—a need for justification, and the brave gesture, the boldness—but no final, no positive, no present comfort.

What are the alternatives?

*Writing was an activity able to hold its shape
in the material world; thus it began to give
shape to an "I" that existed apart from the
responses of its public.*
—Harold Rosenberg on Sartre

*A preoccupation with identity and sometimes its
discord, duality, runs through much of my work.*
—Borges on "Borges and Myself"

Wish I could find a good book—to live in.
—Melanie

3

Two years ago, a producer of educational movies asked me to write program notes for a film called *The Inner World of Jorge Luis Borges*. One scene in that film showed Borges walking down a street in Buenos Aires, reciting a poem in English. Always intent on being Borges, Borges had chosen some lines from Keats which fit snugly into the history of the Eternal Return which Borges has constructed:

> **Perhaps the self-same song that found a path**
> **Through the sad heart of Ruth, when, sick for home,**
> **She stood in tears amid the alien corn. . . .**

Confident that I could ask an appropriate question without knowing the answer, I wrote in the section of the guide devoted to discussion of the movie: "What is unusual about the way Borges recites these lines? (Would you recite them that way?)" I knew I could answer only part of that question: No, I would never read lines that way. Not just because Borges flattened the rhythm as he recited with an elocutionist's care for stress and diction, contradicting everything he has ever said about "the verbal music of English"; not just because he purchased the heft and balance of those words —caring little for the sense—without transmitting any of the spell he put on himself. No, it had more to do with the vision of Borges walking away into the illusionary depths of the screen as he intoned those well-known words while his voice on the sound track stood simultaneous with the visual plane. But that was all. That was as far as I could get.

Early in the spring of last year, Borges and I were walking

52

of one of his editors, who told me how, every time an eager assistant runs into the office offering a new interview with Borges, she says thank you to the assistant's enthusiasm and puts the interview away without reading it. She thinks she has learned that Borges is always repeating himself. What she doesn't realize is the actual dimension of that verb.

Then, too, we must not forget that Borges is probably the most interviewed author alive. He seems unwilling to refuse those occasions, burdensome as they may be, which will evoke dialogues with himself: his identity. But these are interviews *of* Borges, not *with* him. (Etymology is to the point here: *entre,* "mutually," "each other," "between," and *ver,* "to see." Precisely what doesn't happen in a Borges interview.)

What is really interesting, however, is the way this management operates in his creative work. An illustration from an interview, appropriately enough, will clarify my point. Borges is talking with Napoléon Murat, and in part what he says about his beginnings as a storyteller translates:

> ...I had met a man from the Palermo district who talked a little like my good fellow; that is to say, who told stories a little like that story. He was an old murderer.
>
> When I wrote this story ["Streetcorner Man"], my friend was dead. His name was don Nicolás Paredes. At that time, I wrote each sentence very slowly, very painstakingly, because I would reread it, trying to sound it in his voice. If there was anything too literary, I would erase it. That helped me to really strike out the literary phrases—"literary" in the bad sense of the word.
>
> Then I said to myself: "I can write stories," and I had launched myself a bit.[5]

Quite simply, Borges is saying that he became a storyteller by inviting the voice of the dead murderer to invest his, Borges' own, vocal cords. As the voice of his father legitimizes his recitation of poetry in English, so the voice of Paredes warranted his writing the story. Borges justified his own composition by application to a part of himself presented as Paredes; or, to put it another way, he doubled himself as author—"divided" would be the miser's description—and collaborated in the writing.

If we chose to, we might label this generous lending of self

5. "Entretiens avec Napoléon Murat," *L'Herne* (Paris, 1964), p. 379.

important. What counts is his management of self by recourse to some other, a deployment which points to the way Borges experiences himself, his self. On the one hand, the procedure is fundamental and typical, as George Herbert Mead argues:

When a self does appear it always involves an experience of another; there could not be an experience of a self simply by itself. The plant or the lower animal reacts to its environment, but there is no experience of a self. When a self does appear in experience it appears over against the other. . . .[3]

Or the deployment is accomplished in a human reunion, through which man yet grows essential and distinct. This is how, for example, Martin Buber presents it, quoting Friedrich Heinrich Jacobi ("The I is impossible without the Thou"):

In all ages it has undoubtedly been glimpsed that the reciprocal essential relationship between two beings signifies a primal opportunity of being, and one, in fact, that enters into the phenomenon that man exists. And it has also ever again been glimpsed that just through the fact that he enters into essential reciprocity, man becomes revealed as man; indeed, that only with this and through this does he attain to that valid participation in being that is reserved for him; thus, that the saying of Thou by the I stands in the origin of all individual human becoming.[4]

But, on the other hand, what is striking in the case of Borges is that quite often he seems not to experience his self as over against an other who is not himself—a questioner, for example, or "society" in Mead's sense—so much as over against a previously constructed or absorbed self. Just read a couple of interviews with Borges, and you will see what I mean. Borges almost never really talks to the interviewer, almost never responds to the question, but literally echoes his own thoughts and experiences, which were made up long before the interviewer ever appeared. Listen to the tapes of those interviews and the sound of his voice will convince you that what he is doing is listening to the sound of his own voice from some past time and expressing himself as if that past person were the present. He listens to himself—that is, the present Borges is in vital contact with a past or remembered Borges, not with the living other who occasions that contact. Hence the lamentation

3. *Mind, Self, and Society* (Chicago, 1939), p. 195. To Richard Kitzler ("to whom my debt is so great that to specify one part seems to repudiate or silence the others") I owe the suggestion to follow this line of thought.

4. "The History of the Dialogical Principle," in *Between Man and Man,* trans. Maurice Friedman (New York, 1970), p. 209.

along upper Third Avenue in New York after dinner. The evening invited and East-Siders responded, meandering along the familiar street in dull comfort. Borges, who loves to walk, made his way with one arm linked in mine, the other supporting his cane, which he uses more as a divining rod than as a support. We talked of the first time we had met, and he asked if I had come to like *Beowulf* any better. "No," I replied, "and I don't think I ever will." "Well, you should," he countered, and he immediately began to recite in Anglo-Saxon some fifteen or twenty lines from the poem. All the concrete reality of New York dissolved at the sound of his loud, hollow drone, and some passersby lost their dim, twilight numbness at the strange sight and sound of a blind man reciting an anachronistic language to an inattentive companion. Inattentive, I mean, to what Borges wanted me to attend to: the beauty of the language—especially beautiful, he guessed, if I was not altogether familiar with the meaning of the words, as indeed I was not. What I attended to instead was the eerie reawakening of that recitation from the movie; that and my sense of Borges' not being *in* the recitation any more than I was *in* the response to it. Yes, our arms touched, but the distant language, his remote voice, and my estranged understanding rendered our relation metaphysical. Suddenly I knew Borges was not reciting: he was listening in his imagination to someone else recite, and using his own voice as the medium for that other, obviously faraway voice. His resounding monotone resulted, in part, from paying such careful attention to the other voice that his own style could hardly come through.

Some days later, I was reading Borges' "An Autobiographical Essay" and observing how he attributed all the witty remarks and amusing anecdotes to others when I came upon these sentences about his father:

It was he who revealed the power of poetry to me—the fact that words are not only a means of communication but also magic symbols and music. When I recite poetry in English now, my mother tells me I take on his very voice. (A, 206–207)

Whether or not Borges actually does sound like his father is un-

inspiration; but that would be to deny the assertion, the creation of self which only appears to be a giving away of self. In literature, Borges became himself—a storyteller—by including an other within his own boundaries. (Recall Whitman: "I am large, I contain multitudes.") Borges did not become the other: he doubled himself. (Now you see how Whitman asserts less than he seems to.) In short, the procedure seems to demonstrate the thesis of Mead's book, *Mind, Self, and Society:* the self as other.

Don't lose sight of the fact, however, that if Borges seems to be saying that Paredes talks through him, it is Borges who got Paredes to do the talking. All too often one hears about the way in which various collaborators have pulled the strings of Borges' talent, but we must remember that Borges has set himself up so that they could and indeed would pull the strings. If interviewers ask questions of him, Borges' work has invited their inquiry; if collaborators join with him, it is because there is enough of him to share.

Extending the perception inherent in Borges' description of how he began writing fiction, we can now see the basic function of all the literary allusions in those writings where Borges has gained his own voice and doesn't seem to be listening to another voice. Quite clearly, those allusions still echo voices which are *others* in Borges' imagination, against whom he aligns and defines himself. As one critic has put it: "Borges' is the hand that points: his essence is a direction away from his own substance. To see beyond his work— really, to see through it to other writings—is the greatest necessity and achievement of his labor." His substance *is* the others; he has made himself up by communicating through and with the other voices of his reading. Not only in the simple way of imitating Sir Thomas Browne's or Quevedo's style, as he did in his early essays; not only by permitting Paredes' voice to speak through him, as he did in his first story; but rather, and more important, by confirming his own voice, by justifying it in repeated recourse to those others he continually establishes—according to the principle of literary history announced in "Kafka and His Precursors"—as his own self in other times and other places. It is Borges who has remarked that to speak Hamlet's words is to be Hamlet.

Those allusions to other selves in other literatures are his communication arching backward in time rather than pinpointing in the present; and if it is true, as Mead argues, that the "individual experiences himself as such, not directly, but only indirectly, from the particular standpoints of other individual members of the same group, or from the generalized standpoint of the social group as a whole to which he belongs," [6] then we must define "group" and "social" in a literary way so as to make the statement applicable to Borges. The group to which Borges most clearly belongs is the set of all writers and the location of his relation is the library or universal academy. That Borges wants this to be so, wants it to appear so, is evident from his autobiographical statement:

I believed for many years that I had grown up in a suburb of Buenos Aires, a suburb of adventurous streets and showy sunsets. The truth is that I grew up in a garden, inside an iron picket fence, and in a library of unlimited English books. [7]

That relocation is a limitation in one direction only, for, as Mead writes, the individual is aware of himself

not only in political citizenship, or in membership in groups of which he is a part, but also from the point of view of reflective thought. He is a member of the community of the thinkers whose literature he reads and to which he may contribute by his own published thought. He belongs to a society of all rational beings, and the rationality that he identifies with himself involves a continued social interchange. The widest community in which the individual finds himself, that which is everywhere, through and for everybody, is the thought world as such. He is a member of such a community and he is what he is as such a member. [8]

This wider definition of community is important because it gives us the perspective to see at least one fault in such an assertion as Alfred Kazin's that the sense we get in Borges is "of a wholly and obsessively mental world, of a lack of great experience, of any deep sexual concern." [9] Just what Kazin means by "great experience" is unclear, but, as Mead helps us to see, the panorama of Borges' community may be so vast, the range of relation so broad, that no single experience could seem great in proportion to that scale. Surely Kazin is right, however, when in echoing another

6. *Mind, Self, and Society*, p. 138.
7. *Evaristo Carriego* (Buenos Aires, 1955), p. 9.
8. *Mind, Self, and Society*, p. 200.
9. "Meeting Borges," *The New York Times Book Review*, May 2, 1971, p. 5.

reviewer he writes: "Borges has built his work—and I suspect his life itself—out of the same dogged effort to make himself a home in his own mind." To make himself at home in his mind, to make his mind, to make himself—Borges has built that work to create the society in which he can exist, can have a self, can be.

Always, though, with a full consciousness of what it means to make allusions. Borges has read *I and Thou.* The etymon of "allude" is "to play with."

Ponder the fact that the most reverently iconoclastic book about Borges is titled *Borges et Borges,* and that in order to write it Ibarra had to invent, I imagine, a dialogue with himself, had to decompose himself in order to compose Borges.

Borges is not only double in himself, he is the cause of doubling in others.

> *When I wrote "The Circular Ruins"*
> *way back in 1940, the work carried*
> *me away as it had never done before*
> *and as it has never done since. The*
> *whole story is about a dream and, while*
> *writing it down, my everyday affairs*
> *—my job at the municipal library,*
> *going to the movies, dining with friends*
> *—were like a dream. For the space*
> *of that week, the one thing real to me*
> *was the story.*
> *—Borges' Commentary,*
> The Aleph and Other Stories

> *When I finished reading Borges the last*
> *and final draft of the story, sometime*
> *last May, the tears ran from his eyes*
> *and he said, "Caramba, I wish I could*
> *still write like that."*
> *—Norman Thomas di Giovanni*

4

The epigraph to "The Circular Ruins" could well be the epigraph for all Borges' fiction: "And if he left off dreaming about you. . . ." That phrase, from the fourth chapter of *Through the Looking-Glass,* points both to the relation of the author to his fiction and to the interrelation of the characters within that fiction; it comprehends the theme of Borges' major stories as well as the threat to the characters in those stories. At the same time, it embodies the essentially bipartite reality (dreamer/dreamed) and structure of those stories, permitting us to see the narrative it heads as metaphor for all Borges' art.

Thus the aim of the priest in "The Circular Ruins" can be understood as the consuming aim of the writer in general and of Borges in particular:

His guiding purpose, though it was supernatural, was not impossible. He wanted to dream a man; he wanted to dream him down to the last detail and project him into the world of reality. (A, 56)

Moreover, the energy Borges ascribes to the fulfillment of that purpose ("This mystical aim had taxed the whole range of his mind," *A,* 56), and the difficulty by which he qualifies that labor ("the task of shaping the senseless and dizzying stuff of dreams is the hardest that a man can attempt," *A,* 58), both express Borges' literal devotion and lofty aspiration. Significantly, the surrogate artist is a priest.

In a real sense, then, "The Circular Ruins" is a parable. The point being, I think, that it is not *only* a parable—hence Borges' insistent denial of the parabolic nature of his writing. Like much contemporary art, Borges' work is chiefly about itself, that is, about art itself; like many of Borges' stories, "The Circular Ruins" is an affirmation of faith in the metaphysical or magical nature of art, but without the salvation such faith customarily guarantees.

No joyous celebration of the artist as dreamer, such as a Romantic might have written, the story broods on devastation. The fiery hue of the sacred image has faded to the color of ash, the temple is in ruins, and only the mud is said to be sacred, while the priest, like the hero of "The Immortal," is himself quiet and gray, almost entirely lacking a sense of the primary condition of what William James calls "the material self": his body, his clothing, his family, his home, his property. The absence of this part of the self is abundantly indicated, but nowhere more pointedly than when Borges tells us that the priest perhaps did not even feel "the brushy thorns that tore his flesh" (*A,* 55); and this absence

59

coordinates the priest with his temple. Both are in decay, for, as James reminds us, a loss suffered by our material self results in a "sense of the shrinkage of our personality, a partial conversion of ourselves to nothingness. . . ." [10] From an observer's point of view, the priest is more dead than alive, and, in confirmation of this state, Borges tells how the priest (prefiguring the hero of "The Immortal") "searched the crumbling walls for a burial niche, where he covered himself over with leaves he had never seen before" (*A*, 56).

Out of a death in sleep, out of one kind of personal nothingness, the priest is intent on fabricating something by means of what James might label "the spiritual self." In any case, the priest is "laid asleep/ In body and become a living soul," just as Borges would have us believe he dreamed through his ordinary life during the composition of the story; and if we pursue a correspondence between the creation *in* the story and the creation *of* the story, having been almost explicitly invited by the vocabulary of dreaming to do so, we must postulate the "nothingness" out of which the fabrication of the priest arose, a "nothingness" based on a weak sense of the material self (what can you recall about the clothes Borges' characters wear?), a minimal sense of the social self (to what degree and in what ways are Borges' characters *recognized* by other Borges characters?), and a disproportionate sense of the spiritual self—that subjective ability, as James casts it, *"to think ourselves as thinkers."* [11] A "nothingness," in short, which invokes the theme and title of one of Borges' early and crucial essays, "La nadería de la personalidad" (The Nothingness of the Personality), and points us back to the encompassing emotion experienced by character and author in "The Circular Ruins" —an emotion consubstantial with that described in Freud's paper "Mourning and Melancholia," and epitomized by Montaigne when he laments his state after the death of his friend: "I was already so formed and accustomed to being double everywhere, that now I seem to be no more than half."

10. *Principles of Psychology* (New York, 1950), p. 293.
11. *Principles of Psychology*, p. 296.

Borges is often described as a "writer's writer," a peculiarly rational, extraordinarily lucid, intellectual, and philosophic author. In a word, unemotional. Setting aside the obvious objection that "ideas," at least the kind you find in Borges, are emotions, or at least are experienced as such by Borges and his attentive readers, one still cannot describe the man's fiction as cold or unfeeling. The experience of the priest at the end of "The Circular Ruins," for example (and if it is not a "great experience" I don't know what is), is a flood of perceptive feeling: "In relief, in humiliation, in terror, he understood that he, too, was an appearance, that someone was dreaming him" (*A*, 62). The quasi-periodic construction of that sentence places all the emphasis on that relief, that humiliation, that terror, and, in the spatial chronology of prose, makes understanding subsequent to feeling.

But, then, the emotional tone of the story has been established from the moment of the epigraph, for the passage in Lewis Carroll from which Borges is quoting is one in which Alice is first indignantly on the offensive at hearing that if the Red King should leave off dreaming her she wouldn't exist, subsequently tearful as she cries "I *am* real!", and finally defensive in dismissing the whole thing as nonsense:

> "If I wasn't real," Alice said—half-laughing through her tears, it all seemed so ridiculous—"I shouldn't be able to cry."
> "I hope you don't suppose those are *real* tears?" Tweedledum interrupted in a tone of great contempt.
> "I know they're talking nonsense," Alice thought to herself: "and it's foolish to cry about it." So she brushed away her tears, and went on, as cheerfully as she could, "At any rate I'd better be getting out of the wood, for really it's coming on very dark. Do you think it's going to rain?" [12]

Alice, always cheerful and anxious (!) to make the best of things, manages to put at least a comi-tragic face on the situation, but her tears *are* real to her, she *can* only go on "as cheerfully as she could," the landscape *is* "coming on very dark," and the two creatures she confronts *are* weird doubles. The seed Carroll gave to Borges grew, according to Borges' own commentary, because Borges had often thought of life as a dream, but also because the

12. *The Annotated Alice*, ed. Martin Gardner (Cleveland, 1963), pp. 239–40.

emotional tone of Carroll's passage is one that must early have been at the heart of Borges. That seed *did* grow.

What is childlike in Alice—the ridiculous, the nonsense, the foolish, and, ultimately, the tears themselves—is developed by Borges both in circumstance and psychology into elevated terror and humiliation. True, Borges' characters do not cry, nor do they laugh much; and, most of all, they do not have that sense of non-sense and non-sense which Alice has, because they transform her awareness into the adult preoccupations of metaphysics, literature, and theology. But her sense plays over Borges' fiction as irony and humor, in much the same way that Carroll's grasp of mathematics, physics, and philosophy shade in her adventures with tints of mature reflection and speculation. Is it not possible, then, to see how, in a *Wonder*-land so frequently charted by Borges' Chesterton, each man spies through a different end of the same glass? Carroll confronts the abstract and speculative with elementary sense, hence Alice's exaggerated concern with her exaggerated material self; and Borges attacks settled perceptions with evolved non-sense, hence his characters' devotion to all kinds of heresies. In this way, Martin Gardner's elaborate, recondite edition of *Alice in Wonderland* elicits a genuine Borgesian content from Carroll, just as Borges' epigraph from Carroll instills a primary fear into "The Circular Ruins." Of course, Borges gives that seminal passage from Carroll his own special inflection, but there is no doubting that Carroll stands in relation to Borges' story as a confirming, horrific double. Both take their characters into a type of the dark forest; neither acknowledges, but each implies, Pan as source of panic.

"The Circular Ruins" is an allegory for what the artist does; it is also an allegory for what the artist is. Borges dreams his characters in order to project into the real world simulacra which, recognized as fantasmal by all but themselves, will still reflect a measure of reality back upon the author, who will be, at the very least, the projector of those simulacra. What the allegory demonstrates, however, is that the effort is a brilliant, triumphant failure, because it confirms not the projector's reality, but the artist's initial doubts of his own existence. Dreaming and writing are ways in which the artist projects others who reflect the self—but neither way is successful here. Therefore, with *relief* (justification of the original, inspiring doubt), with *humiliation* (a return, as the root of the word reminds us, to the firm ground of reality), with *terror* (the fear of "if not that, what then?"), the priest and the author confront their own existences without even the satisfaction of knowing or believing it is their own terminal selves they confront.

The loneliness at the heart of "The Circular Ruins" is enforced at every turn. The priest is in an isolated spot, the people who come to feed him do so at night, sneaking so as to avoid a genuine contact, and even when he speaks to two of them near the story's end, "he could not see their faces" (*A*, 61). The loneliness is a function of silence in the story. We never hear a single noise in the course of the narrative (what does this have to do with Borges' blindness?); we never directly hear a single voice: the dreamed boy never answers his dreamer, the men in the boat are only reported as having spoken. Surprisingly enough, we never even hear the priest himself. The only voice we do hear is that of the narrator, of Borges himself, so there is no real communication, no "meeting," as Buber would say, between the boy and the priest, only identity—just as there is only identity, or indistinct sameness, resonating between the author Borges and the priest character. The priest is a type of Borges; similarly the boy is not an other created by the priest but merely a reflection. Despite the intimate, although one-sided, connection between them, and despite the lingering affection of the priest for his unbegotten son, the real value of the boy for the priest would be his existence at a remove, where the boy might have been recognized as autonomous and thus lend that quality implicitly to his father. It is precisely not as a relation but as a reflection in "the real world" that the son is intended. In such a looking glass the priest desires to appear; never saying "Thou" to the boy, he only says "I," says "Me." But if the son in the tale is an unsatisfactory projection, ultimately lacking the final requisite for a substantial, independent existence, so the priest is an inadequate projection of Borges, lacking as he does a contact with a physical reality and a voice of his own with which to express what he touches—lacking that dimension we mean when we speak of a "rounded" character. Both are unreal-ized.

The story fails, deliberately, at the same effort for which the priest is unfit: to dream a man "down to the last detail and project him into the world of reality." Brilliant as it is, moving as we know it to be for Borges and for us, the story fails as an act of justification in one existential sense—the one it defines. Rather, it links the informing crisis to the inspiring context in giving mournful, perfect expression to the existential dilemma in the world of Borges.

Montaigne writes, "The soul refines itself by practice."

> *Almost everything written about Whitman is distorted by two interminable errors. One is the summary identification of Whitman, the man of letters, with Whitman, the semi-divine hero of* Leaves of Grass, *just as Don Quixote is the hero of the* Quixote.
> —Borges, Discusión *(1932)*

> *To move from the paradisiacal sphere of his verses to the insipid chronicle of his days is a melancholy transition. Paradoxically, that melancholy is inevitably aggravated when the biographer wants to hide the existence of two Whitmans: "the friendly and eloquent savage" of* Leaves of Grass *and the poor writer who invented him.*
> —Borges, Other Inquisitions *(1952)*

> *Examples can be multiplied endlessly: there is almost no page which does not confound the Whitman of his mere biography and the Whitman he wanted to be and now is. . . .*
> —Borges, Preface to his translation
> *of* Leaves of Grass *(1969)*

5

"The Circular Ruins" failed to project a character into either order of reality—literary or quotidian—and, after that purposeful failure, that demonstration, Borges never tried, never had a character try again; for although he often wrote of novelists and dramatists, they are not concerned with the creation of characters or personalities, just as he was not, but with the execution of plots and systems, just as he was. Of course, you might want to consider his poem about the Golem as a reenactment of the priest's ambition, but in this poem (as in the story "The Intruder," which does at first glance seem to develop characters), what interests Borges is the theme of such relationships and not the "creatures" themselves, as he has called them. All this is perfectly clear to any reader of Borges, but if you are doubtful of his intention in this direction, compare his answer to a student's question about the relevance of "character" in his fiction:

... I'm afraid there are no characters in my work. I'm afraid *I'm* the only character; or rather, I should say a kind of wishful thinking. . . . I don't think I have evolved a single character. I think I'm always thinking in terms of myself, of my limitations, and of the possible lives I should have lived and haven't.

Never tried to project character again, I said; or is it only tried again and again in different ways? Because what becomes increasingly clear as more of Borges' work comes into full view is the autobiographical projection of his fiction. From his early years, when he wrote "All literature is autobiographical, ultimately," up through "Borges y yo" and "An Autobiographical Essay," Borges' impulse toward a presentation of self has been insistent, if often indirect. Now, of course, every writer puts himself into his work and perhaps even lives there the lives he couldn't or didn't want to live, and in this minimal sense Borges' writing is the wish-fulfillment he spoke of in answering the student's question. But in a more profound sense, Borges arranges the separation of his authorial and personal selves—that is, he labors at the creation of an author for this work. That author, the man who has not lived but written and read (Borges doesn't tire of repeating it), that author whom we name when we say "Borges"—that author is the character Borges has created, a character whose *Life* is the *obras completas* of Jorge Luis Borges. Not the author *in* those works—he has made much fun of that Borges—but the author whose identity is the image we trace as we read his words, many of them borrowed from other men in whom he has discovered himself. In other words, he is the *other* Borges. (The distinction deserves skepticism, but test "the other Dickens," or even "the other Kafka," or, best of all, "the other Shakespeare," and perhaps you will see its appropriateness if not its uniqueness. The repercussions of the distinction, at any rate, are significant.) For example, when we view Borges' works as fictive biography or characterization, then questions of genre become pointless. There is no less fiction in the essays of Borges than in the stories, because there is no less projection of the mind originating the verbal concatenation. Moreover, the reciprocal relationship Borges develops between his various works leads the reader away from the distinctness of those individual writings and toward the identity of mind which created them, suggesting in the process that the prepared consequence of Borges' *oeuvre,* the end to which that reciprocity is means, ordains a fictive author whose figure informs each work, which then, in turn, must be read like the catalogued productions of Pierre Menard—as facts toward the biography of a single mind. So we may now wish to think of Borges' writing as *politique du auteur,* learning to speak of this over-all plot as well as the plots (never forgetting Aristotle) of his essays and thus coming closer to the motive and motivator who also issues in poems and stories. At the same time, we will better comprehend Borges' determination to destroy certain parts of that *obra,* because they are aberrations of character, not simply of literary style or critical opinion. The question, of course, is *which* character?

The character Borges has created, then, is precisely not himself but another self—not an anti-self either, but a complementary self who takes up where he leaves off and fulfills that original self by replacing it in the eyes of the world, by usurping the place of the originating Borges.

To create, to extract the literary history of his work's author is a central project of his writing, and in order to accomplish that purpose he must work his past with rigor:

I believed for many years that I had grown up in a suburb of Buenos Aires, a suburb of adventurous streets and showy sunsets. The truth is that I grew up in a garden, inside a wrought iron fence, and in a library of unlimited books.

In this same passage from *Evaristo Carriego,* Borges is choosing which events and circumstances he will allow, in his writing, to be responsible for his authorial personality, and he chooses in such a way that the reader is forced to an awareness of his autobiographical information, not merely as selective and thus part of the narrative falsification essential to all biographies, but as fiction deliberately shaped away from the scenes or realities of social and historical selves. That shift from *belief* to *truth* is the shift from nature or existence to art or authorship—from grace to works. What Borges is asking *us* to believe is that he always was "Borges," while what *is* true is that he created that creature of circumscribed experience ("inside an iron picket fence"), idyllic source ("in a garden"), and vast erudition ("in a library of unlimited books"), and, having created him, chose to nourish and finally project him into the world of "adventurous streets" and "showy sunsets." In other words, Borges' careful elaboration of himself as a writer, his stubborn willfulness to be only that (try having a non-literary conversation with him!) is a demonstration of the primal self, "for the only object of the mirror is to reflect images," as Lawrence wrote, and it is that primal self who comes most into being by and in the procedure of elaborating the other or developed self. "Borges" is the son sent down to the lower temple: he is the justification of that other one.

Whitman is the model for the procedure. Not that Borges merely imitated Whitman. No, but in some sense both created their works not to contain but to establish the voice of those works—an other who guarantees the self. Some of Borges' earliest compositions were Whitmanesque, and some of his later works, like "The Aleph," still bear the imprint of Whitman; but nothing, I think, in all that Borges has written of and through Whitman is more meaningful than the title of his earliest essay on the American poet: "El otro Whitman" (The Other Whitman).

One is accustomed to proof of God by recourse to creation, but it may be startling to glimpse the puppet as evidence of the manipulator.

"Borges y yo" is therefore the critical text. More exactly than any other statement, this brief paragraph-and-a-sentence crystallizes the procedure whereby Borges has realized his self in projecting the other: Borges and Borges, Borges as "Borges," the self as other. More explicitly than any other statement, this essay/fiction evokes the "Borges" hovering in the other fictions, but this time in relation with the genitor, so that we experience the delicate yielding and aggressiveness which is the relationship fulfilling the life of each. And precisely in the conduct of this relationship, the current on-goingness of it, we see the splendid achievement of the piece, at once surmounting the nuclear failure of "The Circular Ruins" and even surpassing the vast precedent of Whitman.

Borges' composition is so just, so clever, so universal, and then, too, so calm, so resigned, that its accomplishment may go unnoticed; yet in concentrating on its elements—the *"Borges,"* the *"y,"* and the *"yo"*—we can at least get near to what he has achieved. Starting with the *"yo"* (I), as Borges pointedly does not, we see how Borges' old theme of denying the self, the individual, is itself denied here, because, of course, the composition points to the way in which that self has been generated. Yes, we do have the parenthetical "if it is so that I am someone" (*A*, 152), but that is only weak scruple, a genuflection to reverenced habits of speaking and thinking. Just look: the title grants a self, a *"yo,"* as the given, and throughout the rest of "Borges y yo" that self is either assumed or, more significantly, seen as surrendering everything to the other, who is named "Borges." But note that for there to be "everything" to lose, there had to be "everything" in the first place, and the ceding is thus a manner of assertion—the having is in the relinquishing.

Englished, the title makes all this clear. In Spanish, we read "Borges y yo," but Borges and di Giovanni have rendered that as "Borges and Myself." There, you see, the self is not only presumptive as it was, implicitly, in the former Spanish; but its *a priori* condition is made explicit by replacing the "I" of other translations with "my-*self.*" After all, Borges had not written—would not have written—"Borges y yo mismo"; nevertheless, that *mismo* is exactly what di Giovanni sought out, as one of his letters makes clear:

"Myself" in "Borges y yo." This was my idea. I simply presented it to Borges as a *fait accompli* **and did question him particularly, saying, is "Borges and Myself"**

better than "Borges and *I*?" He thought so. Here is why I did it. First of all, "Borges y yo" is the only way this can be said in Spanish. I saw three options in English: "Borges and I"; "Borges and Me"; and "Borges and Myself." The first struck me as too formal and much too stiff for the laconic way my inner ear hears Borges. The second sounded too informal. The third seemed ideal because it is informal and also stresses the very heart of the matter: the I and the other self. This is exactly what the piece is about, and the word "self" in the title stresses and clarifies this.

In considering those three options (they were not options, any of them, before this translation), di Giovanni has at once seen the way both to making the latent self manifest and to adjusting more precisely one of Borges' best works to the eponymous theme in most of his writing: *El otro, el mismo*—The Self and the Other.

Just as that Spanish title of Borges' later poetry emphasizes, the other now precedes the Self, although the original order was obviously different. Certainly the first sentence of "Borges and Myself" establishes this reversed order: "It's to the other man, to Borges, that things happen" (*A*, 151); and it is not until the second sentence that we encounter the "I" who "walk along the streets of Buenos Aires." Once we have this order in mind, we are able to see how the tactics of "The Circular Ruins" have been subordinated to the strategy of the double in Borges. Whereas the son had to be created in order to reflect a kind of reality on the priest, here "Borges" is warranted ab-original—that is, anachronistic— by both title and opening sentence. Whereas "The Circular Ruins" adumbrated the creation of an other, "Borges and Myself" presents the prior fact of that other, even to the point of showing the parent figure wishing release from his offspring, since "Borges" is not only *there,* but so much so that he challenges the maker's independence: "Years ago, I tried ridding myself of him and I went from myths of outlying slums of the city to games with time and infinity, but those games are now part of Borges and I will have to turn to other things" (*A*, 152). Thus, unlike the autonomy of the son, which was publicly recognized by the nameless rowers in "The Circular Ruins" but shamefully, privately accused by the priest, "Borges" is attested to by the outside world ("of Borges I get news through the mail and glimpse his name among a committee of professors or in a dictionary of biography," *A*, 151), as well as by

69

the "Myself," who can indeed quibble about his own being "someone" but who can never, not even for a moment, suggest that "Borges" is not someone. In short, "Borges and Myself" is the successful completion of the priest's endeavor in "The Circular Ruins": Borges has managed to dream a man and project him into the real world, and we know it because "Borges" exists among us. If he is but a creature of breath—certainly not of fire—he does not seem aware of it, and can we be sure? Moreover, the whole weight of "Borges and Myself" is directed, not toward projecting "Borges," as "The Circular Ruins" aimed at projecting the son, but rather toward establishing the substance, ironically diminishing, of the "Myself," thereby hinting at a staggering success of Borges' projection. Look at it this way: Milton felt obliged to justify the ways of God to man—but in the same way, Borges writes "Borges and Myself" in order to validate his own self in relationship to his created character. Maybe Emerson was right when he said, "It is a greater joy to see the author's author than himself."

The way Borges has succeeded is encapsulated in the "y," or "and," of his title. In relationship, if not actual dialogue, both Borges and the "Myself" have their existence. Whitman wrote, "I do not understand the mystery, but I am always conscious of myself as two." It is almost as if Borges had written (he hasn't, of course), "I am conscious of myself through the process of being two." At least, that's what "Borges and Myself" seems to say: "I live, I let myself live, so that Borges can weave his tales and poems, and those tales and poems are my justification" (A, 151). Vampiristic though it may be, the relationship does secure the degree and manner of Borges' survival: "In any case, I am fated to become lost once and for all, and only some moment of myself will survive in the other man. Little by little, I have been surrendering everything to him" (A, 151–52). That parasitic tie of creator to created had been suggested in "The Circular Ruins," when the narrator told us the priest "perceived with a certain vagueness the sounds and shapes of the world, for his absent son was taking nourishment from the magician's decreasing consciousness" (A, 60–61); however, that diminishing was not explored, merely terminated in the

70

priest's sense of victory: "His life's purpose was fulfilled; the man lived on in a kind of ecstasy" (*A*, 61). In "Borges and Myself," the real matter, as Buber would have understood (pointing to the active meaning of the conjunction), is the relation *between* "Borges" and the "Myself"; or, as the title of Buber's book has it, *Between Man and Man*. Living, defined as surrender to literature, is what Borges' essay/fiction contemplates, and so *in* the surrendering, *in* the losing, *there* is the life. While "Borges and Myself" defines an opposition, it does so by achieving a grammatical balance in its title, where, if we will just see it, the substantive isocolon is created, maintained, preserved by the catenary "and."

The mystery of it all, to recall Whitman's immense word, is nothing less than the basis of Dante's poem: *"mi ritrovai per una selva oscura,"* which is usually translated as "I came to myself in a dark wood" but must also be understood as "I rediscovered myself (my self) by means of a dark wood." If Mead argues that it is the "reflective process within which a self arises," it is no less important to recall that self is often, as here in the quotation from the *Inferno*, reflexive. In fact, if we look at "Borges and Myself" from Mead's point of view, we can see how the literary theme of the double, far from having the pathological implications usually associated with it, points to a fundamental model in the psychology of selfhood: "It is fair to say that the beginning of the self as an object, so far as we can see, is to be found in the experiences of people that lead to the conceptions of a 'double.' " [13] In short, "Borges and Myself" is a reflection on the nature of self as reflexive, as well as a presentation of the double as means to knowledge and being—an inflection of the theme that is all too rare, or too rarely recognized. The nominative condition of self has been called in doubt throughout Borges' career, but the reflexive process or relation of self (Dante's *camino*, Carroll's dark forest) has been evidenced again and again. To illustrate: Juan Dahlmann, the hero of "The South," is just that, a doll-man whose existence is hallucinatory, while Scharlach and Lönnrot—the protagonists of "Death and the Compass," whose common identity is proclaimed

13. *Mind, Self, and Society*, p. 139.

by the shared "redness" of their names—exist more completely, perhaps eternally, in their relation: " 'The next time I kill you,' replied Scharlach, 'I promise you such a maze, which is made up of a single straight line and which is invisible and unending' " (*A*, 78).

Although the elegiac tone of "Borges and Myself" is not to be ignored, we must not overlook the triumph of the piece in recognizing that recurring tone in Borges. "The Circular Ruins" left the priest with the knowledge that he was not more than his creation, and established the infinite series of phantasms Borges has so often contemplated, as in "Chess":

> **The player too is captive of caprice**
> **(The words are Omar's) on another ground**
> **Where black nights alternate with white days.**
>
> **God moves the player; he in turn the piece.**
> **But what God behind God begins the round**
> **Of dust and time and dream and agonies?** (*SP*, 121–23)

On the other hand, "Borges and Myself" leaves Borges diminished or diminishing—with the sense, that is, that he is outdistanced by his creation, while knowing that he supplies the continuing means for that outdistancing. The process has not been interrupted by space or short-circuited by apocalypse as it was in "The Circular Ruins," and so Borges remains with the knowledge—knowledge, it is true, which is a confusion: "Which of us is writing this page I don't know" (*A*, 152)—that his creation, in being more than himself, is the justification, through absorbing excess, of his labor and his doubt.

Of course there is sorrow here too, because the other is only the self and neither assessing angel nor close friend, and because the communication, the relation, is in the writing, not the reading. Listening to Borges—reading with an ear for that sounding silence of the written word—we hear a monologue. Among the many pages of modern literature consciously and implicitly devoted to alienation and isolation, his are perhaps the loneliest. We hear, we read, a monologue, a voice of rare inflection in the dimness of a still room after dinner, in the selected privacy of a distant

study, in the mute gloom of a library. The privilege of that triumph
—impressive, honorable—has been costly.

> *Where is this division of labor to end and*
> *what object does it finally serve? No doubt*
> *another may also think for me, but it is not*
> *therefore desirable that he should do so to*
> *the exclusion of my thinking for myself.*
> —*Thoreau*

> *Which of us is writing this page I don't know.*
> —*"Borges and Myself"*

6

Among muted charms in "An Autobiographical Essay" appears
the confession: "All the foregoing books I read in English. When
later I read *Don Quixote* in the original, it sounded like a bad translation to me" (*A*, 209).

But that was my reaction, *mutatis mutandis,* when I first
picked up the Borges–di Giovanni version of the stories I had read
in other translations, or in Spanish—in my own English parallel
to the Spanish. The first story I looked at was "The Circular Ruins,"
and where I had always read or heard, "No one saw him come
ashore in the unanimous night," I now found "Nobody saw him
come ashore in the encompassing night" (*A*, 55). Not a *bad*
translation: not a translation at all! Then, when I saw di Giovanni,
his first considered question was "What's all this fuss about
'*unánime*' and 'encompassing'?" Indeed, what was the fuss? Or,
rather, what was being done to Borges? At least, what was being
done to *my* Borges?

Not so simple, the answer is that Borges is not just being translated, moved from one side of the Spanish-language barrier to the
other, as he has in fact been translated before, but truly doubled
in an English text of his own re-creation. These are not translations at all, but *original texts,* different from the previous Spanish
ones, but fully their equal in sanction, dignity, and intention.[14]
Here, in his seventies, with some ten volumes to issue, is a major

14. I said so in a review of *The Aleph and Other Stories* in the *Nation*, March 1,
1971, 282–84, and I now borrow back those words.

73

English author, who, like two other such in our time, emerges bilingually. But in the case of Borges, there is this difference, among others: English is a language he feels "unworthy to handle" (*A*, 258); however, English is also the language of his literary infancy, the language he wishes had been his birthright. Borges' right to that language—that is, nothing less than his *worth*—is established by this translation. In other words, in his English, Borges comes into his own.

Any child knows the answer to "Who did that?"

"Me."

"You and who else?"

"Me, myself, and I."

The formulaic satisfactions of that litany apply to circumstances of this translation, for the "subject" is compound: the Borges who wrote the Spanish text in the past, the Borges who collaborates in the rethinking of "every sentence in English words," and di Giovanni—nominal translator, actual medium—who along with Borges has "shunned the dictionary as much as possible" and cooperated in making "these stories read as though they had been written in English" (*A*, 9). This interrelation, which is chiefly an intra-relation, is evidenced in the preface to *The Aleph and Other Stories,* which Borges and di Giovanni conclude with both their initials but commence with a sentence insinuated around shifting pronouns: "Since *my* fame rests on *my* short stories, it is only natural that *we* should want to include a selection of them among the several volumes of *my* writings *we* are translating for E. P. Dutton" (*A*, 9; italics added). The esthetic, psychological, and critical implications of those pronomial adjectives are dizzying and, of course, playful. Pure Borges. Nevertheless, we can catch that enrichment of Borges by Borges and see at the same time how this work, undertaken "in what may be a new way" (*A*, 9), is confirmation of self through heroic doubling, based on a participating other—no intruder.

Collaborative translation is not an operation *on* Borges' work, but a function *of* it. In his autobiographical sketch, Borges projects "revising and perhaps rewriting my father's novel *The Caudillo,* as

74

he asked me to years ago. We had gone as far as discussing many of the problems; I like to think of the undertaking as a continued dialogue and a very real collaboration" (*A, 259*). Think, then, of this translation as dialogue and very real collaboration. Recall "The Circular Ruins."

Some other qualities of this special labor, noted at random:

1. As much an edition as an Englishing of Borges, this collaboration benefits, in the best manner of his work, from simultaneous scholarly/critical/creative intelligence. Thus some pointless and some invaluable errors are righted. For example, in the story about the Tichborne Claimant in *A Universal History of Infamy,* an entire line crediting one of Borges' sources had been misprinted, leading to inevitable interpretive fictions. Now that opportunity is canceled, and Borges' intention is restored. Borges is restored.

2. Direct access to Borges' meaning is provided, whereas formerly we were in contact with a translator's elucidation or excusable ignorance: in "Death and the Compass," as translated by Anthony Kerrigan, we read: "At four in the morning they came out. In the tortuous Rue de Toulon, as they stepped on the dead serpentines of the dawn . . . ," [15] which is unintelligible, just as it is in the Spanish (*"cuando pisaban las serpentinas muertas del alba"*), if you are relying on a dictionary. Di Giovanni did not understand the phrase and when he was reading from the Spanish, Borges interrupted to say: "Here we have some Ultraism," and then by means of gestures showed that *serpentinas* are streamers used at Carnival time and, in answer to questions, that they were "dawn's" and "dead" because they had been thrown the night before. Di Giovanni then suggested that the word "confetti" be added for greater clarity and accuracy. The line now reads: "as they were stepping over last night's tangle of streamers and confetti" (*A, 71*).

Violence has been done to the former text, I know that. But while it is in accord with di Giovanni's principle of clear, "nonpoetic" English, it is also in agreement with Borges' principle of

15. *A Personal Anthology* (New York, 1967), p. 6. Donald Alfred Yates renders the crucial phrase identically in *Labyrinths* (New York, 1962), p. 81.

eliminating involuted metaphors typical of Ultraism and also of avoiding any looming word or phrase. The latter is a principle adopted from Robert Louis Stevenson, and it explains precisely the substitution of "encompassing" for *"unánime"* in "The Circular Ruins." True enough, the drafts show that "encompassing" is one of two alternatives offered by di Giovanni, but the demand satisfies Borges' own imperative.

(In the meantime, it is possible to see that both are wrong: *"unánime"* may be the wrong word, but there's no doubt it is the *great* word.)

How that offering is made has been described in detail, but too diplomatically, by di Giovanni,[16] while the texture and politics of the collaboration are still to be presented, especially if we are to see this collaboration as that and not as *coup d'état*. The *relation* is what must be guaranteed. Of course, it would take an analyst of dramatic delicacy to establish the rhythms and stresses of that relation, but the following scene, quoted almost verbatim from a tape recording, offers an essence.

[Borges and di Giovanni are at work in the National Library in Buenos Aires. They are translating "The Approach to al-Mu'tasim" and have reached the line *"Atronadora, ecuestre, semidormida, la policía. . . ."*]
di G: Now let's get the string of adjectives.
  B: *Thunderous.*
di G: *Thunderous* is good. Or *thundering?* I think *thunderous* is better.
  B: *Atronadora: thunderous*—better than *thundering.*
di G: *Ecuestre: mounted.*
  B: *Thunderous, mounted.*
di G: *y . . .*
  B: *Semidormida,* no? *Half-asleep,* no?
di G: Yeah, but why? That's all right, but it seems . . .
  B: They were taken by surprise.
di G: Ah-h-h . . . Why not "caught by surprise"?
  B: Yes.
di G: You know why, Borges? Because . . .
  B: No, no, that's right. Go on.
di G: Because *half-asleep*—I don't know whether you're trying to be ironic about the actual physical condition.
  B: No, no, no. I'm thinking of their being quite indifferent to the whole thing, no?
di G: Well, then why not say *indifferent?*

16. "At Work with Borges," *Antioch Review* (Fall/Winter, 1970–1971), pp. 290–98.

B: Well, anyway . . .

di G: No, no: I want it to be expressive. I mean, *semidormida* is fine, but you know I thought you were making fun of the police for being sort of, for not being wideawake *americanos*.

B: Yes.

di G: *Caught napping?*

B: No.

di G: *Caught offguard?*

B: Perhaps *not wholly awake*, no?

di G: You mean *caught offguard*.

B: No, I think of them as men . . . they wake them up, and they have to go and do it. They are still . . . hazy about the whole thing.

di G: Um.

B: How about *half-asleep?*

di G: It seems like you mean it very literally there—a physical condition.

B: Yes. Why not?

di G: I know, but it's sort of strange, isn't it? To just throw in a word like that . . .

B: Yes, that's right.

di G: . . . without its being intelligible. It doesn't illuminate the story.

B: Well, it changes it.

di G: *Taken by surprise: Caught by surprise?*

B: *Un-understanding?* Or can't you say that?

di G: I don't know . . . *un-understanding?*

The drama of that fragment must be played to be felt, and subtle strengths cannot be realized, perhaps, until you know the outcome: in their translation the phrase reads: "mounted, thunderous, and barely awake" (*A,* 47). At any rate, for all the surges of energetic aggression on the one side (*aggression:* to step toward) and all the artful dodging on the other, these two are yoked in effort. The yoke is what matters.

3. In that thorny phrase about the streamers, you noticed the intrusion of a new word, "tangled"; and in the line about the police you saw how the final word-order was changed so that *mounted* now precedes *thunderous.* Both changes reflect an important quality of this translation: concern with sound and rhetorical pattern. While the word *tangled* reintroduces Borges' persistent labyrinth-net-web metaphor (just as it does in "The Intruder," where it transfigures the verb *fought* [*pelearon, A,* 162]), di Giovanni affirms that it was added for the sake of verbal rhythm. Elsewhere he has noted "the carefully constructed, balanced, and rhythmic sentences that are written with the ear and largely modeled

on English sentence structure" [17] which characterize Borges' Spanish style. This translation remembers and institutes those structures brilliantly. For example, the penultimate sentence of "Borges y yo" is one of the most beautiful examples of polysyndeton in all Borges: *"Así mi vida es una fuga y todo lo pierdo y todo es del olvido, o del otro."* The perorative, elegiac solemnity of the construction is betrayed by all other translations which begin "Thus," missing the rhetorical possibility. Borges and di Giovanni's translation reads: "And so, my life is a running away, and I lose everything and everything is left to oblivion or to the other man" (*A*, 152). And this, if it matters, is closer to the Spanish because that opening *"así"* governs the value of the subsequent repetition of *"y."*

What does matter here is that for the first time we are able to take the language seriously—at face value, not as an accident. For instance, certain forms carry over into English coincidentally: repetitions such as the anaphora (fulcrum of balanced clauses) introducing "The Circular Ruins": "Nobody saw him come ashore in the encompassing night, nobody saw the bamboo craft run aground in the sacred mud" (*A*, 55); or the polyptotin near the end of story: "In the dreamer's dream, the dreamed one awoke" (*A*, 59). But other casts are innovated according to Borges' preordaining style. For example, the rough draft of di Giovanni's translation of "Borges and Myself"—the draft he composed before reading the text aloud with Borges—offers two versions of the final sentence:

a. "I don't know which of the two of us is writing this page."

b. "Which (one) of us is writing (writing down) this page I don't know."

The final version reads: "Which of us is writing this page I don't know" (*A*, 152). Least like the anterior Spanish but most like Borges in approximating the period of feeling.[18]

17. "At Work with Borges," p. 292.
18. So great is my debt to the characteristic generosity of Borges and di Giovanni for answering questions and permitting me to quote from tapes, letters, and manuscripts that I should document it everywhere in these notes. The present instance, then, has the minimal virtue of being accurate.

Now the study and appreciation of Borges can really begin for us, since what the man is and what he has made is a way of writing, a way of sounding. To any reader of Spanish, that quality is immediately apparent because Borges' sentences do more than sound as if they had been composed in English; to a reader of English, the question must be, what kind of English? what kind of sentences? to what effect? Now, comparisons, say with Hemingway (to choose one frequent and perverse instance), must wither. Let us instead examine the use of conjunctions in Borges—try "Borges *and* Myself" for a starter—and we will be closer to what the writer is about than any transparent resemblance might hint. There it all is: "Polysyndeton in Borges and Hemingway." Let us ponder the sentence structure of "The Intruder" and face those who find no emotion in such fiction. The figures of Borges' speech do count for more than the figures in his tales; for, ultimately, which constitute the lines of his face?

(One possible reason for rhetorical validity in this translation is its achievement, at least in part, through reading the text and texts aloud. Di Giovanni's repeated "Let's see how it sounds" is precisely the impossible, and we benefit because they must *say* how it sounds. Borges listens to Borges as fulfilled by di Giovanni, and not since the late works of Henry James has oral prose so affected —and effected—the written word. Here perhaps is that judgment, envisioned near the end of "Profession of Literary Faith." Perhaps here too is that brave reading of his justifying page in the dusk. Another is reflected in a remark I once heard di Giovanni make when asked about his Spanish: "I don't have to worry about my Spanish. What matters is this: how good is my English?" Here Paul Goodman's statement is apposite: "The problem of translation is to retreat to a simpler tenor of one's own style and creatively adjust this to one's author." [19] *To, one's, author.*)

4. In clarifying points "taken for granted by any Argentine" (*A,* 10), Borges and di Giovanni shift our position: we are no longer the reader for whom all this is clear; we are no longer on the inside (even though we might really be out in the

19. Paul Goodman, *Five Years* (New York, 1963), p. 128.

cold). More remarkable still, Borges changes sides too: he is no longer the author by whom such things are taken for granted, and the Argentine becomes, for him too, pardonable—that is, minimal and justifiable—local color. Now he's on our side too.

5. This translation of Borges' *oeuvre* discovers themes; it originates them. In that sense it is undeniably new and original. For example, in his article about how they work, di Giovanni comments: "I had happened along, all unwittingly, to help fill those long empty Sundays he so dreaded, to offer him the kind of work he could give his mind to (this in turn earned him much needed self-justification), and to lend him the ear he desperately needed." [20] The choice of "self-justification" is appropriate, since the theme of justifying the self is *in* the works just as much as it is *of* them; and we have only to turn to "The Aleph" to find Borges saying: "I would not be forced, as in the past, to justify my presence with modest offerings of books" (*A*, 16); or to "Borges and Myself" to find him declaring that "those tales and poems are my justification" (*A*, 151); or to "An Autobiographical Essay," where he writes:

> **Throughout my boyhood, I thought that to be loved would have amounted to an injustice. I did not feel I deserved any particular love, and I remember my birthdays filled me with shame, because everyone heaped gifts on me when I thought that I had done nothing to deserve them—that I was a kind of fake. After the age of thirty or so, I got over the feeling. (A, 208–9)**

In a sense, Borges has spent a lifetime creating and sustaining a self worthy of those gifts—someone, at least, to receive them. The theme is pervasive and nowhere more pathetic than in *The Maker,* where we read of Shakespeare (read "Borges"): "By instinct, so as to cover up the fact that he was nobody, he had grown skilled in the trick of making believe he was somebody" (*SP,* 259); and of Dante: "Years later, Dante was dying in Ravenna as unjustified and as alone as any other man." But in *The Aleph and Other Stories,* the theme condenses. "Borges and Myself" refers to the "few worthwhile pages" Borges has written (*A,* 151); and "The Circular Ruins" mentions "a soul worthy

20. "At Work with Borges," p. 290.

of taking a place in this world" as well as "visions of a crude and worthless nature" (*A*, 57). The condensation is remarkable because previous to the English "worth" there were three wandering Spanish words: *"válidas," "mereciera,"* and *"inservibles."*

Borges has said many times that in his successful collaborations he cannot discern or remember who wrote or said what. Here the question is gratuitous. Clearly, the aim of the work is served. Borges is projected.

Another Borges—*one* other Borges, perhaps *the* other Borges —is the English Borges.

The end of every maker is himself.
—St. Thomas Aquinas

7

In April of last year I heard Borges describe his most recent fiction: " 'El Congreso' is a story that has been haunting me for the last thirty or forty years. I thought I should be worthy of that plot, but as time went on I felt that I had no such hope. . . . The story is about a mystical experience I never had, but maybe before I die I'll be allowed to have it. I can say no more—the story hasn't been published as yet. It may be, for all I know, my best story or my justification as a storyteller."

From *Borges et Borges:*
the final dialogues
NÉSTOR IBARRA

Translator's note: *Born in Argentina, but long a resident of France, Néstor Ibarra was an early and close friend of Borges; as translator and critic, he played an important part in bringing Borges to a French audience.* Borges et Borges *consists of a series of dialogues between Ibarra and an interviewer identified only as* L'Herne, *the name of both the journal in which the dialogues first appeared and the house that published them in book form in 1964. But the dialogues are something other than orthodox, and it may be worth considering that if Ibarra's title is meant to echo and comment on Borges' own "Borges y yo," it may also suggest something like "Ibarra and Ibarra."*

L'Herne: This being our last conversation, we should think of some way to conclude. But first I'd like to ask you one question: In your opinion, is Borges "modern"?
Ibarra: I'm not entirely sure what the word means. If "modern" implies a concern with the advent of astronautics or the disappearance of colonialism, the answer is no, *absolument pas!* But you have in mind something else. . . . If it's of any help, I can give you

a short list of figures whom he considers quite impossible—some known to me and others that I ascribe to him on trust: Raymond Queneau, Saint-John Perse, Marcel Aymé, René Clair, Eluard, Ionesco, four-fifths of Gide, Giraudoux, Claudel, four-fifths of any given issue of the *Nouvelle Revue Française* (this, of course, doesn't alter the fact that Borges is himself the very type of an *N. R. F.* writer!).... For convenience, I've limited myself to French names, but they're easily transposable, and at any rate you see my point.

L'Herne: And so "modernism" is more ready to receive Borges than Borges is to be received?

Ibarra: That's the whole business of the "modern," the whole beautiful business! But not always successful.

L'Herne: What kind of Nobel laureate would Borges make? First of all, would you like to see him win the prize? (And please don't answer only as a friend.)

Ibarra: Why, of course, I'd like to see him win it—why on earth not! ... But one would enjoy seeing the Nobel Prize crown that man in him who in some sense shouldn't have gotten it. The Nobel Prize is in large part a prize for virtue, and that's quite the way it should be. I believe, essentially, in Borges' virtue—but in the sense that "virtue" means something more and something different from "merit," the sense in which it questions and threatens the very idea of "merit." ... To exalt his exemplary and well-favored devotion to Letters, to bestow upon him the Distinguished Service Order of the Mind—why, it's perfect, it's exactly right. But for me, with Borges it's above all a question of his *flower*—that inimitable, irreplaceable flower.

L'Herne: But who is in a position to sniff this flower—some chosen few?

Ibarra: On the contrary! Borges could easily be turned into a popular parlor game.

L'Herne: ?

Ibarra: I myself have managed to play "Borges" among friends; it could easily spread. The French radio and television might consider looking into it.

L'Herne: A somewhat televisionary wish! But what does the game consist of?

Ibarra: In its first, and simplest, form, it consists of completing sentences, of finding words. A few examples? [Here Ibarra quotes passages from Borges in which he suppresses one key word; the challenge to fill in the blanks is less a test of memory than of sensitivity to Borges' style. The answers appear at the end of the interview.] Let's begin with some humorous passages:

> He held a minor post in I don't remember which _____ suburban library.

You suspect that Borges doesn't have a very high opinion of this library's holdings.

> A King of the isles of Babylon called together his architects and his _____ and set them to build him a labyrinth so _____ that no wise man would dare enter inside, and so _____ that those who did would lose their way.

Now here we try to find an adjective in a sentence of a totally different style. The word is beautiful, infallible, and probably not to be found.

> On this subject I shall say all that I know; I shall attempt to omit nothing, to interpret nothing, for life is as _____ as a crime, and we know not where God places his accents.

The following passage is part of a text in verse:

> The inwardness of Good-bye is tragic
> Like that of every event in which Time is _____.

The final word could be (but—you could swear by it—was not originally) "palpable."

L'Herne: Might there not be, in your case, an exaggerated tendency to, so to speak, "take Borges at his word"—to see him as a mere master talker?

Ibarra: But I do indeed see him as a master talker. Perhaps one of the great rhetors of literature. I even think that a punctiliously rhetorical study of Borges, one that wouldn't stop short of the definition and classification of his "tropes," would be a work of the liveliest interest. It's a pity that the world of stylistic criticism and the world of literary criticism are so distinct, so far apart!

Someone who can sense that "silent ebony" or "abject in dust" are Latinisms, and someone who can sense the aptness and the beauty of these Latinisms, won't necessarily—won't very likely—be the same person. If they were, his task would be arduous, it's true. To be sure, someone was quick to apply the word "hypallage" to such verbal conjunctures as "quarrelsome alcohol" or "sedentary hospital," and "metonymy" to the invasion of the physical by the moral in "dissolute swamps." But it's likely that we'd need to find a new terminology for "scrupulous insomnia," "profound pistols," "monstrous relief," "avid precautions," "contemplative deserts," "rivers thick with caymans," "intimate knife" (of the cutthroat) . . . for all Borges' dissident and irrevocable adjectives; the adjectives, yes, but no less so the nouns, verbs and verb phrases ("smoke which, in the sky, loses interest"), adverbs . . . ellipses turning sometimes in the direction of creative imprecision. Listen to this one: "Twenty-three hundred years (some of them mythological) of polished manners"—we're in Japan—"had anxiously complicated the ceremonies to be observed upon the occasion." Try saying it some other way, and if possible half as well! And if it were up to you to demonstrate that a certain school of poetry, a certain system of images, forces us to look at the world with a sense of surprise, of strangeness, how could you do better than to invoke this simple phrase, which is neither Spanish nor French nor of any known tongue: "These images amaze us at the world"? I invite the "poeticians" to apply themselves to the case of Borges the stylist. The beautiful, irrational metaphor isn't hard to find among our Surrealists and Sons of Surrealists; but with them, such a metaphor is more often not irreducible, turning its back on one tradition and unable to found another. But Borges is ultimately—or should ultimately be—available for dismantling and demonstration; he is never gratuitous. If no single analysis is capable of "giving" us Borges, if all analysis is slipshod along the way, it in no sense follows that Borges, even Borges the poet, *especially* Borges the poet, should not be subject to arraignment for an "explication," for close and precise commentary. The one condition is that the investigation be free of delirium and imposture, that shrewdness and skepticism work on its behalf, that it partake of the *mens divinior* it investigates. But it's clear to me that all this is not to your taste, correct? Those Greek words, a while back, made your blood run cold. . . . And so too, to begin with, did the very notion of formal rhetoric. Here I'll allow Borges to answer: "They always use the word 'rhetoric' in a negative sense, to designate the lack of rhetoric. It's as if they used 'architecture' to designate bad weather and demolitions."

L'Herne: I admit that trying to picture a writer at his work table, saying to himself, "Ten pages without a single oxymoron! Better do something about *that!"*—Well . . .

Ibarra: Indeed. At the same time that a painter who said to himself, "That corner needs a little burnt sienna ground," or a musician who wondered whether to begin the Allegro with a harmonic modulation, would be entitled to your highest respect. Oh, you're not the only one. To call a pictorial work "a true painting" is an act of exaltation; to call a novel or a poem "truly literary" is an act of annihilation. I myself would like to be able to say of Borges that he's "truly literary" and thereby not only define but exalt him. But don't quote me as saying that I reduce Borges' work to a museum of tropes. I mean that a reader unconcerned with and unaffected by Borges' tropes is unconcerned with and unaffected by Borges. He whom they concern; he who, in the good sense of the word, *worries* about them; he who, even without using them, keeps them in his memory—*he* is ready for Borges, close to Borges. The "flower" of Borges will not be denied him.

L'Herne: But you admit that if Borges were, above all else, that "flower," he couldn't have so vast an audience. His renown, after all, has been created by people patently unable to read him in the original.

Ibarra: My dear fellow, I know you're a connoisseur of coffee, I've enjoyed many an excellent cup in your home. In the entire world, how many people are there who really know what good coffee is? Very few. Most absorb only an execrable liquid traveling under the name of coffee. The prestige of coffee was created and is upheld by a tiny minority; it's worth noting that the majority has been incapable of imposing on us other beverages quite as bad, in general, but lacking only the ability to be delicious to the tiny minority. There is, in Borges' work, a flower whose odor is surely sensed by very few people in the world, but without which his vulgarization (through misunderstanding, through hope, through imposture) would never have come into being. Always, with art—maybe with everything—in the beginning is the flower.

L'Herne: But to limit this flower to nothing but a formal game, however successfully worked out! . . .

Ibarra: What I really mean is this. It has been said, if not in exactly these words, that science is after all nothing more than "a well-made vocabulary" or "a well-made language"; and there exists a literature which is the art of turning a poorly made language to one's own advantage. Borges is one of the most admirable representatives of that literature, and this conception of literature, whatever its value, announces "Borges" to us, brings us close to him, better than any other.

L'Herne: A number of circumstances can make it impossible to pay attention to that particular Borges. Surely there are avenues of access a bit more open to general traffic?

Ibarra: Borges' sense of humor is also an essential trait. It also tells us something essential about him—and, at the very least, it never lies to us. It's far from always being tied to a dissident form, to words that entice us and lead us astray; it works well, or should work well, in French. The sad part is that his work allows it an increasingly narrow range. His humor extends into his poems, even into his most recent ones—humor of the most exquisite dignity and reserve. But one would get a highly inaccurate sense of Borges' humor (and indeed of Borges in general) if one read only his latest works. Borges' humor is multifarious and runs the entire gamut. He can even play with absurdity and eccentricity, annex the incongruities and incontinences of speech; I hear the voice of Borges in such antics as the following:

[It was the period in which it had been decided that Almafuerte, Lugones, and Banchs] constituted the triumvirate (or perhaps the tricorn or the trimester) of Argentine poetry. . . .

87

The phrase is taken from *Evaristo Carriego* (1930); and so too is this one:

[Someone] describes (for a change!) the gaucho of the pampas who, seated in the shade of an ombu, in the infinite calm of the desert, intones, accompanied by a Spanish guitar, the monotonous ten-line stanzas of *Martín Fierro;* but the writer is so monotonous, ten-lined, infinite, Spanish, calm, deserted, and accompanied, that he fails to notice that in *Martín Fierro* there are no ten-line stanzas.

And what have you to say of the lovely aggressive skepticism that opens "The Art of Insult"?

Devoted and assiduous investigation of the other literary genres persuaded me for a time that insult and sarcasm were necessarily of greater worth. . . .

For nonbelievers, the sophisms of theology have always been a rich source of irony. Borges' Voltaireanism, it goes without saying, is not a *table d'hôte* Voltaireanism—that is to say, who *wouldn't* sit down at table with such a host as that?

[To resolve the problem of good men born before the Christian era, theology has recourse to the omniscience of God, which is also the knowledge of all possible things; it "introduces the conditional into Eternity":] Hercules is in heaven . . . because it is clear that he would have observed the ecclesiastical calendar; the Hydra of Lerna is relegated to the outer shades because God is convinced that she would have refused baptism.

Let me ask you one little question in passing: I believe that L'Herne —a word that condenses, as I'm well aware, *L'H* (ydre de L)*erne* †
—should be able to clarify the point. In your opinion, is the drollness of this baptism merely the result of the simple fact that we're speaking of a monster, or (without our being conscious of it, to be sure) do the Hydra's seven heads, which would necessitate a special ceremony, contribute to the effect?

L'Herne: There will follow a consultation of the seven heads in order to come up with an answer.

Ibarra: Now listen to this one. Borges had discovered in some pious text or other that "sin is infinite, because it is directed at God, who is infinite." Borges comments: "This is like claiming that sin is holy because God is holy; like asserting that insults, if addressed to a tiger, will have stripes or, if addressed to Bernard Shaw, a beard."

† If one removes the central letters of the French phrase for "Hydra of Lerna" (as indicated by the parentheses), the name "L'Herne" remains. TRANSLATOR.

88

L'Herne: Aren't we back to that Borges who enjoys picking on weaklings? After all, don't adversaries like these refute themselves without assistance?

Ibarra: There are ways and ways of murdering the dead. But it is true that sometimes Borges limits himself to common sense. There is indeed the Borges who enjoys breaking down open doors. Just the same, there exist some excellent open doors through which no one passes, precisely because they are open. In the right company, one might go through them to one's betterment; they might well open onto the just and the salubrious. What the Borges we're discussing wants to break down is our forgetfulness. As editor, as uncommon phrase-maker, he provides a delightful idea of what one kind of intellectual journalism could be. . . . He certainly has a lot of the journalist in him (think of his remarkable demolitions of films)—that is, first and foremost, insincerity. Is this to be resented? Nonsense. Ferocity, or the desire to be comical, places any dispute on its proper ground. Listen to him attacking Bergson; in order to clarify and refute the Eleatic paradox, Bergson has imagined, in place of Achilles and the tortoise, two tortoises adjusting their footsteps one on top of the other: "Bergson," says Borges, "displays two tortoises instead of one in order to distract the reader's attention."

L'Herne: Borges' humor is thus sufficient unto itself?

Ibarra: Not only his humor. Borges is Borges, Borges is the sound Borges makes, not his ideas. One must seek him out beyond his excessive, unwarranted, immemorial themes. One of Borges' most beautiful lines uses the very stuff of popular songs: it's . . . awaited, commented on, by the tritest of rhymes, *"amour"* and *"toujours."* Here it is, in its magnificence: "Eternity is the style of desire."

L'Herne: Are you aware that you're bringing me to some kind of peace with your quotations? I'd lent some of Borges' works (in their original version) to a good English Hispanist; he returned them with these words, which at the time seemed to me a rather brief, slightly slanderous compliment: "A most quotable writer indeed. . . ." I see much better now what he had in mind. But even so, something bothers me. One fact, I should think, is clear: the various Borgeses out of whom you compose your Borges are always in some way unverifiable. I believe I've read practically all the Borges translated into French, yet your quotations almost always succeed in bewildering me.

Ibarra: What are you trying to say? That there are not three but four sorts of liars, in ascending order: liars, egregious liars, statisticians, and quotation-mongers? I must defend myself. What I quote from Borges is quite often borrowed from works as yet untranslated and which, by all appearances, won't ever be translated; some of these, among them those dating from the twenties, are out of print and even quite literally unavailable. Borges went to considerable expense to buy up the remaining copies in order to burn them! If I still have in my library *El idioma de los argentinos* and *Inquisiciones,* I no longer have *El tamaño de mi esperanza,* though my memory sometimes gives me back little fragments of it. . . .

L'Herne: Calculated to make you regretful?

Ibarra: No, to make me vigilant. Borges was only, or only thought himself to be, concerned with labels (Creolism, Ultraism) in the twenties; never, perhaps, was he more set upon by an essential liberty and—in the grand sense of the word—*secularity.* One might find certain of the irreverences of *The Extent of My Hope* a bit superficial. But it was only the youthful disorder, the precompetition swagger of what is strongest and most precious in Borges, his spirit of free inquiry. Everything invited him to test his strength, whether Populism or Surrealism ("that demagogic heresy of pauperism as a state of grace, of lack of foresight as infallibility") or the "antiquary classicism" of which he wrote:

It has perpetrated such aberrations as the fable, which reduces the denizens of land and air to ornaments of an abject morality. . . . It has proposed for veneration and wonder a world of complex horrors and useless obscenities: an old man endowed with elephantiasis—

(Oedipus = swollen foot)

—an old man with elephantiasis who contracts marriage with his mother after solving a riddle; an ingenious wooden cow which takes care of all the inconveniences of intimacy between a woman and a bull. . . .

L'Herne: You're very fond of this irreverent Borges, eh? You resent him for having watered his wine? One wonders if these preferences and these regrets aren't dictated by the memory of the man, the man of the thirties, the man you knew best?

Ibarra: I saw Borges again around 1940; I saw him again five years ago. I found him practically unchanged, though he had almost completely lost his sight in the meantime. The enthusiast and the iconoclast are always alive in him, and so too is someone who whispers to you that everything is soon, everything is already, everything is, first and foremost, hack work—that one is, almost by necessity, the spokesman of a plot to slander one. Borges is still the most joyously, fruitfully demoralizing man on earth.

L'Herne: But this Borges—do you find him in his work? You're not the man to need reminding that only the work counts.

Ibarra: I find him—and I lose him. In the last few years, I have to admit, I find him only by looking very hard.

L'Herne: Shouldn't you find him in his critical essays, when he happens to know his subject thoroughly, when the subject doesn't lend itself to "reapparitions"?

Ibarra: I know it's odd, but Borges isn't often a good critic, especially when he admires his subject. Look at his essay on Quevedo, where he shows us so well what Quevedo is not, and hurries over, with such brilliance, what he is (and by the way, what is he?). But happily there are days when Borges seems to wake up equitable, charming, profound, naive, adult, quaking, definitive. . . . It's no longer a matter of Borges. He is only a link—but what a link!—in the chain of the eternal intelligentsia. When the spirit of inquiry inhabits someone who *in addition* is Borges, the reader is in paradise.

L'Herne: You couldn't, in any case, seek the spirit of inquiry in his ghost stories and other fantasies?

Ibarra: I don't know. Phantoms and phantasies (that would be the appropriate spelling here) could advantageously have held the place in his work that he gives them in his conversation. It's true that certain pages of "Tlön" or "The Library of Babel," that the

91

exquisite "Lottery in Babylon" (not in fact very phantomly), that the admirable "Secret Miracle" advise us to place his fiction of metaphysics at the very head of his claims to glory. But at other times, and more often, you put the book down, or rather the hand of the reader puts the book down to be taken up again only by the hand of the curiosity-seeker or critic. It's a pity. The supernatural should have remained for Borges a temptation—one of those temptations that one greets with a certain trembling, and with a faint poetic drunkenness, but also with the most unshakable irony. It's a field for Borges the man, not Borges the writer. Out of a seductive lost wager, Borges has made an indefatigable and untenable martingale. But even for Borges the writer, let's not speak of *Unheimlichkeit*. Outside of a few rare exceptions, Borges does not disturb or frighten us—except those of us who are disturbed and frightened on purpose, and them I pity. As you yourself know, there's a whole mob of people who, for want of experiencing literature as it is, determine to make themselves—and us—believe that they experience it as something it isn't. False minds, these; and worse, false souls. Let's forget them. Listen to this brief passage, which more than any other seems to me to symbolize, to define the Borgesian supernatural. The text is entitled "Dead Men's Dialogue" and is found in *El hacedor*. The dead men in question are from an old Argentine civil war; we are in hell.

A group of men, women, and children anxiously waited for him [the tyrant Rosas]. Many had their throats marked with a red line; others were headless and moved uncertainly, like a man walking in the dark.

L'Herne: Now that we've paid tribute to the humorist, the inventor of verbal games, the iconoclast, how do we read Borges? How do we read *any* Borges? How may we enter sufficiently into his game? *Ibarra:* I don't believe it necessary to enter into his game. What is necessary is to give him the best of ourselves, to begin by saying no. Let's not turn him into a good opportunity; he's worth much more than that. Indeed, his most significant victories will be against those who object, those hardest to please. That he may be very vulnerable must not tempt us to generosity. We must charge at him. He'll survive; his survival will be exemplary. I think back on everything I've reproached him with during these conversations. Each reproach has been just. And each has been at the same time, in a certain sense, false. Both the justness and the falseness were good. I take nothing back; it's Borges who takes back everything. By his very presence. The least of his pages literally sweeps away everything one might say against it, against those pages that surround it, against all of them. "In a manner sufficient and secret," he is the stronger.

Solution to the missing-words puzzles on page 84
illegible
wizards; intricate; subtle
chaste
manifest

translated by E. Rubinstein

Borges as reader
ALASTAIR REID

Borges takes pains always to identify himself first as a reader; and the implication is that it is his reading which has caused his writing. I think this is true. But what Borges means by being a reader is something we are losing fast. We no longer live in books. From the earliest incursions into books in his father's library, reading has been to Borges an intense and separate life, a displacement in time, a shift to other dimensions, to a point where for him the borders between imagination and reality fuzz over and actually cease to exist.

I think that Borges, moving among languages, has always seen language itself as a separate plane of existence, on which words can manipulate everything, even the one who uses them; but at the same time, he is conscious always that language is paradox itself. Words like "forever" mock the one who utters them. The image that recurs in Borges' writings so often—that at certain points, one man is all men, that in reading Shakespeare we become Shakespeare—crops up because it has so often cropped up to Borges

Adapted from an introduction to a lecture by Borges on his life in books, London, May 13, 1971.

94

in his reading. He takes in language in all forms—conversation and prayer, algebra and the tango, puzzles, maps, runes, the secret histories in objects, translation and mistranslation. He has even succeeded in making scholarship a device of the imagination.

I see three distinct strains in Borges' reading—first, the language of storytelling, of Kipling, Chesterton, Stevenson, of the sagas, the language of plot and coincidence, the unwinding of crucial events. Then there is the language of high poetry, magic, riddle and spell, words at the highest pitch of all, words as alchemy. We have only to hear Borges read poetry with the incantatory awe he gives it to realize how much it moves him. And third, the language of metaphysical speculation, from Schopenhauer and Berkeley through the curiosities of Coleridge, Quevedo, De Quincey, to Kafka and the fantastic. And, of course, it is in Borges' writings that these three strains converge—or rather in the aura given off by both his writings and his presence.

At a time when the validity of literature is often in question, Borges reads and writes as one who has no doubt at all of the power of words to illumine and disquiet. I always think of him occupying that nether world of the translator and the bilingual, backstage in the great silence behind language, taking his careful daily walk from the silence to the word, to the sentence, to the book, to the library, and back again. I think that what we are most grateful for in Borges' work is that from such disparate elements, such diverse reading, such multilingual experience, he has found a focal point, a mysterious balance, an equilibrium in a way that we, his readers, no longer thought possible in books. Once Borges has infiltrated our awareness, we find ourselves saying so often, in the course of reading other books, seeing films and paintings, "Why, that's Borges!" And it is. We find, in reaching the most secret recesses of the imagination, that Borges has been there already.

It is not always that the presence of a writer illumines his word; in general, writers are at their best in book form. As usual, Borges is the exception. He has made us feel so many things in his work —and they are not comfortable things, not easy things; but his presence generates a feeling on a wholly different plane, a feeling, quite simply, of great and deep affection.

Borges: the reader as writer
EMIR RODRÍGUEZ MONEGAL

1

Like his imaginary Pierre Menard, Borges has enriched the "halt-ing and rudimentary art of reading" with all kinds of public, and some secret, adventures. That apocryphal French writer had in-tended to rewrite *Don Quixote,* but did not want to offer just another personal version of the famous novel, as some imitators (Avellaneda, Montalvo, Unamuno) had done. He wanted to achieve a version that could be both rigorously literal and a com-pletely new work of its own. The stages through which Menard passes to complete his undertaking are charmingly described by Borges in "Pierre Menard, Author of the *Quixote,*" a story he published in the Argentine magazine *Sur* in May 1939, before in-cluding it in his first collection of fantastic narrative, *El jardín de senderos que se bifurcan* (The Garden of Forking Paths, 1942). The key moment of that process takes place when Menard (after tests which cannot be presented in detail here) finally manages

I would like to thank Suzanne Jill Levine for her help in translating this essay. E. R. M.

to reproduce, word by word, a paragraph from Cervantes' novel. Borges writes:

> Cervantes' text and Menard's are verbally identical, but the second is almost infinitely richer. (More ambiguous, his detractors will say, but ambiguity is richness.)
>
> It is a revelation to compare Menard's *Don Quixote* with Cervantes'. The latter, for example, wrote (part one, chapter nine):
>
> > ... truth, whose mother is history, rival of time, depository of deeds, witness of the past, exemplar and adviser to the present, and the future's counselor.
>
> Written in the seventeenth century, written by the "lay genius" Cervantes, this enumeration is a mere rhetorical praise of history. Menard, on the other hand, writes:
>
> > ... truth, whose mother is history, rival of time, depository of deeds, witness of the past, exemplar and adviser to the present, and the future's counselor.
>
> History, the *mother* of truth: the idea is astounding. Menard, a contemporary of William James, does not define history as an inquiry into reality but as its origin. Historical truth, for him, is not what has happened; it is what we judge to have happened. The final phrases—*exemplar and adviser to the present, and the future's counselor*—are brazenly pragmatic.
>
> The contrast in style is also vivid. The archaic style of Menard—quite foreign, after all—suffers from a certain affectation. Not so that of his forerunner, who handles with ease the current Spanish of his time. (*L*, 42–43)

More unexpected than this dazzling exercise in critical jugglery over a fixed text is the story's conclusion:

> Menard (perhaps without wanting to) has enriched, by means of a new technique, the halting and rudimentary art of reading: this new technique is that of the deliberate anachronism and the erroneous attribution. This technique, whose applications are infinite, prompts us to go through the *Odyssey* as if it were posterior to the *Aeneid*.... This technique fills the most placid works with adventure. To attribute the *Imitatio Christi* to Louis Ferdinand Céline or to James Joyce, is this not a sufficient renovation of its tenuous spiritual indications? (*L*, 44)

Another of Borges' *boutades?* That's what some readers believed, and the fact that his "Pierre Menard . . ." was finally included in a collection of stories with the very explicit title, *Ficciones* (1944), helps even more to heighten the impression of game-playing and irresponsible invention that many readers had. Nevertheless, Borges aficionados could have detected in this story some ideas expressed by the writer in earlier essays. There is, for example, one entitled "La fruición literaria" (Literary Fruition), which was published in *La Nación,* January 23, 1927, before being included in *El idioma de los argentinos* (The Language of the Argentines) in

1928. Some twelve years before "Pierre Menard . . . ," Borges
here examines a metaphor to show that every reader places himself, willingly or not, in a conditioned perspective; before judging,
every reader prejudges. The metaphor Borges examines is the
following: "Fire, with ferocious jaws, devours the fields."

He then attributes it to different poets, belonging to different
times and cultures. Here are his arguments:

Let us suppose that in a café on Corrientes or the Avenida de Mayo a writer
presents the metaphor as his own. I would think: Making metaphors is now a
very common task; to substitute "devour" for "burn" is not a very profitable exchange; the mention of "jaws" perhaps will astonish someone, but it shows the
poet's weakness, a mere sequel to the expression "devouring fire," an automatism;
in short, nothing. . . . Let us suppose now that it is presented to me as the work of
a Chinese or Siamese poet. I would think: Everything becomes a dragon to the
Chinese and I'll imagine a fire, lighted like a party and serpentine-shaped, and I'll
like it. Let us suppose that it is used by the witness of a fire or, even better, by
someone who was menaced by the flames. I would think: The concept of a fire
with jaws comes really from a nightmare, from horror, and adds a human, odious
malignity to an unconscious fact. That phrase is almost mythological and powerful. Let us suppose that somebody tells me that the father of the image is Aeschylus and that it was in Prometheus' tongue (which is true) and that the arrested
Titan, bound to a rock cliff by Force and Violence, two very severe ministers,
told it to the Ocean, an aging gentleman who came to visit his calamity in a
winged chariot. Then the sentence will seem appropriate and even perfect to me,
considering the extravagant nature of the characters and the (already poetical) distance of its origin. I'll do what the reader did: suspend judgment until I can be
sure to whom the phrase belongs.[1]

The essay drifts, later, to related subjects, but Borges has already made his point: all judgment is relative; criticism is an activity as imaginary as fiction or poetry. It is possible to recognize
here the critical seed of "Pierre Menard, Author of the *Quixote.*"
The conclusion which Borges implicitly reached in that forgotten
essay is very different from the lessons someone like I. A. Richards
would draw, as for example in his similar exercises of *Practical
Criticism* (1929). Both start from the same experience—the discussion of a text whose author is unknown to the reader and which,
therefore, can only be deciphered by itself—yet the point of arrival
could not be more different. Contrary to Richards, what Borges
postulates is precisely the impossibility of scientific criticism. Five

1. Jorge Luis Borges, *El idioma de los argentinos* (Buenos Aires, 1928). There
is no English translation of this book.

years after this essay, in a text which he never republished and which therefore is even more neglected than the former, Borges developed this theme more directly. It is called "Elementos de preceptiva" and was published in *Sur,* April 1933. After considering some texts, Borges reached these two conclusions:

One, the invalidity of rhetoric, if it is practiced without vagueness; second, the final impossibility of an aesthetics. If there is not a word in vain, if the lyrics of a *milonga* are an orb of attractions and repulsions, how to elucidate that "tide of pomp, that beats upon the high shore of the world": the 1056 pages in quarto minor attributed to Shakespeare? How to judge seriously those who judge it as a whole, without any other method but a marvelous emission of terrified praise, and without analyzing one single line? [2]

This essay, written only six years before "Pierre Menard," agrees on "the final impossibility of an aesthetics." Nevertheless, it is possible to attempt another reading of these texts, and of the famous "Pierre Menard," and instead of taking literally the conclusions of those critical articles, or the ironies of the story, perhaps to see in these short pieces the foundation of another aesthetic discipline, based not on the creation of the literary work but on its reading—instead of an aesthetics of the work of art, an aesthetics of its reading. This approach to Borges' work has been favored by the Nouvelle Critique since Gérard Genette's article, "La littérature selon Borges." Taking as his starting point the final lines of "Pierre Menard," Genette has emphasized the importance of the Borgesian intuition that the most delicate and important operation of all those which contribute to the writing of a book is reading it. He concludes his analysis with these words:

The genesis of a work in the time of history and the life of an author is the most contingent and most insignificant moment of its duration. . . . The time of a book is not the limited time of its writing, but the limitless time of reading and memory. The meaning of books is in front of them and not behind them; it is in us: a book is not a ready-made meaning, a revelation we have to suffer; it is a reservation of forms that are waiting to have some meaning, it is the "imminence of a revelation that is not yet produced," and that every one of us has to produce for himself.[3]

2. Quoted from my "Borges: Teoría y Práctica," *Número,* 27 (Montevideo, December 1955), 138–39.
3. Gérard Genette, *Figures* (Paris, 1966), p. 132. This essay was originally published in *L'Herne* (Paris, 1964), pp. 323–27, under the title quoted in the text.

Genette's last lines contain a reference to a key text of Borges, the sentence which concludes the essay "The Wall and the Books," first published in *La Nación,* October 22, 1950, and later collected in *Other Inquisitions* (1952):

that imminence of a revelation that is not yet produced is, perhaps, the aesthetic reality. (*OI*, 5)

From Genette on, other French critics and almost all those of Latin America have tended to repeat this approach, of whose validity there is no question. Instead of reiterating it here, I would like to examine in some detail the roots of this critical thought within the whole body of Borges' work and outside it, in his own personal experience.

2

Throughout his work, Borges has dropped a series of hints, allusions, and observations which challenge us to reconstruct that aesthetics of reading, ironically expressed in the last paragraph of his "Pierre Menard." Already in 1923, in the preface to his first collection of poems, *Fervor de Buenos Aires,* Borges wrote a paragraph (quoted now from the latest version of *Obra poética*), in which an aesthetics of reading is formulated at the expense of selfhood:

If the pages of this book offer some felicitous line or other, may the reader pardon me the discourtesy of having claimed it first. Our inconsequential selves differ but little; the circumstance that you are the reader and I the writer of these exercises is accidental and irrelevant. (*SP*, 270)

It is possible to recognize in this text Borges' theory (which runs throughout his work) about "the nothingness of personality." Using these words as a title, he was to present in his first book of essays, *Inquisitions* (1925), an outline of his views. This essay and a complementary one from the same book, "La encrucijada de Berkeley" (Berkeley's Crossroads), express his conviction that "there is no such a thing as a complete I." In "The Nothingness of Personality," Borges can then formulate his intuition:

I understood this personality that we used to praise so excessively to be nothing. It occurs to me that my life will never be justified by a full, absolute, instant container of all the other ones; that all of them will be provisional steps, destructive

of the future, and that, outside the episodic, the present, the circumstantial, we are nothing.[4]

In the second essay, "Berkeley's Crossroads," Borges also denies time, with a vehemence that years have pacified but not obliterated. The present is the substance of our life, of this life, he insists:

I am limited to this vertiginous present, and it is unacceptable that its minute narrowness could contain the horrifying multitude of all the other scattered moments.

For this lucid observer of the world and himself, reality isn't much, apart from that "I," living in the present:

Reality is like that image of us that peers out of all mirrors, a simulacrum that exists because of us, that comes with us, makes some gestures, and goes, but in whose search we don't have to do anything but go and find it.[5]

In texts subsequent to these, written when he was twenty-five— texts which appear not only in the pages of his essays, but also in his poems and fictions—Borges will argue and develop these basic intuitions much further. The true nature of reality will be described—for instance, in a poem "Truco," in which he uses that card game to illustrate the theme of the Eternal Return; it will also be presented in that sinister Utopia (*heterotopia*, as Michel Foucault would say) [6] entitled, "Tlön, Uqbar, Orbis Tertius," in which Borges makes fun of those who attempt to find a rational meaning for the universe. It will also turn up in those two parallel stories, "The Lottery in Babylon" (about the blind chance that rules the universe) and "The Library of Babel" (about the book as a symbol of the universe). But it is mainly in his essays, reworked but never really completed, that it is possible to follow more clearly the evolution of some metaphysical preoccupations. Borges reduces this to some constant topics: the discussion of Zeno's second paradox about the race between Achilles and the tortoise, which helps to reveal the illusory nature of space and time (an article collected first in *Discusión* [1932] and twenty years later in *Other Inquisitions*); the doctrine of cycles, linked to

4. Jorge Luis Borges, *Inquisiciones* (Buenos Aires, 1925), p. 90. There is no English translation of this book.
5. *Inquisiciones*, pp. 116, 119.
6. Michel Foucault, *Les mots et les choses* (Paris, 1966), p. 9.

101

the basic theme of the Eternal Return, which seems to negate the notion of an irreversible time (it appears first in an essay in *History of Eternity* [1936], moves then to a 1940 poem, "The Cyclical Night," and is then reiterated in several essays). But the main effort is concentrated in the total refutation of time. It is traceable since the twenties in some texts of *El idioma de los argentinos* ("Sentirse en muerte" is perhaps the first), and it reappears in successive versions of the same subject, to culminate in the most important of his "metaphysical" pieces, *New Refutation of Time* (published in 1947 in a limited edition and, since 1952, included in *Other Inquisitions*). A final conviction is achieved through all these rehearsals: the unreality of the apparent world, the unreality of the individual I. Borges' is a solipsism which goes beyond that of Berkeley or Hume (two philosophers he quotes constantly) and rests on some selected texts of Schopenhauer (always the same ones) to affirm that, outside of the present, time does not exist and that this very present in which we live is by nature illusory. At the root of his speculations there is an intuition of the vanity of all intellectual knowledge and the conviction that it is impossible to penetrate the ultimate core of reality (if there is any).

His "metaphysical" vision also postulates the negation of all supernatural help and the stubborn denunciation of theology's fables. In an article on Edward FitzGerald, included in *Other Inquisitions,* Borges excuses Omar Khayyám's theological incursions with a phrase that could also be applied to him:

... every cultivated man is a theologian, and faith is not a requisite. (OI, 76)

Pursuing this ambivalence, Borges insists on the examination of historical heretics, like Basilides (to whom he devotes an essay in *Discusión*), or like John Donne, whose *Biathanatos* he discusses in an essay in *Other Inquisitions*. Borges' work also proliferates with apocryphal registers of heresies, generally invented by him as witty variations of the historical ones, as in the story "The Theologians" (in *El Aleph*), or in "Three Versions of Judas" (in *Ficciones*), which postulate the existence of a certain Nils Runeberg, a heretic who carries Donne's ideas to their final (theological and existential) consequences. Borges also dedicates essays and poems to meditations on the *Inferno,* comments on other key passages of the *Divine Comedy,* and even writes an Introduction, in 1949, to an Argentine edition of the famous poem. In an article, "The Mirror of the Enigmas," published in *Sur,* March 1940, and now in *Other Inquisitions,* Borges will pursue one image through several of Léon Bloy's texts, to discover with him that

"The joys of this world would be the torments of hell, seen *in reverse,* **in a mirror."** *(OI,* **127)**

As Bloy points out, this idea contains an echo of a famous passage by the apostle Paul; a text which Borges also likes to quote, as he does in his essays on Pascal in the same book:

"For now we see through a glass, darkly; but then face to face: now I know in part; but then shall I know *even as also I am known.***"** *(OI,* **94)**

Perhaps this ultimate "theological" conviction can be found in a terrible phrase of his most important story, "Tlön, Uqbar, Orbis Tertius," originally published in *Sur,* May 1940, and now collected in *Ficciones:*

How could one do other than submit to Tlön, to the minute and vast evidence of an orderly planet? It is useless to answer that reality is also orderly. Perhaps it is, but in accordance with divine laws—I translate: inhuman laws—which we never quite grasp. *(L,* **17)**

Perhaps all these speculations of Borges' completely lack philosophical value, and hence the occasional quotation marks which I have used. Borges probably hasn't added a single new idea, a single lasting intuition, to the vast corpus compiled by the West and the East since the meditations of the pre-Socratics or the passive hallucinations of Buddha. But his speculations, although modest, are essential to an understanding of the ultimate meaning of his work, and in particular of his novel aesthetics of reading. Borges himself tends to speak with irony about his philosophical speculations. Upon correcting the proofs of *Other Inquisitions,* he admits he has discovered the tendency in these essays

to evaluate religious or philosophical ideas on the basis of their aesthetic worth and even for what is singular and marvelous about them. *(OI,* **189)**

103

We also know that he has defined these same speculations, assuming a falsely apologetic air, as the

feeble machination of an Argentine adrift on the sea of metaphysics. (*OI*, 171)

But these self-ironies do not succeed in invalidating the importance of his intuitions for a more precise understanding of his aesthetics. Here rests his concept of a need to reconsider again "the halting and rudimentary art of reading."

3

Before going on with any further examination of this theme, it will be helpful to see how Borges conceives reality. To do this, it will be necessary to examine, in some detail, his "New Refutation of Time." There Borges sums up his most lasting metaphysical obsession. The points of departure are some key texts of idealist philosophers. According to Borges,

Berkeley denied that there was an object behind sense impressions. David Hume denied that there was a subject behind the perception of changes. Berkeley denied matter; Hume denied the spirit. Berkeley did not wish us to add the metaphysical notion of matter to the succession of impressions, while Hume did not wish us to add the metaphysical notion of a self to the succession of mental states. (*OI*, 183)

Following these two who deny space and the spirit, Borges will also deny time:

Nevertheless, having denied matter and spirit, which are continuities, and having denied space also, I do not know with what right we shall retain the continuity that is time. Outside of each perception (actual or conjectural) matter does not exist; outside of each mental state the spirit does not exist; nor will time exist outside of each present instant. (*OI*, 183–84)

To reinforce his arguments, Borges quotes Schopenhauer:

"No one has lived in the past, no one will live in the future; the present is the form of all life, it is a possession that no misfortune can take away." (*OI*, 186)

This conviction, which Borges reasons through and shares with Schopenhauer, is not just the end product of his readings or the final step of an intellectual speculation. It has its roots in an experience which it would perhaps be fitting to qualify as illumination, if the word didn't carry certain occult connotations which

Borges would flatly reject. He describes it in the same essay. It all began, literarily speaking, one night in the late twenties in a suburb of Buenos Aires. The immense metropolis was still a city which faded into the surrounding countryside: the streets brusquely ceased to be streets and began to be roads, paths, trails barely traced across the boundless plains which are called the pampa. In 1928, Borges walked alone and without any set destination along the streets of the suburbs. He stopped for a moment, to contemplate a rose-colored wall:

I stood there looking at that simplicity. I thought, no doubt aloud, "This is the same as it was thirty years ago." I guessed at the date: a recent time in other countries, but already remote in this changing part of the world. Perhaps a bird was singing and I felt for him a small, bird-sized affection. What stands out most clearly: in the already vertiginous silence the only noise was the intemporal sound of the crickets. The easy thought, "I am in the eighteen hundreds," ceased to be a few careless words and deepened into reality. I felt dead—that I was an abstract perceiver of the world; I felt an undefined fear imbued with knowledge, the supreme clarity of metaphysics. No, I did not believe I had traveled across the presumptive waters of Time; rather I suspected I was the possessor of the reticent or absent meaning of the inconceivable word *eternity*. Only later was I able to define that imagining.

And now I shall write it like this: that pure representation of homogeneous facts—clear night, limpid wall, rural scent of honeysuckle, elemental clay—is not merely identical to the scene on that corner so many years ago; it is, without similarities or repetitions, the same. If we can perceive that identity, time is a delusion; the indifference and inseparability of one moment of time's apparent yesterday and another of its apparent today are enough to disintegrate it.   (*OI*, 179–80)

One of the literary sources of this passage had its origin on another night in another suburb, more than one hundred years before, when an English poet heard a nightingale sing in Hampstead. In the interpretation of this incident Borges presents, "The Nightingale of Keats," now published in *Other Inquisitions,* the poet discovered that the bird which was singing that night for him was the same bird which had sung for kings and buffoons, and for Ruth

> ... when, sick for home,
> She stood in tears amid the alien corn.

Each nightingale is every nightingale; its immortality and the immortality of its song is guaranteed by the immortality of the species.

In Borges' text, the allusion to the famous ode is found in a single phrase: "Perhaps a bird was singing . . . ," a phrase which immediately leads to an observation, both prosaic and ironic: "What stands out most clearly: in the already vertiginous silence the only noise was the intemporal sound of the crickets." (Borges knows that there are no nightingales in Argentina, but that there are crickets.) If Keats discovers his own mortality by listening to the song of the immortal bird, Borges, on the contrary, feels annihilated in the face of mortal time; he feels transformed into an "abstract perceiver of the world" and discovers not the personal identity which the romantic poet seeks and which Proust manages to escape only through art; what Borges discovers is something else—the impersonal identity of the perceiver and the object perceived:

> . . . that pure representation of homogeneous facts—clear night, limpid wall, rural scent of honeysuckle, elemental clay. . . . (*OI*, 180)

Time is thus abolished, not because Borges feels eternal or because his art is capable of preserving him forever in the eternity of his work, but because he, Borges, isn't anybody. Or, better said, *is* nobody.

It would be impossible to quote all the places in Borges' work in which he discusses personal identity only to deny it. It will be enough to remember one of his most famous stories, "The Shape of the Sword." This story can be considered the prototype for so many others like "Theme of the Traitor and the Hero," "Three Versions of Judas," and "The Theologians"—all stories in which personal identity is subtly questioned. In a more indirect form, the subject was already present in "Death and the Compass," "The Circular Ruins," "The Garden of Forking Paths," "The Waiting," and even "The House of Asterion"—which deal (apparently) with two individuals but really explore the notion of the double, or *Doppelgänger*. From this point of view, in all these stories the protagonist is both a hero and a coward, a victim and a victimizer, a creator and the creature created. Thus John Vincent Moon will say in "The Shape of the Sword":

> "Whatever one man does, it is as if all men did it. For that reason it is not unfair that one disobedience in a garden should contaminate all humanity; for that rea-

son it is not unjust that the crucifixion of a single Jew should be sufficient to save it. Perhaps Schopenhauer was right: I am all other men, any man is all men, Shakespeare is in some manner the miserable John Vincent Moon." (*L*, 70)

Already in "Tlön, Uqbar, Orbis Tertius," Borges had borrowed the same concept from Schopenhauer, but with an interesting variation. While describing this imaginary planet, Borges comments in a footnote:

Today, one of the churches of Tlön Platonically maintains that a certain pain, a certain greenish tint of yellow, a certain temperature, a certain sound, are the only reality. All men, in the vertiginous moment of coitus, are the same man. All men who repeat a line from Shakespeare *are* William Shakespeare. (*L*, 12)

Many readers have taken these phrases as *boutades:* a verbal game of the impenitent joker. But for Borges these phrases enunciate a tautology. For him it is obvious that all men are one man and that nobody is somebody. In his effort to deny time, this disciple of Berkeley has not arrived at solipsism but at the severely impersonal. While the English philosopher only admits the existence of an individual I, because his reality is sustained on the existence of God (after all, Berkeley was a bishop), Borges concludes precisely that there is no such thing as an individual I. To arrive at this conclusion, he departs considerably from Berkeley, but Berkeley was undoubtedly Borges' starting point. And it doesn't seem accidental to me that the name of the general in whose villa John Vincent Moon hides is "Berkeley."

The theme of the man who is nobody and is all men finds its most elaborate formulation in "The Immortal," published under the title of "The Immortals" in *Los Anales de Buenos Aires,* February 1947, and later incorporated in *El Aleph.* The protagonist lives throughout the centuries and takes almost as long as the confused reader to discover that in a previous incarnation he has been Homer, and that much later he will be one of the subscribers to the eighteenth-century translation of Homer by Pope. Borges' immortal will also be a Roman tribune, a troglodyte, a Jewish antique dealer, and (perhaps) the very author of the story. The meaning of this rather long narrative metaphor (to call it an allegory would be excessive) is quite clear: every man is all men, the author and the translator, and even the reader, of a certain book are one and

107

the same man. The doctrine of the Eternal Return, which Borges has discussed in several essays, allows him to give another metaphysical turn to his theory. Everything returns; we all return.

Because of that, the hallucinatory experience of time standing still, of the visible and palpable eternity, which Borges had that suburban night in 1928 helped him to erase his personal identity.

Nevertheless, we must not forget that his essay on time does not end on this note. In a somersault which is very characteristic of all his work, Borges denies in a last paragraph all that the long essay has tried vainly to prove:

And yet, and yet—To deny temporal succession, to deny the ego, to deny the astronomical universe, are apparent desperations and secret assuagements. Our destiny (unlike the hell of Swedenborg and the hell of Tibetan mythology) is not horrible because of its unreality; it is horrible because it is irreversible and ironbound. Time is the substance I am made of. Time is a river that carries me away, but I am the river; it is a tiger that mangles me, but I am the tiger; it a fire that consumes me, but I am the fire. The world, alas, is real; I, alas, am Borges. (OI, 186–87)

This is not his only denial. The whole essay lies under the sign of contradiction. In a preface to it, Borges had already taken it upon himself to emphasize the joke the title contains:

A word about the title. I am not unaware that it is an example of the monster which logicians have called *contradictio in adjecto*, because to say that a refutation of time is new (or old) is to attribute to it a predicate of a temporal nature, which restores the notion that the subject attempts to destroy. But I shall let it stand, so that this very subtle joke may prove that I do not exaggerate the importance of these word games. Apart from that, our language is so saturated and animated with time that it is very possible that not one line in this book does not somehow demand or invoke it. (OI, 172)

Neither the irony of the title nor the final rectification succeeds, however, in obliterating his basic intuition of the irreality of the world, of one man's identity with all men. Against what the arguments of metaphysics, or logic, or language, point out in a contrary or deflating sense (the world is real, time exists; Borges, alas, is Borges), the inner vision, the hallucinatory experience, and the literary fiction continue to struggle, offering the opposing theses. It is upon these persistent intuitions that Borges will sustain his aesthetics of reading.

108

4

Although "Pierre Menard, Author of the *Quixote"* is (as we have already seen) his most important text on the limitless possibilities of improving that "halting and rudimentary art of reading," there are other texts which help to clarify the problem from a different angle. Before writing "Pierre Menard," Borges had attempted to produce some more or less fictional narratives. The first was called "Hombres de las orillas" and was published in the September 16, 1933, supplement of *Crítica,* a very popular newspaper, under the pseudonym of "Francisco Bustos." The title was later changed to "Hombre de la esquina rosada" (Streetcorner Man). But it was not this line of realistic and, apparently, genre literature that Borges was to follow in the near future. His next story, "The Approach to al-Mu'tasim," would define a much more personal line of writing. The form it takes is that of a book review of a nonexistent detective novel. To perfect the hoax, Borges buries the "review" in a book of essays, *History of Eternity*. The road to a new narrative development lay in this direction. We will return to it later.

Another of Borges' narrative experiments proceeds in a different manner, although it combines something of the two previous ones. For the same popular newspaper he wrote a collection of "biographies" of infamous men: gangsters, slave dealers, cowboy outlaws, Chinese pirates, and assorted crooks, collected in 1935 under the title of *A Universal History of Infamy*. A list of sources at the end of the volume indicates that each story is supposed to be "real" and is based on well-known articles and books. Borges pretends to be only the reader and editor of the stories, not their maker. There is in the book a section of texts which are, according to Borges, mere translations or adaptations of existing books. In the preface, Borges calls his stories "exercises in narrative prose" and indicates the general sources: "my rereadings of Stevenson and Chesterton, and also from Sternberg's early films, and perhaps from a certain biography of Evaristo Carriego." In his eagerness to acknowledge other people's inventions, he forgets (or prefers not to say) that Carriego's biography was written by him in 1930. He

109

also emphasizes even more his position as reader, not author, of these other texts:

> As for the examples of magic that close the volume, I have no other rights to them than those of translator and reader. Sometimes I suspect that good readers are even blacker and rarer swans than good writers. Will anyone deny that the pieces attributed by Valéry to his pluperfect Edmond Teste are, on the whole, less admirable than those of Teste's wife and friends? Reading, obviously, is an activity which comes after that of writing; it is more modest, more unobtrusive, more intellectual.[7]

The image of himself Borges wants us to have is that of another reader, barely preceding us and without any privilege of invention. If one goes back to the words placed at the beginning of *Fervor de Buenos Aires,* it is possible to see the persistence of an attitude of criticism and denial of authorship. For a 154 edition of *A Universal History of Infamy,* Borges added a second preface which clarifies the problem of his psychological attitude toward fiction. Upon referring to the stories the volume includes, he points out:

> They are the irresponsible game of a shy young man who dared not write stories and so amused himself by falsifying and distorting (without any aesthetic justification whatever) the tales of others.[8]

In many cases, as in "Tom Castro, the Implausible Impostor," his story is infinitely superior to his mediocre sources (in this case, in the Eleventh Edition of the *Encyclopaedia Britannica*). But even Borges admits he falsified and distorted (that is, he changed and invented) other people's stories. Implicitly, he admits that to reread, to translate, to retell are part of the literary invention. And perhaps that to reread and translate *are* what literary creation is about. An aesthetics of reading is implicit here.

To formulate that aesthetics, it will be necessary to examine some essays in *Other Inquisitions,* three of which deal explicitly with the same theme, literary tradition, but implicitly they constitute the basis of an aesthetics of reading. The first, "The Flower of Coleridge," was originally published in *La Nación,* September 23, 1945; the other two, "On the Cult of Books" and "Kafka and

7. Jorge Luis Borges, *A Universal History of Infamy* (to be published by E. P. Dutton in 1972), pp. 7–8 (page numbers to correspond to the 1954 Emecé edition). Translations supplied by Norman Thomas di Giovanni.
8. *A Universal History,* p. 10.

His Precursors," were also published in that newspaper, on July 8 and August 19, 1951, respectively. I underline the exact dates of the first publications because it strikes me as significant that they were composed during Borges' most active period of essay and narrative production.

"The Flower of Coleridge" visibly sets out to trace the evolution of an idea through the heterogeneous texts of three English authors. From this point of view, the essay corresponds perfectly to that type of study that tries to place a topos, a motif, or an image in a certain literary tradition. But Borges' goal is nothing quite so innocent. More important than the evolution of an idea across a century of English texts (from Coleridge to Henry James to H. G. Wells) are the general observations which open and close the essay. The first paragraph states:

> Around 1938 Paul Valéry wrote that the history of literature should not be the history of the authors and the accidents of their careers or of the career of their works, but rather the history of the Spirit as the producer or consumer of literature. He added that such a history could be written without the mention of a single writer. It was not the first time that the Spirit had made such an observation. In 1844 one of its amanuenses in Concord had noted: "I am very much struck in literature by the appearance that one person wrote all the books; ... there is such equality and identity both of judgment and point of view in the narrative that it is plainly the work of one all-seeing, all-hearing gentleman" (Emerson, *Essays: Second Series*, "Nominalist and Realist," 1844). Twenty years earlier Shelley expressed the opinion that all the poems of the past, present, and future were episodes or fragments of a single infinite poem, written by all the poets on earth. (*OI*, 10)

This introduction to the subject (despite the fact that it already establishes the ternary system of authors and contains, in emblematic synthesis, the later subject of the evolution of an idea) goes much further than the explicit intention of the article. It postulates an *impersonal* view of literature; it substitutes for the multitude of authors only one, the Spirit. Borges' article returns to this subject, after running through the three versions of an idea. And upon returning, he clearly indicates the metaphysical basis of this literary concept:

> ... the pantheist who declares that the plurality of authors is illusory finds unexpected support in the classicist, to whom that plurality matters but little. For classical minds the literature is the essential thing, not the individuals. George

Moore and James Joyce have incorporated in their works the pages and sentences of others; Oscar Wilde used to give plots away for others to develop; both procedures, although they appear to be contradictory, may reveal an identical artistic perception—an ecumenical, impersonal perception. Another witness of the profound unity of the Word, another who denied the limitations of the individual, was the renowned Ben Jonson, who, when writing his literary testament and the favorable or adverse opinions he held of his contemporaries, [limited himself to combining] fragments from Seneca, Quintilian, Justus Lipsius, Vives, Erasmus, Machiavelli, Bacon, and the two Scaligers. (*OI*, 12–13) [9]

This last text is worth a closer look. The pantheistic approach which the quotes from Valéry, Emerson, and Shelley, all a bit tainted by romanticism, sketched out at the very beginning of the essay is finally contrasted now with the rigorously classical hypothesis that it is not the individual authors but literature which matters—which is not contradictory but complementary to the pantheistic notion. Metaphysical pantheism and literary classicism are, then, paradoxically conciliated: Shelley and Ben Jonson share the same aesthetics. But there is something else in the text, or in its allusions. When speaking of Jonson, Borges underlines (as if in passing) two essential characteristics of this writer; he calls him

Another witness of the profound unity of the Word, another who denied the limitations of the individual. . . . (*OI*, 13)

Thus, the apparent literary speculation is linked, obliquely, to the metaphysical speculations of his essay on time: to deny the personality of each writer is to deny any individual personality. The description of Jonson is almost more important than the whole essay.

"On the Cult of Books" carries the argument one step further. The obvious purpose of the essay is to indicate the difference between literature and poetic creation, and thus to show that the book (both the literary text and the physical object) has become something sacred.

In Book VIII of the *Odyssey* we read that the gods weave misfortunes into the pattern of events to make a song for future generations to sing. Mallarmé's statement that the world exists in order to . . . [end] in a book seems to repeat, some thirty centuries later, the same concept of an aesthetic justification for

9. I have changed a couple of words where there was an obvious mistake in the translation; where Borges wrote: *"se redujo a ensamblar fragmentos,"* the translation reads: "was obliged to combine."

evils. The two teleologies, however, do not coincide fully; the Greek's belongs to the era of the spoken word, and the Frenchman's, to an era of the written word. One mentions song and the other mentions books. A book, any book, is a sacred object for us; Cervantes, who perhaps did not listen to everything people said, read even "the scraps of torn paper in the streets." *(OI, 116)* [10]

Thus the central theme of the essay is defined. Although Borges meanwhile continues to explore another theme (the ancients' lack of trust in writing, the slow substitution of reading aloud by silent reading, with the eyes only), the essay is really directed toward another goal: the concept of the book as an end in itself.

Superimposed on the notion of a God who speaks with men to order them to do something or to forbid them to do something is the notion of the Absolute Book, the notion of the Sacred Scripture. For the Moslems the Alcorán (also called The Book, *Al Kitab*) is not merely a work of God, like men's souls or the universe; it is one of the attributes of God like His eternity or His ire. . . .

Even more extravagant than the Moslems were the Jews. The first chapter of the Jewish Bible contains the famous sentence: "And God said, Let there be light: and there was light." The cabalists reasoned that the virtue of that command from the Lord proceeded from the letters of the words. The *Sepher Yetzirah* (Book of the Formation), written in Syria or Palestine around the sixth century, reveals that Jehovah of the Armies, God of Israel, and God Omnipotent created the universe by means of the cardinal numbers that go from one to ten and the twenty-two letters of the alphabet. That numbers may be instruments or elements of the Creation is the dogma of Pythagoras and Iamblichus; that letters also may be used in the Creation is a clear indication of the new cult of writing. . . .

The Christians went even further. The thought that the divinity had written a book moved them to imagine that he had written two, and that the other one was the universe. At the beginning of the seventeenth century Francis Bacon declared in his *Advancement of Learning* that God offered us two books so that we would not fall into error. The first, the volume of the Scriptures, reveals His will; the second, the volume of the creatures, reveals His power and is the key to the former. Bacon intended much more than the making of a metaphor; he believed that the world was reducible to essential forms (temperatures, densities, weights, colors), which integrated, in a limited number, an *abecedarium naturae* or series of the letters with which the universal text is written. *(OI, 118–19)*

Borges' essay continues developing this double idea of the Book and the universe as parallel creations of God, supported with quotes from Galileo, Sir Thomas Browne, Carlyle, Léon Bloy, and concluding with Mallarmé:

10. Again I have changed a word in the translation's text. Borges makes an explicit reference to Mallarmé's phrase: *"Le monde n'existe que pour aboutir à un livre";* the English translation says "Mallarmé's statement that the world exists in order to be written . . . ," which is not the same thing.

> According to Mallarmé, the world exists for a book; according to Bloy, we are the versicles or words or letters of a magic book, and that incessant book is the only thing in the world: or, rather, it is the world. *(OI, 120)*

The identification of the universe with the Book has permitted Borges to introduce into his essay (somewhat laterally) a different and complementary theme: we ourselves are a kind of writing. The complete quotation from Bloy is very illuminating in this sense, since it relates the theme of the Book to the identity of each individual:

> "There is no human being on earth who is capable of declaring who he is. No one knows what he has come to this world to do, to what his acts, feelings, ideas correspond, or what his real *name* is, his imperishable Name in the registry of Light.... History is an immense liturgical text, where the *i*'s and the periods are not worth less than the versicles or whole chapters, but the importance of both is undeterminable and is profoundly hidden." *(L'Ame de Napoléon, 1912)* *(OI, 120)*

The Spirit as producer of literature, which Valéry had discovered, appears in this essay transformed into the Spirit which has created two "books": the Sacred Scriptures and the universe. Hidden behind all these quotes, Borges has been leading his reader to the point at which the personality of the writer is totally dissolved in a pantheistic and classicist concept.

In "Kafka and His Precursors," Borges approaches the subject from another angle. Once more, the obvious purpose of the essay seems very simple: the examination of a given writer's precursors.

> At first I thought he was as singular as the fabulous Phoenix; when I knew him better I thought I recognized his voice, or his habits, in the texts of various literatures and various ages. *(OI, 106)*

The rest of the essay is dedicated to the singling out and evaluation of texts which anticipate, in some way, those of Kafka. Thus Borges reviews one of Zeno's paradoxes, a fable by the Chinese prose writer Han Yu, two parables from Kierkegaard, a story by Léon Bloy, another by Lord Dunsany, a poem by Browning. The conclusion of this brief examination is very important:

> If I am not mistaken, the heterogeneous selections I have mentioned resemble Kafka's work: if I am not mistaken, not all of them resemble each other, and this fact is the significant one. Kafka's idiosyncrasy, in greater or lesser degree, is present in each of these writings, but if Kafka had not written we would not perceive it; that is to say, it would not exist.... The word "precursor" is indis-

pensable in the vocabulary of criticism, but one should try to purify it from every connotation of polemic or rivalry. The fact is that each writer *creates* his precursors. His work modifies our conception of the past, as it will modify the future. (*OI*, 108)

In a footnote, Borges indicates that one of the sources of this passage is an article in T. S. Eliot's *Points of View* (1941) entitled "Tradition and the Individual Talent." Although there is some coincidence between Eliot's and Borges' views of literary tradition as a two-way system (Homer influences Virgil, but our reading of Virgil influences our reading of Homer), Eliot underlines the stately aspect of this system, while Borges emphasizes the paradoxical nature of it. His concept that each writer creates his precursors is more challenging.[11]

Other Inquisitions also includes an essay, "For Bernard Shaw," which in a certain way helps to close this series of statements. It was originally published in *Sur,* June 1951, on the death of the Irish playwright. The first paragraph, as is usual with Borges, goes much further than the occasion itself and opens a wide perspective.

At the end of the thirteenth century Raymond Lully (Ramon Lull) attempted to solve all the mysteries by means of a frame with unequal, revolving, concentric disks, subdivided into sectors with Latin words. At the beginning of the nineteenth century John Stuart Mill expressed the fear that the number of musical combinations would some day be exhausted and that the future would hold no place for new Webers and Mozarts. At the end of the nineteenth century Kurd Lasswitz played with the overwhelming fantasy of a universal library that would record all the variations of the twenty-odd orthographic symbols, or rather everything that can be expressed, in all languages of the world. Lull's machine, Mill's fear, and Lasswitz's chaotic library may make us laugh, but they merely exaggerate a common propensity to consider metaphysics and the arts as a sort of combinatory game. Those who play that game forget that a book is more than a verbal structure, or a series of verbal structures; a book is the dialogue with the reader, and the peculiar accent he gives to its voice, and the changing and durable images it leaves in his memory.... Literature is not exhaustible, for the sufficient and simple reason that a single book is not. A book is not an isolated entity: it is a narration, an axis of innumerable narrations. One literature differs from another, either before or after it, not so much because of the text as for the manner in which it is read. If I were able to read any contemporary page—this one, for example—as it would be read in the year 2000, I would know what literature would be like in the year 2000. (*OI*, 163–64)

Here we return to "Pierre Menard" and to the "halting and rudimentary art of reading." For Borges, reading a book is doing some-

11. Harold Bloom (no admirer of Eliot's critical standing) uses Borges' text as the starting point of his *Yeats* (New York, 1970), p. 4.

thing more than exercising a passive activity. It's a more intellectual activity than that of writing it, as he paradoxically points out in the first preface to the *A Universal History of Infamy;* reading participates in the creation itself, since it is a dialogue with a text, as the just-quoted essay points out. But it is much more than the creation of literature if one sees the universe as a book and each individual (be he writer or reader) as simply letters or signs of that book.

5

In several of his most famous stories, Borges develops the theme of the universe as book. The best known is, perhaps, "The Library of Babel," which was published for the first time in *The Garden of Forking Paths* (1942) and since 1944 has been included in *Ficciones.* The first line of the story is sufficiently explicit:

The universe (which others call the Library).... (L, 51)

From there on, the description of a total library, along the lines of Kurd Lasswitz's chaotic library described in "For Bernard Shaw," is really turned into an allegory of the universe. Less analyzed from this point of view are two other stories which deal with the parallel creation of the universe and the book. They are "The Garden of Forking Paths" (which gives the volume its title) and "The God's Script," which was published in *Sur,* February 1949, and was included the same year in *El Aleph.* In the first of these two stories, a rather complicated and at the same time excessively symmetrical detective plot camouflages the central theme of the-book-and-the-universe. When the main character (and narrator) Yu Tsun reaches the town where his victim lives, he discovers that to get to his house he must take the left fork and at each intersection turn always to the left. Yu Tsun then observes:

The instructions to turn always to the left reminded me that such was the common procedure for discovering the central point of certain labyrinths. I have some understanding of labyrinths: not for nothing am I the great grandson of that Ts'ui Pên who was governor of Yunnan and who renounced worldly power in order to write a novel that might be even more populous than the *Hung Lu Meng* and to construct a labyrinth in which all men would become lost. Thirteen

years he dedicated to these heterogeneous tasks, but the hand of a stranger murdered him—and his novel was incoherent and no one found the labyrinth. Beneath English trees I meditated on that lost maze: I imagined it inviolate and perfect at the secret crest of a mountain; I imagined it erased by rice fields or beneath the water; I imagined it infinite, no longer composed of octagonal kiosks and returning paths, but of rivers and provinces and kingdoms . . . I thought of a labyrinth of labyrinths, of one sinuous spreading labyrinth that would encompass the past and the future and in some way involve the stars. *(L,* 22–23)

Although this passage seems a digression (which it is, from the point of view of the spy story), it is possible to find in it the key to the "other" story the tale includes. It is not surprising, then, that having confronted him, Yu Tsun discovers that his victim is a sinologist and hence knows very well (perhaps too well) the story of Ts'ui Pên. As in a dream, the coincidences surprise no one, and the sinologist is more than willing to comment on the double task Ts'ui Pên set himself:

"An astounding fate, that of Ts'ui Pên," Stephen Albert said. "Governor of his native province, learned in astronomy, in astrology and in the tireless interpretation of the canonical books, chess player, famous poet and calligrapher—he abandoned all this in order to compose a book and a maze. He renounced the pleasures of both tyranny and justice, of his populous couch, of his banquets and even of erudition—all to close himself up for thirteen years in the Pavilion of the Limpid Solitude. When he died, his heirs found nothing save chaotic manuscripts. His family, as you may be aware, wished to condemn them to the fire; but his executor—a Taoist or Buddist monk—insisted on their publication." *(L,* 24)

As a true member of the family, Yu Tsun interrupts Albert to criticize his ancestor's novel, "an indeterminate heap of contradictory drafts." In turn, Albert interrupts him to explain the secret of the book of the lost labyrinth:

"After more than a hundred years, the details are irretrievable; but it is not hard to conjecture what happened. Ts'ui Pên must have said once: *I am withdrawing to write a book.* And another time: *I am withdrawing to construct a labyrinth.* Everyone imagined two works; to no one did it occur that the book and the maze were one and the same thing. The Pavilion of the Limpid Solitude stood in the center of a garden that was perhaps intricate; that circumstance could have suggested to the heirs a physical labyrinth. [T]s'ui Pên died; no one in the vast territories that were his came upon the labyrinth; the confusion of the novel suggested to me that *it* was the maze." *(L,* 25)

It is impossible to follow in detail here all the dialectical wanderings of Albert's explanation of that labyrinth. It will be enough to say that, after having proved why Ts'ui Pên's book, a novel, is

117

labyrinthine, he shows that the total absence of one word, "time," in the text of the novel indicates precisely that this is its central theme.

"The Garden of the Forking Paths **is an enormous riddle, or parable, whose theme is time; this recondite cause prohibits its mention. To omit a word always, to resort to inept metaphors and obvious periphrases, is perhaps the most emphatic way of stressing it. That is the tortuous method preferred, in each of the meanderings of his indefatigable novel, by the oblique Ts'ui Pên. I have compared hundreds of manuscripts, I have corrected the errors that the negligence of the copyists has introduced, I have guessed the plan of this chaos, I have re-established—I believe I have re-established—the primordial organization, I have translated the entire work: it is clear to me that not once does he employ the word 'time.' The explanation is obvious:** *The Garden of the Forking Paths* **is an incomplete, but not false, image of the universe as Ts'ui Pên conceived it. In contrast to Newton and Schopenhauer, your ancestor did not believe in a uniform, absolute time. He believed in an infinite series of times, in a growing, dizzying net of divergent, convergent and parallel times. This network of times which approached one another, forked, broke off, or were unaware of one another for centuries, embraces** *all* **possibilities of time."** (L, 27–28)

The labyrinth and the book are, therefore, one and the same. But they are also something else, as Borges insinuates—the universe. The solution reached intellectually by Albert is the same which, intuitively and as in a dream, Yu Tsun had grasped while he walked toward Albert's house. Upon meditating on the lost labyrinth of his ancestor, he imagined it not only as a labyrinth in space but also as

one sinuous spreading labyrinth that would encompass the past and the future and in some way involve the stars. (L, 23)

Such a labyrinth exists: it is the world. The solution to the sinologist's riddle was already there, although presented in an indirect, oblique, conjectural way.

"The God's Script" is, apparently, a simpler story. A Mayan priest, locked up in a prison by the Spanish conquerors, meditates his revenge. On the other side of a long window with bars he sees a jaguar who measures with "secret and even paces the time and space of captivity." The priest's meditations, prolonged during years of captivity, bring him to evoke an old tradition of his people:

The god, foreseeing that at the end of time there would be devastation and ruin, wrote on the first day of Creation a magical sentence with the power to ward

off those evils. He wrote it in such a way that it would reach the most distant generations and not be subject to chance. No one knows where it was written nor with what characters, but it is certain that it exists, secretly, and that a chosen one shall read it. (L, 170)

In the story, the priest then conjectures several possible forms of that magical writing and finally arrives at the conclusion that his god had entrusted the message to the skin of jaguars. It is not necessary to continue the examination of the story any further. Its symbolical meaning is sufficiently clear:

Gradually, the concrete enigma I labored at disturbed me less than the generic enigma of a sentence written by a god. What type of sentence (I asked myself) will an absolute mind construct? I considered that even in the human languages there is no proposition that does not imply the entire universe; to say *the tiger* is to say the tigers that begot it, the deer and turtles devoured by it, the grass on which the deer fed, the earth that was mother to the grass, the heaven that gave birth to the earth. I considered that in the language of a god every word would enunciate that infinite concatenation of facts, and not in an implicit but in an explicit manner, and not progressively but instantaneously. In time, the notion of a divine sentence seemed puerile or blasphemous. A god, I reflected, ought to utter only a single word and in that word absolute fullness. No word uttered by him can be inferior to the universe or less than the sum total of time. Shadows or simulacra of that single word equivalent to a language and to all a language can embrace are the poor and ambitious human words, *all, world, universe.* (L, 171)

Borges' well-known pantheism reappears here to produce a very skillful transition between the magical scripture of a god which the priest searches for, and the vision of the universe as a total scripture of God. Most of us are probably indifferent to the Mayan context of the story; it is what transcends this circumstance, and makes the story valid in any context, that is significant. The tale ends with a mystical vision, similar to those Borges explores in "The Aleph" and "The Zahir," but in a different order of images.

6

A final aspect of this theme remains to be explored. As far as I know, it has still to be examined by the critics: the relationship Borges establishes between literary creation and paternity. We have already seen in "The Shape of the Sword" that, aided by an allusion to Schopenhauer, John Vincent Moon can say:

"Perhaps Schopenhauer was right: I am all other men, any man is all men, Shakespeare is in some manner the miserable John Vincent Moon." (*L*, 70)

The same concept has been used in "Tlön, Uqbar, Orbis Tertius," with a significant variant:

All men, in the vertiginous moment of coitus, are the same man. All men who repeat a line from Shakespeare *are* William Shakespeare. (*L*, 12)

The final identification between author and reader, based in the first example on a Schopenhauer quote, is enriched, or duplicated, by another type of identity in the second example, which also uses a parallelistic form to emphasize the syntactical identity. All men who perform the same basic and ritual act are the same man. The theme is not new in Borges, and one of his earliest and best poems, "Truco" (from *Fervor de Buenos Aires*), is based on that feeling of a loss of individual identity. Borges' poem describes, very metaphorically, a card game very popular in the River Plate area. The last verses read as follows:

> **as the ups and downs of the game**
> **are always the same**
> **the players in their present zeal**
> **repeat distant moves:**
> **a fact that immortalizes a bit,**
> **not much,**
> **the dead companions who are quiet now.**[12]

By repeating the same moves, today's players are yesterday's players. Or, if you prefer, the dead players live again in the living players. The repetition of an act, the conversion of an act into ritual, helps to immortalize it and confers a kind of eternity upon those who practice it. We recognize here once more the ideas underlying some passages of "New Refutation of Time." But the link with the last quotation from "Tlön, Uqbar, Orbis Tertius" is even more revealing. By pointing out the simultaneous identity of author-reader, on the one hand, and that of all men in the moment of coitus, Borges insinuates another identity that encompasses both —the identity of the creative act. The reader recreates Shakespeare's lines; he is, therefore, Shakespeare. Every man in the instant of coitus is fulfilling a basic act of genesis; he is, therefore,

12. *Obra poética* (Buenos Aires, 1964), pp. 27–28.

all men. To see to what extremes Borges is willing to carry these identities, we should examine a story from the second edition of *Ficciones* (1956), one which still has not been sufficiently studied by the critics. It is "The Sect of the Phoenix" (originally published in *Sur,* September–October 1952). In a 1956 postscript to the foreword introducing the second edition of *Ficciones,* Borges explains his purpose in composing this story:

> In the allegory of the Phoenix I imposed upon myself the problem of hinting at an ordinary fact—the Secret—in an irresolute and gradual manner, which, in the end, would prove to be unequivocal; I do not know how fortunate I have been. (*F,* 105)

"The Sect of the Phoenix" is filled with insinuations, camouflaged under the guise of archeological observations which are not always false. Borges' technique of allusion could not be more Jamesian, recalling the vacillations of the author of *The Ambassadors* when asked to reveal what the protagonist's father manufactured (James supposedly told his most intimate friends it was chamber pots). Borges, however, elevates euphemism to allegory:

> Once, in addition to the Secret, there was a legend (and perhaps a cosmogonic myth), but the shallow men of the Phoenix have forgotten it and now only retain the obscure tradition of a punishment. Of a punishment, of a pact or of a privilege, for the versions differ and scarcely allow us to glimpse the verdict of a God who granted eternity to a lineage if its members, generation after generation, would perform a rite.... The rite constitutes the Secret. This Secret... is transmitted from generation to generation, but good usage prefers that mothers should not teach it to their children, nor that priests should; initiation into the mystery is the task of the lowest individuals. A slave, a leper or a beggar serve as mystagogues. Also one child may indoctrinate another. The act in itself is trivial, momentary and requires no description. The materials are cork, wax or gum arabic. (In the liturgy, mud is mentioned; this is often used as well.) There are no temples especially dedicated to the celebration of this cult, but certain ruins, a cellar or an entrance hall are considered propitious places. The Secret is sacred but is always somewhat ridiculous; its performance is furtive and even clandestine and the adept do not speak of it. There are no decent words to name it, but it is understood that all words name it or, rather, inevitably allude to it and thus, in a conversation I say something or other and the adept smile or become uncomfortable, for they realize I have touched upon the Secret.... A kind of sacred horror prevents some faithful believers from performing this very simple rite; the others despise them, but they despise themselves even more. Considerable credit is enjoyed, however, by those who deliberately renounce the custom and attain direct contact with the divinity; these sectarians, in order to express this contact, do so with figures taken from the liturgy and thus John of the Rood wrote:

121

May the Seven Firmaments know that God
Is as delectable as the Cork and the Slime.

I have attained on three continents the friendship of many devotés of the Phoenix; I know that the Secret, at first, seemed to them banal, embarrassing, vulgar and (what is even stranger) incredible. They could not bring themselves to admit their parents had stooped to such manipulations. What is odd is that the Secret was not lost long ago; in spite of the vicissitudes of the Universe, in spite of wars and exoduses, it reaches, awesomely, all the faithful. Someone has not hesitated to affirm that it is now instinctive. (*L*, 102–4)

The Secret—whose gradual revelation Borges wishes to produce in his reader—is none other than copulation, which insures the reproduction of the species and, therefore, grants "eternity to a lineage if its members, generation after generation, would perform the rite." The Secret is the mystery of paternity. Ronald Christ, like others, was puzzled by the Secret, and, in his book on Borges, he has told how and when he dared to question the author on the Secret:

When Borges was in New York in 1968, I asked him if he ever revealed the answer to the riddle. "Yes, sometimes." Would he tell me? And I knew, at once, my error: he turned and looked at his wife for a moment and then said, "Not now; tomorrow. I'd like to keep you guessing for one more day." The following day at a reception I reminded him of his promise. He leaned over and whispered into my ear so that no one else could hear: "Well, the act is what Whitman says 'the divine husband knows, from the work of fatherhood.'—When I first heard about this act, when I was a boy, I was shocked, shocked to think that my mother, my father had performed it. It is an amazing discovery, no? But then too it is an act of immortality, a rite of immortality, isn't it?" [13]

Christ then comments:

Borges' sense of decorum further explains the form of the story while his childhood shock helps explain the appearance of dirt in the rite itself.

In the story, Borges underlines the surprise of some of the faithful believers when told of the act: "They could not bring themselves to admit their parents had stooped to such manipulations" (*L*, 103). The same shock is found in one of the few stories by Borges which touches on a sexual theme, "Emma Zunz," first published in *Sur*, September 1948, and later included in *El Aleph*. It presents a young woman whose father was forced to commit suicide; to

13. Ronald Christ, *The Narrow Act: Borges' Art of Allusion* (New York, 1969), p. 190.

122

avenge his death, she plans an elaborate scheme, one of the steps of which is to be raped by an unknown sailor (the plot is the weakest part of the story, I admit). In describing her reactions during intercourse, Borges writes:

> During that time outside of time, in that perplexing disorder of disconnected and atrocious sensations, did Emma Zunz think *once* about the dead man who motivated the sacrifice? It is my belief that she did think once, and in that moment she endangered her desperate undertaking. She thought (she was unable not to think) that her father had done to her mother the hideous thing that was being done to her now. She thought of it with weak amazement and took refuge, quickly, in vertigo. (*L*, 135)

I would like now to recall another text, a brief poem which closes Borges' *Obra poética*. The original title, which is in French, is "Le Regret d'Héraclite," and it is attributed to an apocryphal European poet, Gasper Camerarius:

> I, who have been so many men, have never been
> The one in whose embrace Matilde Urbach swooned. (*DT*, 92)

By placing this poem at the end of his collection of verses and, at the same time, by attributing it to a nonexistent poet, Borges both underlines and denies (or tries to deny) the importance of that text. The paradox implied in his attitude, whereby repudiation is contained in the acknowledgment, is paralleled by the stylistic periphrasis in his conversation with Ronald Christ, and by the somewhat grander "obscurantism" of the "The Sect of the Phoenix." It is impossible to point out all the allusions that the story contains; it will be enough, I think, to indicate one: the "John of the Rood" whose verses he quotes near the end is none other than Saint John of the Cross. The scholarly joke and the deliberate anachronism, which were already employed in "Pierre Menard," are used here to beg the reader's complicity. These tricks reveal rather than hide Borges' basic preoccupation with the subject of paternity, literary or otherwise. One further observation: in a passage at the beginning of "Tlön, Uqbar, Orbis Tertius," there is a different testimony about the shocking link between copulation and paternity. In the story, Borges (a fictitious character, not the author himself) is talking to his friend Bioy Casares (also a fictitious character) about mirrors and encyclopedias:

> From the remote depths of the corridor, the mirror spied upon us. We discovered (such a discovery is inevitable in the late hours of the night) that mirrors have something monstrous about them. Then Bioy Casares recalled that one of the heresiarchs of Uqbar had declared that mirrors and copulation are abominable, because they increase the number of men. **(L, 3)**

Let me insist upon the fictitious character of this conversation. It is possible that a somewhat similar one took place in similar circumstances; but what is impossible is that Bioy Casares (the real one) could have attributed that phrase to an Uqbar heresiarch. He would have known that the phrase is from another of Borges' stories. Originally, it appeared in "The Masked Dyer, Hakim of Merv," first published in *Crítica* under the simpler title, "The Face of the Prophet" (January 20, 1934), and later collected in *A Universal History of Infamy.* Summing up the protagonist's cosmology, Borges writes:

> The world we live in is a mistake, a clumsy parody. Mirrors and fatherhood, because they multiply and confirm the parody, are abominations. Revulsion is the cardinal virtue.[14]

Perhaps the phrasing is more precise and elegant in "Tlön, Uqbar, Orbis Tertius," but the earlier formulation has the virtue of being more revealing: the use of the word "fatherhood" instead of "copulation" and the mention of "revulsion" in the last line are not casual. Hakim of Merv's idea of the universe and the heresy of an unknown Uqbar theologian come to coincide with what Emma Zunz felt in the act of being raped. What Gaspar Camerarius-Heraclitus felt about not having held Matilde Urbach becomes a gloss on what some followers of the Phoenix felt upon discovering the Secret. Which is also what Borges felt, according to what he himself told Ronald Christ.

7

Coming back to "Pierre Menard, Author of the *Quixote,*" the curious circumstances in which this story was written can probably shed some light upon its limitless projections. Borges has referred to the origins of the story on more than one occasion. In inter-

14. *A Universal History,* p. 90.

124

views with James E. Irby, Napoléon Murat, and Georges Charbonnier, he has gone over it in some detail. But perhaps Borges' best account of the story's genesis occurs in "An Autobiographical Essay":

> It was on Christmas Eve of 1938—the same year my father died—that I had a severe accident. I was running up a stairway and suddenly felt something brush my scalp. I had grazed a freshly painted open casement window. In spite of first-aid treatment, the wound became poisoned, and for a period of a week or so I lay sleepless every night and had hallucinations and high fever. One evening, I lost the power of speech and had to be rushed to the hospital for an immediate operation. Septicemia had set in, and for a month I hovered, all unknowingly, between life and death. (Much later, I was to write about this in my story "The South.") When I began to recover, I feared for my mental integrity. I remember that my mother wanted to read to me from a book I had just ordered, C. S. Lewis' *Out of the Silent Planet,* but for two or three nights I kept putting her off. At last, she prevailed, and after hearing a page or two I fell to crying. My mother asked me why the tears. "I'm crying because I understand," I said. A bit later, I wondered whether I could ever write again. I had previously written quite a few poems and dozens of short reviews. I thought that if I tried to write a review now and failed, I'd be all through intellectually but that if I tried something I had never really done before and failed at that it wouldn't be so bad and might even prepare me for the final revelation. I decided I would try to write a story. The result was "Pierre Menard, Author of *Don Quixote*." (A, 242–43)

There are three moments in this episode which I would like to consider separately. First, the accident itself; then, the reading of C. S. Lewis' science-fiction book; and last, the writing of "Pierre Menard." The accident (as Borges reminds us) was used by him, literarily transposed, in the story "The South." After introducing the protagonist, Juan Dahlmann, in the first paragraph, Borges describes in the second an accident which happens to Juan during "the last days of February 1939." There is a change of dates, perhaps to avoid the Christmas Eve aura, and to mark (secretly) Borges' own recuperation.

> Dahlmann had succeeded in acquiring, on that very afternoon, an imperfect copy of Weil's edition of *The Thousand and One Nights.* Avid to examine this find, he did not wait for the elevator but hurried up the stairs. In the obscurity, something brushed by his forehead: a bat, a bird? On the face of the woman who opened the door to him he saw horror engraved, and the hand he wiped across his face came away red with blood. The edge of a recently painted door which someone had forgotten to close had caused his wound. (F, 167–68) [15]

15. There is an obvious mistake in the English translation; instead of "a recently painted window," it refers to a door.

125

If one compares the version in "The South" with the one in "An Autobiographical Essay," it is possible to believe that Borges felt compelled to invent some narrative details to make the story more concrete and believable: the finding of a copy of a German translation of *The Thousand and One Nights* (one of his favorite books); the avidity which that discovery awakens in Dahlmann; Dahlmann's discovery of his wound, dramatized by the expression on the face of the woman who opens the door to him. But another testimony on Borges' accident will show that the fictional version is perhaps closer to reality than the autobiography. It comes from Borges' mother, doña Leonor Acevedo:

> He had another horrible accident. He began to write fantastic stories afterward, a thing that had never happened to him before; I believe that something had changed in his brain. Anyway, he was for a time between life and death. It was Christmas Eve, and Georgie had gone to pick up a girl who was coming to lunch with us. But Georgie didn't come back! I was in anguish till we had a call from the police. . . . It seemed that, the elevator being out of service, he had climbed the stairs very quickly and did not see an open window; pieces of glass had gotten into his head. The scars are still visible.[16]

In explaining the context of the accident, doña Leonor contributes important details which complement those in both the story and the autobiography. In the story, the girl Borges had gone to pick up is reduced to the horrified anonymous face; the anticipated emotion of the visit is transferred (very adequately, one would say) to Dahlmann's enthusiastic discovery of a rare copy of *The Thousand and One Nights*. Even more significant is the omission of all references to the somewhat romantic context of the accident in the autobiographical essay.

On the reading of the C. S. Lewis novel two observations should be made. The first is obvious: this book is undoubtedly one of the sources (but not the only one) of the story, "Tlön, Uqbar, Orbis Tertius," which also deals with an imaginary planet and was written by Borges immediately after "Pierre Menard." The second observation refers to the bliss which overcomes Borges when he realizes he hasn't lost the faculty of understanding. A passage of "The God's Script" will help to illuminate this feeling of bliss. Near the

16. Leonor Acevedo de Borges, "Propos," in *L'Herne* (Paris, 1964), p. 11.

end, when the protagonist of that story has a mystical vision of the Wheel (which is the universe, which is his god), he exclaims: "O bliss of understanding, greater than the bliss of imagining or feeling" (*L,* 172).

From the torture of fever, from that zone between life and death in which he has been existing, Borges slowly returns. The bliss of understanding is what first possesses him: the reader is the first personality to recover from pain and hallucination and near-death. The second one to return is the writer. In his mother's testimony, more so than in his own, it is possible to see to what extent Borges' accident radically changed that second personality, the writer:

As soon as he was back home, he began to write a fantastic story, his first one. ... And afterward, he wrote only fantastic stories, which scare me a little because I don't understand them very well. I asked him once: "Why don't you write again the same things you used to write?" He answered: "Nonsense, nonsense." And he was right.

We have already seen in the autobiographical essay that Borges offers a rationalization to explain his change of genre, and even of style: the fear of no longer being able to write a poem or a review. It is possible that this rationalization had been very much in his consciousness while he was lying, wide awake, in the clinic. But it seems to me that another more important circumstance motivated the change. To attribute the transformation to the reading of C. S. Lewis' fantastic novel is to emphasize the work of chance. It would be like believing that, had doña Leonor read him a play by Shaw, Borges would have decided to try his hand at a comedy, also a genre he had not attempted before. No, it is better to search for an explanation in the accident itself, and in the exact context in which it happened. In retelling the episode, Borges points out that it took place on Christmas Eve, 1938, and he adds, "the same year my father died." It is this fact which opens a new perspective for the analysis. There is also another consideration: Borges had the accident when he ran up the staircase of a strange house to pick up a young woman he was going to take home to lunch with his mother. Combined, the two elements suggest a completely different interpretation than the one given in the autobiographical essay, and even more complex than the one presented in "The South." To

127

understand the meaning of this double circumstance we should recall the real nature of Borges' relationship with his father.

8

In "An Autobiographical Essay," Borges speaks in some detail about his father. Some of the things he says are very relevant to the understanding of their relationship.

> My father, Jorge Guillermo Borges, worked as a lawyer. He was a philosophical anarchist—a disciple of Spencer's—and also a teacher of psychology at the Normal School for Modern Languages, where he gave his course in English, using as his text William James's shorter book of psychology.... (A, 204)

> His idols were Shelley, Keats, and Swinburne. As a reader, he had two interests. First, books on metaphysics and psychology (Berkeley, Hume, Royce, and William James). Second, literature and books about the East (Lane, Burton, and Payne). It was he who revealed the power of poetry to me—the fact that words are not only a means of communication but also magic symbols and music. When I recite poetry in English now, my mother tells me I take on his very voice. He also, without my being aware of it, gave me my first lessons in philosophy. When I was still quite young, he showed me, with the aid of a chessboard, the paradoxes of Zeno—Achilles and the tortoise, the unmoving flight of the arrow, the impossibility of motion. Later, without mentioning Berkeley's name, he did his best to teach me the rudiments of idealism. (A, 206–7)

> My father wrote a novel, which he published in Majorca in 1921, about the history of Entre Ríos. It was called *The Caudillo.* He also wrote (and destroyed) a book of essays, and published a translation of FitzGerald's Omar Khayyám in the same meter as the original. He destroyed a book of Oriental stories—in the manner of the Arabian Nights—and a drama, *Hacia la nada* (Toward Nothingness), about a man's disappointment in his son. He published some fine sonnets after the style of the Argentine poet Enrique Banchs. (A, 210–11)

Don Jorge undoubtedly wanted to be a writer and, despite his extreme modesty ("My father was such a modest man that he would have liked being invisible," his son tells us), his literary ambition followed him well into maturity. Total blindness alone forced him to give up writing. But already the ambition to be a writer had become the ambition to make his son a writer. The son's vocation was only the reflection and the confirmation of the father's frustrated vocation. If we accept, as Sartre confesses in *Les mots* (and confesses for all of us), that we write *in imitation,* then it is true that don Jorge is to Georgie what grandfather Schweitzer is to the child Jean-Paul: the Pygmalion, the Svengali who awakens the

128

hidden gift. In the autobiographical essay, Borges describes the stages of that awakening. His father used to give him philosophy lessons as if they were just children's games. Borges was to continue speculating (playing) on those themes all his life.

Also very important is the presence of an enormous library of English authors. In the preface to the second edition of his *Evaristo Carriego* (1955), Borges wrote:

I believed for many years that I had grown up in a suburb of Buenos Aires, a suburb of adventurous streets and showy sunsets. The truth is that I grew up in a garden, inside an iron picket fence, and in a library of unlimited English books.[17]

Fifteen years later, writing his autobiography, he says in an even more forceful way:

If I were asked to name the chief event in my life, I should say my father's library. In fact, I sometimes think I have never strayed outside that library. (*A*, 209)

It is not accidental, for that reason alone, that his father's image and that of the library end by merging into one image in the child's consciousness, and that the frustrated vocation of the father becomes the fulfilled vocation of the son. Recalling this aspect of their relationship, Borges says:

From the time I was a boy, when blindness came to him, it was tacitly understood that I had to fulfill the literary destiny that circumstances had denied my father. This was something that was taken for granted (and such things are far more important than things that are merely said). I was expected to be a writer.

I first started writing when I was six or seven. I tried to imitate classic writers of Spanish—Miguel de Cervantes, for example. I had set down in quite bad English a kind of handbook on Greek mythology, no doubt cribbed from Lemprière. This may have been my first literary venture. My first story was a rather nonsensical piece after the manner of Cervantes, an old-fashioned romance called "La visera fatal"—(The Fatal Helmet). I very neatly wrote these things into copybooks. My father never interfered. He wanted me to commit all my own mistakes, and once said, "Children educate their parents, not the other way around." When I was nine or so, I translated Oscar Wilde's "The Happy Prince" into Spanish, and it was published in one of the Buenos Aires dailies, *El País*. Since it was signed merely "Jorge Borges," people naturally assumed the translation was my father's. (*A*, 211)

This last confusion is portentous because Borges (the son, of course) was to carry the art of literary mystification to its highest

17. Jorge Luis Borges, *Evaristo Carriego* (Buenos Aires, 1955), p. 9.

point of aesthetic elaboration. The fact that his translation of Wilde's story was attributed to his father is an anticipation of the false attributions he himself was to make throughout his work (and also of the even falser attributions with which Borges would inspire his readers and critics). He himself has noted that upon publishing his story "The Approach to al-Mu'tasim" as a review of a nonexistent Hindu novel, a friend hurried to order the book (*A*, 240). More recently, in a bibliography of Borges' work, three of his stories ("An Examination of the Work of Herbert Quain," "The Sect of the Phoenix," and "Three Versions of Judas") were classified as essays. In the same bibliography (and this makes the full circle), don Jorge's translation of FitzGerald's Omar Khayyám was attributed to his son.[18] The vertiginous play of perspectives which fate initiates by attributing the son's translation of Wilde to his father contains a key to that aesthetics of reading which we are trying to examine.

As Georgie develops his own literary career, don Jorge continues his subtle watching. In his autobiography, Borges tells what followed the award of his bachelor's degree in Switzerland:

...it was now understood that I should devote myself to writing. I wanted to show my manuscripts to my father, but he told me he didn't believe in advice and that I must work my way all by myself through trial and error. (A, 218)

But if his father doesn't want to act like a teacher, mentor, or a guide, he still takes care to create a favorable atmosphere in which his son's work may develop. He relieves the young man of all economic worry, allows him to dedicate himself completely to literary creation, and even pays for the publication of his first book—he plays Maecenas to his own son. The friendship between them (both personal and literary) is so important that they even share friends. Two of the most decisive writers in Borges' early career are Macedonio Fernández and Evaristo Carriego; both are don Jorge's friends, and in adopting them as literary models (one for his metaphysical vision of the world, the other for his early poetry of

18. Nodier Lucia and Lydia Revello, "Contribución a la bibliografía de Jorge Luis Borges," in *Bibliografía argentina de artes y letras*, No. 11 (Buenos Aires, April–September 1961), pp. 60, 64, 65, 75.

the slums), Borges is indicating, very subtly, his father's influence.[19]
Even today, when he remembers the happy days of his literary beginnings, Borges recalls that

> **These years were quite happy ones because they stood for many friendships.**
> **There were those of Norah Lange, Macedonio, Piñero, and my father.** (A, 235)

But the relationship with his father—the literary relationship, of
course—was even more complex. Discussing the novel his father
had published in Majorca, Borges says:

> My father was writing his novel, which harked back to old times during the civil
> war of the 1870's in his native Entre Ríos. I recall giving him some quite bad
> metaphors, borrowed from the German expressionists, which he accepted out of
> resignation.

> Now I repent my youthful intrusions into his book. Seventeen years later, before
> he died, he told me that he would very much like me to rewrite the novel in a
> straightforward way, with all the fine writing and purple patches left out. (A,
> 219–20)

And further on, when Borges talks about his present projects, he
adds:

> I have another project that has been pending for an even longer period of time—
> that of revising and perhaps rewriting my father's novel *The Caudillo*, as he
> asked me to years ago. We had gone as far as discussing many of the problems;
> I like to think of the undertaking as a continued dialogue and a very real col-
> laboration. (A, 259)

Dialogue, collaboration: Borges could not have found better
words to define his very intimate literary relationship with his
father.

9

Nevertheless, some aspects of this relationship do not cease to be
puzzling. To understand it better, it will be necessary to return to
some of the texts already quoted and also introduce some new
ones. In the first place, don Jorge's excessive modesty, which to a
certain extent his son has inherited, should be emphasized. It is a
modesty which, undoubtedly, prevented him from developing all
his potential as a writer. Second, we should point out the father's
unmistakable skepticism toward the very activity of writing, or (at

19. Emir Rodríguez Monegal, *Borgès par lui même* (Paris, 1970), pp. 20–22.

least) toward writing in Argentina. There is a very revealing statement of his which Borges quotes in a text written for the magazine *Latitud* (February 1945), where he remembers a discussion with don Jorge about the meaning of an oracular phrase of San Martín, Argentina's national hero—"You will be what you must be, and if not you will be nothing":

My father discussed that interpretation with me: he asserted that San Martín said more or less: *You will be what you must be*—you will be a gentleman, a Catholic, an Argentine, a member of the Jockey Club, an admirer of General Uriburu, an admirer of the vast genre paintings of Quirós—*and if not you will be nothing*—you will be an Israelite, an anarchist, a simple jerk, a humble clerk; the National Commission of Culture will ignore your books and Dr. Rodríguez Larreta will not send you his, valued for the autograph....

Perhaps the father's interpretation of San Martín's dictum was wrong, as Borges suggests in the article, but what was right was his image of the person he himself was. The second prototype, and not the first, was nearer to his modesty and skepticism, to his philosophical anarchism, to his almost invisible sense of irony. Perhaps don Jorge was skeptical also about his son's literary gifts. Perhaps he believed that his son was also destined to be a frustrated second-rate writer. We will never know. Even so, I don't think it excessive to recognize something more than modesty in some statements the son attributes to him, and which I have already quoted. I quote again three of these statements:

I wanted to show my manuscripts to my father, but he told me he didn't believe in advice and that I must work my way all by myself through trial and error....

My father was writing a novel.... I recall giving him some quite bad metaphors, borrowed from the German expressionists, which he accepted out of resignation....

Seventeen years later, before he died, he told me that he would very much like me to rewrite the novel in a straightforward way, with all the fine writing and purple patches left out. (A, 218–20)

Perhaps this is just idle conjecture. But a fact one must not forget is that don Jorge witnessed only the beginnings of Borges' career. The books which he could have read—three slim volumes of verses, five volumes of brief essays, a biography of a quite second-rate Argentine poet, and one volume of short biographies of infamous people—although they reveal here and there the greatness of the future author of *Ficciones, The Aleph, Other Inquisitions,* and *Dreamtigers,* are obviously not works which an impassioned admirer of Shelley, Keats, and Swinburne could consider major. Even today, Borges has condemned to oblivion his three earliest volumes of essays, has severely reduced and revised the three first volumes of poetry, and has given only halfhearted approval to *Evaristo Carriego* and *A Universal History of Infamy.*

Besides, if one remembers that his father's main ambition was to write a novel and that Borges, despite some more or less burlesque attempts with Bioy Casares, never completed one, one can then better understand the almost invisible sense of reticence one finds in don Jorge's statements. An examination of two of his son's texts which deal with the subject of a man who is dreamed or made by another will help, I hope, to clarify the conjecture. The older text is the story "The Circular Ruins," which was published for the first time in *Sur,* December 1940, two years after his father's death. The theme of the story is well known: a magician whose god is fire decides to dream a man (a son) and interpolate him into reality so that he'll continue, somewhere else, his father's vocation. After many tests, the magician manages to dream a son, and succeeds in erasing in him all knowledge of his origin. His ghostly condition will be unknown to all, except to fire, the god. The feat achieved, the magician sends his son elsewhere. The end of the story is not too difficult to guess; the sanctuary where the magician lives is threatened by fire:

For a moment, he thought of taking refuge in the river, but then he realized that death was coming to crown his years and to release him from his labors. He walked into the leaping pennants of flame. They did not bite into his flesh, but caressed him and flooded him without heat or burning. In relief, in humiliation, in terror, he understood that he, too, was an appearance, that someone else was dreaming him. (*A*, 61–62)

Another version, both comical and pathetic, can be found in the poem "The Golem," which Borges wrote in 1958. The poem is based on the Czech legend which Gustav Meyrink had used in his novel *Der Golem,* one of the first works Borges read in German. But the same poem cites another source: Gershom Sholem's *Major Trends in Jewish Mysticism* (1941). In the poem, Borges recreates the legend of a certain Judah Löw, rabbi of Prague, who had made a clay figure in whom he tried to inculcate the "Secrets of Time, Space, Being, and Extension."

> **The rabbi revealed to it the universe**
> *(This is my foot; that's yours; this is a log)*
> **And after years of training, the perverse**
> **Pupil managed to sweep the synagogue.**

The poem's conclusion is predictable:

> **The rabbi gazed on it with tender eyes**
> **And terror.** *How* **(he asked)** *could it be done*
> *That I engender this distressing son?*
> *Inaction is wisdom. I left off being wise.*

> *To an infinite series why was it for me*
> *To add another integer? To the vain*
> *Hank that is spun out in Eternity*
> *Another cause or effect, another pain?*

> **At the anguished hour when the light gets vague**
> **Upon his Golem his eyes would come to rest.**
> **Who can tell us the feelings in His breast**
> **As God gazed on His rabbi there in Prague?**   *(SP, 113, 115)*

These are not the only texts in which Borges develops this theme, although they are the best known. In poems dedicated to chess and in essays on literary and dramatic fiction, Borges has emphasized several times this unreal condition of the human being dreamed (made) by someone, his father, who in turn was dreamed by another—God perhaps—who (vertiginously) was dreamed by another, and so on to infinity. It is possible to believe that, in some way, Borges has felt himself not only engendered by his father in the flesh and spirit, but also in his other existence as a writer. His career is the development and perfection of his father's frustrated one; his duty as a writer is to carry out the work his father couldn't do because of adverse circumstances (blindness at an early age being the main one); even now, when his fame as a writer has surpassed whatever he and his father had ever dreamed, Borges continues thinking modestly of completing a thorough revision of his father's novel and along the frugal lines his father wanted.

That Borges more than once must have had the feeling that he had been "dreamed" by his father seems to be undeniable. That he had had the feeling of being inferior to that dream, to his father's expectations, can also be conjectured. Almost all the texts he has written speak of failure, unfulfillment, betrayal, secret and overwhelming guilt. Even in the friendly and luminous reminiscences of his autobiographical essay, a chilly note is struck; the chill is only momentary, but it is worth underscoring. Speaking of the works his father undertook and then destroyed, Borges soberly names "a drama, *Hacia la nada* (Toward Nothingness), about a man's disappointment in his son" (*A*, 211). The theme of the misfit son in "The Golem" is sketched here.

10

To reconsider the accident after this excursion is to bring back to our attention its hidden meaning. Symbolically, the accident dramatizes both Borges' feelings of guilt over his father's death and his very deep, almost inexplicable need to be free of his father's subtle guidance. In a sense, the accident represents a symbolic action: death and rebirth. After the accident (the trial), Borges re-emerges transformed into a different writer, engendered by *himself*. Before the accident he is a poet, a book reviewer; after the accident he will be the inventor of the most arduous and exciting labyrinths, the creator of a new art form, the short story that is, at the same time, an essay. The new Borges (the new writer) goes much further than anything planned by his father. The fact that the accident also happens in somewhat romantic circumstances (he was going to pick up a young woman, we mustn't forget) only adds the necessary erotic element to the symbolic parricide that the accident (as death and rebirth of the hero) implies. But in assuming his new identity, Borges doesn't dismiss the old one. On the contrary, he publicly emphasizes it by pretending that his fantastic stories are only reviews of nonexistent books, essays on imaginary writers, descriptions of apocryphal planets. The new Borges will want to be seen as the old one, "the other, the same," as the title of one of his last volumes of verses puts it.

135

To re-examine "Pierre Menard, Author of the *Quixote*" after this excursion through so many texts means rereading it with different eyes. In the character of Menard, Borges has not only perfected the "pluperfect Edmond Teste" (as he himself calls him), giving his protagonist a comical power completely lacking in the tenuous ironies of Valéry; not only has he carried to its extremes the portrait of the intellectual à la Mallarmé, obsessed with perfection, the pursuer of the page's impeccable whiteness, of absence, of nothingness. But he has also given a portrait in code of his father—and of himself, of course. Above all, he has given a model of the art of writing which (for Menard, as for himself) is inseparable from the art of reading. For a man who believes himself to have been dreamed by someone else, whose literary vocation seems to be only the replica of the literary vocation of the man who engendered him, whose work is (in some way) the realization of a work sketched but not completed by his father, a man who has never participated in some of men's most common activities and who has converted his own bookish specialization into a symbol of the human condition—for such a man, literary creation must be "repetition" not "creation," "editing" not "inventing," "reading" not "writing." Therefore, his aesthetics must be, finally, an aesthetics of reading. Moreover, Borges' aesthetics of authorship, of creativity, is based on and nourished by his aesthetics of reading (the humbly borrowed heritage), in much the same way as his modesty in the role of the son as a receiver of gifts and unfinished projects conceals the shunning of paternity (origination, "originality"). This is why, in the famous piece "Borges and Myself," he expresses the wish to exist only as a percipient, not as creator—in the present, not in the past—anxious to live laterally and not in the causal sequence of lineage:

Spinoza held that all things try to keep on being themselves; a stone wants to be a stone and the tiger, a tiger. I shall remain in Borges, not in myself (if it is so that I am someone), but I recognize myself less in his books than in those of others or than in the laborious tuning of a guitar. (A, 152)

A similar thought is presented in the epilogue to *Dreamtigers:*

136

> **Few things have happened to me, and I have read a great many. Or rather, few things have happened to me more worth remembering than Schopenhauer's thought or the music of England's words.** (*DT*, 93)

The last version (so far) of the same thought can be found in his latest book of poems, *Elogio de la sombra* (In Praise of Darkness). It reads:

> **Let others boast of pages they have written,**
> **I take pride in those I've read.**[20]

The poem was written in 1969, and its title is, of course, "A Reader."

---

20. Jorge Luis Borges, *Elogio de la sombra* (Buenos Aires, 1969), p. 151. The English translation of this book is in progress; I quote here from Norman Thomas di Giovanni's translation in *Harper's*, December 1970.

The past tense
THREE POEMS
BY R. H. W. DILLARD

1. Rain

(After the Spanish of Jorge Luis Borges)

The afternoon produces a rain.

It also falls in the past.

You hear it. You remember the day
You first saw the color of a rose,
Saw the flower (you knew the name).

This rain closes the window,
But it opens tiny lenses in the screen
Of the room you knew, slicks the plums
On a bent tree that is no more.

This wet afternoon brings you the sound
You have been listening for:

Your father's voice, alive in the rain.

2. She

(After the English of Jorge Luis Borges)

In town or field, or by the insatiate sea,
Men brood on buried loves, and unforgot....
                                    —H. Rider Haggard

You want her.
You have little to offer:

Your hour under the moon,
The blue asphalt like steel,
The memory you hold of a smile,
Caught like silver in your eye,
A touch of fingers, her hand
Held out from the window
As she leaves (the last time).

A past: dead men, ghosts,
An odor of verbena, "dying thunder of hooves,"
The charge of three hundred men in Peru,
Your father's father wrapped in the hide of a cow,
A soldier shot at Gettysburg,
Caught among boulders, his leg stiff as leather,
The knife his son fashioned,
Touched now with rust, sharp as an eye.

The expression of your books,
The books themselves, green, orange, gold,
The paper stiff as a knee.

Your loyalty
And the fact of your betrayals.

Yourself, the smile no mirror shows,
Safe from time, from joy, from pain.

A glimpse of a yellow rose
In a goblet by a bed.

Your theories of her:
News that opens like a knife, a window,
Authentic and surprising news.

The loneliness that wakes you late and lonely,
The hunger that wakes you,
The lure of uncertainty, danger,
The possibility of defeat.

3. A world

El anverso y el reverso de esta moneda
son, para Dios, iguales.

Borges speaks of a world
Of bored barbarity, of monotonous
Savagery, of dull cruelty.

True enough.

He continues
But the world remains.

A leg breaks lazily,
Splitting the long way
Like the branch of a walnut
With the weight of ice.

In the dark building
They tie you to a chair
And edge you, straining,
To the edge of the stairs.

The long rows blur
To a grey serpent, sliding
Crookedly across the mud,
The chains lashing
Like ground teeth,
Sharp as your fear,
The water of your nerve.

The prevalence of blood,
Spreading on the highway,
Pooling in the sour cellar,
Draining under the locked door,
A heart pumps wildly
Into the stained air.

Words that strike
Like shaggy spears, like stones,
Like short, honed swords,
The quiet words that stick
In the comfortable air
Like clumsy darts.

The eyes of animals swell
In their heads, their lips
Tug nervously back, hackles
Stiff as dry blood. A wind
Rises and clatters the dark wood.
Grasses snarl in the clearing.
Rain stings like lead pellets.
The walls of the house strain
Like foundering ships.

Your side cracked like a husk,
Jesus, sprayed the soldier's
Face with blood and water:

Cracked like graves
With the bodies of waking saints,

Like rent garments,
Like the rotten temple wall:

Cracked like dry skin,
Dry dirt around the base
Of the skull:

Cracked like a caul,
Like the sweet taste
Of walnuts, of water,
Cracked like parting waters,
Like the scales of a new bud
Hot in the darkened air.

The final creole: Borges' view of Argentine history
HUMBERTO M. RASI

The general direction of the studies devoted to Borges' writings, as well as the preferences of certain of his translators, has contributed to an unbalanced view of his total work, and has tended, for various reasons, to create the image of a countryless writer, one foreign to the literature and the realities of his homeland.

This same charge, along with those of Byzantinism and dehumanization, is one that the Argentine critic Adolfo Prieto directs at Borges in the first book devoted entirely to his work.[1] Prieto, who writes in 1954 from a fiery existentialist perspective, is joined in his attack by Jorge Abelardo Ramos, author of a sociopolitical diatribe also leveled at Borges. To Ramos, Borges is a "systematic denigrator of everything Argentine," a man who has "lived his whole life with his back turned against the Nation." He adds ironically, "It is not a matter of denying Borges' patriotism. The truth is that he is a British, French, German patriot." After reviewing the main periods of Borges' productivity, Ramos con-

---

1. Prieto, *Borges y la nueva generación* (Buenos Aires, 1954). All translations from the Spanish are mine unless otherwise noted. My warm thanks to Mr. Richard K. Emmerson for his help in the final preparation of this essay.

cludes, "Since 1939 [Borges] has been willfully and decidedly a foreign writer." [2]

Studies favorable to Borges, by generally overlooking what is Argentine in his work, have also helped perpetuate this unbalanced view of his writings. Some have stressed the role that certain themes—time, eternity, infinity, personal identity—play in his production; others have analyzed in detail the peculiarities of his style; and still others have underlined his interest in foreign authors, tracing their effect on his work.

The apologists, finally, have emphasized the non-Argentine factors of Borges' life, education, and literary sources with the intent of stressing both his singularity in the Hispanic literatures and his importance with regard to other contemporary Western writers. Néstor Ibarra, who was the first to bring Borges to the attention of the French, calls him *"homme de lettres européen,"* [3] and states that *"personne n'a moins de patrie que Jorge Luis Borges."* [4] In his foreword to Borges' *A Personal Anthology,* editor Anthony Kerrigan says that the pieces that make up the book were translated by several men "who have put into American and into English some of the thoughts Borges has had in various languages— even in English—before he wrote them down in Spanish." [5] And Emir Rodríguez Monegal, one of the most knowledgeable students of Borges' work, declares in a recent book that: *"l'exotisme de Borges consiste à être étranger à la littérature de son propre pays."* [6]

2. Ramos, *Crisis y resurrección de la literatura argentina,* 2d ed. (Buenos Aires, 1961), pp. 27–28, 57–58. Both Prieto and Ramos were reviving an objection raised more than twenty years earlier, before Borges had taken up the short story. The young Enrique Anderson Imbert had claimed that "Argentine reality is absent from his essays" (*Megáfono,* Buenos Aires, August 11, 1933).

3. Ibarra, Preface to Borges' *Fictions* (Paris, 1952), p. 7.

4. Ibarra, "Jorge Luis Borges," *Lettres Françaises,* Buenos Aires, IV, 14 (1944), 9.

5. *A Personal Anthology* (New York, 1967), p. vii.

6. Rodríguez Monegal, *Borgès par lui même* (Paris, 1970), p. 7. He was closer to the truth in 1952, when he wrote: "Although Borges populates his stories with Scandinavian or Oriental names, from under the elaborate and (almost always) apocryphal erudition emerges the typical viewpoint of [a man from] the Río de la Plata area: the insatiable cultural avidity, the nostalgia for a time of violence and crime (a time when something happened), the color and the landscape of Buenos Aires and even of Uruguay, which so many days of repeated observation and experience have preserved in the retina of this retentive creator." *Narradores de esta América* (Montevideo, 1962), p. 20.

I believe that an impartial and thorough study of Borges' writings invalidates all the above statements, both the condemnatory and the apologetic. There is certainly *one* Borges saturated with foreign intellectual influences, but there is also another equally important Borges deeply interested in and attracted by the landscape, the history, the human types, the language, and the literature of his country. His true literary profile emerges only when these two partial and complementary images are superimposed. A study of his view of Argentine history will reveal some features of this less known figure—Borges the Argentine writer.

1

From the beginning of Borges' literary production, three sustained interests appear in full interdependence: a fondness for the city of Buenos Aires, a feeling for the history of his homeland, and an evocative admiration for his military ancestors. Significantly, the two poems opening his first book, *Fervor de Buenos Aires* (1923), seek to communicate these emotions. In "The Streets," Borges presents the territorial essence of his early poetic world, centered in the outskirts of his native city. In "The Recoleta," he reflects on the passage of time and on the men buried in this old patrician cemetery of Buenos Aires.[7] (Years later he would write that one of his ancestors was executed against the Recoleta's walls [8]). Walking pensively through its paths, he feels the "many confirmations of final dust," and alludes to the numerous military men whose bodies now rest in those tombs. Borges concludes the poem with a reference to the crypt containing the remains of his own ancestors: "These thoughts came to me in the Recoleta,/ in the place where my ashes will lie." [8] Thus geography, history, and family are tied together from the start, and must be considered facets of a single emotional unit in his work.

The basic factor in Borges' view of Argentine history is his constant awareness of being the descendant of men who were prominent during the conquest, colonization, and revolutionary and

7. Borges, *Fervor de Buenos Aires* (Buenos Aires, 1969), pp. 19–20. This is a revised version of his first book.
8. Borges, *Elogio de la sombra* (Buenos Aires, 1969), p. 127.

145

civil wars of southern South America. He looks upon the heroes and the episodes of his country's past as part of the tradition of his own family. Once, during an interview, Borges sought to correct his friend and translator Ibarra, who had presented him as a foreigner in Argentina:

I have an English grandmother, who married an Argentine colonel, and then the rest of my family—in a more distant way, of course—is of Spanish-Portuguese descent. But all are, essentially, Argentines. They are the men who fought in the wars of independence, in the war with Brazil, who fought against the Indians, who have been ranchers in this country. We have been in South America for several centuries.[9]

Genealogy confirms these assertions.[10] Paternally, the writer is the grandson of Colonel Francisco Borges; and, through a great-grandmother, he is related to the Argentine poet and philosopher Juan Crisóstomo Lafinur, who lived in the early nineteenth century. Borges is also related to men like Gerónimo Luis de Cabrera y Toledo (founder of the Argentine city of Córdoba in 1571), Juan de Garay (founder of the second settlement of Buenos Aires in 1580), Hernandarias (first creole, or native-born, governor of the Río de la Plata area), and Gerónimo Luis de Cabrera y Garay (governor of the Río de la Plata in 1641, and of Tucumán in 1646).

On his mother's side, Borges is the great-grandson of Colonel Isidoro Suárez (a hero in the wars of independence), whose wife was related to both Francisco Narciso de Laprida (the lawyer who presided over the Congress of Tucumán, which in 1816 proclaimed the independence of the United Provinces of the Río de la Plata) and to Brigadier General Miguel Estanislao Soler (who fought with General José de San Martín, liberator of Chile and Peru). So closely related were early Argentine settlers that, through the mother of Colonel Suárez, Borges is even a distant relative of the dictator Juan Manuel de Rosas.

These deep family roots, planted for centuries in South American soil, make Borges an authentic *criollo*—a bedrock Argentine.

9. James E. Irby, Napoleón Murat, and Carlos Peralta, *Encuentro con Borges* (Buenos Aires, 1968), p. 59.
10. See Manuel Mujica Láinez, "Borges et les ancêtres," and Carlos T. de Pereira Lahitte, "Généalogie de Jorge Luis Borges," both in *L'Herne* (Paris, 1964), pp. 151–58.

"I have been an Argentine for many generations," he once wrote in a moment of discouragement, stressing his right to criticize what he considers wrong in the affairs of his country.[11] Moreover, being a creole of long ancestry has imbued him with certain fundamental values—courage, dignity, friendship, generosity, individualism— and provided him with a peculiar feel for his country. "You . . . carry history in your blood," concedes one of the characters of his story "Guayaquil," speaking to the protagonist whom Borges has endowed with several autobiographical features; "You have only to listen closely to an inner voice" (*DBR,* 104).

The yellowing portraits and the swords of his ancestors decorating the walls of his paternal home in Palermo; the military anecdotes told by his maternal grandfather; the paternal grandmother's tales of her adventures as the wife of a frontier commander fighting the Indians;[12] the walks through the Recoleta cemetery; the nearness of the former estate of the dictator Rosas— all these instilled in the future writer a vivid consciousness of Argentine history. Years later, after returning from his second trip to Europe, Borges would transfer the experience to his homeland and write: ". . . only new countries have a past; that is to say, an autobiographical memory of it; in other words, only they have a living history."[13]

This living heritage emerges repeatedly throughout Borges' work. The names of his ancestors are sometimes mentioned in his stories, thus contributing to the verisimilitude of the fictional narrative. Three of them appear in "The Life of Tadeo Isidoro Cruz (1829–1874)." "[T]he gauchos," writes Borges, "were routed by a detachment of Suárez's cavalry," and the man who fathered Cruz "died in a ditch, his skull split by a saber that had seen service in the Peruvian and Brazilian wars." Later Cruz goes to Buenos Aires "on a cattle drive from the ranch of Francisco Xavier Acevedo," and fights against the Indians "led by Sergeant Major Eusebio Laprida . . ." (*A,* 81–83). In other cases, as in "Guayaquil,"

11. Borges, *Discusión* (Buenos Aires, 1932), p. 17.
12. See "Story of the Warrior and the Captive" (*A Personal Anthology,* pp. 170–74), in which Borges utilizes one of her tales as the basis for the second half of the narrative.
13. Borges, *Evaristo Carriego* (Buenos Aires, 1930), p. 27.

Borges utilizes family memorabilia as the inherited background for a character:

> On display in my study are an oval portrait of my great-grandfather, who fought in the wars of Independence, and some cabinets containing swords, medals, and flags. I showed Zimmerman those old glorious things. . . .

> "Here my great-grandfather lay down his sword, which saw action throughout the continent. Here I have pondered the past and have compiled my books. I can almost say I've never been outside this library. . . ." (*DBR*, 102, 103)

It is in Borges' poetry, however, that evocations of Argentina's past most persistently appear. Unlike the analytical intellectualism of most of his essays and stories, this poetry is intuitive, and it reflects Borges' mythological view of men and events that emotionally attract him. In *Fervor de Buenos Aires,* besides "The Recoleta," he devotes a pair of compositions, both entitled "Sepulchral Inscription," to his military ancestors Suárez and Borges, and another to "Rosas," the dictator. In *Luna de enfrente* (Moon Across the Way), published in 1925, are "Dulcia Linquimus Arva," [14] a remembrance of hardy forefathers who were soldiers and ranchers on the pampas; "The Year 1840," about the time of Rosas; and two poems centered on the tragic career of Facundo Quiroga, "The Plains" and "General Quiroga Rides to His Death in a Carriage." *Cuaderno San Martín* (1929) contains "The Mythical Founding of Buenos Aires" and "Isidoro Acevedo," in which Borges evokes the deathbed agony of his maternal grandfather. Later, in an unusual prose poem composed in English, Borges asks his love:

> What can I hold you with? . . . I offer you my ancestors, my dead men, the ghosts that living men have honoured in marble: my father's father killed in the frontier of Buenos Aires, two bullets through his lungs, bearded and dead, wrapped by his soldiers in the hide of a cow; my mother's grandfather—just twenty-four—heading a charge of three hundred men in Perú, now ghosts on vanished horses. (*SP*, 77)

In one of his best poems, "The Cyclical Night" (1940), Borges presents three of his leitmotifs—Buenos Aires, his military ancestors, and Argentina's past—definitively united in a conjecture on the possibility of circular time:

14. The title is from Virgil: "We depart from our own country, from the sweet fields [of home]."

> This, here, is Buenos Aires. Time, which brings
> Either love or money to men, hands on to me
> Only this withered rose, this empty tracery
> Of streets with names recurring from the past
>
> In my blood: Laprida, Cabrera, Soler, Suárez...
> Names in which secret bugle calls are sounding,
> Invoking republics, cavalry, and mornings,
> Joyful victories, men dying in action. (*SP*, 79)

Three years later, in the haunting "Conjectural Poem," Borges evokes the last pathetic moments in the life of Dr. Francisco Laprida. During the dictatorship of Juan Domingo Perón, he composes the significant "Page to Commemorate Colonel Suárez, Victor at Junín" (1953), and, some time later, "Allusion to the Death of Colonel Francisco Borges (1833–1874)." With "Sarmiento" (1961) he celebrates the sesquicentennial of the birth of a towering figure of Argentina's history, and between 1966 and 1971, in "Junín," "Acevedo," and "La Busca" (The Search), he poetically reinhabits the lands of his grandparents to evoke their memory. Thus Borges fulfills, across half a century, a duty of filial and patriotic devotion which he had taken upon himself in 1925: "To the ancestors of my blood and spirit, I have made an offering of verses." [15]

Several factors converge in Borges' insistent return to the past of family and country. Basically, this return springs from his vehement desire to capture the essence of the *patria* through an identification with some of the men who participated in its inception. In this attempt to define and establish a personal relationship with his homeland, Borges shares the preoccupation of many writers in young countries; the search for national identity appears early in Argentina's literature and becomes painfully evident after the political crisis of 1930.[16] Borges' literary preference for military figures and events is also a psychological compensation for his physical limitations, prompting him to extol courage and heroism above all other virtues. "As most of my people had been soldiers . . . and I knew I would never be," he wrote recently, recalling his with-

15. Borges, *Luna de enfrente* (Buenos Aires, 1925), p. 28.
16. See, for example, Raúl Scalabrini Ortiz, *El hombre que está solo y espera* (1931); Ezequiel Martínez Estrada, *Radiografía de la pampa* (1933); and Eduardo Mallea, *Historia de una pasión argentina* (1937).

drawn boyhood, "I felt ashamed, quite early, to be a bookish kind of person and not a man of action" (*A*, 208). Of course, this ancestor cult may be the result of a defense mechanism as well. Many writers, reacting against the European immigrants flooding Argentina (and particularly Buenos Aires) in the first decades of the century, insisted upon their deep ancestral roots in an effort to mark differences and to defend their social positions. There is a definite sense in which Borges' ancestors shielded him from an indistinct populace. But when fascism and later Peronism came to dominate Argentine politics in the forties and fifties, Borges was to invoke his forefathers primarily for the inspiration to survive spiritually in those difficult years.

2

Borges has remarked that a close reading of his *Obra poética* reveals that several poems deal with the same theme or figure. "It is," he said, "as if I had spent my life writing seven or eight poems, as if each book were a rough draft of the next one." [17] This statement is particularly true of the successive compositions he devotes to various ancestors. (These poems make up the bulk of his poetry concerned with Argentina's past.)

The first of these figures to attract Borges' interest is Isidoro Suárez, who in August of 1824 played a key role in the battle of Junín, in Peru. Suárez commanded a squadron of the revolutionary cavalry fighting for the independence of Spanish America. After the brief but bloody encounter, which resulted in the defeat of the royalist forces, General Simón Bolívar came to the battlefield and congratulated the young Argentine officer before the troops for his audacity at the decisive moment. Borges' poetic tribute to his maternal great-grandfather, who later died in exile during Rosas' dictatorship, is crystallized in two poems written over an interval of thirty years. The first, "Sepulchral Inscription" (1923), stressed Suárez's personal courage in each verse:

> **His valor passed beyond the Andes.**
> **He fought against mountains and armies.**

17. Rita Guibert, "Jorge Luis Borges," *Life en Español,* XXI, 5 (1968), 55.

> Audacity was a habit with his sword.
> At Junín he put a lucky end to the fight
> and gave Spanish blood to Peruvian lances.
> He wrote his roll of deeds
> in prose inflexible as battlesinging trumpets.
> He died walled in by implacable exile.
> Now he is a handful of dust and glory. (*SP*, 5)

The second poem, "A Page to Commemorate Colonel Suárez, Victor at Junín" (1953), is prompted by a double stimulus, evocative and political—Borges' memory of this valiant ancestor and his reaction to the oppressive Perón regime, under which he had to live. Both motifs are projected against the sinister background of recurring Argentine dictatorships. Longer and freer than the earlier tribute, this poem consists of three parts. The opening enumerates the deprivations and exile suffered by Suárez after returning to his homeland in 1827, "the ignominies of growing old, / the dictator's shadow spreading across the land." But all this, the poet says, can be endured because the man "had at least his burning hour on horseback, / on the plateau of Junín." And Borges insists: "What is time's monotony to him, who knew / that fulfillment, that ecstasy, that afternoon?" In the middle part, the poet alludes to Suárez's distinguished military record, and then recalls with vivid, flashing strokes

> the crimson battle of Junín, the enduring moment
> in which the lances crossed, the order of battle,
> defeat at first, and in the uproar
> (as astonishing to him as to the army)
> his voice urging the Peruvians to the attack,
> the thrill, the drive, the decisiveness of the charge,
> the seething labyrinth of cavalries,
> clash of the lances (not a single shot fired),
> the Spaniard he ran through with his spear,
> the headiness of victory, the exhaustion, the drowsiness
>   descending,
> and the men dying in the marshes. . . .

In the final section of this vibrant poem, Borges identifies his own predicament with that of Suárez: "His great-grandson is writing these lines, / and a silent voice comes to him out of the past, / out of the blood. . . ." He then refers to Perón's dictatorship and the constant fight for liberty:

["]The battle is everlasting and can do without
the pomp of the actual armies and of trumpets.
Junín is two civilians cursing a tyrant
on a street corner,
or an unknown man somewhere, dying in prison." (*SP*, 89–91)

Borges' maternal grandfather, Isidoro Acevedo, who fought in
several military encounters during the Argentine civil wars from the
late 1850's to 1880, appears in a poem in which the writer records
a memory from infancy. Acevedo died in 1905 at the Borges home
after an unusual agony filled with hallucinations and patriotic
fervor. After summarizing in the second stanza the highlights of
his grandfather's life, the poet concentrates on Acevedo's revealing
last hours.

His dream was of two armies
entering the shadow of battle;
he enumerated the commands, the colors, the units.
"Now the officers are reviewing their battle plans,"
    he said in a voice you could hear,
and in order to see them he tried sitting up.

He seized a stretch of the prairie,
scouting it for broken terrain, where the infantry could
    hold their ground,
and for a flat place so that the cavalry charge could not
    be turned back.
. . . .

[He] rounded up an army of Buenos Aires ghosts
so as to get himself killed in the fighting.

That was how, in a bedroom that looked onto the garden,
he died out of devotion for his city. (*SP*, 53–55)

The two underlying emotions of this narrative poem, which Borges
may later have used as a point of departure for his story "The
Other Death," are admiration for this ancestor—courageous even
in his last agony—and regret for not having lived in those years
of adventure.

Undoubtedly, Borges' favorite ancestor is his paternal grandfather, Colonel Francisco Borges. He refers to him several times
in his prose and, perhaps trying to capture the essence of the man,
portrays him in four successive poems written over a period of
some forty-odd years. Francisco Borges was born in Montevideo,

Uruguay, in 1833, while the city was under siege by a Federalist army. He participated in his first battle as a boy of fifteen. Later he fought against the forces of Rosas in the battle of Caseros; after that, in the War of the Triple Alliance, in Paraguay, where he was wounded; next, in Entre Ríos against López Jordán's gaucho militia; then on the pampa against the Indians. By 1872 he was the commander of a post located on the western frontier of the Province of Buenos Aires, defending the settlers from Indian attacks. When, in 1874, a revolt led by General Bartolomé Mitre against President Sarmiento broke out prematurely, Colonel Borges left the command of his government troops and went alone to join Mitre's forces. During the battle of La Verde, the insurgent army was defeated. After the defeat, Borges, dressed in a white poncho, rode out unarmed toward the victorious troops and was killed.

The attractive figure of this young soldier, whose forty years begin and end amid the clash of battle, appears in an early poem from the first edition of *Fervor de Buenos Aires:*

> **The easy hills of Uruguay,**
> **Paraguay's burning swamps**
> **and the vanquished prairies**
> **to your mind were**
> **a single unending violence.**
> **In the fighting at La Verde**
> **death made inroads on so much bravery.** (*SP*, 247)

The timidity of these youthful verses disappears when Borges next takes up the subject. The expression is now more resolute and martial:

> **For your life was this:**
> **an object dragged from battle to battle.**
>
> **Honor, poignancy, loneliness**
> **and courage that served no end.** (*SP*, 247)

The nucleus of this poem repeats images from the earlier one, and its structure reveals an attempt to convey the impression of a military report. But not even this new version satisfied Borges, and it was eliminated from the 1967 edition of his collected poems. (The earlier poem was never reprinted after its initial appearance.) Around 1960, convinced that he could not communicate directly

153

the emotion that this figure awakens in him, the poet settles for an "allusion":

> I leave him on his horse on that evening
> In which he rode across the plain to meet
> His death, and of all the hours of his fate
> May this one, though bitter, go on living.
> ....
> What closed on him, the Remingtons' crackle,
> What his eye took in, endless grazing land,
> Are what he saw and heard his whole life long.
> Here was his home—in the thick of battle.
> In his epic world, riding on his horse,
> I leave him almost untouched by my verse.   (*SP*, 135)

The conciseness and controlled emotion of this poem make it the most arresting of the series. And yet, in 1966, the poet returns for the fourth time to this same subject, dealing with it now from another perspective. A visit to Junín in the Province of Buenos Aires, where his grandfather had been a frontier commander, prompts Borges to identify his destiny with that of this ancestor: "I am myself and I am him today, / The man who died, the man whose blood and name / Are mine. . . ." The poet attempts an impossible dialogue with him, then closes the poem with a conjecture regarding his grandfather's true character: "I picture you as sad and somewhat stern, / But who and what you were, I'll never learn" (*SP*, 211).

Two opposing but sometimes complementary emotions, pride and frustration, are present in Borges' fervid evocations of his military ancestors. He feels pride in the distinguished heritage left to him by Suárez, Acevedo, and Francisco Borges, through whom he reaches back to the beginnings of Argentina. But he also manifests the frustration of having arrived too late to participate in those virile campaigns, the sorrow of being unable—owing to physical as well as temperamental limitations—to demonstrate that total courage he so much exalts. These feelings explain the "noble sadness of being a creole" he experiences in 1921,[18] and they also explain the "charge at Junín in your blood" that spurs and inhibits him (*SP*, 93).

18. Borges, *Inquisiciones* (Buenos Aires, 1925), p. 83.

We touch here the emotional core of Borges' attitude toward his civic and familial heritage, which to a large extent are one and the same for him. Conscious of being the last link of a long line of brave men who fought and died for his *patria,* Borges sees himself as a "final creole." [19] This sentiment, expressed early in his work, becomes more intense as he melancholically approaches a childless old age and foresees the unavoidable extinction of his name.

> **The valiant men are all finished**
> **and they have not left descendents.**
>
> **. . . . .**
>
> **Where are those who left this land**
> **to liberate other nations,**
> **or those who went to the South**
> **to confront Indian lances?**
> **Where are those who marched to war**
> **in well-organized batallions?**
> **Where are those who died**
> **in other revolutions?** [20]

In these verses Borges projects his sad realization of physical weakness upon the decline of Argentine society as a whole. *"Je crois qu'au XIXe siècle nous étions un pays plutôt dur,"* he has stated in an interview with a French critic; *"nous sommes malheureusement devenus un pays veule, très mou et très sentimental."* [21]

A comparable atmosphere of decadence and extinction infects his narrative "The Elder Lady" (1970), in which Borges tells the story of the daughter of a minor hero of Spanish-American independence whose hundredth birthday is celebrated with official pomp. There are several autobiographical features in this somewhat ironic yet pathetic portrait of a blind and antiquated old woman who endures oblivion with dignity. In the concluding paragraph Borges suggests what it means, for himself and the old lady, to be a "final creole":

19. Borges, *Obra poética 1923–1967* (Buenos Aires, 1967), p. 88. The lines containing these words were deleted from the 1969 revision of the poem.
20. *Obra poética 1923–1967,* p. 301.
21. Jean de Milleret, *Entretiens avec Jorge Luis Borges* (Paris, 1967), pp. 149–50.

I think back on the dead soldiers of Big Hill; I think of the nameless men of America and of Spain who met their deaths under the hooves of the horses; I think that the last victim of that throng of lances high on a Peruvian tableland was, more than a century later, a very old lady. (*DBR*, 96)

But nowhere else in his work does Borges express his "yearning for that epic destiny which my gods denied me" [22] as fully as in his prose poem "The Dagger." In this piece Borges first recounts the history of the weapon he received from his father and now keeps in a drawer of his desk. Whoever sees it, Borges says, "has to pick up the dagger and toy with it, as if he had always been on the lookout for it. The hand is quick to grip the waiting hilt, and the powerful obeying blade slides in and out of the sheath with a click." Its basic purpose, however, is not to be played with or to open envelopes; the dagger "wants to kill, it wants to shed sudden blood." The final lines express the conviction that this dagger-Borges was born with another destiny, somehow frustrated:

In a drawer of my writing table, among draft pages and old letters, the dagger dreams over and over its simple tiger's dream. . . . At times I am sorry for it. Such power and single-mindedness, so impassive or innocent its pride, and the years slip by unheeding. (*SP*, 95)

"Conjectural Poem," one of Borges' best compositions, centers on the tragic figure of Francisco Narciso de Laprida, a remote ancestor of Borges, with whom, more than any other, the poet identifies his own destiny. First published on July 4, 1943, this poem integrates several Borgesian motifs—cyclical time, the inscrutable labyrinth, the key that in the final moment reveals the meaning of life—and relates them to the classic Argentine ideological dilemma, civilization vs. barbarism, which, during the Second World War, took on universal dimensions. The poet's choice of Laprida as a symbol was a felicitous one. Laprida had been the president of the congress which in 1816 declared Argentine independence, and, in addition, was one of the few men in his country's history who are above political dispute. Using a rich interior monologue, Borges imagines the circumstances of Laprida's death—never fully clarified—while fleeing in 1829 from Aldao's gaucho militia, who finally kill him:

22. Victoria Ocampo, *Diálogo con Borges* (Buenos Aires, 1969), p. 19.

> Bullets whip the air this last afternoon.
> A wind is up, blowing full of cinders
> as the day and this chaotic battle
> straggle to a close. The gauchos have won:
> victory is theirs, the barbarians'. (*SP*, 83)

In view of subsequent events in Argentina, Borges' forebodings by mid-1943 seem powerfully accurate. Exactly one month before the publication of "Conjectural Poem" in the literary supplement of *La Nación,* a successful coup, carried out by ultra-nationalistic and pro-fascist officers of the armed forces, with the intent of preparing the country for what then seemed the inevitable triumph of the Axis powers, had opened a new and ominous chapter in Argentine political evolution.[23] Primitivism and violence, which in "The Dagger" attract him mysteriously, are seen in this poem as negative qualities; but their repercussions are assumed by Borges (as by Dahlmann in "The South") with resignation and fortitude:

> I, Francisco Narciso Laprida,
> who studied both canon law and civil
> and whose voice declared the independence
> of this entire untamed territory,
> in defeat, my face marked by blood and sweat,
> holding neither hope nor fear, the way lost,
> strike out for the South through the back country.

Borges, who saw in the contemporary surge of militarism and fascism a rebirth of the dark forces of barbaric oppression, feels that after the lapse of one century *he* is reliving Laprida's lot:

> I who longed to be someone else, to weigh
> judgments, to read books, to hand down the law,
> will lie in the open out in these swamps;
> but a secret joy somehow swells my breast.
> I see at last that I am face to face
> with my South American destiny. (*SP*, 83)

23. In a final word appended to a lecture delivered at the University of Montevideo, Uruguay (October 29, 1945), a few months before Perón's accession to the presidency of Argentina, Borges alluded to his frame of mind in 1943 when he wrote this poem. "Many nights revolved over us and something happened that is now well known. It was then I realized that my country had not been spared its bitter cup. I realized that we were once again facing the unknown. I felt that the tragic year 1820 was returning; I felt that the men who then faced barbarity had also been bewildered by the countenance of an unexpected destiny, from which they nonetheless did not flee," *Aspectos de la literatura gauchesca* (Montevideo, 1950), p. 34.

The fate of the Argentine or Latin American intellectual, Borges tells us in this poem, is inevitable and essentially tragic: it implies frustration, struggle, suffering, and sometimes violent death. But this destiny can be manfully assumed, as the sacrifice demanded at times, by an ethic of dignity. In this sense, the ultimate message of the poem transcends national or temporal boundaries, and involves an affirmation of man's highest values.

In his "Conjectural Poem" Borges descends to the hell of national reality, guided by his ancestor Laprida, and returns to this world with a deeper understanding of the poles of Argentine tradition—light and darkness, book and dagger—a dialectic which he accepts with all its consequences. Family and country, history and personal destiny, will be, from now on, a clearer poetic unity in his work.

3

Although attenuated, the ideological conflict that divided Argentines during the first decades of their nationhood is still in force. More than a prolonged dispute over the model to be used in the political organization of the country, the confrontation between *unitarios* and *federales*—those favoring a strong central government versus those defending states' rights—involved the tension between two nineteenth-century life styles: between Buenos Aires, with its modern, liberal, European sympathies, and the interior, with its traditional, conservative, Spanish leanings. This still unresolved dichotomy, which has been retarding Argentina's full development, tacitly demands that every citizen take sides.

Borges, although his writings are not ideological in character, has not remained aloof from this controversy. Every time he touches upon themes, events, or figures of Argentine history, he implicitly assumes a position in the polemic. A chronological reading of his work reveals a basic change in orientation that began in 1930 and became more marked in the following quarter of a century. In September of that year, a military coup toppled President Hipólito Yrigoyen, thus breaking half a century of constitutional government and initiating a period of political instability from which Argentina has not yet recovered. Borges, then sympathetic to the nationalistic and populist Radical Party that supported Yrigoyen, reacted bitterly to the pro-fascist coup and withdrew to his literary world. But as fascism and nazism found more admirers in Argentina during the late thirties and early forties, Borges condemned these ideologies outright in several essays, warning of their implicit burden of tyranny, oppression, and inhumanity.

There are three Argentine historical figures who allow us to follow the reorientation of Borges' ideological stance, and to trace the effect of political change on his work. Two of them are, in themselves, symbols of the national Federalist-Centralist polarization: Juan Manuel de Rosas (1793–1877), a reactionary rancher and businessman who ruled the country with an iron hand between 1829 and 1852, and Domingo Faustino Sarmiento (1811–1888), a progressive teacher, writer, and diplomat who served as constitutional president between 1868 and 1874. The third figure, whose existence was related to the lives of the other two, is Juan Facundo Quiroga (1790–1835), the embodiment of all the qualities and defects of the Argentine gaucho. Both Rosas and Quiroga were caudillos, that is, charismatic political leaders who exerted their absolute power with the blind support of the masses.

Borges was disposed by family tradition to sympathize with the views of *unitarios.* His great-grandfather Suárez died in exile during the Rosas tyranny; his grandfather Borges fought against Rosas' forces in the siege of Montevideo and at Caseros; his grandfather Acevedo had in his childhood seen a bloody example of the methods used by Rosas' henchmen against the opposition. This clear political leaning of the family was even reflected in their literary tastes. Borges remembers that he had to read *Martín Fierro,* José Hernández' classic Argentine gaucho poem, "on the sly" because "Hernández was militant in the cause of the evil ones—he had belonged to the Federalist Party, to the party of Rosas." [24] Not even private life escaped this all-embracing rift. For example, in a sketch far removed from politics, Borges recalls:

Around 1927 I met a sombre girl, first by telephone (for Julia began as a nameless, faceless voice), and, later, on a corner toward evening. She had alarmingly

24. Irby, Murat, and Peralta, *Encuentro con Borges,* p. 62.

large eyes, straight blue-black hair, and an unbending body. Her grandfather and great-grandfather were *federales*, as mine were *unitarios*, and that ancient discord in our blood was for us a bond, a fuller possession of the fatherland.[25]

Prompted, however, by a youthful rebellion against his family's "timorous" anti-Rosas tradition,[26] by his admiration for a man he considered then a prototype of creole virility, and by a naive nationalism, Borges felt the magnetism of the powerful figure of Rosas. This almost mythical caudillo was the object of hero worship by the young poet during the first decades of his literary production. In an early poem entitled "El truco" (a Spanish card game), Borges refers to the power of the ace and adds admiringly that it is, "like don Juan Manuel [de Rosas], omnipotent. . . ." There is also in *Fervor de Buenos Aires* a poem devoted entirely to Rosas. Someone in the paternal living room, says Borges, "pronounced that familiarly sinister name," and Rosas' huge frame emerged "like a darkening mountain," evoking "Conjecture and memory. . . ." The poem echoes heated family arguments and reveals a young man searching for an unbiased appraisal of the figure "Famous in infamy. . . ." He views Rosas both as a man who left his bloody signature on national history and as an object of "the gaucho idolatry." Furthermore, we now lose count of his killings, which, compared with those perpetuated by time, are minimal. The poem closes with a hint of skepticism, and with an invitation to forgive the dictator's crimes:

> Perhaps Rosas
> was only the implacable butcher our grandfathers
> thought him;
> I think of him now, like ourselves, as
> a creature of chance enclosed in an action's parentheses. . . .
> . . . .
> Even God has forgotten him. (*SP*, 11–13)

In an essay from *Inquisiciones* (1925), Borges presents Rosas as the personification of basic creole qualities and, together with Yrigoyen, as "one of the two great caudillos to embrace the soul of Buenos Aires." [27] In a poem from *Luna de enfrente* (1925),

25. *Dreamtigers*, p. 27.
26. Borges, *El tamaño de mi esperanza* (Buenos Aires, 1926), p. 145.
27. *Inquisiciones*, p. 132.

entitled "The Year 1840," the poet seems to forget that this year had marked the pinnacle of Rosas' tyranny of systematic intimidation and political murders, and instead chooses to dwell on the picturesque features of the time. Rosas and his actions are viewed as the manifestation of popular beliefs and practices. In 1926 Borges expresses a similar opinion in his nationalistic book *El tamaño de mi esperanza* (The Extent of My Hope): "Our greatest male is still don Juan Manuel, a great model of individual courage"; Rosas' political system was "an authentic creole organism," and even his secret police were an incarnation of "creole" mentality.[28] In the volume's initial essay, Rosas and Sarmiento are compared, for the first time, and, with a single disparaging sentence, Borges dismisses former president Sarmiento as a "North-Americanized, untamed Indian, who greatly hated and misunderstood everything creole," and who set out to Europeanize Argentina prompted by a "blind faith, typical of a man just arrived to culture, and who expects miracles from it."

Borges later repents his naive and astigmatic view of Argentine history, which continued up to his biography *Evaristo Carriego* (1930). He was to reject his first two books of essays (*Inquisiciones* and *El tamaño de mi esperanza*), delete virtually all of his third (*El idioma de los argentinos*), and eliminate "The Year 1840" when he first collected his poems. But before analyzing this total reorientation of Borges' point of view of Argentine history, and particularly his concept of Rosas and Sarmiento, we must refer briefly to his changing attitude toward Facundo Quiroga, who also attracted him in the early years of his enthusiastic *criollista* stance. Borges' interest in these particular nineteenth-century figures is not accidental, since their names have remained linked in national history. Quiroga exerted his autocratic rule over a wide area in northwestern Argentina, but his influence reached even farther in the 1820's and 1830's. Rosas' domain included central-eastern Argentina, and, after Quiroga's assassination in 1835, the entire nation was subject to his power. Sarmiento, younger than both, was forced into exile by one of Quiroga's satraps. As a writer

28. *El tamaño de mi esperanza,* pp. 6, 8, 34.

in Chile, he attacked both Quiroga and Rosas, and plotted with other liberal exiles until Rosas was toppled in 1852.

Like Sarmiento in his biographical essay *Facundo, civilización o barbarie* (1845), Borges feels alternately fascinated and repelled by Facundo Quiroga. Two pieces in *Luna de enfrente* reflect this fluctuation. In "The Plains," the poet stresses the cruelty and senselessness that characterized the raids carried out by Quiroga's gaucho army. The plains witness their arrival, wanton destruction, and departure with total indifference. "It is sad that memory would include everything," concludes Borges, "especially if the recollection is embarrassing." [29] The second poem, however, is far from abject. "General Quiroga Rides to His Death in a Carriage" evokes the final moments of the caudillo who rides knowingly and fearlessly into an ambush. In the first stanza, Borges sketches the desolate landscape through which the stagecoach relentlessly advances with its "six souls in terror and one wide awake and bold." This dauntless courage redeems the man and raises him to the category of a creole myth: "General Quiroga had in mind to approach the haunts of death/ taking six or seven companions with slit throats as escorts" (*SP,* 35). Quiroga's audacity prompts him to brave even the world beyond. This early ambivalence of the poet toward barbarous courage—rejected in the first poem and admired in the second—anticipates a recurrent play of attitude in Borges, already pointed out in the case of the opposing views contained in both "Conjectural Poem" and "The Dagger," and reflects his thoroughly Argentine constitution.

After this first approach to Rosas, Quiroga, and Sarmiento, two decades went by before Borges again took up these subjects. Meanwhile, several important events and trends had affected Argentina's socio-political and ideological climate: the military coup of 1930, the growth of fascism, the emergence of a vocal ultra-nationalistic faction that exalted Rosas, the surge of an active Germanophile sector during the Second World War, the new military coup of 1943, Perón's accession to power in 1946, and the appearance of a revisionist historical school bent upon condemning liberal

29. *Luna de enfrente,* p. 12.

Argentine tradition and determined at the same time to vindicate Rosas.[30]

When all these elements are taken into account, the factors behind Borges' radical about-face become clear. By 1941 he is ready to accept Paul Groussac's ironic definition of Rosas as a "rear-guard militiaman" (*OI*, 28). After the fall of Perón, when Borges again contrasts Sarmiento and Rosas, the latter is no longer the admired prototype of the creole caudillo, but the incarnation of several national defects which the Argentines bring back to the presidency with masochistic passion:

Two tyrannies had their day here. During the first some men coming from the Plata market hawked white and yellow peaches from the seat of a cart. A child [Borges' maternal grandfather] lifted a corner of the canvas that covered them and saw *unitario* heads with bloody beards. The second, for many, meant imprisonment and death; for all it meant discomfort, a taste of disgrace in everyday acts, an incessant humiliation. (*DT*, 40)

From this new viewpoint, Rosas is no more the all-powerful man of Argentine history, but a coward who was able to escape from the defeat of his forces at Caseros, and sail on a British ship to England, where he died peacefully a quarter of a century later. To sharpen the contrast, Borges confronts Rosas with Quiroga in a parable entitled "Dead Men's Dialogue," which is a continuation of the last stanza of his poem "General Quiroga Rides to His Death in a Carriage." The first paragraph suggests the atmosphere of the world beyond, where the encounter takes place. Quiroga instructs Rosas—who, according to popular tradition, ordered Quiroga's elimination—on the meaning of their past lives:

"Rosas, you never did understand me. . . . Your lot was to command in a city that looks toward Europe and will someday be among the most famous in the world. Mine was to wage war in America's lonely spots, on poor earth belonging to poor gauchos. . . . I live and will continue to live for many years in the people's memory because I was murdered in a stagecoach at a place called Barranca Yaco, by horsemen armed with swords. It is you I have to thank for this gift of a bi-

---

30. A favorable view of Rosas would credit him with having prevented the territorial disintegration of the country and with having maintained a considerable degree of internal order, benefiting those who supported his regime. But an impartial view would also blame him for having set back the cultural and economic development of the nation, besides having used systematic oppression and political assassination as a means of remaining in power.

zarre death, which I did not know how to appreciate then, but which subsequent generations have refused to forget." (*DT*, 33–35)

Rosas looks at him disdainfully and remarks that posterity's judgment is worth not much more than contemporary flattery, which one can buy with a few presents. But Quiroga (and Borges) insists: "In 1852, destiny, either out of generosity or out of a desire to sound you to your depths, offered you a real man's death in battle. You showed yourself unworthy of that gift: the blood and fighting scared you" (*DT*, 34). Borges condemns Rosas to shame and hell because he views him now as the embodiment of cowardice—a most despicable defect. Quiroga, on the other hand, is redeemed, thanks to his courage, which, in a future time not bent upon violence, may manifest itself in a more civilized manner. Years later, Borges returned to the epoch of Rosas in a brief narrative entitled "Pedro Salvadores," dramatizing the cruelty of a regime that forced a peaceful citizen to live hidden in the cellar of his own home for nine years to escape political assassination.

Implicit in his subsequent execration of Rosas and his regime are Borges' fresh and somber memories of his own experience under the dictatorship of Perón. Most of his later pieces dealing with Rosas, including "Pedro Salvadores," may be read as fragments of his own spiritual autobiography. The truth is that the parallels between Rosas and Perón—allowing for a century of intervening time—are remarkable. The two are similar in ideological stance, political methods, the role played by their respective wives, and the circumstances of their downfall and escape. "Destiny takes pleasure in repetition, variants, symmetries" (*DT*, 36), wrote Borges, and in his final appraisal Rosas and Perón are viewed as "the same coward and sly dictator" who cyclically comes to power in Argentina.[31]

Rosas' vertical drop in Borges' esteem is accompanied, predictably, by a corresponding rise in his regard for Sarmiento. Accordingly, Borges now considers Sarmiento's classic *Facundo* a clear-sighted prophecy of Argentina's future, not understood until a century later.

31. Borges, "1810–1960," *Sur*, 267 (November–December 1960), 2.

In our childhood *Facundo* gave us the same delectable taste of fable as the inventions of Verne or the piracies of Stevenson; the second dictatorship taught us that violence and barbarism are not a paradise lost, but an immediate risk. Since the 1940's we have been the contemporaries of Sarmiento and of the historical process he analyzed and anathematized; before that time we were also his contemporaries, but we did not realize it.[32]

This prophetic aspect is the point of departure for an admiring poem that Borges wrote to commemorate the sesquicentennial of Sarmiento's birth. Sarmiento appears as the prodigious and solitary patriot who cannot be silenced even by predictable official ceremonies:

> ... He is not an ancient echo
> Multiplied by hollow fame
> Or, like many others, a colorless symbol
> That dictators can manipulate.
> He's himself. He's the witness of our homeland,
> The one who sees our infamy and our glory,
> The light of May and the horrors of Rosas' time
> And that succeeding horror, and the secret days
> Of our elaborate future.

Sarmiento still lives, "hating, loving, and fighting," causing veneration or antagonism, and following with deep interest the evolution of the country to which he devoted his best energies, and whose trajectory he so accurately foresaw: "Sarmiento the dreamer is still dreaming us." [33]

Borges' meditations on the Argentine past are one of the basic themes of his literary work—particularly of his poetry—which now spans half a century. In it he offers an intimate vision of men and events connected to his family and to his own experience. Family tradition thus becomes for Borges another equivalent of national history, and his approach, although circumscribed, has depth, insight, and authenticity. Argentine political change must be taken into account to understand the variations that occur in Borges' assessment of certain key figures, just as his ambivalence toward figures like Rosas modulates his understanding of bravery, destiny, and repetition. The artistic quality of his literary evocations of the Argentine past makes him his country's best contemporary civic poet.

32. Borges, "Sarmiento," *La Nación*, Buenos Aires (February 12, 1961), section 4, p. 1.
33. Borges, *Obra poética 1923–1967*, pp. 229–30.

165

On fantastic literature
ADOLFO BIOY CASARES

History

Stories of the fantastic, as old as fear itself, antedate the invention of writing. Apparitions inhabit all literatures: they may be found in the Zend-Avesta, the Bible, Homer, and the *Arabian Nights*. Perhaps the first specialists in the genre were the Chinese. The admirable *Dream of the Red Chamber,* even erotic and realistic novels such as *Chin P'ing Mei* and *Shui Hu Chuan,* as well as philosophical works, are rich in ghosts and dreams. But how representative of Chinese literature these books are we do not know; in our ignorance, unable to experience that literature first-hand, we must settle for what dumb luck grants us via learned professors, cultural exchange committees, and Mrs. Pearl S. Buck. Turning to Europe and America, we can say that as a more or less defined genre fantastic literature makes its appearance in the nineteenth century and in the English language. Of course, there are fore-

This essay served originally as introduction to the *Antología de la literatura fantástica* (Buenos Aires, 1940), edited by Jorge Luis Borges, Silvina Ocampo, and Adolfo Bioy Casares. TRANSLATOR.

runners: in the fourteenth century, the Spanish Infante Don Juan Manuel; in the sixteenth, Rabelais; in the seventeenth, Quevedo; in the eighteenth, Defoe [1] and Horace Walpole [2]; and by the nineteenth century, E. T. A. Hoffman.

Technique

In writing, the possible existence of a set of fixed, general rules should not be equated with the possible existence of rules. Aristotle's *Poetics* and *Rhetoric* are perhaps no longer applicable, but rules nonetheless exist, and to write is continually to discover these rules or to fail. If we study the use of surprise effects or plots, we shall see how literature goes about changing readers and, consequently, how readers demand continual change in literature. As for rules for the fantastic story, there is no one kind of fantastic story, but many. General rules for each kind of story, then, and special rules for each story must be investigated. The writer's problems are solved in part by general, preestablished rules and in part by special rules that he must discover for himself.

1. Overall Observations:

Ambience, or atmosphere. Fantastic literature's first plots were simple. They recorded, for example, the mere fact of the appearance of a ghost, and their authors tried to create a suitable ambience of fear. The creation of ambience, of atmosphere, is still the concern of many writers. A banging window blind, rain, a recurring phrase—or, more abstractly, the memory and patience to repeat such leitmotifs every so many lines—create the most cloying of atmospheres. Some of the genre's very masters have, nonetheless, not been disdainful of these means. Exclamations such as "Horrors!" "Dreadful!" "Imagine my surprise!" abound in Maupassant. Poe—not, certainly, in the limpid M. Valdemar—makes

---

1. *A True Revelation of the Apparition of One Mrs. Veale, on September 8, 1705* and *The Botetham Ghost,* both poor in invention, appear to be little more than anecdotes related to the author by persons claiming to have seen apparitions, or—as it turns out—to have seen persons who had seen apparitions.

2. *The Castle of Otranto* should be regarded as the predecessor of that whole treacherous breed of Gothic castles, abandoned to decay amid cobwebs, the elements, chains, and bad taste.

frequent use of abandoned mansions, hysteria and melancholy, and autumnal gloom.

Later, a number of writers discovered the advantage of producing, in a wholly believable world, but a single unbelievable event— in other words, of introducing a ghost into a normal, everyday world exactly like the reader's. By contrast, this gave a more heightened effect, leading eventually to a realistic tendency in fantastic literature (the prime example is H. G. Wells). But in time, scenes of peace and happiness, and projects planned to follow crises in the lives of the characters, became clear forewarnings of the worst calamities. In this way, the contrast formerly achieved and its surprise effect disappear.

The surprise effect. The surprise effect may come as a parenthetical revelation, in the way a story is written, or in its ending. Like all literary effects, but more than any other, it eventually wears thin. Rarely, however, does a writer forgo making use of surprise effects. There are exceptions: Max Beerbohm in "Enoch Soames" and W. W. Jacobs in "The Monkey's Paw." Beerbohm deliberately and sensibly suppresses any possibility of a surprise in Soames's voyage to 1997. Even the least sophisticated reader will find few surprises in "The Monkey's Paw," one of the most impressive stories in this collection. This is upheld by the following anecdote, told by John Hampden: A playgoer (Jacobs had made an adaptation of his story for the stage) complained after a performance that the terrible ghost, seen when the door was opened, was an offense to art and good taste; the author should not have shown the fantasm but let the audience imagine it. Which is exactly what Jacobs had done.

For a surprise ending to be effective, it must be prepared, foreshadowed. Nevertheless, the sudden surprise at the end of Leopoldo Lugones' "Los caballos de Abdera" (The Horses of Abdera) is remarkably effective. So is the one at the end of this sonnet by Enrique Banchs from his book *La urna* (The Urn):

> Tornasolando el flanco a su sinuoso
> paso va el tigre suave como un verso
> y la ferocidad pule cual terso

topacio el ojo seco y vigoroso.
Y despereza el músculo alevoso
de los ijares, lánguido y perverso,
y se recuesta lento en el disperso
otoño de las hojas. El reposo . . .
El reposo en la selva silenciosa.
La testa chata entre las garras finas
y el ojo fijo, impávido custodio.
Espía mientras bate con nerviosa
cola el haz de las férulas vecinas,
en reprimido acecho . . . así es mi odio.

[Its flank turning iridescent in its sinuous / pacing, the tiger moves as smoothly as a verse / and its ferocity burnishes, like polished / topaz, its dry and vigorous eye. / And it stretches the treacherous muscles / of its loins, languid and perverse, / and slowly it lies down again in the scattered / autumn leaves. At rest . . . / At rest in the silent forest. / Its flat head between its slender claws / and its eye fixed, undaunted watchman. / It watches while it beats with a nervous / tail the faggots of nearby ferula / in a suppressed crouch—so lurks my hate.]

The Yellow Room and the Yellow Peril. With this formula, Chesterton points out a desideratum (something happens, in a limited space, with a limited number of characters) as well as a mistake in detective-story plots. It seems to me that the formula may also be applied to the plots of fantastic stories. It is an updated version—both journalistic and epigrammatic—of the principle of the three unities. Wells would have fallen into the yellow peril had he created, instead of a single invisible man, hordes of invisible men invading and conquering the world (a tempting plan for current German novelists); or had he, instead of soberly suggesting that Mr. Lewisham was able to leap from one body to another ever since the beginning of time, and of putting him immediately to death, made us participate in each and every story of that continually renewed ghost's passage through time.

2. Kinds of Fantastic Plots:

Those in which ghosts appear. In this anthology there are two (and one is a variation on the other), both perfect and extremely brief: I. A. Ireland's "Ending for a Fantastic Story" and George Loring Frost's "A Believer." [3] The fragment from Carlyle's *Sartor*

3. These selections are apparently extracted by the editors from longer works— the former from Ireland's *Visitations,* the latter from Frost's *Memorabilia.* TRANSLATOR.

Resartus which we include has the same plot, but in reverse.

Travels in time. The classic example is *The Time Machine.* In this unforgettable story, Wells uses a machine that he does not explain, and he never deals with the changes that his time travels produce on the past or future. Max Beerbohm, in "Enoch Soames," uses the devil, who requires no explanation, and he not only discusses his voyage but also makes use of its effects on the future. For its plot, its over-all conception, and its details—which are well thought out and greatly stimulate both thought and imagination— for its characters, dialogue, and description of the English literary scene at the end of the past century, I consider "Enoch Soames" one of the best of the longer stories in this anthology.

Kipling's " 'The Finest Story in the World' " is also rich in invention of detail. But in one of its most important points it is flawed. Charlie Mears, states Kipling, is about to tell him a fine story. But can we believe the author? If Charlie did not resort to the fact of his poor inventive powers, he would have but a few faithful details to relate or, at most, a story with all the imperfection of reality, or something equivalent to a bundle of old newspapers, or—according to H. G. Wells—the work of Marcel Proust. We would not expect the secrets of a local Paraná delta boatman to make up the finest story in the world. Why should we expect the same of the secrets of a Greek galley slave, who lived in a poorer, less civilized world? In this story, there is actually no voyage in time; there are fragmentary memories of a quite remote past.

In "El destino es chambón" (Destiny Is a Bungler) by the Argentine writers Arturo Cancela and Pilar de Lusarreta, the voyage is hallucinatory.

Of all stories of travels in time, perhaps the most elegant in inventiveness and execution is "The Wizard Postponed" by don Juan Manuel.[4]

4. This refers to Borges' adaptation, collected in *A Universal History of Infamy.* It appears in English translation in the *New Yorker*, January 1, 1972, p. 25. TRANSLATOR.

170

The Three Wishes. This story was first set down some ten centuries ago by illustrious writers of far-flung times and places; a little-known contemporary writer has brought it to a skillful conclusion. Its earliest versions are pornographic; we find them in the *Sendebar,* in the *Arabian Nights* (Night 596), and in certain parts of Firuzabadi's *al-Qamus.* Later, in the West, a vulgar version appears, which, according to Burton, degraded the story of the three wishes to a matter of flesh. In 1902, W. W. Jacobs, an author of humorous sketches, comes up with a third version—this one tragic and admirable. In those early versions, wishes are asked of a god or talisman that remains in the world. Jacobs, however, writes for more skeptical readers. After his story the talisman's power, which was to grant three wishes to each of three persons, ends. (The story concerns only those who asked for the last three wishes.) We may yet come across the monkey's paw, since Jacobs does not destroy it, but we shall find it powerless.

Stories that take place in hell. There are two in the anthology, both remarkable: the fragment [5] from Swedenborg's *Arcana Coelestia* and "Where Its Fire Never Ends" by May Sinclair. The latter's theme is from Canto V of Dante's *Inferno:*

Questi, che mai, da me, non fia diviso,
La bocca mi baciò tutto tremante.

Stories with a dreamed character. We include the impeccable "Pao Yu's Infinite Dream" [6] by Ts'ao Hsüen-ch'in, a fragment from Lewis Carroll's *Through the Looking-Glass,* and Giovanni Papini's "The Sick Gentleman's Last Visit."

Stories with metamorphoses. Examples are Kafka's "Metamorphosis," Silvina Ocampo's "Sábanas de tierra" (Sheets of Earth), Santiago Dabove's "Ser polvo" (Turning to Dust), and David Garnett's "Lady into Fox."

---

5. Titled "A Theologian in Death," this is another Borges adaptation found in *A Universal History.* It is not, however, from the *Arcana Coelestia,* as Borges misleadingly (deliberately so) credits it, but from section 797 of Swedenborg's *True Christian Religion.* An English version of it appears in the *New Yorker,* January 1, 1972, pp. 25–26. TRANSLATOR.

6. Excerpted by the editors from *The Dream of the Red Chamber.* TRANSLATOR.

Stories with parallel acts that operate by analogy. "La sangre en el jardín" (The Blood in the Garden) by Ramón Gómez de la Serna and "The Sect of the White Lotus." [7]

The theme of immortality. The Wandering Jew, "Mr. Elvisham" by H. G. Wells, "Las islas nuevas" (The New Islands) by María Luisa Bombal, *She* by H. Rider Haggard, *L'Atlantide* by Pierre Benoit.

Metaphysical fantasies. Here, more than in what takes place, the fantastic is in the reasoning. Our anthology includes "Tantalia" by Macedonio Fernández, a fragment from Olaf Stapledon's *Star Maker,* the story of Chuang Tzu and the butterfly, the story of the denial of miracles,[8] and "Tlön, Uqbar, Orbis Tertius" by Jorge Luis Borges.

With "The Approach to al-Mu'tasim," "Pierre Menard," and "Tlön, Uqbar, Orbis Tertius," Borges has created a new literary genre, part essay and part fiction. These stories, exercises in unceasing intelligence and buoyant imagination, devoid of heaviness or of any human element—either emotional or sentimental—are destined for intellectual readers, for students of philosophy, and almost for specialists in literature.

The stories and novels of Kafka. These are marked by obsessions with infinity, endless postponements, and bureaucratic subjugation. In scenes of mediocre, bureaucratic everyday life, Kafka achieves a sense of depression and horror. His methodical imagination and colorless style never interfere with the unfolding of his plots.

Vampires and castles. Their passage through literature has not been felicitous. Let us mention Bram Stoker's *Dracula* and *Mrs. Amworth* by Benson. They do not figure in this anthology.

Fantastic stories may also be classified according to the explanations they offer:

7. The former an apparent excerpt from *Los muertos, las muertas y otras fantasmas;* the latter from Richard Wilhelm's *Chinesische Volksmärchen.* TRANSLATOR.

8. A fragment quoted from H. A. Giles's *Confucianism and Its Rivals.* TRANSLATOR.

a. Those that are explained by the agency of a supernatural being or deed.

b. Those having a fantastic but not a supernatural explanation. ("Scientific" does not seem to me the apt term for such rigorous, realistic, and grammatically structured inventions.)

c. Those that are explained by the intervention of a supernatural being or deed but that also hint at the possibility of a natural explanation (Saki's "Sredni Vashtar"), and those that are explained by a hallucination. This possibility of natural explanations is sometimes an achievement, offering a greater complexity, but in general it is a weakness, an evasion on the part of the author, who is otherwise unable to present the fantastic believably.

The present selection

In making this selection, we have followed a criterion of self-indulgence; we did not begin with the intention of publishing an anthology. One night, in 1937, talking about fantastic literature, we discussed those stories which to us seemed best. One of us said that if we were to collect and to add to them certain fragments of the same character that were jotted in our notebooks, we could end up with a good book. This is that book. From a historical or geographical viewpoint, it will seem uneven. We have neither sought out nor rejected well-known names. This volume is, simply, a collection of what strikes us as the best pieces of fantastic literature.

Omissions. We have had to resign ourselves, for reasons of space, to a number of omissions. Enough material was left over for a second selection. We have deliberately omitted the following: E. T. A. Hoffman, Sheridan Le Fanu, Ambrose Bierce, Montague Rhodes James, and Walter de la Mare.

A clarification. The narrative titled "El destino es chambón" belongs to a projected novel by Arturo Cancela and Pilar de Lusarreta on the Argentine revolution of 1890.

Acknowledgments. To Mrs. Juana González de Lugones and Mr. Leopoldo Lugones, Jr., for permission to include a story by

Leopoldo Lugones. To friends, writers, and readers for their collaboration.

Buenos Aires, 1940 [9]

translated by Norman Thomas di Giovanni

9. In 1965, in an enlarged second edition of the anthology, Bioy added to his original preface a three-page postscript in which, among other things, he deplores his description of Borges' stories, regrets his judgment of Kipling's " 'Finest Story in the World,' " and repents of certain other statements. But more important, he has this to say:

"What threw me so repeatedly into error was my well-intentioned, sectarian zeal. The compilers of this anthology believed then that the Argentine novel, in our time, suffered from a great lack of plotting. Writers had forgotten the fundamental aim of their profession—that of telling a story. Out of such oblivion emerged monsters—novels whose secret plan consisted of either a verbose record of types, legends, objects, and representatives of this or that folklore, or simply of a plundering of the dictionary of synonyms. . . . Because we needed a less absurd adversary, we lashed out against the psychological novel, to whose construction we imputed a lack of rigor. In it, we argued, plot was no more than a string of episodes—comparable to adjectives or illustrations—that served to define the characters; the invention of such episodes was shaped by little else than the whim of the novelist, since psychologically anything is possible and even believable. . . . As a cure-all, we recommended the fantastic story.

"Of course, the psychological novel was not endangered by our attack. Its survival is assured, for, like an inexhaustible mirror, it reflects different faces, in which the reader always recognizes himself. Even in fantastic stories we find characters in whose reality we irresistibly believe; we are drawn to them, as to flesh and blood people, by a subtle combination of known elements and of mysterious destiny. . . .

"Nor is the fantastic story endangered by those who scornfully demand a more serious kind of writing, which will come up with answers to mankind's problems. . . . Only rarely will these answers bring forth solutions—all of which is beyond the aim of the novelist or storyteller. Such writing will, more likely, insist on commentary, reflections, and digressions . . . on the theme of the moment—politics and economics today, some corresponding obsession yesterday or tomorrow. But throughout life and throughout history, the fantastic story has been part of a less obsessive, more lasting desire of man's—the unflagging desire to hear stories told—and it satisfies this desire better than any other kind of tale because the fantastic story is the storyteller's story, the tale of the ancient collections of the East, and . . . the golden fruit of the imagination." TRANSLATOR.

Business from Porlock
KENNETH FIELDS

I, alas, am Borges

The universal author of a plurality of texts, breathing through an ingenious Argentine, has recorded his fascination with the famous dream of Coleridge. Certainly the universal history provides us with few images more arresting or more profound. Falling into a narcotic sleep, the poet had "the most vivid confidence" of composing an entire poem of two or three hundred lines—a poem, one assumes, of Oriental and architectural magnificence. The vision, whole and complete, remained with him when he awoke, but as he was beginning to write it down he was interrupted by an unsuspecting agent of the prosaic world. It is thus (and not for the first time) that literary investigators have been left with a beguiling fragment: much as if one had but a single clue for the perfect crime. Coleridge's poem is fifty-four lines long, a mere one-sixth or, at best, one-fourth of its archetype. As for the progenitive vision itself, "all the rest had passed away like the images on the surface of a stream into which a stone has been cast, but, alas! without the after restoration of the latter!"

The waters of oblivion have always run deep; and hence the

profundity of what, in another culture, would surely have been transformed into a parable. Who does not understand Jung when in *Memories, Dreams, Reflections* he speaks of the "inner security" attending the perception of the wholeness of his life, his own destiny? *"I* did not have this certainty, *it* had me." And a few sentences later: "I was outside time, I belonged to the centuries." The perception is doubtless the common experience of all men. Most of us, at one time or another, have felt like Flann O'Brien's John Furriskey, who "was born at the age of twenty-five and entered the world with a memory but without a personal experience to account for it." This particular feeling, particular and therefore unique, is the collective and lonely burden of mankind.[1] It is a fact which, according to Jung, "it is neither possible nor meaningful to doubt," and I myself do not think it is going too far to suggest that the feeling has been at the heart of nearly all our philosophies and religions. But two apparently insurmountable considerations remain. The first is that such an experience (or its illusion—I am not prepared to say which) is beyond the realm of words; or, to use Jung a final time, "It is a subjective affair quite beyond discussion." The second, which we have already learned from Coleridge, is that we often forget the experience.[2]

Human nature is fortunately so curious that such facts do not deter, but rather intensify, our fascination. As Henry James makes the author in *The Middle Years* exclaim, "The pearl is the unwritten—the pearl is the unalloyed, the *rest,* the lost." One of the most intrepid adventurers into the lost was Descartes, whom Voltaire called "an arguer, half geometrician, half chimerical." In the fifth of his marvelous *Meditations,* Descartes has given us this sentence, charming but weighted with frustration: "And as regards God, if my mind were not preoccupied with prejudices, and if my thought did not find itself on all hands diverted by the continual

---

1. Octavio Paz, in *The Labyrinth of Solitude,* believes the experience to be "a revelation [that] almost always takes place in adolescence."
2. Cf. Wordsworth, *The Prelude,* II, ll. 315 ff:
> . . . the soul
> Remembering how she felt, but what she felt
> Remembering not, retains an obscure sense
> Of possible sublimity. . . .

176

pressure of sensible things, there would be nothing which I could know more immediately and more easily than Him." Reading Descartes with Voltaire's description in mind, one begins to understand that perhaps to be *"moitié géomètre, moitié chimérique"* is not to be first one thing and then another, but to be both at once.

Accordingly, it is from the Greek mathematicians that we inherit many of our chimeras—those infinite regressions that comprise, together with the prints of M. C. Escher, the unmoving arrow of Zeno and the divine Cartesian flight of Plotinus ("detachment from all things here below, scorn of all earthly pleasures, the flight of the lone to the Alone"). It is the breath of Porphyry and Thomas Taylor that fills the lungs of New England's frailest ghost (a man startlingly blessed with a robust style); only Emerson, who believed that the world is the incarnation of a thought and returns to a thought again, could write while in Venice (June 2, 1833): "I collect nothing that can be touched or tasted or smelled. . . ." Thirty-six years earlier, in a trance the Concord water-drinker would have flatly shunned, Coleridge had been collecting the same stuff.

Coleridge's dream appears to have much in common with the mystical vision, and it reflects many of the Neo-Platonic interests of his century. According to Plotinus (who was apparently ashamed, as we learn from his handsome biographer, to have a body), this vision is marked by its wholeness, by its unity: there are no longer any distinctions between subject and object. *Forgetting* is therefore an inevitable consequence, for the One cannot be known: "When the soul knows something, it loses its unity; it cannot remain simply one because knowledge implies discursive reason and discursive reason implies multiplicity. The soul then misses the One and falls into number and multiplicity" (*Enneads,* VI, 9). If applied rigorously, the terms of the text are clear: Coleridge plainly had his vision of Kubla's palace, and had it so distinctly that he even knew the length of his poem; but, visitor or no visitor, we were never to have it from him.

This view was not the only one available to the century. In the same way that the Greeks had not only the Mathematician but the Biologist as well, the nineteenth century had an alternative to the

Neo-Platonic conception of the universe; and the two, taken together, are so comprehensive that they nearly circumscribe the period. I refer, of course, to the notion that inverts the Platonic scheme; according to the second, the soul does not "fall" into number and multiplicity, but rather finds there its true and proper home. Its chief spokesman is that most avid reader of nature's varied texts, the eloquent apologist of the earthworm, Charles Darwin.

To be sure, the young Darwin had speculated that "we may be all melted together," but since our first great progenitor appears to be unknowable—and the beauties of life so endlessly beguiling—it is multiplicity and not unity that holds his scrupulous gaze: "It is interesting to contemplate an entangled bank, clothed with many plants of many kinds, with birds singing on the bushes, with various insects flitting about, and with worms crawling through the damp earth. . . ." And according to one view of evolution, the world is growing more complex, its fragments ever smaller and more beautiful. "The old, stiff, sky-reaching wooden world," writes Loren Eiseley in *The Immense Journey,* "had changed into something that glowed here and there with strange colors, put out queer, unheard-of fruits and little intricately carved seed cases. . . ." The age of the dinosaurs, of monolithic unity, had ended as if by an explosion: "Intricate mechanisms splashed pollen on the breasts of hummingbirds, or stamped it on the bellies of black, grumbling bees droning assiduously from blossom to blossom." Eiseley, a more skeptical man than Darwin, knows very well the arbitrary terrors of being set adrift in a universe of enchanting fragments, and we see his desperation clearly in his latest book, *The Unexpected Universe.* But Darwin, imbibing from the Victorian cup of progress, could conclude his major work confidently: "There is grandeur in this view of life, with its several powers, having been originally breathed by the Creator into a few forms or into one; and that, whilst this planet has gone cycling on according to the fixed law of gravity, from so simple a beginning endless forms most beautiful and most wonderful have been, and are being, evolved."

As Darwin's last sentence suggests, the two positions (the Neo-

Platonic and the evolutionist) imply each other and are not exclusive. It is simply a matter of emphasis.[3] One may tend (with Taylor and Emerson) to look to that beautiful and immobile realm of contemplation, where Zeno's arrow, regressing backward out of time and movement, strains at the drawn weapon, but without the least thought of release. Or, choosing from a shifting world, one may send the arrow straight to its mark. The first offers the milk of Paradise, which no man has drunk; the second, business from Porlock.

The dangers and clarities of the two positions should not suggest to the wary (or unwary) eclectic that there is security in homogenizing them. As I have remarked, the two positions do mirror each other; further, when the cake is an idea, few people will see the harm in trying to have it and eat it. Ezra Pound's sentence fragment is explicit: "Man drunk with god, man inebriated with infinity, on the one hand, and man with a millimetric measure and microscope on the other" ("Neo-Platonicks, Etc.," *Guide to Kulchur*). Despite Pound's implicit scorn for the second man, I suspect him of trying to be both, that is to say, Zeno and Iambilichus as well as Linnaeus and Agassiz. In the note that opens *Kulchur* he writes of perhaps his favorite work of architecture, the Tempio of Malatesta: "If the Tempio is a jumble and junk shop, it nevertheless registers a concept." Coming at the problem from the other direction, he begins the first section of the book with a passage from the Confucian Analects:

Said the Philosopher: You think that I have learned a great deal, and kept the whole of it in my memory? Sse replied with respect: Of course. Isn't that so? It is not so. I have reduced it all to one principle.

The *Cantos*, Pound's "ragbag" of anecdotes, images, and odds and ends of learning may attempt to register a concept, one principle; and perhaps God perceives it, much as he is said to perceive the randomness and confusion of a man's entire life as a single, perfect

3. "What consciousness overlooks is the fact that all boundaries and divisions are held in common by their opposite sides and areas, so that when a boundary changes its shape both sides move together. It is like the *yang-yin* symbol of the Chinese— the black and white fishes divided by an S-curve inscribed within a circle." Alan W. Watts, *The Joyous Cosmology* (New York, 1962).

polygon. But it is clear that Pound, looking back over his life's work (and the life's work of innumerable critics, present and future), has difficulty making out the figure. In what must surely be one of the last Cantos (CXVI), he is lamenting his failure to realize his paradise:

> Justinian's,
> a tangle of works unfinished.
> I have brought the great ball of crystal;
>   who can lift it?
> Can you enter the great acorn of light?
>   But the beauty is not the madness
> Tho' my errors and wrecks lie about me.
> And I am not a demigod,
> I cannot make it cohere.

The confession, coming so late in the life of one of the century's most earnest poets, is more than touching, for it is the confession of a failure that makes Coleridge's seem domestic and occasional. When Pound says, "I cannot make it flow thru," he is speaking of his greatest and perhaps his only artifact—his life. The book in which these admissions occur is called, with grim appropriateness, *Drafts & Fragments of Cantos CX–CXVII*. In the end, he assures us that even though his life's work appears to be a failure, the paradise of his private vision is still whole, "i.e., it coheres all right / even if my notes do not cohere." [4]

A tangle of works unfinished—this might be the motto of modern literature, which is preoccupied with process and fragmentation. We hear it in Coleridge and in Wordsworth, whose major work is called *The Prelude;* in Pound and in Wallace Stevens, who made what he could of a final statement in that strange poem with the tentative title. (How many modern works might be called

---

4. Recall that the first division of Pound's major work is *A Draft of XXX Cantos,* and that "Kubla Khan" has the subtitle, "Or a Vision in a Dream: A Fragment." For an excellent discussion of the lines in question, see James McMichael's "Pound and Others," *Southern Review,* III (Spring 1967), 425–34: "The *Cantos* are perhaps the most private literary document of our century. No amount of intelligent explicating will make the poem more public, nor should we ask that it do so." I suppose that explications make "Kubla Khan" more public, but they can scarcely clarify the vision itself. *That* road is a dead end. (I mention here that McMichael's review is merely a fragment of a book that will probably never be published. Had this been a fiction, I would have omitted the detail as too perversely smacking of contrivance. In an essay, however, one has the simple task of telling the truth.)

Notes Toward a Supreme Fiction?) When Durrell's Pursewarden confesses that completing a work makes him feel suicidal (and this is his fate, you will recall), he is revealing the fear of completion, artistic and sexual, that may be shared by at least two other writers of his acquaintance: Darley, who tells us Pursewarden's story, and Durrell, who tells us Darley's. And what are we to make of Mark Twain (that double of the famous lecturer), who left at his death all those unfinished manuscripts? Who can believe the boast (I wonder which of them made it?) that he could have finished them any time he wished?

"Opium-eaters, though good fellows upon the whole, never finish anything." Most of the writers I have mentioned were not opium-eaters, but the author of the sentence and his subject were: it is Thomas De Quincey on Coleridge. The pure voice that speaks in narcotic reveries is, by all accounts, univocal and compelling. Like the dream of Plotinus, it is whole—that is, subject and object vanish as distinctions—and it is insular. *"Istigkeit"*—the term offered by Aldous Huxley in *The Doors of Perception*— "wasn't that the word Meister Eckhart liked to use? 'Is-ness.' " "Significance here," he writes later, "is identical with being; for, at the mind's antipodes, objects do not stand for anything but themselves." In such states the instant is elevated and isolated to a microcosmic eternity, and the universe seems composed of discontinuous fragments: it is as if one's mind were a movie projector, with each printed frame of the film followed by a black one. Each frame would be complete in itself, and not connected to those preceding or following. Stroboscopic lights often produce the same effects; Théophile Gautier uses similar terms to describe hashish: "I considered everything in the gleaming of a remnant of reason which went and returned by instants like a candle ready to gutter." Here we have the "hard, gem-like flame" of Pater. Removed to this realm, the mind focuses on the moment (which, in Huxley's terms, is "self-luminous"), sometimes with the awareness that the full import of that instant, so clear in the present, will in another moment be gone. Truth to say, even before Scotus, man must have loved the quidditous. Anyone who has undergone sur-

181

gery will understand the feelings alluded to in this paragraph. Likewise anyone who has, as Coleridge had, a prescription. The others must suffer, as admixture, the dubious delights of criminality.

But perhaps not. For aren't we back to the islandic experience of man?—whether it is the inner security of fate, laudanum, hashish, mescalin, lysergic acid, the god of Thomas Taylor and Plotinus, or the privacies of adolescence? The illicit experiences, I think, must only heighten or sometimes introduce the licit. Or, put another way, perhaps the drug experience is sufficient but unnecessary.

Let me illustrate with an experience of my own, a kind of momentary hallucination, certainly not drug induced. The other day while I was going out of my upstairs bedroom, I happened to look into a full-length mirror. I did not hesitate and continued walking toward the stairs, but I had seen staring back at me a young man who did not look like the man I was, say, a year ago. (I now have, for example, gold-rimmed glasses and I wear my hair moderately long.) The image stayed with me, for as I reached the top of the stairs I had my vision. Suddenly I perceived that a friend, who had been dead for two years, was dreaming me. In his dream he saw me standing before him, outwardly changed but essentially the same man he had known in life—he knew all this though we had not said a word to each other. I wanted very much to say goodbye to him, which I had not done at our last meeting, and he knew this too with the sureness that one has about one's own dreams. But just as I was beginning to speak, he awoke. The vision ended as I stepped down the first stair.

Last night I fell asleep pondering the termination of the problems I have been raising. I dreamed that I was downstairs at my typewriter (where I am at this moment), trying to conclude my essay. To my left was my desk, which was piled high with the books I have used for reference, scraps of paper stuck in them here and there. One of the books I picked up (*The Marihuana Papers,* edited by David Solomon) contained the following remarkable statements by Baudelaire:

182

It sometimes happens that your personality disappears, and you develop objectivity—that preserve of the pantheistic poets—to such an abnormal degree that the contemplation of outward objects makes you forget your own existence, and you soon melt into them. . . . By a singular transposition of ideas, or mental play upon words, you will feel [while you are smoking] that you yourself are evaporating, and that your pipe (in which you are huddled and pressed down like the tobacco) has the strange *power to smoke you.*

Luckily this apparently interminable fancy has lasted only for a single minute —for a lucid interval, gained with a great effort, has enabled you to glance at the clock. But a new stream of ideas carries you away: it will hurl you along in its living vortex for a further minute; and this minute, too, will be an eternity, for the normal relation between time and the individual has been completely upset by the multitude and intensity of sensations and ideas. You seem to live several men's lives in the space of an hour. You resemble, do you not? a fantastic novel that is being lived instead of being written. . . .

The other text I consulted in my dream was even more astounding, for it was an essay entitled "Business from Porlock," and its author none other than myself. With considerable interest I read the words that were identical to my own, for I was anxious to see how the author would settle these perplexing matters. I followed him through the by-now-familiar hallucination, his dream, and his citation of the passages from Baudelaire that you have just seen. He was sitting at his desk in *his* dream, and he was reading his own essay. Before he came to the passage describing the dream and the discovery of his own text, however, on an unaccountable impulse he looked up. There on the wall just above his head he saw a photograph of himself, reading at his desk. He could not tell whether his eyes were open or closed.

Now a less scrupulous writer (such as the canny Argentine) might adduce this last curiosity to support the theory of the universal history, according to which we are all the dreams of God and all authors have been at work on the same text. The argument, I believe, goes something like this.

Borges and the Kabbalah
JAIME ALAZRAKI

When asked a few years ago about his interest in the Kabbalah,
Borges replied, "I read a book called *Major Trends in Jewish
Mysticism* by Scholem and another book by Trachtenberg on Jewish superstitions.[1] Then I have read all the books on the Kabbalah
I have found and all the articles in the encyclopedias and so on.
But I have no Hebrew whatever."[2] These remarks, considering
the number of interviews Borges has given, come rather late. Except for this single statement, nothing else has been added on the
subject since Rabi's essay "Fascination de la Kabbale,"[3] and Rabi's
contribution lies in his merely having called attention to Borges'
familiarity with Kabbalistic texts. I shall attempt to show how far
Borges' acquaintance with the Kabbalah goes beyond the few
accidental tracks left in his writings as a result of his readings.

1. Borges is referring to Joshua Trachtenberg's *Jewish Magic and Superstition:
A Study in Folk Religion* (New York, 1939).
2. See Ronald Christ, "Jorge Luis Borges, an Interview," *The Paris Review,* 40
(Winter–Spring 1967), 162.
3. See Rabi, "Fascination de la Kabbale," *L'Herne, J. L. Borges* (Paris, 1964),
pp. 265–71.

Ultimately, as André Maurois puts it, "Borges has read everything" that exists ("and all the books that don't exist," adds John Barth), and it would be unusual not to find in his prose some imprints of the material which, as is the case with the Kabbalah, exerted on his mind such an enthralling fascination.[4]

The impact of the Kabbalah on Borges' work far exceeds the random quotations or allusions the casual reader may find and which, after all, only confirm the interest Borges conceded above. Behind his transparent texts there lies a stylistic intricacy, a certain Kabbalistic texture, a spellbinding characteristic to which Borges finds himself attracted.

To the question, "Have you tried to make your own stories Kabbalistic?" he replied, "Yes, sometimes I have." [5] For the Kabbalists, as one of their classic texts shows, "every word of the Torah has six hundred thousand faces—that is, layers of meaning or entrances," and the ostensible aim of the Kabbalah seems to be to reach these profound layers. Borges' writings offer the reader a similar challenge. Most of his narratives do not exhaust themselves at the level of literal meaning—they present an immediate and manifest layer and a more oblique and allusive one. It is the latter which generates in his stories a Kabbalistic aura whose source goes far beyond a fortuitous familiarity with the Kabbalah.

1. A scrutiny of Borges' Kabbalah library

In "Death and the Compass," Borges examines some books on the Kabbalah from his own library. Echoing Cervantes' device,[6] Borges includes among the volumes of the murdered rabbi's complete

4. See J. L. Borges, "Una vindicación de la cábala," *Discusión* (Buenos Aires, 1957), pp. 55–60.

5. Christ, *ibid.,* p. 161.

6. As every reader of the *Quixote* knows, in Chapter VI the curate and the barber perform a thorough scrutiny of the library "of our ingenious gentleman." The scrutiny represents a critical examination of romances of chivalry and pastoral novels to whose tradition Cervantes himself contributed *La Galatea*. This book, too, falls into the hands of the scrutinizers who decide to keep it because, the curate says, "that fellow Cervantes and I have been friends these many years, but, to my knowledge, he is better versed in misfortune than he is in verses. His book has a fairly good plot; it starts out well and ends up nowhere." Borges himself has referred to the effects of this "play of mirrors" in his essay "Partial Enchantments of the *Quixote*."

185

works his own essay, "A Vindication of the Kabbalah," collected in the volume *Discusión*. Contrary to what happens in *Don Quixote,* where Cervantes' pastoral novel *La Galatea* receives from the curate a favorable although not excessively generous comment, the reference to Borges' essay in the story goes without any remark at all. However, the mere inclusion of an essay written by the same author who now writes the story produces an effect similar to the one achieved by Cervantes in the famous passage. Essentially it is the effect produced by the theater within the theater, by literature becoming the subject of literature. In this operation, Borges attains a literary magic he himself has poignantly described:

> **Why does it make us uneasy to know that the map is within the map and the thousand and one nights are within the book of A Thousand and One Nights? Why does it disquiet us to know that Don Quixote is a reader of the Quixote, and Hamlet is a spectator of Hamlet? I believe I have found the answer: those inversions suggest that if the characters in a story can be the readers or spectators, then we, their readers or spectators, can be fictitious. (OI, 46) [7]**

Among the books that Borges attributes to Rabbi Marcelo Yarmolinsky there figures "a literal translation of the *Sefer Yetsirah*." The Book of Creation is a brief treatise on cosmologic and cosmogonic matters. It was written between the third and sixth century and represents, with the Book *Bahir* (twelfth century), the embryo out of which the bulk of the Kabbalah grew and developed. Its chief subjects are the elements of the world, which are sought in the ten elementary and primordial numbers—Sefiroth—and in the twenty-two letters of the Hebrew alphabet. Together these represent the mysterious forces whose convergence has produced the various combinations observable throughout the whole of creation; they are the *thirty-two secret paths of wisdom,* through which God has created all that exists. In his essay "On the Cult of Books," Borges again refers to the *Sefer Yetsirah*. This time the reference is a long paragraph in which he furnishes some basic information on the book, describes its purpose and method, and brings in a quotation which may or may not be taken directly from the text, since this is the most widely cited passage of the Book of Creation

7. I have further discussed the effects of this device in *La prosa narrativa de Jorge Luis Borges* (Madrid, 1968), pp. 87–88.

and Borges might well have found it in the books and articles he read on the subject: "Twenty-two fundamental letters: God drew them, engraved them, combined them, weighed them, permuted them, and with them produced everything that is and everything that will be." At any rate, the long reference is an indication that the inclusion of this title in Yarmolinsky's bibliography is as important with regard to the murdered Talmudist as it is with respect to Borges' own interest in the Kabbalah. It shows also, however, that the aura of fantasy created by those enigmatic and often esoteric books springs, rather than from Borges' intention, from the reader's unfamiliarity with these works and authors, although Borges—undoubtedly—is aware of their puzzling impact on the reader.[8] The same holds true for the other books mentioned in the list. Thus the *History of the Hasidic Sect* and the *Biography of the Baal Shem,* attributed to Yarmolinsky, are slightly modified versions of two works by Martin Buber: *The Origin and Meaning of Hasidism* [9] and *The Legend of Baal Shem.*[10] Borges' acquaintance with Buber becomes apparent in the story "The Sect of the Phoenix," where he quotes him, and in the essay "On Chesterton," where he directs the reader to Buber's classic *Tales of the Hasidim.*[11]

The last book mentioned in the list, *A Study of the Philosophy of Robert Fludd,* although not directly concerned with the Kabbalah, is not foreign to its doctrine. Several of Fludd's (1574–1637) postulates are amazingly close to those of the Kabbalah. The English Rosicrucian maintained that the universe proceeds from, and will return to, God; that the act of creation is the separation of the active principle (light) from the passive (darkness) in

8. The last sentence was written before the appearance of *The Aleph and Other Stories* (New York, 1970). There Borges provides, for the first time, some enlightening "commentaries" on the background of the short stories collected in that volume. On "Death and the Compass," he says: "No apology is needed for repeated mention of the Kabbalah, for it provides the reader and the all-too-subtle detective with a false track, and the story is, as most of the names imply, a Jewish one. The Kabbalah also provides an additional sense of mystery" (*A,* 269).

9. Although this book was published in English in 1960, it collects essays published (1927) in Buber's *Die chassidischen Bücher* and his *Der grosse Maggid und seine Nachfolge* (1921).

10. The German edition dates from 1907.

11. There may be other references to Buber that I have overlooked.

the bosom of the divine unity (God); and that the universe consists of three worlds: the archetypal (God), the macrocosm (the world), and the microcosm (man). He was a follower of Paracelsus, whose prescriptions for the making of the homunculus bear astonishing similarities to the golem-making formulae of the Kabbalists.[12]

Lönnrot, the "pure logician" of "Death and the Compass," carries these books off to his apartment, "suddenly turning bibliophile and Hebraic scholar" (*A, 67*). Borges could as well have said "Kabbalist," since Lönnrot attempts to solve the mysteries of the seemingly ritualistic murders in the same manner that a Kabbalist deciphers the occult mysteries of the Scripture. The arithmetic value of the dates of the murders and their geometric location on the map become important and revealing. Before Lönnrot can establish these symmetries in time and space, he devotes himself to perusing Yarmolinsky's books. Borges does not miss the chance to unfold his erudition on the subject. Thus, one book revealed to the investigator "the doctrine that God has a secret name in which . . . His ninth attribute, Eternity, may be found—that is to say, the immediate knowledge of everything under the sun that will be, that is, and that was" (*A, 68*). The ninth attribute mentioned in the story takes us to the very core of the Kabbalah's cosmogony—the theory of the *Sefiroth*.

2. The doctrine of the *Sefiroth*

Borges' first explorations into the subject of the Kabbalah are found in his second collection of essays, *El tamaño de mi esperanza* (The Extent of My Hope), published in 1926. There, in an article entitled "A History of Angels," Borges leaves a testimony to his first readings on the Kabbalah. He mentions two books, Erich Bischoff's *Die Elemente der Kabbalah* (1914) and *Rabbinical Literature* by Stehelin; even more important is the fact that the passage contains the germ of his more mature essay, "A Vindication of the Kabbalah," of 1931. Yet it is in the earlier article, "A History of Angels," where he writes literally about the theory of the *Sefiroth*.

12. For further information on this subject, see Scholem's *On the Kabbalah and Its Symbolism* (New York, 1969), pp. 197–98.

Relying on Bischoff and Stehelin, Borges explains that "to each one of the ten *Sefiroth,* or eternal emanations of the godhead, corresponds a region of heaven, one of the names of God, one commandment of the decalogue, a part of the human body, and a class of angels." He adds that Stehelin "links the first ten letters of the Hebrew alphabet to these ten heavenly worlds. Thus the letter Aleph looks toward the brain, the first commandment, the heaven of fire, the second name 'I Am That I Am,' and the seraphim called Holy Beasts." [13]

Perhaps the most direct bearing the doctrine of the *Sefiroth* has on Borges' work emerges in the story "The Aleph." The theory of the *Sefiroth* postulates that there are two worlds and that both represent God. "First a primary world, the most deeply hidden of all, which remains insensible and unintelligible to all but God, the world of *En-Sof* (Infinite); and secondly, one joined unto the first, which makes it possible to know God, the world of attributes." [14] The ninth *Sefirah,* as pointed out by Borges, is the source from which the divine life overflows in the act of mystical procreation. The world of *Sefiroth* is described as a mystical organism, and the most important images used in this connection are those of the tree and of a man. This tree is the unknown and unknowable God, but it is also the skeleton of the universe—it grows throughout the whole of creation and spreads its branches through all its ramifications. All mundane and created things exist only because something of the power of the *Sefiroth* lives and acts in them.[15] This notion of God's externalization is summarized in a passage of the *Zohar* (Book of Splendor): "The process of creation has taken place on two planes, one above and one below, and for this reason the Torah begins with the letter Beth, the numerical value of which is two. The lower occurrence corresponds to the higher; one produced the upper world (of the *Sefiroth*), the other the nether world (of the visible creation)." [16] The pantheistic character of this outlook comes openly to the surface in the Spanish Kabbalist Joseph

13. J. L. Borges, *El tamaño de mi esperanza* (Buenos Aires, 1926), p. 67.
14. Scholem, *Major Trends in Jewish Mysticism* (New York, 1961), p. 208.
15. For comprehensive information on the *Zohar,* see Chapters V–VI in Scholem's *Major Trends.*
16. Scholem, *ibid.*, p. 222.

Gikatila's formula, "He fills everything and He is everything." The theogony of the *Sefiroth* and the cosmogony of creation represent two aspects of the same act. "Creation," says Scholem, "mirrors the inner movement of the divine life. . . . It is nothing but an external development of those forces which are active and alive in God Himself. . . . The life of the Creator pulsates in that of his creatures." [17] The last assertion does not differ, even in its formulation, from Borges' own pantheistic formula, "Every man is an organ put forth by the divinity in order to perceive the world" ("The Theologians," *L*, 124). [18]

The Kabbalistic notion that conceives the Torah as a vast *corpus symbolicum,* representative of that hidden life within God which the theory of the *Sefiroth* attempts to describe, is paraphrased in Léon Bloy's *L'Ame de Napoléon* (as quoted by Borges in his essay "The Mirror of the Enigmas"): "History is an immense liturgical text, where the *i*'s and the periods are not worth less than whole verses or chapters, but the importance of both is undeterminable and is profoundly hidden. . . . Everything is a symbol." Borges' own comments underline the affinity between Bloy and the Kabbalah:

Bloy . . . did nothing but apply to the whole Creation the method that the Jewish cabalists applied to the Scripture. They thought that a work dictated by the Holy Spirit was an absolute text: a text where the collaboration of chance is calculable at zero.[19] The portentous premise of a book that is impervious to contingency, a book that is a mechanism of infinite purposes, moved them to permute the scriptural words, to sum up the numerical value of the letters, to consider their form, to observe the small letters and the capital letters, to search for acrostics and anagrams. . . . (*OI*, 128)

17. *Ibid.*, pp. 223–24.
18. This is not the place to elaborate on Borges' fertile use of pantheism in his fiction. I have treated this aspect of his work in my book *La prosa narrativa de J. L. Borges,* pp. 60–73. Here it will suffice to observe that the pantheistic notion that frames several of his stories stems from Plotinus, Spinoza, Sufism, Hinduism, Buddhism, and other sources, as well as from the doctrines of the Kabbalah. In some instances, Borges' contacts with the Kabbalah are indirectly established through authors who in one way or another echo Kabbalistic theories. Thus the world of *Sefiroth,* as described above, is found in Francis Bacon's *Advancement of Learning,* but now the theosophic symbols "tree" and "man" are replaced by the image of a book: "God offered us two books," writes Borges quoting Bacon, "so that we would not fall into error. The first, the volume of the Scriptures, reveals His will; the second, the volume of the creatures, reveals His power" (*OI*, 119).
19. The seed of this idea is already found in "A History of Angels," and is literally reproduced in "Una vindicación de la cábala."

190

For the Kabbalists, the letters of the Torah are the mystical body of God, and from this it follows that the Creation is just a reflection or emanation of the Holy text; hence the Midrash "God looked into the Torah and created the world," and the story told in the Mishnah about a scribe (of the Scripture) who, when asked about his occupation, received from his teacher the following advice: "My son, be careful in your work, for it is the work of God; if you omit a single letter, or write a letter too many, you will destroy the whole world. . . ." [20] The whole idea is put in a nutshell in the Kabbalistic axiom: "What is below is above and what is inside is outside," [21] from which the *Sefer Yetsirah* infers that "on the basis of the lower world we understand the secret law according to which the upper world is governed." The Kabbalist Menahem Recanati adds his own exegesis to the axiom: "All created being, earthly man and all other creatures in this world, exist according to the archetype (*dugma*) of the ten *sefiroth*." [22] The text that best shows the spell of the *Sefiroth* on Borges is a passage from his story "The Theologians," in which he gives in a condensed formula the pantheistic essentials of the theory. "In the hermetic books," he says, "it is written that what is down below is equal to what is on high, and what is on high is equal to what is down below; in the *Zohar,* that the higher world is a reflection of the lower" (*L,* 123). From this Borges derives one of his favorite motifs—"every man is two men"—which has ingenious and fertile effects on his narratives. [23]

3. The legend of the golem

Borges' debt to Gershom Scholem is acknowledged in a couplet from his poem "The Golem": "But all these matters are discussed by Scholem / in a most learned passage of his book" (*SP,* 113). The book is Scholem's *Major Trends in Jewish Mysticism,* un-

20. Quoted by Scholem in *On the Kabbalah . . .* , p. 38.
21. *Ibid.,* p. 122.
22. *Ibid.,* p. 124.
23. In addition to "The Theologians," the motif can be traced in the following stories: "The Shape of the Sword," "Theme of the Traitor and the Hero," "Three Versions of Judas," "Story of the Warrior and the Captive," "The End," "The Life of Tadeo Isidoro Cruz," "The South," and "The Other Death."

doubtedly the most authoritative work on the subject and a model of scholarship. Borges could not have chosen better. Paradoxically, however—and this is one of the voluntarily involuntary mistakes in which Borges delights—the information for the poem does not arise from the "learned book," *Major Trends . . .* , which hardly devotes a few lines to the question of the golem, but from other sources.[24] Later Borges resourcefully explained in his "Autobiographical Essay" that he twice used Scholem's name in the poem "as the only possible rhyming word" for golem.

The poem represents one of the most felicitous expressions of a main theme in Borges' work—the world as a dream of God. More than in a *topos* of seventeenth-century literature, Borges finds in the religions of India a new foundation for his idealist outlook on reality.[25] Nevertheless, this theme of the world as God's dream is not motivated by only one doctrine, or "perplexity," as Borges calls it. "The Circular Ruins," for example, embodies the Buddhist belief in the world as the dream of Someone, or perhaps no one, but at the same time it casts in the mold of fiction the idealist notion which postulates the hallucinatory character of all reality. Borges' avid erudition, however, does not stop at these two sources. He searches for new formulations of the same basic idea, for new versions of a same metaphor, until he arrives at a brilliantly concise assertion—"Perhaps universal history is the history of the diverse intonation of a few metaphors" ("Pascal's Sphere," *OI,* 6). Therefore, it would be mistaken to point to one source as the motivation of the poem or the story, or to single out one exclusive intonation of a metaphor as the only "perplexity" Borges intends to reinterpret in his fiction. One of the enchanting features of Borges' art is precisely the combination of very diverse constituents, the blending of various intonations into one unified tone. In this process, the metaphors of history were converted into what they essentially are—into metaphors of literature.

Thus the story "The Circular Ruins," which seems to be inspired

24. One of them was undoubtedly Gustav Meyrink's novel *Der Golem,* which young Borges read while still a student in Geneva.

25. A concise exposition of this outlook as conceived by Eastern thought may be found in Borges' essay "Forms of a Legend."

by Eastern beliefs,[26] is no less imbued with the doctrines of the Kabbalah than the poem "The Golem." Tale and poem are variations of the same theme: a man (a magician in the story, a rabbi in the poem) dreams another man into existence, only later to find that he too, the dreamer, is but a dream. In both instances, the creative powers of man seem to be competing with the creative powers of God. In reconstructing the legend of the golem in the poem, Borges makes use of a long Kabbalistic tradition from which the legend originates. This tradition has its beginnings in an old belief according to which the cosmos was built chiefly from the twenty letters of the Hebrew alphabet as presented in the *Sefer Yetsirah* (Book of Creation). If man can learn how God went about his creation, he too will be able to create human beings. This power is already attributed, at the end of the *Sefer Yetsirah,* to Abraham, who "contemplated, meditated, and beheld, investigated and understood and outlined and dug and combined and formed [i.e. created] and he succeeded." [27] A Midrash from the twelfth century goes even further by stating that "when God created His world, He first created the *Sefer Yetsirah* and looked into it and from it created His world. When he had completed His work, he put it [the *Sefer Yetsirah*] into the Torah [Pentateuch] and showed it to Abraham. . . ." [28] The secret is therefore in the Torah, which is not only made up of the names of God, but is, as a whole, the one great Name of God, and yet no one knows its right order, for the sections of the Torah are not given in the right arrangement. If they were, everyone who reads it might create a world, raise the dead, and perform miracles. Therefore the order of the Torah was hidden and is known to God alone.[29] The Kabbalists strove to find that hidden order, and the tradition of the Golem goes back as far as the

26. I have discussed this in some detail in *La prosa narrativa de Jorge Luis Borges,* pp. 53–59.

27. *Le Sepher Yetsirah,* Texte hébreu intégral, lu et commenté d'après le code originel de la Cabale par Carlo Suarès (Geneva, 1968), p. 122. I use the English translation as it appears in Gershom Scholem's *On the Kabbalah and Its Symbolism,* p. 169.

28. The Midrash is "Neue Pesikta." Quoted by Scholem, *On the Kabbalah . . . ,* pp. 177–78.

29. Scholem, *ibid.,* p. 167.

prophet Jeremiah, who busied himself with the *Sefer Yetsirah* until a man was created. For the Hasidim the creation of a golem confirmed man in his likeness to God. Through Jakob Grimm's version of 1808, the legend achieved wide popularity and exerted a special fascination on authors like Gustav Meyrink, Achim von Arnim, and E. T. A. Hoffmann. This is not to say that "The Circular Ruins" is strictly an avatar of the legend, although the poem certainly is, but rather that Borges' familiarity with the legend of the Golem has impregnated his story.

The creation of a golem by man is parallel to the creation of Adam by God. As the golem is made from clay or mud, so Adam was made from the matter of the earth, literally from clay. The etymological connection between Adam and earth (Hebrew, ADAM*ah*) is very much stressed in the rabbinical and Talmudic commentaries on Genesis. Furthermore, in the Aggadah (the narrative branch of the Jewish oral law), Adam is designated as *golem,* which means the unformed, amorphous. Adam was said to be golem before the breath of God had touched him; and in a Midrash from the second and third centuries, Adam is described not only as a golem, but as a golem of cosmic size and strength to whom, while he was still in this speechless and inanimate state, God showed all future generations to the end of time. It was only after the Fall that Adam's enormous size, which filled the universe, was reduced to human proportions.[30] "His size [explains Scholem] would seem to signify, in spatial terms, that the power of the whole universe is concentrated in him. He receives his soul only at the end of Creation." [31]

In describing the efforts the magician makes to dream his creature in "The Circular Ruins," Borges interpolates this digression: "In the cosmogonies of the Gnostics, the demiurges mold a red Adam who is unable to stand on his feet; as clumsy and crude and elementary as that Adam of dust was the Adam of dreams wrought by the nights of the magician" (*A,* 59). Here Borges refers to

30. On the subject of the golem, see the chapter "The Idea of the Golem" in Scholem's *On the Kabbalah . . .* , pp. 158–204.
31. *Ibid.,* p. 162.

certain Gnostic ideas, originally of Jewish extraction, according to which "the angels of Elohim took some of the best earth and from it formed man." [32] As in the traditional Midrash, this Gnostic Adam did not receive his soul until God and earth joined to make it. The idea that such an act of creation might be repeated by magic or other arts represents the backbone of the Kabbalistic tradition of the golem. It is this idea which one can perceive in Borges' story.

At first glance, the kinship of story and legend is hardly noticeable; "The Circular Ruins" is the story of a magician who sets himself the task of dreaming a man to later project him into reality, but the core of its theme is revealed only in the last paragraph: the dreamer too is but a dream; the creator too is but the imperfect creation of another creator; reality as a whole is but a dream of someone or no one. Thus focused, Borges' story begins to move toward the legend of the golem. Although the magician does not shape his intended son with mud or clay, as in the legend, but dreams him, the goal is still the same—the creation of a man. Yet the magician's dreams are not treated as such—that is, as intangible material—but rather as very concrete clay, as moldable substance: "He realized that, though he may penetrate all the riddles of the higher and lower orders, the task of shaping the senseless and dizzying stuff of dreams is the hardest that a man can attempt. . . ." (Recall that "golem" means "unformed matter.") And further on: "He then swore he would forget the populous vision which in the beginning had led him astray, and he sought another method." Before taking up his task again, "he cleansed himself in the waters of the river, worshiped the gods of the planets, uttered the prescribed syllables of an all-powerful name, and slept" (*A*, 58). When Borges writes "the prescribed syllables of an all-powerful name," we may surmise that he is thinking of the *Shem Hamephorash* or Tetragrammaton, which the Kabbalists sought by combining the letters of the Hebrew alphabet. Borges himself has paraphrased the Kabbalistic belief that when the miraculous *Shem Hamephorash* is pronounced over the golem made of clay or mud he must come to life: he "pronounced the Name which is the Key,"

32. *Ibid.*, p. 164.

Borges wrote in the poem "The Golem" (*SP*, 111). In his essay "The Golem" he had also pointed out that golem "was the name given to the man created by combinations of letters." [33] In "The Circular Ruins," the magician succeeds in dreaming a beating heart only after he has uttered "the prescribed syllables of an all-powerful name."

The description of the magician's dream is also reminiscent of the process of transformations (*temuroth*) of the letters as described in *Sefer Yetsirah*. Borges writes: "On the fourteenth night he touched the pulmonary artery with a finger and then the whole heart. . . . Before a year was over he came to the skeleton, the eyelids. The countless strands of hair were perhaps the hardest task of all" (*A*, 58–59). Similarly, in the *Sefer Yetsirah*, the letters of the Hebrew alphabet correspond to different parts of the human organism. Thus the double letters (beth, gimmel, daleth, caf, pei, reish, and taf) produced the seven planets, the seven days, and the seven apertures in man (two eyes, two ears, two nostrils, and one mouth). The twelve simple letters, on the other hand, created the twelve signs of the zodiac and thence the twelve months in time and the twelve "leaders" in man; the latter are those organs which perform functions in the body independent of the outside world—the hands, feet, kidneys, gall, intestines, stomach, liver, pancreas, and spleen (*Sefer Yetsirah*, IV–V). "One prescribed order of the alphabet produces a male being, another a female; a reversal of these orders turns the golem back to dust." [34]

Finally, Borges' magician dreams a complete man, but the dreamed being "could not stand up or speak, nor could he open his eyes." He resorts to the effigy in the destroyed temple, and the multiple god reveals to him that "its earthly name was Fire . . . and that through its magic the phantom of the man's dreams would be wakened to life in such a way that—except for Fire itself and the dreamer—every being in the world would accept him as a man of flesh and blood" (*A*, 59). In the Kabbalistic tradition, too, the act of animation comes with finding the right combination of let-

33. J. L. Borges, *The Book of Imaginary Beings* (New York, 1969), pp. 112–14.
34. Scholem, *On the Kabbalah . . .* , p. 186.

ters as prescribed in the Book of Creation, an undertaking which normally demands three years of studying the *Sefer Yetsirah,* just as it takes a thousand and one nights for Borges' magician to produce his dreamed son. In both cases, animation comes only after exercising the divine power generated by the "all-powerful name."

Borges suggests in his tale that the dreamed man himself eventually becomes a dreamer and repeats the magic operation, and so will his son, and the son of his son, and so on *ad infinitum.* The golem of the Kabbalists does not reproduce, but it may grow endlessly in size. The only way of controlling this demiurgic growth is by erasing from his forehead the first letter of the word *Emeth* (truth), which makes the word read *meth* (he is dead). Once this is done, he collapses and turns to clay again. As fire can reveal that the magician's created son is a simulacrum, so the dropping of one letter can return the golem to his previous state as dust. Borges goes further by granting the dreamed man all the qualities of human life, thus bringing the golem-maker to a status no different from that of God. In the Kabbalah, on the other hand, the golem remains at a speechless level, a kind of docile Frankenstein,[35] with the exception of one Kabbalistic source—the *Pseudo Saadya,* where the golem is granted soul and speech.

Before sending his created son to another temple, "the magician imbued with total oblivion his disciple's long years of apprenticeship" (*A,* 60)—an idea of deep Kabbalistic roots. The "Midrash on the Creation of the Child" relates that "after its guardian angel has given it a fillip upon the nose, the newborn child forgets all the infinite knowledge acquired before its birth in the celestial houses of learning."[36] In a parenthesis Borges explains that the oblivion is needed "so that the boy would never know he was a phantom, so that he would think himself a man like all men" (*A,* 60), thus integrating a seemingly bizarre and unconnected idea into the sequential "rationale" of the narrative.

The exegesis of the Midrash comes from Eleazar of Worms

---

35. Notice that Mary W. Shelley's creature is also a close descendant of the golem.

36. Scholem, *Major Trends . . . ,* p. 92.

(1232?), one of the pillars of German Hasidism: "Why, Eleazar asks, does the child forget? Because, if it did not forget, the course of this world would drive it to madness if it thought about it in the light of what it knew." [37] So no matter how different the two explanations may seem and how unlike their purpose, both share a common ground—the acceptance of a golem-making stage in which the dream and the child knew the mysteries of Creation. To be able to bear this world, the oblivion of that celestial or magical stage becomes inevitable. Scholem has observed that "in the root of the Midrash lies a remarkable variant of the Platonic conception of cognition as recollection, as anamnesis." [38] There is a moment in Borges' tale when the magician is about to recover the effaced awareness of that early stage, as if suddenly the recollection were to yield to a total illumination in which his origins became unveiled: "From time to time," writes Borges, the magician "was troubled by the feeling that all this had already happened. . . ." The revelation does not occur, but the hint provides one more clue to what Borges discloses only in the last line: the magician's own condition as phantom.

There is, however, one difference that separates the world-view of the Kabbalah from the outlook presented in "The Circular Ruins." In his story, Borges suggests that every man's reality is a dream and the god who is dreaming us is himself a dream. In the Kabbalah, God makes His creatures according to secret formulas that He alone knows; the first golem He created—*Adam Kadmon* (the primeval Adam)—was a creature of cosmic size and strength, and, furthermore, that first man was God Himself. It is in this light that one may understand the Midrash; "While Adam still lay as a golem before Him who spoke and the world came into being, He showed him all the generations and their wise men, all the generations and their judges and their leaders." [39] The Kabbalists managed to demonstrate this identity between God and Adam by means of *gematria* (isopsephism): they found that the numerical

37. *Loc. cit.*
38. *Loc. cit.*
39. Quoted by Scholem in *On the Kabbalah . . .*, p. 162.

value of YHWH is 45 and so is ADAM's. As the Torah is but the name of God, Adam is God Himself. Before Adam, God dwelled in the depths of nothingness, and it is this abyss within God that was overcome in the Creation. Borges takes up where the devotion to monotheistic belief reined-in the imagination of the Kabbalists. The Kabbalah goes as far as identifying Adam—God's golem—with God Himself. Beyond this point we are confronted with an infinite abyss of nothingness which is but the primeval and chaotic state of God before the Creation. Borges, on the other hand, echoing old Gnostic beliefs, implies that behind his dreamer there are perhaps innumerable dreamers: his golem-maker is a mere link in a long golem-making chain. He has said it masterfully in the last lines of a memorable sonnet, "Chess":

> **The player too is captive of caprice**
> **(The words are Omar's) on another ground**
> **Where black nights alternate with whiter days.**
>
> **God moves the player, he in turn the piece.**
> **But what god beyond God begins the round**
> **Of dust and time and sleep and agonies?** (*SP*, 121–23)

4. The doctrine of the Ibbür

Borges has written, "In the history of philosophy are doctrines, probably false, that exercise an obscure charm on human imagination, [for example] the Platonic and Pythagorean doctrine of the transmigration of the soul through many bodies" (*OI*, 37). Flashes of this doctrine flicker throughout his fiction, converting the revelations of theology into nuances of the fantastic. In several stories and essays, the transmigration of the soul is presented as a possible resolution of incoherent situations or conflicting circumstances.[40]

40. Here are a few examples to illustrate Borges' use of the doctrine. To explain the poem "Kubla Khan," dreamed by Coleridge, and the palace Kubla Khan dreamed and then had built, Borges suggests: "The Emperor's soul penetrated Coleridge's, enabling Coleridge to rebuild the destroyed palace in words that would be more lasting than marble and metal" (*OI*, 16). In "The Theologians," one of the sects postulates that "most [men], like Pythagoras, will have to transmigrate through many bodies before attaining their liberation; some, the Proteans, 'in the period of one lifetime are lions, dragons, boars, water and a tree' " (*L*, 123). In "The Shape of the Sword," Borges mentions " 'enormous epic poems which sang of the robbing of bulls which in another incarnation were heroes and in others fish and mountains. . . .' " (*L*, 68).

Borges himself has disclosed the sources of this doctrine in "The Approach to al-Mu'tasim," but, as in other instances, here too the motif is a synthesis in which not two but several sources are cohesively blended. In the last paragraph of "The Approach . . . ," Borges supplies the Kabbalistic version of the doctrine of transmigration: "With due humility, I suggest a distant and possible forerunner, the Jerusalem Kabbalist Isaac Luria, who in the sixteenth century advanced the notion that the soul of an ancestor or a master may, in order to comfort or instruct him, enter into the soul of someone who has suffered misfortune. *Ibbür* is the name given to this variety of metempsychosis" (*A*, 51–52). This Kabbalistic version of the transmigration of the soul enriches the doctrine substantially, adding to it original and highly imaginative elements. Thus, according to Luria (the leading figure of the Safed School), each soul retains its individual existence only until the moment when it has worked out its own spiritual restoration. Souls which have fulfilled the commandments are exempted from the law of transmigration and await, each in its blessed place, their integration into Adam's soul, when the general restitution of all things shall take place. As long as the soul has *not* fulfilled this task, it remains subject to the law of transmigration.

This banishment into the prison of strange forms of existence, into wild beasts, into plants and stones, is regarded as a particularly dreadful form of exile. As to how souls can be released from such an exile, Luria refers to the relationship between certain souls, in accordance with their original place in the undivided soul of Adam, the father of mankind. There are, according to Luria, relationships between souls, and even families of souls, which somehow constitute a dynamic whole and react upon one another.[41] These souls have a special aptitude for assisting and supplementing each other's actions. Also, by their piety, they can lift up those members of their group or family who have fallen to a lower plane and can enable them to start on the return journey to higher forms of ex-

41. Cortázar's idea that individual destinies cluster together in *figuras* whose shape and interaction they ignore, just as the stars or a constellation do not know they are part of such a group, may well find in Luria's text a suitable Kabbalistic explanation.

istence.[42] These are the essentials of the Kabbalah's interpretation of the doctrine which is called *gilgul* or *ibbür,* as Borges refers to it.

Kabbalists of the Lurianic School also held the belief that "everybody carries the secret trace of the transmigration of his soul in the lineament of his forehead and his hands, and in the aura which radiates from his body."[43] I fail to find any traces of chiromancy in Borges writings, but the idea that man's soul and its wanderings in search of total fulfillment or, what amounts to the same thing, that man's destiny is drawn in the lines of his forehead, provides a Kabbalistic clue to one of the most beautiful passages written by Borges: "A man," he says in the epilogue to *Dreamtigers,* "sets himself the task of portraying the world. Through the years he peoples a space with images of provinces, kingdoms, mountains, bays, ships, islands, fishes, rooms, instruments, stars, horses, and people. Shortly before his death, he discovers that that patient labyrinth of lines traces the image of his face" (*DT,* 93).[44] What in the Kabbalah is an ingeniously imaginative thought, in Borges becomes poetry at its best. Yet in the context of the Kabbalah, Borges' text regains the full measure of its implied and perhaps hidden significance. Like God, man creates his own universe, his own labyrinth which, unlike God's, he can penetrate and decipher. Like God, who revealed Himself in the Creation, man reveals himself (his face) in the world he creates (his work). In few writers' work do all the threads of the variegated texture interlock so tightly and firmly as they do in Borges'. This inner unity constitutes another pleasure among the many that Borges' work offers the patient reader.[45]

42. Scholem, *Major Trends . . .* , pp. 282–83.
43. *Ibid.,* p. 283.
44. An early formulation of this thought is found in "Ars Poetica," one of Borges' finest poems. The pertinent stanza reads:

> At times in the evenings a face
> Looks at us out of the depths of a mirror;
> Art should be like that mirror
> Which reveals to us our own face. (*SP,* 143)

45. Like many others in Borges' work, this idea cannot be restricted to one exclusive source. In addition to its bearings on Luria's version of metempsychosis, other connections are disclosed by Borges himself. In his essay on Oscar Wilde, he

5. Reality of the unreal

Another link between Borges and the world of the Kabbalah is the invention of authors and books which do not exist but could. Borges has explained that "The composition of vast books is a laborious and impoverishing extravagance. To go on for five hundred pages developing an idea whose perfect oral exposition is possible in a few minutes! A better course of procedure is to pretend that these books already exist, and then offer a summary, a commentary" (*F*, 15). This effort to abbreviate responds not only to an ideal of verbal economy and density of style, but is also one of the many ways Borges chooses to efface the bounds between what we call the real and the unreal. If life becomes an illusion when presented as a dream somebody is dreaming or as a line of a book somebody is writing, a summary or commentary of a nonexistent book produces the opposite effect: the summary or commentary ends by imposing on us the reality of the imagined book. We can see the device at work in the preface to an anthology devoted to Almafuerte and compiled by Borges himself:

Among the works I have not written and shall not write, but which in some way justify me—-though in an illusory or ideal way—there is one that could be titled *Theory of Almafuerte*. Drafts of it in an early handwriting prove that this hypothetical book has haunted me since 1932. It has, say, some hundred-odd octavo pages; to imagine it as any more extensive would be exorbitant. Nobody should regret its nonexistence or its existence only in that strange motionless world of possible objects. The summary of it that I am now going to give might prove identical to what one remembers over the years of a long book. Furthermore, its state as an unwritten book aptly fits it; the subject under examination is less the letter than the spirit of its author, less the notation than the connotation of his work. The general theory of Almafuerte is preceded by a particular conjecture about Pedro Bonifacio Palacios [Almafuerte], but (I hasten to add) the theory can do without the conjecture.[46]

---

has commented on some perspicuous observations left by the author of *De Profundis*. From this posthumous book Borges quotes Wilde's assertion that "there is no man who is not, at each moment, what he has been and what he will be," to explain later in a footnote: "Compare the curious thesis of Leibnitz, which seemed so scandalous to Arnauld: 'The notion that each individual includes *a priori* all the events that will happen to him'" (*OI*, 80). Borges alludes to the letters Leibnitz wrote to Arnauld (in one of which the famous statement was made), and to the negative reaction of the French Jansenist. Here, in the Leibnitz letter, the relationship is more abstract. Borges' memorable page and the Kabbalistic text share the striking image, in addition to the idea of a destiny conceived *a priori*, of a man's destiny traced in the lines of his face.

46. J. L. Borges, *Prosa y poesía de Almafuerte* (Buenos Aires, 1962), p. 6.

The same pseudepigraphic attitude was adopted by the author of the *Zohar,* although motivated by a different purpose. Moses de León came from the world of philosophic enlightenment against which he subsequently conducted an unremitting fight. In his youth we see him brooding over Moses Maimonides' *Guide for the Perplexed,* which he translated into Hebrew in 1264. Somewhat later, de León is turned by his mystical inclinations in the direction of Neo-Platonism, reading extracts from Plotinus' *Enneads,* which in the Middle Ages were commonly known by the title *The Theology of Aristotle.* But at the same time, he was more and more attracted to the mystical side of Judaism and gradually he came to ponder the mystery of the godhead as it was presented by the Kabbalistic theosophy of his age. Moses de León wrote the *Zohar* in order to stem the growth of the radical rationalistic mood which was widespread among his educated contemporaries. "If I told the people," he is quoted as saying, "that I am the author, they would pay no attention nor spend a farthing on the book, for they would say that these are but the workings of my own imagination." To capture the attention of a small and select circle of Jewish readers, Moses de León sets his book against the background of an imagined Palestine, where the famous Mishnah teacher of the second century A.D., Rabbi Simeon ben Yohai, is seen wandering about with his son Eleazar, his friends and his disciples, and discoursing with them on all manner of things human and divine. To further mislead the reader, Moses de León used Aramaic, the language spoken in Palestine during the second century A.D. Now, of course, it is known that "The Aramaic of the Zohar is a purely artificial affair, a literary language employed by a writer who obviously knew no other Aramaic than that of certain Jewish literary documents, and who fashioned his own style in accordance with definite subjective criteria. The spirit of medieval Hebrew, specifically the Hebrew of the thirteenth century, is transparent behind the Aramaic facade." [47] And yet Moses de León's literary artifice succeeded; until the overwhelming evidence presented by Gershom Scholem, the question of the *Zohar's* authorship bore much re-

47. For a detailed discussion on the subject of the *Zohar's* authorship, see Scholem, *Major Trends . . . ,* pp. 156–204.

semblance to the puzzling problem of Shakespeare's or Homer's identity. Was there one author or were there several? Was the *Zohar* the work of many generations, or a compilation from more than one author, rather than the work of one man? Do its several parts correspond to different strata or periods? Many scholars and students of the *Zohar* still hold the belief that the *Zohar* represents only a final edition of writings composed over a long period; others candidly accept Moses de León's own version—that is, the legendary origin of the book according to which Simeon ben Yohai and his son, sentenced to death by the Romans in the Palestine of the second century A.D., fled to a cave and hid there for thirteen years, in which time the *Zohar* took form.

One of the factors that led to the success of Moses de León's pseudepigraphic efforts was his firm consistency in the references and allusions he made to the *Zohar* and its author within the frame of his own works. Borges refers to this equipoise when examining the "enchantments of the *Quixote*": "we are reminded of the Spanish Rabbi Moises de León, who wrote the *Zohar* or *Book of the Splendor* and divulged it as the work of a Palestinian rabbi of the third [*sic*] century" (*OI*, 46). It is at this point that the author of the *Zohar* comes close to some of Borges' own enchantments. Like Borges, who offers to the reader the summary of a novel which exists only in his imagination, Moses de León supplies fantastic references to nonexistent sources. The whole *Zohar* is full of bogus references to imaginary writings which have caused even serious students to postulate the existence of lost sources.[48] In this respect we cannot help recalling that some of Borges' naive readers have also made diligent attempts to obtain "the first detective novel to be written by a native of Bombay City," Mir Bahadur Ali's *The Approach to al-Mu'tasim,* whose summary Borges offers in his story. But Bahadur Ali's novel as well as Moses de León's cited sources exist only in that Borgesian "motionless and strange world of possible objects."

Like Borges, who delights in intermixing fictional characters with real people, in confounding dummy authors with illustrious ones and hypothetical books with existing ones, the author of the

48. *Ibid.,* p. 174.

204

Zohar has produced an entire library of apocryphal books, and somebody has gone so far as to compile a catalogue of this "library from the upper world"—a tempting idea for a student of Borges. Next to works such as the "Book of Adam," the "Book of Enoch," the "Book of King Solomon," the "Book of Rav Hammuna Sava," and others that Moses de León comments on and profusely quotes —to the perplexity of the reader who knows nothing and can know nothing about them, simply because they exist only in the fancy of the mischievous Kabbalist—we can place Nils Runeberg's *Kristus och Judas* and his major work, *Den hemilge Frälsaren* (with its German translation); Herbert Quain's *The God of the Labyrinth, April March, The Secret Mirror,* and *Statements;* Volume XI of the *First Encyclopedia of Tlön;* the nineteen listed items of Pierre Menard's visible works, not to mention his unfinished masterpiece, *Don Quixote;* and several others that Borges quotes and paraphrases throughout his narratives. Yet these libraries of fictitious books, of nonexistent but possible books, acquire in their respective contexts a reality which makes them as real as those catalogued in, say, the Library of Congress—perhaps more real, since readers of Borges and the *Zohar* know much more about those nonexistent books than they will ever get to know about those millions of volumes in a library as bewildering as the Library of Babel. So what has been said of Moses de León's quotations from his "celestial library" can also be said of Borges' imaginary books: "They are entirely of a piece with the context in which they stand, both in style and terminology, and as a rule they are part of the argument as well." [49] In "Three Versions of Judas," the review of Nils Runeberg's books forms the argument as well as the body of the story.

Often the devices used by Moses de León to attain this effect are similar to those employed by Borges. As in the case of *Theory of Almafuerte,* a book which Borges has not written but of which he gives us a comprehensive summary, Moses de León widely quotes from imaginary books he may have written or may have intended to write. Thus, for example, the long passages quoted by him from the *Book of Enoch,* about which Gershom Scholem says: "There

49. *Ibid.,* p. 174.

can be no question of his having used an Arabic *Book of Enoch* unknown to us, or anything else of the sort; nor is it necessary to assume that he had himself written such a book before he quoted it, although he may have intended to do so or even have begun writing it; also Moses de León is the first to quote from the 'Testament of Eliezer ben Hyrkanus' which must have been written by the author of the *Zohar* himself." [50]

6. Style

To these contextual resemblances between Borges' work and the Kabbalah, stylistic similarities can be added. Thus, it has been said of the language of the *Zohar:* "It runs all the way from serene beauty to labored tortuousness, from inflated rhetoric to the most paltry simplicity, and from excessive verbosity to laconic and enigmatic brevity." [51] The reader familiar with Borges' development as a prose writer will immediately recognize in this definition some of the most distinctive traits of Borges' style. His early prose is pompous, strained, and exhibits a too obvious effort to astonish. Borges himself has referred to those years of his earlier volumes of essays in the bluntest terms: "I used to write in a very baroque and tricky way. Out of timidity I used to believe that if I wrote in a simple way people would think that I did not know how to write. I felt then the need to prove that I knew many rare words and that I was able to combine them in a very startling fashion." [52] That inflated and often tortuous style has nothing in common with the restrained, precise, and condensed prose of his short stories and later essays. The Borges of the Ultraist experiments has yielded to a Borges whose terse and pregnant style has all the marks of the best prose.

The oxymoron figures among the fondest stylistic devices used by Borges. [53] This preference has very little to do with rhetorical excesses or baroque mannerism whose intention is "to surprise, to

50. *Ibid.,* p. 200.
51. *Ibid.,* p. 163.
52. James E. Irby, "Encuentro con Borges," *Vida universitaria,* Monterrey, México (April 12, 1964), p. 14.
53. The reader interested in the use and effects of the oxymoron in Borges' narrative prose may see the subchapter "Oximoron" in *La prosa narrativa de J. L. Borges,* pp. 186–99.

astonish, to dazzle," [54] nor has Borges' oxymoron any ornamental or embellishing purpose—its use in his prose is definitely expressive and functional. The encounter and reconciliation of two notions which normally contradict or reject each other is, for Borges, a way of expressing at the level of style the paradoxical reality of his fictions. In his stories, frequently, the material of the fable organizes as a huge oxymoron. Style, then, restates and reinforces what is suggested by the theme of the narrative: eternity held in an instant, the chaos of our ordered universe, a dot which contains the universe, a library of illegible books, a pursued pursuer. The author of the *Zohar* also shows a definite predilection for oxymora and paradox, elements that Scholem defines as a "characteristic peculiarity of his style": " 'It is and is not' signifies, not that something exists, as it were, only partially, but that its existence is of an exquisitely spiritual nature and cannot therefore be properly described." [55] "Properly described," one could add, by means of the normative alternatives offered by language and whose limitations and barriers the Kabbalists, as well as Borges, strive to overcome.

7. Unveiling the seventy faces of a text

In the *Zohar,* as in Borges' fiction, one also finds the use of an old myth or motif and its subsequent reshaping into a new mode of thought. Moses de León takes the materials from the Aggadah and with them weaves his own fabric. He uses them freely for his own purposes and gives free rein to his imagination in making vital changes, emendations, and reinterpretations of the original. One example of this occurs in *Zohar* II, 124a. There, Moses de León converts a brief Talmudic tale which appears sporadically in the treatise of *Pesahim* 3b into a lively story on the same subject. When the Aggadah already contains mystical elements, these are duly emphasized and occasionally changed into an entirely new myth. A case in point is the mythology of the "great dragon" in the *Zohar* II, 35a, which has evolved from the Aggadah on the *Or ha-Ganuz*

---

54. E. R. Curtius, *European Literature and the Latin Middle Ages* (New York, 1963), p. 282.
55. Scholem, *Major Trends . . . ,* pp. 166–67.

in the Talmudic treatise of *Hagigah* 12a. Borges' treatment does not differ essentially from Moses de Léon's. In the recreation of the myth of the Minotaur in the story "The House of Asterion," Borges' purpose is not mere virtuosity. Borges himself has suggested that the idea "of a monster wanting to be killed, needing to be killed" [56] is the fictional reverse or paraphrase of another idea stated in his article "A Comment on August 23, 1944," written during the war. There he said that Hitler would be defeated because he wanted to be defeated: "Hitler is collaborating blindly with the inevitable armies that will annihilate him, as the metal vultures and the dragon (which must not have been unaware that they are monsters) collaborated, mysteriously, with Hercules" (*OI*, 136). Yet Borges' own interpretation of his story far from exhausts its far-reaching implications. I believe it is in this story more than in any other that Borges' labyrinthine outlook has been most fully and richly developed.[57] The old and weary myth has become here an effective medium for bringing forth his own worldview. Like the Kabbalist, Borges creates a new myth out of the old one. He has read into the legend of the Minotaur a new meaning which not only redeems the old myth, but also justifies it. Borges, indeed, fulfills here a task similar to Pierre Menard's in undertaking to write a contemporary *Quixote*. In "Pierre Menard, Author of the *Quixote*," Borges tells us that "Cervantes' text and Menard's are verbally identical, but the second is almost infinitely richer." This is just an exacerbation of the same attitude, of the same concept of literature according to which "one literature differs from another, either before or after it, not so much because of the text as for the manner in which it is read." "If I were able to read any contemporary page," explains Borges to prove his point, ". . . as it would be read in the year 2000, I would know what literature would be like in the year 2000" (*OI*, 164). In a strict sense, Borges' own narratives could be defined—applying this criterion—as different ways of reading the systems of philosophy and the doctrines of

56. See Richard Burgin, *Conversations with Jorge Luis Borges* (New York, 1969), p. 41.
57. See my essay "Tlön y Asterión: anverso y reverso de una epistemología," *Nueva narrativa hispanoamericana*, I, 2 (September 1971), 21–33.

theology. "I am," Borges has said about himself, "a man of letters who turns his own perplexities and that respected system of perplexities we call philosophy into the forms of literature.[58] His stories are postures for reading those theories (which have made man what he is), but in the process the claimed "absolute truths" have become myths and marvels, humble intuitions of man's fantasy. Perhaps in this wise and skillful turn of the kaleidoscope lies the revelation of Borges' art. If the essence of this revelation resides in the act of reading the new in an old text, we have simply come to the very point where the Kabbalah begins. These beginnings are described by Borges himself in his essay "The Mirror of the Enigmas":

The notion that the Sacred Scripture possesses (in addition to its literal meaning) a symbolic one is not irrational and is ancient: it is found in Philo of Alexandria, in the cabalists, in Swedenborg. . . . The portentous premise of a book that is impervious to contingency, a book that is a mechanism of infinite purposes, moved them [the Kabbalists] to permute the scriptural words, to sum up the numerical value of the letters, to consider their form, to observe the small letters and the capital letters, to search for acrostics and anagrams. . . . (*OI*, 125–28)

Now, one should ask what the Kabbalists achieved by means of this mystical hermeneutics. The *Zohar* is undoubtedly the most representative work of many centuries of Kabbalistic exegesis, but it is far from being the only one—there are literally hundreds of such books, many of them still in manuscript form. The *Zohar* shares some basic characteristics with most of those books: thus, for instance, a deliberately unsystematic construction, a tendency —rooted in Jewish thought—to avoid logical systematization. Scholem has illustrated the method (or rather the method's lack of method) of the *Zohar* with a very eloquent comparison: "Most of the fundamental ideas found in the *Zohar*," he says, "were expressed only a little later in a systematically constructed treatise, *Maarekheth Ha-Elohuth* (The Order of God), but how dry and lifeless are these bare skeletons of thought compared with the flesh and blood of the *Zohar!*" And he goes on: "In the *Zohar* the most unpretentious verses of Scripture acquire an entirely unexpected

---

58. J. L. Borges, "Foreword" to Ronald Christ, *The Narrow Act: Borges' Art of Allusion* (New York, 1969), p. 9.

meaning. . . . Again and again a hidden and sometimes awful depth opens before our eyes, and we find ourselves confronted with real and profound insight." [59] The foundation of this imaginative wealth and fertility of thought lies in the belief that "the Torah is an inexhaustible well, which no pitcher can ever empty." [60]

Borges proposes a similar premise. When he says that "perhaps universal history is the history of the diverse intonation of a few metaphors," he appears to be postulating the opposite case, since he seemingly underlines the exhaustible character of *human* imagination.[61] But it is only the oblique formulation that creates this impression; actually, Borges is saying exactly the opposite. In the essay "The Metaphor," written in 1952, he offers the reader the prolegomenon of his idea, explaining that

The first monument of Western literature, the *Iliad*, was composed some three thousand years ago; it seems safe to surmise that during this vast lapse of time every familiar and necessary affinity (dream-life, sleep-death, the flow of rivers and time, and so forth) has been noted and recorded by someone. This does not mean, of course, that the number of metaphors has been exhausted; the ways of stating or hinting at these hidden sympathies are, in fact, limitless.[62]

Consequently, "perhaps it is a mistake to suppose that metaphors can be invented. The real ones, those that formulate intimate connections between one image and another, have always existed; those we can still invent are the false ones, which are not worth inventing" (*OI,* 47). Taking this one step further, Borges implies that the task of the writer is not to invent new and original works but rather to reinterpret old ones, or—in John Barth's words—"to write original works of literature whose implicit theme is the difficulty, perhaps the unnecessity, of writing original works of literature." [63]

Borges' concept of metaphor (which for him is only a metaphor for literature) does not differ essentially from the *Zohar's* outlook on the Scripture: as the whole world is for the Kabbalists a *corpus*

59. Scholem, *Major Trends . . .* , p. 158.

60. Scholem, *On the Kabbalah . . .* , p. 60.

61. For a penetrating article on this question, see John Barth's "The Literature of Exhaustion," *Atlantic* (August 1967), pp. 29–34.

62. Jorge Luis Borges, "The Metaphor," in "Up from Ultraism," *New York Review of Books* (August 13, 1970), p. 4.

63. Barth, *ibid.,* p. 31.

symbolicum (an idea that Borges has repeatedly quoted),[64] so the Torah is conceived, and to interpret it is, consequently, to unveil its "seventy faces" (i.e., infinite levels). Borges has referred to himself as "the man who weaves these symbols" (*A*, 95), and in a different context he has said that "art operates necessarily with symbols"; [65] in addition, he has insisted on the idea that universal history is "a Sacred Scripture: one that we decipher and write uncertainly, and in which we also are written" (*OI*, 120), and he has likewise endorsed the belief that "we are the versicles or words or letters of a magic book, and that incessant book is the only thing in the world; or rather, it is the world" (*OI*, 120). For the Kabbalists, similarly, God looked at the Torah and created the world. The *Zohar,* like the literature of the Kabbalah at large, is an attempt to penetrate the hidden layers of that holy text; the results are those coined symbols and sometimes elaborated allegories by means of which a new, lucid, and original interpretation of the Scripture has been produced. Borges' narratives and symbols represent a similar attempt, with the difference that the text Borges reads encompasses "the almost infinite world of literature."

It has been asked whether the true interpretation of certain passages of the Scripture may not be found in the *Zohar* and nowhere else; I would like to ask if Borges' symbols—which claim not to be a reflection of the world but rather something added to it —do not imply a new understanding of man's confrontation with the world. Some of these symbols suggest that since man can never find the solution to the gods' labyrinth, he has constructed his own labyrinth; or, in other words, that since the reality of the gods is impenetrable, man has created his own reality. He lives, thus, in a world which is the product of his own fallible architecture. He knows there is another world, "irreversible and iron-bound," which constantly besieges him and forces him to feel the enormity of its presence, and between these two worlds, between these two stories —one imagined by God and the other fancied by man—flows the agonizing history of mankind.

64. In a book review in his collection of essays, *Discusión,* p. 164, he says: ". . . for the mystics the concrete world is but a system of symbols."
65. *Discusión,* p. 141.

The enigmatic predicament: some parables of Kafka and Borges
BEN BELITT

PART I

PART I

1

To make up stories, rather than to tell the truth, is presumably to dissimulate, and all dissimulation, rationally viewed, confounds, rather than assists, reality. In this sense, fiction adds to the riddle-someness of things; or it elects to make up stories about riddles— stories of gods, demons, causality, destiny, "life." From this point of view, Oedipus is our exemplary hero of the antifiction. His confrontation with the Theban Sphinx not only destroyed the sanctity of the enigmatic way, but constituted a revolution in the criteria of knowledge itself. Until the advent of Oedipus, to tell a story of men or gods, to be "true to life," was to engage the enigmatic with a fiction. All storytelling was a venture into the Inscrutable, in which the storyteller said, with Saint Paul: "Behold, I will show you a mystery." After Thebes, the great custodians of the Mysteries— oracles, libation bearers, sibyls—gave way to the Answerer and the defeat of enigma. Presumably, the era of dialectic was at hand.

The fictive art with which I am here concerned is specifically literary. It pertains to those artifacts of narrative prose subsumed under the function of storytelling, as long or short as you please— that self-extending "tapeworm" (of which Forster has written [1] with such amused tolerance), which exacerbates and gratifies the "primeval curiosity" of the reader; asks "What next?" through a thousand and one nights; saves the life of Scheherazade; and transforms us "from readers into listeners, to whom 'a' voice speaks, the voice of the tribal narrator squatting in the middle of the cave, and saying one thing after another until the audience falls asleep among their offal and bones."

Hans Vaihinger learnedly reminds us [2] that the artificial character of these verbal ventures is already implicit in the Latin of *"fictio,* as an activity of *fingere,* that is to say, of constructing, forming, giving shape, elaborating, presenting, artistically fashioning; conceiving, thinking, imagining, assuming, planning, devising, inventing." The movement toward the *enigmatic* is similarly suggested by the Latin: "conceits, figments of the brain, phantasies, phantastic ideas, imagination, imaginary ideas . . . counterfeit ideas, stratagems, dodges . . . chimaera." It is precisely this relationship between fiction and enigma, the contrived and chimerical thing, that I wish to examine in the work of two contemporary masters whose express intent seems to have been to compel a simultaneous awareness of both: to bombard fiction with enigma and enigma with the fictive in the service of some insight which needs to be better understood. For this purpose I have chosen the parables of Kafka and Borges—because, supposedly, their explanations are offered in the guise of enigmas, and their insights are enacted in the form of miniature fictions.

2

First, a word regarding the rhetoric and strategy of parable. Parable, we can say academically, is a fiction implying a comparison, a similitude in the guise of a fable, a plot permeated with symbolic meaning. In a time of little faith, it is a means of addressing, "in

1. E. M. Forster, *Aspects of the Novel* (New York, 1927).
2. Hans Vaihinger, *The Philosophy of "As If"* (New York, 1966).

code," as it were, a message to men of perfect faith and of screening out the skeptic, the hypocrite, the informer, and those not "in the know." For example, in a time of Soviet repression of public criticism of the status quo, on the part of a regime demanding the conformity of the artist, *The Cancer Ward* of Solzhenitsyn is a mode of parabolizing the sickness of the time under the guise of a story about cancer. It provides a means of public double-talk in which a dissenter and a teacher in constant peril of his life can communicate with other dissenters on a closed circuit, "in code," on the Christian principle that "to whosoever hath, to him it shall be given" and that pearls are not to be cast before swine. The parable, then, is a hermetic directive to the "elect" through which action is turned into fable.

The parables of Jesus—flung, as it were, in handfuls, as if the Sower took no account of where they fell—show us fable at all stages of completion, incompletion, compression, and suspension. At times the "plots" that we have come to expect of fable have been so compacted or abbreviated that there is little likelihood of putting them to edifying use. Even a full-dress parable—like the parable of the Sower—which takes its time and proceeds by stages so explicit in their imagery that they may be construed dialectically —aroused the instant consternation of the Disciples, to whom, said Christ, it was "given to know," and required the detailed exposition of the teller. Lacking the glosses of the master, the purport of Christ's parables apparently remained inaccessible. The hoped-for transformation of perception did not occur.

Or, as Kafka remarked, "In parable, you have lost." In fiction, however, the confusion is fruitful. In fiction, the problem is increasingly polarized as fable turns into fiction, and parable into enigma. Fiction asks: How much *plot* is needed for the mind to manipulate if we are not to revert to the riddling hallucinations of the Sphinx? How are we to cover chaos with a plot, to deliver us from the inscrutable? Where does the enigmatic factor of an *unknown intent,* on the way to making itself known, set in? Are we all agreed about the common "meaning" which a "right" reading of the fiction should produce? Or is enigma forced upon us because we find ourselves in essential disagreement and all the disagreements are true?

214

At this point I should like to allow Kafka to raise and resolve contingent issues in his own way in his parable on parable. The essential concern of "On Parables" is epistemological. That is to say, it asks, with St. Paul, "whether there be knowledge," and if there be knowledge, what it is good for—whether it is tentative, terminal, or illusory. Presumably, if it is illusory, it would constitute an order of *fiction,* and fiction might then claim for itself a *fait accompli:* that it is "true" in the sense that it constitutes a mode of *surrogate* or fictive knowing or, at the very least, illusory knowing.

In all fiction, as in all assumptions of knowledge, there would remain for both the philosopher and the writer of fiction the problem explored in such depth by Nietzsche in his "will to illusion,"[3] as to whether in myth, art, and metaphor there is always a kind of "lying, in the extra-moral sense"; whether such "delusional conceptions [are] necessary and salutary provisions of the instinct"; whether all life and all knowing *"needs* illusions, i.e., untruths regarded as truths"; whether we habitually "operate with things that do not exist, with lines, surfaces, bodies, atoms, divisible time, divisible space"; whether "error might [not] be one of the conditions of life"; whether "the recognition of delusion and error as conditions of knowing and feeling" would be "endurable" without art.

Nietzsche goes on to observe that "we must love and cultivate error: it is the mother of knowledge"; and doubtless the novelist would similarly concede that the cultivation of error (or "illusion") is the mother of fiction, however "realistic" its pretensions. "Without the assumption of a kind of being which we could oppose to actual reality, we should have nothing by which we could measure, compare, or picture it; error is the presupposition of knowledge." For Nietzsche, thinking was moreover contingent upon language:

We are continually seduced by words and concepts, into imagining things as simpler than they really are.... A philosophical mythology lies hidden in language which breaks through at every moment, no matter how careful we may be.... Indeed, the most erroneous assumptions are precisely the most indis-

3. The extrapolations from the Collected Works of Nietzsche are from Hans Vaihinger's discussion of *The Will to Illusion,* in *op. cit.,* Part III, Section D, pp. 341–62.

pensable for us. . . . Without granting the validity of the logical *fiction,* man could not live. . . . A negation of fiction . . . is equivalent to a negation of life itself. . . . There is nothing but a moral prejudice that regards truth as of more value than illusion. . . . There would be no life at all were it not on the basis of perspective valuations and semblances . . . the perspective is the basic condition of all life.

Thus, supposedly, the philosopher—and it may be, the inducer of esthetic fictions, the novelist so-called—places himself not only beyond "good and evil" but beyond "truth and falsehood" as well. If this seems too shocking a heresy for esthetic idealists, or too will-fully symptomatic of modern relativism, it is worth remembering that 2,500 years ago Aristotle placed tragedy above epic precisely for the reason that its "imitation" was *fictive,* and as such con-stituted a more universal, more *plausible* mode of the truth than "history."

But why talk in parables at all? It is the essence of parable to avoid showdowns of this nature, and leave the issues suspended. But certain implications of Kafka's little parable should be para-phrased for what they are worth. In the first place, its effect is to suggest that parables are a species of nonfunctional "wisdom"—that is to say, one does not acquire the wisdom of parable in order to deplete or discredit it. Parables are *fabulous* ("he means some fabulous yonder"); [4] *unknown* ("something unknown to us"); *imprecise* ("something that he cannot designate more precisely"); and *useless* ("merely parables and of no use in daily life"). Par-ables are *exceptional* rather than daily, in the sense that a work of literature is less daily than an empirical act of thought. Conversely, parables are *truisms* already deeply known to us all ("We *know* that already"). All they "really set out to say" is "merely that the in-comprehensible is incomprehensible." Parables, moreover, appear to have a way of rendering the knower himself *unreal:* "If you only followed the parables you yourselves would become parables," and all existence would be *parabolized.* Finally, as insights, parables serve what might be called an epistemology of *loss.* Their value, as knowledge, is to enhance our "consciousness of ignorance"—

4. All quotations from the parables of Kafka are from Franz Kafka, *Parables* (New York, 1946), with translations by various hands.

but that is the beginning of philosophy. The vocation of Socrates began with a visit to the Oracle at Delphi and a "parable," and ended with a philosopher's conviction that "I know that I do not know."

3

A sequence of corollaries can be traced to make clearer the parabolic stance of Kafka as a whole—what, in his preface to larger fictions to come, he is saying about fiction as a mode of knowledge. In "An Imperial Message," for example, Kafka's premise is that there is an unimpeachable Source to whom all is known: an "Emperor," removed, remote, infallible, mortal, in whom all data originate. From Him proceeds all knowledge; and all knowledge leads to messages. The known thing is not only communicable, but exists to be communicated. Messages, in turn, lead to message-bearers, and this in its turn leads to "journeys"—a search for those for whom the known thing was intended.

The parable makes it clear that the message is also momentous, and must be exactly imparted to the message-bearer. That it is "whispered" on a deathbed suggests that there is something profoundly confidential about all knowledge; and that it must be confirmed suggests that the datum is profoundly misinterpretable. Kafka goes on to say that though the messenger is "powerful," "indefatigable," "cleaving a path through the throng," to the "chambers of the innermost palace," he will "never get to the end of them," for the resistance of circumstances and things would be infinitely multiplied: more courts, more stairs, more palaces, more years, more gates, more cities, "to the center" of the imperial capital and a "world crammed to bursting with its own refuse."

Two questions are relevant to the parable in hand: (1) For whom was the knowledge intended? And (2) if knowledge is not communicated, does it really exist? Kafka gives them both short shrift; indeed, it may appear to some that he begs questions rather than confronts them. His answer is that the journey, the datum at its mysterious point of origin, and its communication by the messenger were all unnecessary. Anyone can "dream it to himself" by his window. Thus, all apparent knowledge is a dream, by the self, in the self, to the self—what Nietzsche called "mythological dreaming," the "invented world of the unconditioned, the self-identical man," "the will to deception," which is indeed "the soul of art." "It is our laws and our conformity to the laws that we read into the world of phenomena—however much the contrary seems true." There is no Emperor, no messenger, no single mind for whom the message was intended. "The 'agent' has merely been read into the action—the action is all there is. . . . There is only a naive, human manner of arranging things."

In "The News of the Building of the Wall" we have another "epistemological" parable regarding messages, "news," knowledge. Here the effect of "The Imperial Message" is, as it were, reversed, as Kafka reflects on an alternate possibility: "What if the message *had* been delivered?" In the present case, the message arrives "late, some thirty years after its announcement." It is received, not by the storyteller himself (who is barely ten at the time), but by his father. The child, however, is witness to the event, of which he "remembers the smallest circumstances"; and the circumstances are almost conspiratorial in their secrecy. A boatman approaches and beckons, messenger and father meet in the middle of a slope, and, once again, the message is whispered "into my father's ear."

The results of the messenger's mission, however, are ambiguous and unexpected. The son himself "did not understand what was said," the father "did not seem to believe the news," the messenger "tried to convince him that it was the truth, but Father still could not believe it," even though the message-bearer "almost tore open his clothes . . . in order to convince him that it was so." The problem for parable, then, is altered. Has the messenger communicated at all, and is his mission accomplished? If he has indeed communicated, why was he not believed? And if the father believed, what was his knowledge "good for"? Was it truth or illusion?

Characteristically, the issues are left suspended. The fiction moves steadily toward the enigmatic, to which it apparently surrenders, even though its content is supposedly knowable, positive, terminal. The father remains "meditative," the boatman sails away,

218

the recipient of the message returns home and straightway "reports from the threshold what he had heard." The child, as bystander, has "no exact recollection of his words," but "because of the extraordinary circumstances . . . their meaning sank into me so deeply that I still feel able to give a kind of verbatim version of them." He proceeds to do so, and his words pass into the stream of "popular interpretation." The message proves to be little more than a rumor, at once threatening and reassuring. The Emperor, in whom all knowledge is vested, is being threatened by "infidel nations with demons among them" who "shoot their black arrows at the Emperor." It is rumored that "a great wall is going to be built to protect" him. That constitutes the whole of knowledge.

In a further parable on "Couriers," Kafka continues to speculate on the discomfort of messengers, deputies, couriers—that is, on the sources and the terminal aspects of knowing. His misgivings at this stage appear desperate, as well as implacable. Is *anything* known at all? Are there even directions, journeys, goals? The effect of his answer is to turn fiction into phantasmagoria. We all wish to be message-bearers of the King, he argues, rather than kings. "Like children," we wish to receive, disseminate, and communicate knowledge, rather than create it. But there are no kings from whom true knowledge may be said to derive; our messages are "meaningless" and invalid. All that really exists is an enigmatic "oath of service," a commitment to "shout the King's messages" to one another and thereby incur the "misery" of things. Human knowledge is nothing more than the compulsive "shouting" of unauthorized "messages."

4

A final cluster of parables will, I think, help to consolidate the nature of Kafka's commitment to enigmatic fictions. The first, "The Invention of the Devil," is essentially a parable on the anguish of the enigmatic predicament as such, the "misery" of things already imputed to the delusory mission of the "courier." The "Devil" of the title is clearly the demon of the ambiguous, the multiple, the contradictory—of the heterogeneity and pluralism of the world

219

in the presence of a mind that longs for homogeneity, for unity. Here, knowledge is viewed as "possession" in the demonic sense of the word. To "know" is to be appropriated by the irreconcilable pluralism of things, to be dis-possessed of one's own identity—or of the unifying delusion of the rational process—and to be made legion. In this sense, Kafka repeats the formula for demoniacal possession—or, if you wish, for schizophrenia—to which Luke refers in 8:30: "And Jesus asked him, saying, What is thy name? And he said, Legion; because many devils were entered into him." In the same way, Kierkegaard was led to wonder: "Can you think of anything more frightful than that it might end with your nature being resolved into a multiplicity, that you really might become many, become, like those unhappy demoniacs, a legion, and you thus would have lost the inmost and holiest thing of all in a man, the unifying power of personality?" [5]

In "The Invention of the Devil," such a state has actually come to pass: a sense of possession, deprivation, alienation; a sense of the "diabolic" character of this intrusion; of "earthly misfortune" incurred by an act of knowing that leaves the knower without choice, conviction, or the rational subordination of expendable or contingent things to what is irreducibly constant—hence, "deceived." The deception would seem to lie not in the *data* by which the knower is "possessed," but in the temptation to know, *itself*—the trustful and "scrupulous attention" with which the knower has opened himself to the appropriation of data, in which nothing "exterminates" anything else, or "subordinates" itself to the co-existing multipleness of things, as would be the case in syllogistic or dialectical thinking. It is in this sense that one has "become legion," and perhaps it is also in this sense that the enigmatic factor in all art partakes of the "diabolic." The engimatic works in *multiples:* it aims at the "suspension of disbelief" or the "possession" of the reader; and it goes on multiplying its multiples. It not only retains all that it evokes, but resists every effort on the part of the knower to dispose of the content of knowledge in such a way that

5. Søren Kierkegaard, *Either/Or* (Princeton, N.J., 1944), Vol. II, 135.

one thing "exterminates . . . another until only a single one is left . . . or they subordinate themselves to one great devil."

The second parable is devoted to yet another fictive variation, the *legendary,* and may serve to mitigate somewhat the despairing pluralism of "The Invention of the Devil." Here it is the nature of a God, rather than the devil, that demands to be known, and the parable's medium is Prometheus, a defier of "emperors" and absolutes, whom legend assumes to be the tutelary spirit of the whole human condition. The properties of Prometheus, however, are of less concern to Kafka than the mode by which his story has passed into common knowledge. And in the beginning, we are told that "there are four legends concerning Prometheus," just as, presumably, there are four gospels concerning Jesus which must be put "in accord with" their tellers or messengers: the "gospel *according to* Matthew, Mark, Luke, and John."

The implications are again multiple. There is a pluralism of knowledge; but there is also a hope that the truth of the God may be arrived at "orchestrally," by a synoptic reading of all four— arranged in parallel columns, as it were, like the synoptic reading of the gospels. Kafka proceeds to so arrange them, as four variations on a single message. The question in all this, of course, is whether four legends constitute one truth. If not, how many legends are needed? Or is this another parable about the essential unknowability of Prometheus and the defeat of knowledge?

We have only the final paragraph to guide us. Here we meet, in another guise, the essential *paradox of parable:* that legend, like parable, tries to "explain the inexplicable." The fact is well known to all mythologists and historians of religion; all gods have their "aetiological" or explanatory myths, which generally constitute the service of the god. It has always been the task of religious ritual to explain the inexplicable, and, in more secular terms, it may also be the function of all fiction and all knowledge. The reader can only set down faithfully the contradictory import of Kafka's parable: (1) that all legend contains a "substratum of truth" (and all truth a substratum of legend?); (2) that all truth is inexplicable; (3) that therefore all legend which turns into apparent truth turns itself into the "inexplicable"; and (4) that therefore truth and legend are equally fictive and enigmatic. The "inexplicable mass of rock"—the brute substantiality of things untouched by the operations of thought, belief, fiction, delusion, truth—*remains*.

Finally, "The Problem of Our Laws." There may be some question as to whether this is a parable at all, since the speculative cast of the piece outweighs—or outpaces—the parabolic. Nevertheless, it synthesizes many of the concerns which have already furnished Kafka with occasions for parable: messages; messengers; mysteries; wisdom; truth; fiction; interpretation; presumption; traditions; an "elite" from whom all knowledge derives, who originate, administer, and "rule"; and the "ruled," who "live on a razor's edge" of incertitude, and submit.

One must first opt for a meaning, or a complex of meanings, within which one is content to see the key word—LAW—operate. Perhaps the most obvious and convenient meaning should be the first to go: "law" in its literal sense as *legislation* or *litigation*. Juristic procedure for the purpose of defining rectitude and judging deviations from it—the tactic "of bringing a single case under some law in order to apply its theory of rewards and punishments" (Vaihinger)—is merely one permutation of the intended meaning. As the parable makes clear, Kafka has in mind all movements of the reason and the psyche which (according to Vaihinger) "deliberately substitute a fraction of reality for the complete range of causes and facts": abstractive fictions, practical fictions, mathematical fictions, heuristic fictions, scientific fictions," as well as "legal fictions" as such.

In this vein, Kafka goes on to remark that we are all "ruled by laws that [we] do not know"; that "only a few and not the whole people are allowed to have a say in their interpretation"; that "their interpretation has been the work of centuries" and has now "acquired the status of law"; and that "the very existence of these laws . . . is at most a matter of presumption." As usual, Kafka postulates an elite of the intellect—"a small group of nobles who rule

222

us"—philosopher kings; princes of the intellect and administrators of syllogistic propriety; benevolent despots and guardians of the "law and order" of logic, who preside over a "mystery confided to the nobility." He then goes on to question, heretically, whether "when in accordance with these scrupulously tested and logically ordered conclusions, we seek to orient ourselves somewhat toward the present or future, everything" is not "only an intellectual game" —in other words, a system of *fictions,* delusions, arrangements of convenience. Perhaps "these laws that we are trying to unravel"— the right action of the human reason which is compatible with reality and should legitimize all truths—"do not exist at all."

It is here that Kafka gives fullest play to his discomfiture and skepticism. After all, he remarks, "The Law is whatever the nobles do"—i.e., whatever Socrates and Aristotle "did" with their reasoning faculties are the "laws" of right reasoning because they did it. He makes mention of a "party" of dissenters or anarchs of the reason who "see everywhere only the *arbitrary* acts of the nobility." These anti-intellectuals, or antinomians, duly warn their fellow plebeians against a "false, deceptive, and over-confident security." They remind the gullible that "the tradition is far from complete" —as, indeed, sophisticated scientific thought today constantly cautions the vulgar. The nature of inductive scientific procedure as such is inherently fragmentary, nonterminable: a work-in-progress that, like Zeno's arrow, mathematically shortens the distance between itself and the target toward which it travels but, by the same mathematical logic, can never reach it. They challenge that "preponderance of evidence" by which science, at a given point of its trajectory, regards its case as "demonstrated" or "proven," announces a terminal datum—or "law"—and functions in relation to it as one would to a "truth." They even go an irrational step further to envision a time when the "law" will "belong to the people and the nobility will vanish."

Here Kafka recoils. He reminds us that the "party which believes that there is no law"—the anarchs and the heresiarchs—has, after all, "remained small." It is small because of a universal craving for the postulate that Knowledge Does Indeed Really Exist Somewhere

—even if it must do so enigmatically, with the "nobility." We would all rather have enigma—the enigma of the law—than anarchy or nullity. Therefore, "nobody would dare to repudiate the nobility" that rules, pontificates, governs, coordinates, orders, and consoles with a "fiction" of orientation and knowledge, and renders the world bearable. The essential "divinity that doth hedge a King" hedges all knowledge; it is *all* divine. No knowledge is secular. Knowledge is innately mysterious, arcane, privileged, arbitrary, unknowable; and the conviction of knowledge must therefore remain a fiction to all except the nobility, who will never divulge the "mystery" over which they preside during their lifetimes and which they take with them into their death.

PART II

1

The case for Kafka as "precursor" to Jorge Luis Borges would be apparent to those familiar with the enigmatic fictions of both, even without Borges' little essay on "Kafka and His Precursors." In that knowledgeable and crotchety piece, Borges admits to a long predilection for the art of Franz Kafka, which has left him with a dowser's instinct for "his voice, or his practices in texts from diverse literatures and periods" (*L,* 199). He goes on to cite six such texts, with a preciosity which will surprise no one familiar with the encyclopedic habits of the Director of the Argentine National Library and laureate of the chair of English and North American Literature at the University of Buenos Aires.

Similarly, the reader of Borges is constantly aware of the "voice, or . . . practices" of Kafka in that labyrinthine world over which Borges presides as presumptive heir and successor. The scope of this essay permits only the most cursory look at the continuities of Kafka and Borges, but even a cursory look will serve. For one thing, to supplement, or to polarize, the import of his longer fictions, Borges has often chosen to write in "parables," like Kafka. That his parables concern himself—are, in effect, "explanatory myths" of his double stance as artist in fiction and the "other Borges," now legendary for his taste for "hourglasses, maps, eighteenth-century typography, the taste of coffee and the prose of Stevenson" (*L,* 246) and the language of Anglo-Saxon epics—is clear from the title of his parable, "Borges and I."

In a sense, "Borges and I" continues Kafka's long meditation on the theme of knowledge and enigma—this time with a shift of emphasis to the artist as knower. Borges surmises, as Kafka foresaw, that the artist in parable must reckon with two consequences he is destined to invite: (1) "If you follow parable, you yourself become parable"; and (2) "In parable, you have lost." Similarly, the "daily" Borges speaks to the Borges whose "perverse custom" it is to "falsify" and "magnify" things, to conjure up "games with time and infinity" which volatilize or liquidate the identity. "I am giving over everything to him," he confesses. "I live, let myself go on living, so that Borges may contrive his literature." And his conclusion is literally Kafkaesque: "I lose everything," including the conviction of knowledge itself. "I do not know which of us has written this page" (*L,* 247).

It should not escape us that Borges was content to call his most celebrated collection of stories and parables simply *Ficciones,* as if he wished to ally himself generically with the world of illusion, rather than a premise of truth or reality. His point, in this shadow-play, is that fiction makes the maker of fictions fictitious—just as, in another parable entitled "Everything and Nothing," he contends that drama, as another mode of fiction, rendered Shakespeare "fictitious" to himself. The paradox in each case is the same: in fiction (Kafka would say in parable) one "has everything and nothing." On the one hand, fiction liquidates the identity of the teller and invests him with identities not his own; and, on the other, it induces an omniscience which is no longer partial or adventitious, but totally known to the teller of fictions. For the duration of the fiction—as in Kafka's "Invention of the Devil"—he is a congeries of personae, an "invention," a *fait accompli* of fictive clairvoyance. The devil of the ambiguous, the multiple, and the heterogeneous has preempted the consciousness of the storyteller and reduced him to "nothing"; but it has also endowed him with the infallibility and entirety of his fiction: "everything."

In "Everything and Nothing" Borges goes a step further and identifies the artist's faculty for self-surrender as histrionic. "At the age of twenty-one," he writes, Shakespeare

had already become proficient in the habit of simulating that he was someone, so that others would not discover his condition as no one; . . . but once the last verse had been declaimed and the last dead man withdrawn from the stage, the hated flavor of unreality returned to him. . . . Thus hounded, he took to imagining other heroes and other tragic fables. . . . At times he would leave a confession hidden away in some corner of his work, certain that it would not be deciphered; Richard affirms that in his person he plays the part of many and Iago claims with curious words, "I am not what I am." (*L*, 248–49)

Thus, the fictions of drama, like the fictions of the novelist, are viewed as "controlled hallucinations," leading to the old terror of the loss of self, of which both Kafka and Kierkegaard spoke—the pandemoniac state of "being so many," of being legion, of being "possessed." The implications are that the fictive way—if not the function of fiction itself—is essentially enigmatic: that only fiction, as a mode of knowledge, leaves us with the *certainty* that, for the duration of the fiction or the play or the parable, illusion is totally ours. "We are not what we were," says reader to writer with a shock of unprecedented recognition; "we are many. Reality is not our concern." Theirs is the enigmatic predicament in which they have "everything and nothing."

The enigmatic predicament of all things—actor, action, scene, purpose, cognition—the *enigmatizing* of existence—is the supporting vision of the *"ficciones"* of Jorge Luis Borges. Compared with the radical bleakness of Kafka's characteristic manner, however, his approach is baroque, subliminal, "poetic." Whatever his debts to Kafka, and they are considerable, the mode of Borges is Spanish rather than Gothic; that is to say, his precursors are Calderón, Góngora, Quevedo, Cervantes, Unamuno, even Maimonides—that confluence of erudition, dandyism, the balladic, the gauchoesque, and the *mozárabe,* shifting its densities and surfaces as the need requires, but supporting the skipped heartbeat that sustains the Spaniard's sense of reality: *La vida es sueño.*

In his parable on "Inferno I, 32," Borges will invoke Dante, as he did Shakespeare in "Everything and Nothing," only to say of the dying Dante that "In a dream, God declared to him the secret purpose of his life and work; Dante, in wonderment, knew at last who and what he was and blessed the bitterness of his life. Tradition relates that, upon waking, he felt he had received and lost an infinite thing . . ." (*L*, 237). He will exhume the "story of a broken and scattered God" of Diodorus Siculus, only to add that "something infinite has been lost. . . . Men have lost a face, an irrecoverable face. . . . Who knows whether tonight we shall not see it in the labyrinths of our dreams and not even know it tomorrow?" (*L*, 238–39). He will paraphrase Coleridge: "In our dreams . . . images represent the sensations we think they cause; . . . we dream of a sphinx in order to explain the horror we feel" (*L*, 240). In his "Parable of Cervantes and the *Quixote*" he will conclude, "For in the beginning of literature is the myth, and in the end as well" (*L*, 242) (thereby implying the pluralism of Kafka's Prometheus, who steadfastly rejects the expectation of terminal outcomes and opts for the multiplicity of the mythic way). He will insist, in his parable of "The Witness," that ". . . one thing, or an infinite number of things, dies in every final agony . . ." (*L*, 243). In another parable on Cervantes he will say that "Don Quixote . . . senses, standing before the dead body of his enemy, that killing and engendering are divine or magical acts. . . . He knows that the dead man is illusory, the same as the bloody sword weighing in his hand and himself and all his past life and the vast gods and the universe" (*L*, 245). He will remind us, in "The Zahir," that "the words 'live' and 'dream' are rigorously synonymous" (*L*, 164). The fictions of Borges multiply their permutations tirelessly—"enigmatic circumlocutions, or 'kennings' " in which one hears the tumblers of dream and reality shifting in their great locks and engaging their secret components as if to spring open to the keys of the Borgesian mystique. In this sense, the bedeviled protagonist of "The Waiting" has written the epitaph for all artists in fiction: "He was in this act of magic when the blast obliterated him" (*L*, 168).

2

In an essay on "The Mirror of Enigmas," Borges handily furnishes the critic with an apparatus of metaphor, precedent, and learned example worthy of Maimonides the Cordovan's *Guide for the*

Perplexed, playing the critic's advocate to an undertaking which he knows to be impervious to elucidation. Beginning in his accustomed manner with "the thought that the history of the universe—and in it our lives and the most tenuous detail of our lives—has an incalculable, symbolical value" (*L,* 209), he invokes the anguish of Kafka's plebeians in "The Problem of Our Laws," or the dilemma of the child in his "Imperial Message." The anguish of both writers is clearly epistemological, hinting darkly at some scale which weighs all actions by balances unknowable to us, and at messages whose pathos is mysteriously heightened by the impossibility of our ever receiving them. Thus, Borges catches a plane of light from Arthur Machen ("The outer world . . . is a language we humans have forgotten or which we can scarcely distinguish"); flashes it scarily on a surface of De Quincey ("The least things in the universe must be secret mirrors to the greatest"); and then concentrates its total glare on the celebrated passage from I Corinthians, 13:12, which he fussily renders in two limping translations, as though he himself could not produce the Elizabethan touchstone in 1611 English: "Now we see through a glass darkly; but then, face to face: now I know in part; but then shall I know even as also I am known."

Borges then moves on to a parabolic tactic learned from Kafka and Kierkegaard—the synoptic multiplication of alternatives, the building of a labyrinth of instances. Rabbinically, pedantically, ironically, he combs the indices of Léon Bloy for six "different versions or facets" of the *speculum in aenigmate* (the "mirrors and enigmas" of St. Paul), which he arranges in parallel columns, as it were, like a kind of *Midrash.* In the first, dated June 1894, the mirror is seen as a " 'skylight through which one might submerge himself in the true Abyss, which is the soul of man. The terrifying immensity of the firmament's abysses is an illusion, an external reflection of *our own* abysses, perceived "in a mirror" ' " (*L,* 210). The second, from November of the same year, apparently concerns a fanciful meditation on the Czar as " 'the leader and spiritual father of a hundred and fifty million men. . . . In the mysterious dispositions of the Profundity, who is really Czar, who is king, who can boast of being a mere servant?' " (*L,* 210). The third, from a letter written in December, returns to Paul's " 'enigma by means of a mirror' " and maintains that " 'Everything is a symbol, even the most piercing pain. We are dreamers who shout in our sleep.' " The fourth is from May 1904. " *'Per speculum in aenigmate,* says St. Paul. We see everything backwards' " (*L,* 210–11). The fifth is from May 1908. " 'A terrifying idea of Jeanne's, about the text *Per speculum.* The pleasures of this world would be the torments of Hell, seen backwards, in a mirror' " (*L,* 211).

The sixth is dated 1912; apparently concerned with *"L'Ame de Napoléon,"* the passage is made to illuminate another of the recurring preoccupations of Borges, the theme of "precursors": "another hero—man and symbol as well—who is hidden in the future." Borges quotes two passages from Bloy: (1) " 'Every man is on earth to symbolize something he is ignorant of and to realize a particle or a mountain of the invisible' "; and (2) " 'There is no human being on earth capable of declaring with certitude who he is. No one knows what he has come into this world to do, . . . his sentiments, his ideas, or what his real name is. . . . History is an immense liturgical text where the iotas and the dots are worth no less than the entire verses or chapters, but the importance of one and the other is indeterminable and profoundly hidden' " (*L,* 211).

The upshot of this tactic and these examples vindicates all those convinced that Borges is writing synoptically rather than "serially": the *simultaneity* of his six contexts not only constitutes a mode of knowledge but confirms the strategy of its magic. The insight they serve, however baffling their reversals and multiplications, composes like a mosaic in the "mirror" of the intended "enigma." In his own words, the six contexts taken together constitute an "angelic cryptography" for a "hieroglyphical world," and support a conviction which profoundly concerns the nature of all fictions, whether of art or of reality. They align Borges among the "heresiarchs" who "permute" words, "add up the numerical value of letters, consider their form, observe the small letters and capitals, seek acrostics and anagrams and perform other exegetical rigors" (*L,* 212).

In this respect, at least, Borges' position differs markedly from the enigmatic pluralism of Kafka's "Prometheus." It is as though, committed to the premise—impenetrable to Kafka—that all legend contains a "substratum of truth" and therefore must founder on the "inexplicable mass of rock," Borges has found a magical way out that turns him into an exegete of the inexplicable. With an incandescence unthinkable to Kafka's Prometheans, he passes on to that "substratum" of numbers, letters, astrological and orthographical "rigors" where the "truths" of myth may be engaged as cryptograms interpretable by the elite, to whom it is given to crack codes without ever disclosing their "message" and to triumph over the "rock" by becoming custodians of the priestly tablets.

The effect is to deny the relevance of manifest meanings to the world: "It is doubtful that the world has a meaning. . . . *No man knows who he is.*" According to Borges, it is the purpose of fiction to render that ignorance *intimate;* to hold the mirror up, not to nature, but to the dream of the heart's conjunction with the world; to compel the heart to take up the "burden of the Mystery," each out of his own dream, and imagine the common dream of the world's knowledge. Like Kafka's questioner in "The Imperial Message," each may "sit at [his] window when evening falls and dream it to [himself]." Knowledge is a multiplication of instances, images, illusions (Blake's "minute particulars of mankind," or Yeats's "Path of the Chameleon"). Its tension lies in their co-existence, its insight in their contradictions. Only in a fictive complex of this nature can any "man know who he is"; and only by these signs can his "character" be absorbed into his collective humanity. Literature is greatest, "truest," most archetypal, when it is most enigmatic.

3

In this sense, the total canon of Jorge Luis Borges constitutes a "synopticon" of parables, a Kabbalah or *Book of Splendor* which repeats the lineaments of that Cosmological Man in whose limbs, says the *Zohar,* are incorporated all the attributes that pertain to being a man at large in an inscrutable cosmos. One is tempted to say of it, as Rabbi Simeon ben Yohai says of the hidden meaning of the Torah, "How precisely balanced are the upper and lower

230

worlds!" and then add, "The garment is made up of tales and stories; but we are bound to penetrate beyond." [6] Touched at any point, Borges' work gives back the same geometrical pathos, "vertiginous symmetries," the same content of knowledge, the same dynamic of contradiction and diversity, the same secret, as though a single enigma were central to all, and all lines intersected at the center. It is as though Borges wrote of "forking paths," "circular ruins," lotteries, libraries, compasses, searches, miracles, spheres, avatars, mirrors, selves—gave us "everything and nothing"—in order to maximize the Unknown and confront it as we cannot in reality.

One case in point must suffice: for this purpose I have chosen the fable of "The God's Script." The prevailing image of "The God's Script" is *scribal,* if not actually orthographic. Its concern is with the *written* rather than the "whispered" word of Kafka's "The News of the Building of the Wall," and the writing is literally "hieroglyphical"—a "god's script," or a priest's. In this sense, it recapitulates the themes of "Tlön, Uqbar, Orbis Tertius" and "The Library of Babel"—the search for an "Ursprache," or absolute of gnomic discourse, which would contain in its very orthography the signature of the Unknown, which is also the signature of Borges himself.

It is significant that the place and the circumstance chosen for "The God's Script" is a prison—a circle divided by a wall, on one side of which sits, ponders, "perishes," a captive "magician of the pyramid," and on the other side of which a caged jaguar paces. Both are reiterated motifs of Borges' "destiny" as poet and artificer of the Labyrinth; but the conjunction of jaguar and magician is the uniquely mystifying economy of the present tale. Readers of Borges have long been familiar with the omnipresence of the feline principle—in its savage state—in the fictions and poems of his *oeuvre.* If writers can be assigned to tutelary animals, as totems of the scribal mysteries, the jaguar or tiger [7] is the sign of Jorge Luis Borges, as unmistakably as the burro presides over the fictions of

6. *Zohar: The Book of Splendor,* ed. Gershom Scholem (New York, 1963), pp. 121–22.
7. *"Tigre"* is also the local Argentine word for jaguar.

Juan Ramón Jiménez and the bull over the domain of Greek tragedy, or, for that matter, Blake's "Tyger" over the prophecies of
Golgonooza. Nor will readers of Kafka have to be reminded of the
curious coincidence of three different parables which similarly un-
leash the "animal in the synagogue," the "leopards in the temple,"
and the tiger in the "training cage" of Burson, to stalk the unknown
in feral ambiguity. All are heraldic beasts of the pre-verbal, guard-
ing the fictive way.

The track of the tiger is seen again and again in the fictions of
Borges. It is written into the total fable of Borges by Borges the
poet, in the "three tigers" of "The Other Tiger," where it would
appear that the "third tiger" is specifically enlisted for the fictive
mysteries of "The God's Script":

> We'll hunt for a third tiger now, but like
> The others this one too will be a form
> Of what I dream, a structure of words, and not
> The flesh and bone tiger that beyond all myths
> Paces the earth. (*SP*, 131)

It is seen again in the conclusion of Borges' "New Refutation of
Time": "Time is the substance I am made of. . . . It is a tiger
which destroys me, but I am the tiger . . ." (*L*, 234). It recurs in
the guise of the "infinite Tiger" of the Muslim Fakir of "The
Zahir": "This tiger was composed of many tigers in the most vertiginous fashion: it was traversed by tigers, scored by tigers, and
it contained seas and Himalayas and armies which seemed to reveal still other tigers" (*L*, 162). It stalks through the memory of
Otto Dietrich zur Linde of the "Deutsches Requiem": "I can still
repeat from memory many hexameters from that superb poem
Tse Yang, Painter of Tigers, which is, as it were, streaked with
tigers, overburdened and crisscrossed with transversal and silent
tigers."

The jaguar of "The God's Script" belongs among the "silent
tigers"; indeed, its posture seems heraldic, as well as hermetic, as
if to give a certain opulence of design to an otherwise abstract and
vortical composition. For Tzinacán, the magician of the pyramid
of Qahalom, it seems to constitute no threat as, say, does the double

door of Frank R. Stockton's "The Lady or the Tiger?" Indeed, Tzinacán comes to dwell on the presence of the jaguar last of all, among the many "anxieties" which "consume" him; and when he does so, he remembers him piously and "with pity" as "one of the attributes of the god." For a fleeting moment, one remembers the avidity of the leopards in Kafka's parable who "break into the temple and drink to the dregs what is in the sacrificial pitchers"; but these leopards also "become part of the ceremony" in a sacramental act of compassion.

The attention of Tzinacán, however, is fixed on other matters—terminal and eschatological matters, ultimately to be polarized, as the title suggests, in the calligraphy of a "single magical sentence," a "formula of fourteen words," "a single word," a "script" or alphabet of letters, or in a "single sound." All are recognizable permutations of the writer's predicament in the presence of the closure of *language*—a *written* language whose relation to knowledge as such still eludes the understanding—hence, a "prison."

Borges quickly dispenses with the "lateral" exigencies of his story. Time is at once excised from his fiction ("I have lost count of the years") and the antecedent circumstances, or what remains of them as "history," speedily dwindle to a point: "On the eve of the burning of the pyramid," the magician was tortured, his god was overturned, and he "awoke in this prison from which I shall not emerge in mortal life" (*L*, 170). The remainder of the tale, vortical as Poe's "Descent into the Maelstrom," concerns the speculative anguish of the protagonist—the attempt on the part of Tzinacán to arrive at some terminal datum of knowledge by the magic of intellect. Its development would have to be called labyrinthine, for unlike Poe's rider of the Maelstrom, pitting his powers of ratiocination against a spatio-temporal deadline which steadily narrows the cycles of his descent by discernible laws of momentum, the predicament of Tzinacán is timeless, directionless, *stilled*. The mathematics of centripetality, so intriguing to Poe, accomplish nothing for the magician. His thinking is neither syllogistic nor serial; it is not even circular. It is, like the thought process in a Borges parable, synoptic and adventitious. It can be said to

233

proceed in phases, bursts, ricochets; or else it spreads, like ink in blotting paper, and is suddenly folded over to reveal the enigmatic symmetry of the psyche.

The phases of Tzinacán's thinking, tangential and helic by turns, can be retraced as a kind of diagram of the enigmatic process. The first impulse of "the architect of the pyramid" is, understandably, a search for order and number; "the order and the number of stone-carved serpents or the precise form of a medicinal tree." Hours later, however, he senses that he is "approaching the threshold of an intimate recollection" as a "traveler feels a quickening in the blood." Instead of pressing for an order already present in art and nature, he "begins to perceive," in the free-flowing proliferations of his own psyche, "the outline of a recollection. It was the tradition of the god"—a god who "on the first day of Creation wrote a magical sentence" with the power to ward off all evil. As Borges goes on to explain, the god's sentence is secretive, infallible, and terminal—one of those "messages" Kafka ascribes to the Emperor of his parable, irresistibly intended for a single, elect listener, the destined vessel of the god's enigma. Of it, Tzinacán can only say, "No one knows where it was written nor with what characters, but it is certain that it exists, secretly, and that a chosen one shall read it." And he grasps at once that his own "destiny as the last priest of the god" is the "privilege of intuiting the script."

There follows what is described (characteristically) as "a kind of vertigo." Its appropriateness is at once apparent from the spiraling movement of his thought—the vatic "spreading of the inks" of sensibility and the intuitional thrust of his "magic." For a moment, he feels lost in the enormity of the Unknowable: "the generations of cereals, of grasses, of birds, of men." He remembers ancient forms, "any one of which would be the speech of the god"—mountains, rivers, empires, stars, "mutations and havoc." At the conclusion of the cycle, however, he is ready to predicate a "magic written on my own face, perhaps I myself was the end of my search" (*L*, 170).

And then he remembers the jaguar.

4

Here we have what Borges might have called a "compass point" in the labyrinth, in which excitement spreads rapidly to all sides, and all composes itself with a kind of zodiacal fatality in the "sign of the jaguar." The intricacies of Borges' speculations need not be pursued in detail. What is important is the passion with which an image, ingenious and reckless in its conjunction of the visceral and the metaphysical, is pursued to its last shock of revelation. The image is that of a jaguar as cosmos—an enormous palimpsest into whose "living skin," as into a hieratic parchment, has been inscribed the design of the god. A host of possibilities is vertiginously suggested in the paragraphs which follow: that there is a secret "order and configuration of the spots"; that the "black forms running through the yellow fur" constitute a single word, or even a single sound, a text to be deciphered, "a generic enigma," an "infinite concatenation of facts," a "divine sentence, "shadows or simulacra" of *"all, world, universe"* (*L,* 171).

At this point, parable, in its usual sense of enigmatic preachment, might be assumed to have accomplished its objectives. The remaining half of the story, however, seems bent on subverting its own closure, dislodging the structures of metaphor and allegory which are the triumph of its rational magic, magnifying chaos. The story swirls with contradictory and disjunct sensations: dream, nightmare, sleep, "indifference," suffocation, "loss," panic, death —the pathos and the dismemberment of the "heresiarch," the compulsive keeper of the heresies. The discharge is wildly visionary. One thinks of the recondite terrors of another voyeur of the hermetic way, William Butler Yeats, who under the "frenzy of the fourteenth moon," in his castle at Lough Key, became "lost in that region a cabalistic manuscript had warned me of," in which "image called up image in an endless procession and I could not choose among them with any confidence"; Yeats said he had strayed "upon the Path of the Chameleon, upon Hodos Chameliontos." [8]

Near the end of "The God's Script," Tzinacán wakes to a realiza-

8. W. B. Yeats, *Autobiographies* (New York, 1927).

tion that might be called terminal if it were not so impenetrably ambivalent. On the one hand he is aware that "more than a decipherer or an avenger, more than a priest of the god, I was one imprisoned. From the tireless labyrinth of dreams I returned as if to my home, to the harsh prison." On the other hand, he is aware he has not *"awakened to wakefulness, but to a previous dream. This dream is enclosed within another, and so on to infinity"* (*L*, 172). He blesses the jaguar, blesses his "old, suffering body," blesses all the modes of closure which he had previously sought to transcend or transpose. He is content to "let the days obliterate" him in his prison, with its incomprehensible duality of jaguar and magician.

Here again, Borges might have settled for the pittance of an edifying conclusion. What actually follows is a shaking of the total fabric of the meaning—a "union with deity," an "ecstasy," a rending of the veils, a kind of doxology of visionary assertions. The language and the imagery are conventionally apocalyptical: blazing lights, wheels, roses, circles, fires—a lyric improvisation on the mystery of "origins," causes, and effects. But the effect is oddly conclusive. It is as though, having submitted to all closures, all modes of incarnate humanity, all incarcerations, all "prisons," the wall which divided the magician from the jaguar has been dissolved. Only then does the import of Borges' conjunction of jaguar and magician become clear, and the enigma of his prison surrender its secret. The "prison" is the *prison of language,* which divides magician and jaguar as language itself divides the artist from the fictions he would create or the message he would whisper. With the dissolution of the wall, language and fiction are made one. They join in an animal mystery and embody the god's enigma as a truth of immediate knowledge.

Borges' trope for the enigma is, of course, the "sign of the tiger." His secret purpose, inscribed into a corner of his composition, like a mandala or a water-mark, promised the reader, midway in his story: "In the next cell there was a jaguar; in his vicinity I perceived a confirmation of my conjecture and a secret favor." At the conclusion of the story, the "favor" is apparent. It grips the reader

236

like an intuition that illuminates the whole character of fictive writing. It suggests that all Borges' fictions are "tigers," and all literature a "teeming labyrinth of jaguars," repeating "the generic enigma of a sentence written by the gods," each in his own spots, "the black forms running through the yellow fur," to the cursive vanishing point of man's dream of knowledge.

It is this exuberance of *unknowing,* the almost predatory gusto of his conjunction with the Beast of Enigma, which distinguishes the fictions of Borges from the fictions of Kafka. Presumably, both enact the anguish of ungratified ignorance and the malaise of the anomalous predicament. In the case of Borges, it is a vertigo whose circuitions lead to magical breakthroughs of the psyche; with Kafka, it is a *nausée,* with no exit from the windowless room or the carapace of the cockroach. Both enter a labyrinth and toil toward some act of epistemological violence which leads to a prison, a circular ruin, a bestiary, a cathedral, a lumber room, a stone quarry. Both whisper messages out of range of our hearing—with a difference, however. One feels it first as a phenomenon of *tone,* or what Herbert Tauber calls the "atmosphere of silence and taciturnity" that haunts the desolation of Kafka: the despairing cold of cathedrals, courtrooms, corridors, attics, unpeopled streets lit only by a single, enigmatic window. By contrast, the world of Jorge Luis Borges, for all its patina of Anglo-European erudition, is Byzantine in its passion for arabesque and metaphysical mosaic. As Lorca would put it, his is the provenance of the Duende, rather than the Angel or the Muse. For one, the sacred books remain sealed, the door of the Law slams shut, and the burrowing beast accomplishes marvels of self-entrenching panic. For the other, the Duende of the ambiguous points the way out toward those wheels of water and fire, the "faceless god concealed behind the other gods," and the "infinite processes that formed one single felicity," whereby Tzinacán, the magician of the pyramid, having understood all, can now understand the jaguar's inscription.

Borges/Unamuno
ANTHONY KERRIGAN

> *To dream that one exists . . . Well and good!*
> *But to be dreamt by someone else . . . !*

Jorge Luis Borges or Miguel de Unamuno? The epigraph, it so happens, belongs to the latter. But merely because he came first. For his part Borges wrote ("The Circular Ruins"): ". . . to be the projection of another man's dreams—what a feeling of humiliation, of vertigo!" (*L*, 50).

Borges has almost infinite affinities ("on the intellectual globe everything comes from everything and leads everywhere," as Valéry once remarked). But he has a special set of affinities with the forebears of his language (which is "the blood of the soul" in Unamuno's eyes), and most concretely with Miguel de Unamuno. Like Unamuno, who was Basque, Borges is a non-Castilian writing in the language of a Castilian world.

Early on, Borges penned a couple of spirited and colorful defenses of Castilian Spanish ("the language of nihilism and preachment") as spoken in America, and stoutly defended the inflnite future of "Argentine" usage. He quickly agreed, how-

238

ever, in still another piece, that local color, including Argentine local color and speech, was superfluous, drawing on the analogy that a desert work like *The Koran* characteristically contained, as Gibbon has noted, no camels. Latterly, Borges says he has begun to feel Spain as a place of infinite residence. On the last day of January 1963, he told the Madrid press as he landed in Spain for the first time since his youth, "I have the sensation of continuing to be, of having been, in some way always in Spain." And while in Madrid, he referred in a prepared speech to "The Spanish earth, where there are few things, but where each one seems to exist in a substantive and eternal way." He had, with cyclical priority, first formulated this notion some sixteen years before in the opening of his "Averroes' Search."

Parallel to a continuous and unfolding argument about the comparative merits of Castilian Spanish as spoken on the plains of Castile or on the remarkably similar plains of South America, Borges developed what seems to be an atavistic memory for, and sensory appreciation of, original English, Anglo-Saxon, while pondering the merits of its derivatives on both sides of the Atlantic. He exercised this atavistic memory to the point where it allowed him to get drunk on the epical words and run down Peru Street in Buenos Aires shouting Anglo-Saxon at the top of his voice. After the 1963 Madrid visit and his rediscovery of Spain, Borges went to England, where he soon repaired to a church in the West. "For the past nine centuries no one had prayed in the ancient language of King Harold in that tiny church. Borges, profoundly affected, recited in a proud and solemn voice the Paternoster in Anglo-Saxon." [1]

Borges discovered Unamuno early in his life; he read him and wrote to him. As far back as 1927, in *El idioma de los argentinos,* he spoke of "Don Miguel de Unamuno, the only Spaniard who feels and senses metaphysics [*"único sentidor"*] and is therefore—and because of other sensibilities—a great writer." Unamuno sensed metaphysics, truly enough, but with certain never-to-be-satisfied reservations; he "sensed" the rest of philosophy with even greater

1. María Esther Vázquez, "Everness," *TriQuarterly* 15 (Spring 1969).

239

reservations. And Borges, after him, treated philosophy in a strikingly similar way. On the imaginary planet Tlön, "the metaphysicians . . . do not seek for the truth or even for verisimilitude, but rather for the astounding. They judge that metaphysics is a branch of fantastic literature" (*L*, 10).

In his *Diario intimo* (1895–1902, published for the first time in 1970, after nearly seventy years of secrecy), Unamuno points out the virtues of meditation over thought, which simply leads to philosophy. And what is philosophy anyway?, Unamuno asks in adumbration of Borges. He answers himself: "Metaphysics, perhaps." A class of fiction, perhaps.

Unamuno and Borges both, forcibly and perforce, were using a basic Castilian Spanish. The former, a native Basque, had taken Castilian as his language by force—"by right of conquest," as he put it. The latter, an Argentine of mixed descent, declared that "willfully to desert the near-universality of Spanish . . . would be suitable only to begrudgers." Using a language that each looked upon with a certain almost foreign self-consciousness, they both also used and abused the generalizing language of philosophy to supplement their more real language of fiction. The dream and the fiction served them as well as, if not better than, their paraphrases of philosophy.

Castilian, in any case, was the language used to express their peculiar sense of infinity. Was not Castilian the language of the inner world, of mysticism—of the ecstasy among the earthen pots of Santa Teresa, of the thick-thighed quietism of Miguel de Molinos? Castilian was also the language of adventure and unreason, of the "warlike idleness" which Unamuno identified as a way of life in Castile—it was the language of the *non sequitur* and of virility, of the oxymora "conjugated" (or "inflected") by sleepless men on horseback, around a fire, and fused in the twlight of dawn. Used by cloistered monks and bookmen, Castilian hailed back to the indefinite geography of the quest. Epic journeys into the infinite arena of the New World were the natural extension of the limitless horizon of the plains of Castile. And the language began at that local level; it had the urgency of a monotonous landscape built into

240

it. Castilian was the natural-son language, the Latin bastard of the proto-pampas of Spain. It was a non-imagist, un-couple-able, monotonously voweled language of the flat tablelands—a plains language.

For most of his life, Unamuno held that Spain lived, would always live, and live more Hispanically, in the New Spain across the water. Borges seconded him in affirming that American Spanish was more alive than Peninsular Spanish—that Castilian lived better outside Castile than in it. (He told Ronald Christ in his *Paris Review* interview: "I prefer South American speech. I always have." This statement followed his rousing "America must save the [English] language.") And yet, in his terrorist attack in *Other Inquisitions* on the written style of Américo Castro, Borges seems to claim (irony within his over-all irony) that only Hispanic-Americans conserve the classic forms and words of Castilian. He takes "El Doctor Castro" to task for suggesting that the rationale for vocabulary and usage was only to be found in Spain, so that, for example, if the natives of some lost town in Castile have lost a word from their memories, it would be well for the Argentines to do likewise. Borges implies that Argentines would be best advised to act in the true tradition—and retain the word until *they* forget it.

And so in his piece on Unamuno as poet,[2] Borges, an Hispanic-American conserving the classic forms, counts himself with Unamuno among those "practicing contemporary Spanish literature." It is in this 1923 article that Borges acknowledges—more than interests shared by him and Unamuno—a peculiar debt to him. "The man Miguel de Unamuno," he wrote, "bound to his time and place, has thought all the essential thoughts." Borges was suggesting that there was no need for Unamuno to proceed to develop a body of philosophy, nor to build any structure to—or in—its name. This is hardly inconsequential praise. The very lack of structure, of positive systematic fulfillment in Unamuno's meditations, accommodated a quite "Borgesian" sense of flux. Unamuno's humble *intrahistoria,* the unrecorded flow of life in its contradictions, creations, and quotidian epiphanies, becomes for Borges, at one re-

2. "Acerca de Unamuno," *Nosotros,* 175 (December 1923).

move, the theory of "the modesty of history," a history whose dates are secret and whose path is an "inconceivable figure."

Both Hispanic writers were fascinated by the marvels of heterodoxy and heresy. Unamuno seemed appalled, Borges gladdened by the phenomena in this field of speculation. Or perhaps Unamuno was made melancholy with sympathy, Borges made euphoric with what might have been or still might be. Time had always seemed a river-in-flow in Hispanic lyricism (adumbrated by Virgil, in his "numerous Latin," as Borges remarked); but Unamuno, as Borges saw it, was the first to direct the river upstream—have it flow from an upstream after us, from an upstream of the future:

> **nocturnally the river of hours flows**
> **from its source, which is the eternal**
> **tomorrow. . . .**[3]

"The River of Hours," Borges comments, had always been the classic example of the justified equation of time with space, an equation Schopenhauer had declared "indispensable to a sure comprehension of both."

Unamuno, then, appeared to be the first to change the direction of the current. It had always flowed *toward* the future. Unamuno made it flow from the future toward us. Unamuno abused philosophy, execrating all systems based on reason alone and referring all questions back to the a-virginal ("Spinoza . . . like Kant . . . may have died a virgin"), propagating, eternity-loving total man who never could be man-as-philosopher. Borges follows down the same road, where, in the end, man is only playing a game and is neither the proof, nor the victim, of philosophy.

Both Unamuno and Borges played within the same context, the Spanish context (as opposed to the Anglo-Saxon context) of the dream. They were able to postulate indefinitely that they themselves might be the dreamed ones—not merely dreams or dreamers. But before taking up where our epigraph begins, let us note that in the same *Nosotros* piece cited above, Borges speaks of the "Hegelian configuration of Unamuno's spirit"—but only when Unamuno is considered as a prose writer, *not when he is a poet.*

3. Unamuno, *Rosario de sonetos líricos,* 88.

Borges does not favor this "Hegelian spirit," which he understands to consist of a permanent postulation of thesis/antithesis, leading in Unamuno's case to his well-known paradox ("the religiosity of atheism," "the illogic of logic," and so forth). He prefers Unamuno the poet, in whom this "Hegelian spirit" was presumably not to be found. Since, in the final analysis, Unamuno was the most un-Hegelian of men, Borges must consider him such where the context makes this obvious—in his poetry.

In truth, Unamuno was totally incapable of Hegelian synthesis: he insisted—even in his prose—on the absolute necessity for unresolvable contradiction in all things. The "tragic sense of life" is nothing but the necessary tension and agony produced in all men by the inability to resolve the inevitable, natural contradictions between reason and faith, between the head and the heart, between philosophy and passion. As regards history, there was no synthetic solution possible either. There was innate contradiction between humanity's humble "intrahistory" and the larger history of mankind which is also the history of thought, of analytic and therefore self-destructive civilization.

In presenting Unamuno as poet, Borges also gives us a Hegel, uncharacteristically bereft of his syntheses, to compare with a dialectical and Hegelian Unamuno. Further, he inverts the importance of poetry and prose for the role Unamuno played in life and literature. The exercise only emphasizes the finely casual philosophical nature of both Borges and Unamuno.

Borges points out in his 1923 essay that Unamuno affirms concepts by asserting that they cannot be negated if they are capable of being once, or ever, or so much as, asserted at all. The words would fail us—in Unamuno's view—in our denial, if we did not first possess the concept which we deny (as well as the concept "to deny"). In the early 1900's, Bertrand Russell, in his Theory of Descriptions, held that the phrase "The golden mountain does not exist" is invalid because it presumes the existence of a golden mountain which may well be no such thing, may be nothing at all. The descriptive phrase, which is considered legitimate in its place, is nihilist as far as the emotions are concerned. For his part,

Unamuno remained content to describe the passion he found native in man—the passion forever to be and to be more oneself forever, and to be others, the Other, as well.

Borges goes on to say that Unamuno should not affirm something merely because it has been denied. But it will remain a fascinating pastime for Borges himself, in his fond speculations on the legitimacy and possible corollaries (even when they never come to fruition) of all the frustrated and denied heresies which sprinkle his work, to affirm and even dramatize what others have renounced.

In his "Vindication of the False Basilides," Borges writes: "I am aware that there have been many who have denied Ireneus' account of the cosmogony of Basilides, who have invalidated it, but I suspect that this disordered revision of defunct dreams may still admit of a dream which, for all we know, was never dreamed by any dreamer whatever." If the dream were not previously dreamed, Borges would dream it now, dream the possible triumph of the Basilidean heresy, of a victory of the Gnostics over the Church, which held them to be a scandal and an abomination.

For Unamuno's taste also the description of a concept (preferably of one officially denied) would most naturally take the form of a fiction, a dream-fiction, a novel—the novel of oneself in book form or in life form (life-as-one-creates-it, the *"vivencia"* postulated by his friend and correspondent Ortega y Gasset). In describing this peculiar novelistic view, the Spaniard-in-America José Ferrater Mora, biographer of Unamuno's vital philosophy, has observed that human death, for instance, is not really a valid term: "human death" does not exist, but only the death of each person. A novel, therefore, will provide a truer description than any chapter of philosophy of how a person himself dies, dies "for himself." For it is death "from oneself and for oneself" which characterizes "human death as compared to all other forms of death." [4]

Unamuno wrote his novel of himself—and of his own death—in his *Cómo se hace una novela* (The Making of a Novel, or How Is a Novel Made?, depending on the reading of Unamuno's equivocal

4. Unamuno, *El sentido de la muerte* (Buenos Aires, 1947).

punctuation). On the last page the reader, who is the exiled man Unamuno himself, after buying a certain book on a Paris quay, reads in the words of the author that he will die—along with the author—when he reaches the last page. Here Unamuno, as author, asks: "Reader, you who have come this far, are you really alive?" Does he thus beg the question, or does he thereby postulate that there is no such question; does he not simply suggest that the question—or answer—is beside the point, suggesting, too, that we are all caught up in a dream state? In his story "The South," Borges presents the man Dahlmann, who had suffered an accident of a kind apparently not unknown to the author himself. Dahlmann goes out into the pampas, into the brainless night (is he dreaming?) with a-never-to-be-known antagonist, to die in a knife fight —dying as he had lived, an amateur player in an immortal drama or dream: "if he had been able to choose then, or to dream his death, this would have been the death he would have chosen or dreamt" (*F,* 174).

The truest testaments from these two meditative Spanish bookmen are necessarily in their fictions. Unamuno practiced the novel, and he initiated the "novel of one's self" as well as the novel of the Other. He also kept a semi-lyrical gloss on his reading (even his philosophical reading), much as Borges was later to do; it constituted *his* Theory of Descriptions. Borges became interested in the brief histories of metaphor, glosses on legend and on deviant belief (Unamuno was similarly moved by all creeds before they became dogmas). To Unamuno's novel of the Other and I, Borges added (in many guises and disguises) his Borges and I.

There is a curious biological, physiognomical totality to the characters in both men's fiction. Joaquín Monegro, in Unamuno's *Abel Sánchez,* is no evolutionary character, but a man obsessed with jealousy, who needs no other emotion. Rather, he *is* jealousy. And Funes, the memorious (who will contribute a better adjective?)—what has he to do with anything but his memory? He *is* memory—or insomnia, or the prisoner of them both. These entities of "fiction" are true, real, in a world which exists because of them, and whose creators exist because of them, or by the same token.

Since they are nothing but jealousy or memory, they are also almost nothing—with the implicit potential of the inchoate.

Pirandello wrote *Six Characters in Search of an Author* (1921) after Unamuno's *Mist* (*Niebla*, 1914), wherein the protagonist, Augusto Pérez, turns on the author, Unamuno, and demands to know by what right he plans to kill him off. Unamuno, after denying "his" character the right even to commit suicide, suddenly doubts whether or not he himself has any more rights than the invented protagonist. And Borges, relating the story of the golem invented by a rabbi in Prague, asks gently whether someone else has not invented the inventive rabbi. (That characters should get free of their authors is something of a commonplace since Unamuno and Pirandello; for example, in the remarkably underrated *At Swim Two Birds*—a novel about a man writing a novel about characters who get free of their creator—by Brian O'Nolan, who got free of his characters by signing his work Flann O'Brien, Myles na Gopaleen, and Cruiskeen Lawn.) Borges enters a demurrer along the way, as is his wont, noting that "to judge that life is a novel is as adventurous as thinking it is a colophon or an acrostic."[5]

In all the life-is-a-dream commentary in English, from Shakespeare to Edgar Allan Poe, the point is made that we are such stuff as dreams are made on, or that all we seem is but a dream within a dream. Life, in short, is theatre. Shelley, setting eschatology aside, writes that Adonais has awakened from the dream of life. Browning, morally condemning life, like any of a certain type of Christian, calls life, which Joyce amplified to include history, an insane dream. But Browning would have us awake, and so would Joyce. So, of course, would Calderón in his *Life Is a Dream,* in the Spanish tradition, and so would Santa Teresa. But Unamuno, and then Borges, both wonder (Unamuno, desperately; Borges, deviously) whether we have anything whatsoever to do with molding and imagining life—either in terms of dreams or dreamers or (and herein is the essential and annihilative doubt) as dreamed.

Not until after Borges, after Unamuno, does it come naturally

5. Borges, *Sur,* No. 129.

for someone to write—as does, for example, the Yorkshire-poet-in-Canada, Robin Skelton (after his wife "eases her corset down")
—that

> **I sleep**
> **heavily as God sleeps**
> **who dreamed us all**

—suggesting possible procreation of further dream states.

To go back to the beginning, Unamuno is made somewhat desperate by the idea of our epigraph, "But to be dreamed by someone else . . . !" Borges finds the same suspicion "humiliating," "vertiginous." And yet, although their reactions differ in quality and pitch, their preoccupation with the idea of powerlessness, of the oppression of a dreaming universe, is equally severe. Against the inscrutability of such suspicions, Unamuno and Borges have no defense. There is no moderation, no control, which can prevent repetitions. For Borges it is mirrors and procreation which are the abominations—signs of repetitious immortality. Still, one cannot ignore the repetitions; one cannot forget that the world is a series of copies with man among the series. The *intrahistoria* of Unamuno and the modest history of one life's aimless steps in Borges place both authors beyond the pale of inconsequence. "One thing," says Borges, "does not exist: Oblivion." There is no *"olvido,"* no oblivion; there is no way to circumvent

> **. . . the shadows in the glass**
> **Which, in between the day's two twilights, you**
> **Have scattered by the thousands, or shall strew**
> **Henceforward in the mirrors that you pass.** ("Everness," *SP*, 187) [6]

Unamuno, too, thought there was no forgetting. In the Gothic cathedral of León in 1905, Unamuno discovered that every prayer ever uttered there, as well as longings never uttered, every secret desire, every secret of the confessional, every loving importunity whispered (in the Spanish fashion) to a girl in church, were all still there—just as, "in the sounding box of a guitar [adumbrations

---

6. It is interesting that, twenty-eight years before Borges' far more subtle sonnet, Pablo Neruda, who *wanted* to forget death, published a "Sonata" in which he admits that *"No Hay Olvido"* (There Is No Forgetting).

of the guitar in Borges], in its very entrails, all the notes ever struck on it lie sleeping. . . . In the same way, if all the sentiments sleeping in the womb of the cathedral, that stone guitar, were to awake . . . the cathedral would be brought down. . . ." [7]

"No man has died in time, no woman, no, none of the dead." This is a thought common to Unamuno and Borges, though taken in this case from Borges. Unamuno has repeatedly written that nothing which once existed ever ceased to exist in its own character, as it had always been. Thus the mind becomes too crowded, and mirrors serve only to multiply us. Unamuno had fled them before Borges reiterated (and he spoke as a near-blind man who never showed himself much loath to blindness) that mirrors were monstrous, eternal, destroying oblivion, including the oblivion which Funes sought. They exercised the double fascination of no surcease and of immortality:

> **. . . fame, that reflection**
> **Of dreams in the dream of another**
> **Mirror . . . ("Spinoza," SP, 193)**

The Seine, for Unamuno, in his novel of death-on-the-last-page, was a mirror, and he longed to throw himself into it. Borges, blind, need not look into mirrors, but Unamuno, in real life, fled them (just as a contemporary, Ramón Pérez de Ayala, also fled them— though he had been in and of the world enough to serve in London as last ambassador of the last Spanish Republic and had written a score of acceptable novels—and in his own last days refused ever to see himself reflected in one). Unamuno and Pérez de Ayala fled them before Beckett, as scriptwriter, filmed a film called *Film* in which the seeing eye refused, finally, to be seen by itself. Unamuno's contemporary, Antonio Machado, wrote:

> **The eye you see**
> **is not an eye because you see it**
> **but an eye because it sees you . . . ,[8]**

but Unamuno and Borges, and Beckett too, qualified that thought with the notion that the "you" might well be *yourself*. To see your-

---

7. *Cf.* Unamuno, *The Life of Don Quixote and Sancho,* trans. Anthony Kerrigan (Princeton, 1967), p. 203.
8. Machado, *Campos de Castilla* (1912).

self—put together piece by piece in a dream, perhaps coming apart piece by piece—was to know the final truth of your own radical nonexistence.

Borges raised the level of these dread suspicions by suggesting that the greatest man of all, Shakespeare, was the sum of Nobody. This was a compulsory suspicion which had always attracted certain lesser pre-Borgesians, but Unamuno, in his magnificent chapter-by-chapter gloss of the book which involved both author and "fictional" character, had already caused Don Quixote to beget Cervantes. Unamuno had even previously pronounced himself on Shakespeare, before Borges' remarkable discovery that Shakespeare was *Nobody*. And Unamuno had added to the intuition that Shakespeare was no one the belief "that Hamlet, Macbeth, King Lear or Othello created Shakespeare, rather than he them." Unamuno insists that he means no figure of speech, but is expounding his "agonic doctrine." [9] And in his story of Don Sandalio, chess player, he gives us a man who is totally empty, a character of whom we know nothing. As the poet Pedro Salinas pointed out, his "human activity outside the realm of chess disappears in impenetrable shadow, so that he embodies precisely the possibility of everything, of being nothing." Napoleon, speaking as a man from Nowhere on Everything, called poetry *"la science creuse"*—"the void science." And Unamuno, the poet, proffers us a novel which is, as Salinas remarks,

like a novel of a novel which might have been ... and the hollow which Unamuno so masterfully forms with his character ... constitutes an incitement to fill it in with a thousand possible contents, and constitutes an incomplete creation, open to all continuations or continuity.[10]

The Spanish mystics had already, some time before Unamuno, refined the sense of Nothingness in such admonitions as the reverberating sentence of Fray Juan de los Angeles: "Be nought, and thou shalt be mightier than aught that is!" (Here again, as regards the perfect Nought, the Church itself, in its early green days of mythologizing, had come upon a counter for the perfect Nothing

9. Cf. *The Agony of Christianity*, IV (in press).
10. Pedro Salinas, "Tres aspectos de Unamuno," *Literatura española siglo XX* (Madrid, 1970).

—in the communion wafer. It had invented this perfect nought, Nought, *Nada,* of a ritual wafer in the form of a sphere: tasteless —"melodramatically tasteless," writes Lawrence Durrell—tiny, lacking any "color," and yet containing *Nada menos que todo un Hombre:* Nothing less than a whole Man: "your Man, so!") From Fray Juan de los Angeles to Borges is a large step in time, but not when the mystic's intimations had been continued down through Spanish literature across the pages of Unamuno's *Tragic Sense of Life,* so that Borges could readily imagine or find—in the language of Castile—that Shakespeare was "mightiest" precisely because he was "not."

That the nihilist negative leads to the highest good was an early Spanish "discovery," most preposterously stated in the Spanish tongue—as witness the quietist Miguel de Molinos, who postulated that we must detach ourselves from all things, *including God Himself,* to attain godliness. For "Nothingness [*Nada*] is the way to reach the high state of a re-formed mind, the highest good. . . ." And ". . . only the soul that attains to losing itself succeeds in finding itself." [11]

Borges adds and expatiates upon a Nowhere, as well as a Nothing (in 1961 he wrote a preface to a book by "Ulysses Nobody"). He traces the metaphor's history in his quintessential "The Fearful Sphere of Pascal." [12] In this piece, a succinct history of a key metaphor in Western thought, Borges takes St. Bonaventure's description of *God* as a "circle of which the center is everywhere and the circumference is nowhere," through its variation in Giordano Bruno's "the center of the *universe* is everywhere and the circumference nowhere." Tracing the thought from Xenophanes of Colophon to Pascal, Borges shows the latter applying it to nature, a "fearful" thought opening the abyss before him, so that he had written "Nature is a fearful [the adjective later struck] sphere, whose center is everywhere and whose circumference is nowhere."

The "color of seed" is an old refrain in Spanish,

11. *Guía espiritual,* 20:187 and 18:176 (Madrid, 1676).
12. The adjective "fearful' was added to the original title by the present writer in his own translation of the essay—a license which was based on the fact that Borges, reading from the MS pages of the Tourneur edition of Pascal, discovered that Pascal had started to write this adjective.

> **The brook's without water,**
> **the bull without breed,**
> **without shade grows the poplar**
> **the color of seed.**

So Camilo José Cela puts it in his positive compilation of negatives in his book on Castile, *Viaje a la Alcarria* [13] (the vagabond wandering nowhere; the peg-legged man who goes fishing with his "one leg the less"—and drowns; the villages which are left over from some other History; the births as pointless as deaths). But it is precisely the "color of seed" (the color of the Castilian plains— or the Argentine pampas), this nihilist seed the color of mysticism, which engenders endless associations, endless negations. *Nada,* Nothing, is here all One, an all-encompassing Nought or Whole, a self-sufficient Forever. And all books are one book, the *same* book.

Unamuno had one obsessive passion, and held on to it in several works. Borges acknowledges his own repetitiousness. The Spaniard Quevedo enjoyed minting new coins, and so he minted coins but without changing the coinage; the images were all old effigies which he delighted to refurbish, or even to copy, since he held it useless to improve on the perfect. María Rosa Lida de Malkiel notes [14] that, faced with Virgil as Virgil was with Homer, Borges judges it frivolous to vary on the model—that in transporting intact the already perfect to "the maternal language," he reveals that he has consulted with the original "distractedly," merely cultivating or recultivating its unattended loveliness. She also notes Borges' fondness for Emerson's transcendentalist theory that one single person had written all the books extant, there being such a central unity to them all that their author is undeniably singular. José Luis Ríos Patrón says [15] that Borges simply transposes from book to book, from piece to piece, "an author devoid of amazement or rebellion." And when Borges has Pierre Menard re-do *Don Quixote,* Menard has no occasion to improve upon a single word.

Unamuno, the agitator, the *agent provocateur,* the moralist, was disquieted by books (any thought of his set in motion its own

13. (Madrid–Palma de Mallorca, 1958).
14. In her *Contribución al estudio de las fuentes literarias de Jorge Luis Borges* (Buenos Aires, 1952).
15. In *Jorge Luis Borges* (Buenos Aires, 1955).

disquiet): "In the end, the human race will fall exhausted at the foot of libraries, entire forests having been leveled to make the paper stored in the libraries in the form of books; at the foot of museums . . . which have been erected for bequeathing to . . . whom?" Unamuno could not leave the future alone, even if it was our source. In a story by Borges, this Library of Libraries, this Library of Babel, was merely "The universe (which others call the Library). . . ." The Library has grown, in Babel, to be as large as Unamuno's repositories of books: a universe. Strictly speaking, Borges says, "one single volume should suffice." For his part, Unamuno, too, believed that everything ever conceived will one day live, or rather has never ceased living—the one book of the history of the world. Among contradictory texts, Borges cites in his "New Refutation of Time" an Eastern refutation: the man of a past moment has lived, but does not live nor will live. If there is any life at all, any "life" as we conceive it when we grant it a holy meaning, it can only be eternal—since any known life delimited forever in past, present, or future, totally spent or to be spent, is not "life." One of the most authentic of Borgesians, of the voices speaking as witnesses for Borges, María Esther Vázquez, holds in her study of "Everness" that Borges' "prophetic memory" is not simply a description of "divine timelessness" (it is certainly not merely an oxymoron), but rather that this recollected prescience is also "his personal self projected." It is his, and the Other's and Shakespeare's, history which he "predicts," reenacts; in other words, the history which is Nobody's and Everyman's. (Borges himself speaks with equivocation of this "agreeable faith," that every man is all men and that there is no one who is not the universe, in his prologue to Emerson's *Representative Men.*)

It is perhaps curious that in the world of Borges one feels the lack of that drive so crucial in Unamuno: an absence in the world of Borges of the sexual urge to best beat, or even borrow, time by procreation. Borges' verse does, however, appear more sensory and sentient than Unamuno's. In one of Borges' verses the speaker finds "a fair girl, already mine," in a house like an Angel, merely by pushing back the screen of iron and entering the

252

patio—an entry both yielding and sensual. The patio, too, in its endless shifts in light and dark, as well as in its shining brightness under the moon, suggests a responsive mirror to the universe. Borges' poetic speaker also renders himself trembling like a flame as "immediate joy pales into that past." But the Borges who portrays emotions of sentiment in such a deliberately, particularly analogous way will feel no passion to live on, but only an urge for sexual dalliance. He devotes the verse reconstructions of his youth to sweet wastes of time, without the hope of outwitting the sequence by making claim on the memory of the blood.[16]

The furious passion of Unamuno to live on in flesh and blood is at the opposite, passionate extreme from dalliance. Lineages in Borges are aristocratic blood games, purely parallel strains of names, but not, further, reproducible, so that, despite his use of his familial past, Borges has nowhere made a play in the manner of Unamuno, who wrote a death notice for himself (*"esquela"*) in which all the patronymics mix with all the matronymics in the final announcement of who Unamuno—and the Other—was, or added up to, in the imperfect un-novelistic world. Ancestors, as for the Chinese in the "Garden of Forking Paths," are arbitrary counters, not containers for the continuation of the flesh. In short, the appetite to bite into time differentiates Unamuno and Borges; for Borges, metaphysics remains a branch of fantastic literature.

Another Hispanic-American (in the broad sense), George Santayana, thought eternity a dilemma, one to be solved if Time is to exist: either there is an eternity or there is no Time at all. The search for time, for eternity, is an implacable metaphysical need, whether Time flows toward us from the future or not.

Time is fell (felon) death; for Borges it is a knife in a drawer (as in his poem "The Dagger"), crying out for use in its temporary uselessness, crying out to be used to the end it was made and intended for—a refutation, of a sort, of a present time. For Unamuno, who preceded him in the same thought (though the

16. Though Borges' Gnostic in "Tlön" is not "dallying" when he proclaims that "Mirrors and fatherhood are abominable" because they multiply and extend the illusion of the universe.

thought is not overt in Unamuno), it was a loaded pistol: "There is nothing worse than a loaded pistol left lying idle in some corner," he wrote in *The Tragic Sense of Life* (Chapter XI).

We return to our epigraph with a parallel epigraph:

And what if everything were but a dream of G., and G. were to wake some day? Would he recall his own dream?

Unamuno completes the "G." in this quotation, spelling out "God," but Borges also writes of a creator, more terrestrial, who dreams someone else—almost a clay Adam himself, the red Adam of the Gnostics, a dream Adam; but this creator may in turn be dreamed —is, in fact, as he realizes one day, altogether dreamed: ". . . someone else was dreaming him" ("The Circular Ruins").

Unamuno had already thought that we might be dreaming others, that we ourselves might be dreamers of others: ". . . do we not perhaps sustain some alien well-being with our suffering?" But for Unamuno there was the additional danger mentioned above: ". . . what if everything were but a dream of God and God were to wake some day? Would he recall his own dream?" And yet Unamuno thought he must believe, perhaps in order to *deserve* to believe, that "God does not exist, but rather super-exists, and He is sustaining our existence by existing us, making us exist." Unamuno rewrote this thought endlessly, like an obsessive. Even in his letters hither and yon, as in one to Walter Starkie in 1921: "And I say that we are a dream of God. God is dreaming us and woe to that day when he awakes: God is dreaming. It is better not to think of that but continue to dream that God is dreaming."

And now that we have two epigraphs, why not a third?

. . . the hint that the Almighty is also in search of Someone, and that Someone of Someone above him (or Someone simply indispensable and equal) and so on to the End (or rather, Endlessness) of Time, or perhaps cyclically.

Borges or Unamuno? The Almighty is directly cited. And it is from the pen of Borges, "The Approach to al-Mu'tasim." Gnosticism apart, do we not find here a common Hispanic theme of God's need?—a theme which in Unamuno includes God's needs for us? Unamuno postulates that such a need complements the compassion we feel for Him, the pity, eventually the Love. *Pitié pour Dieu.* God suffers, and hence needs us. He needs us so desperately that

He becomes, as Borges proposes later, not the crucified Jesus but the more abominable Judas—the lowest of the low. Hence the self-abased Saviour. Unamuno had already called Jesus necessarily "the most guilty." For Unamuno wrote in *Tragic Sense of Life:* "The innocent Christ, since he felt the intensity of guilt most, was in a certain sense the most guilty." Borges' Judas serves as a more obvious Saviour. (In his book on Judas, however, the Israeli writer Igal Mossinsohn postulates that Barabbas was the true leader in the movement to crucify Jesus—with the consent of Jesus—and that Judas was a mere soldier carrying out orders, no more guilty than a Storm Trooper. The revolt thus planned was a national conspiracy, something in the manner of Borges' idea of revolutionary Ireland as one vast conspiratorial theatre.) Where Unamuno thought that God needs us as we need Him, reciprocally, Borges goes a step further and feels that God needs more than us—He needs also some higher god or gods. (Again, we omit the Gnostic connotations.) Moreover, Borges at one stage suspects that "God has lost Himself, and the despair in our eyes seeks Him." The relationship remains mutual. If God is to find Himself, we shall have to find Him—for His sake as well as our own.

As for final death, at least *one* Borges is dubious. But there are so many Borgeses, as we see from the anti-nihilist proof offered by his own testimony. He first prophetically memorizes (or memorializes) his own previous nonexistence or future nonexistence as Borges, asserting that if there had ever been another Borges, then there has never been a single or singular one at all. But thereafter, writing further in the novel of himself, he reveals that there have been at least two.

Unamuno, *one* Unamuno (whose unity the name suggests but cannot responsibly promise) was more forthright, more sanguine. If life is a dream, so is death.

> **[B]ut if one dreams
> of dying, death is a dream.**

Death, in short, can also be dreamed. By oneself, or by Another; by an Author. Calderón is turned on his head, literally, and not merely dialectically. Death is a dream.

255

The greater voice:
on the poetry of
Jorge Luis Borges
JOHN C. MURCHISON

Not much has been written about Borges' poetry in Spanish, and still less in English.† Borges himself has done a fair job of belittling his own production, dismissing most of it with a sad, slightly contemptuous gesture; but it is this very depreciation that illuminates certain aspects of his poetry. We cannot, after all, lightly gloss over Borges' poetic production; that privilege may be his but not ours, since the poetry itself looms large in his work, and steadily. His first book of poems, *Fervor de Buenos Aires* (Fervor of Buenos Aires), was published in 1923, shortly after his return from Europe; his latest, a mixture of prose and verse—like the earlier *El hacedor* (The Maker)[1]—*Elogio de la sombra* (In Praise of Darkness), appeared in 1969. Over the intervening forty-six years, several others appeared—*Luna de enfrente* (Moon Across the Way), *Cuaderno San Martín* (San Martín Copybook), *El otro, el mismo* (The Self and the Other), *Para las seis cuerdas* (For the Guitar)—

† This article was written for publication in 1970. Since then, of course, Seymour Lawrence has brought out a splendid edition, *Jorge Luis Borges: Selected Poems 1923–1969* (New York, 1971), to which I refer the reader.

1. Published in English as *Dreamtigers*.

well over two hundred poems, and Borges is still going strong. For a writer who professes to be no more than a versifier, such zeal in versifying seems suspect. One can legitimately claim that Borges is, in fact, being too modest in his own appraisal, and even a cursory glance at the poems is enough to convince one that here is a rich terrain indeed, and virtually unexplored.

But Borges' modesty is a major clue to understanding his poetry. It is a peculiar modesty, grounded not only in character but also in metaphysics. Time and again, Borges has stated that he would like to be remembered as the creator of a few good lines; even in his own terms, this, as we shall see, is asking a great deal.

Borges' fictions very often are, in effect, parables of the creative process, its possibilities and limitations. Stories—meditations—on the writing of stories, they deal at heart with the power of the word to capture and re-create a reality which might be termed "objective" when it lies within. This, which may seem no more than a quibbling way to speak about "reality" and "fantasy," nevertheless reflects a vital point; for Borges, *both* are equally real. If "the fantastic" seems a quality inseparable from Borges, it is owing precisely to the fact that fantasy is as real to him, as immediate and pervasive, as a blade of grass is to Whitman.

The problem, then, lies in using words in order to re-create an ambient state, whether objective or subjective. For that re-creation to be effected, the *anima* becomes the decisive factor, the telling element without which the re-creation is stillborn. And the search for that *anima,* that spirit, is what moves Borges, and brings him at last to the realization that the spirit, not the poet, is the creator of the living lines. The potential of enormous power lies within the word, and thus poetry, dealing more closely even than prose with the power of words, has always been a predominant mode of expression for Borges.[2] Indeed, so vital is poetry to Borges that even in the earliest poems we come across the idea of poetry as an all-encompassing phenomenon which antedates the poem and culls

---

2. Between 1929 and 1943, it is true, Borges wrote exactly five poems; but considering the fourteen-year gap, the extent of his poetic output is all the more remarkable.

from it some of that poetry, while at the same time making the poet aware of the encompassing existence of Poetry. Tacitly, these poems reflect a Platonic idea of Poetry as an archetype from which all poems derive, and are thereafter more or less perfect reflections of the whole; though never quite perfect, since by their nature they are limited in time and space, in opposition to the archetype which necessarily transcends these limitations. The heart of the matter— what Borges is *about*—lies in the adjustment of the poem to Poetry, in the transcendence of the work of man, and thus of man himself. In the splendid, early "Vanilocuencia" (Vain Words), from *Fervor de Buenos Aires,* Borges says:

> **The city is within me like a poem**
> **I've not been able to catch in words.**[3]

Seen within this context, his love for that city, for Buenos Aires, grows beyond the proportions of the parochial; the city is a surrounding symbol of Poetry, an endless spatial dimension which indeed spontaneously brings the endless temporal dimension—and the concomitant awareness of a limited self on the part of the poet —into play:

> **On one hand, the exception of a few lines;**
> **on the other, cornering them,**
> **life hastens over time**
> **like a terror**
> **overtaking the soul.**

The City, as a felt presence, is seen as an intimation of Poetry, and it is the latter, more than Buenos Aires itself, which is the subject of the poem. This helps to explain why, in a book ostensibly dedicated to Buenos Aires, we surprisingly come across a poem to "Benares," in which Borges writes about a city as distant and unreal as Samarkand. The poem sings that city into being for us, and, as in "Vain Words," the City—the Poetry—is richer than the poem:

> **And to think that,**
> **while I play with uncertain metaphors,**
> **the city I sing, lives. . . .**

3. Unless otherwise credited, all translations are by the author and are from Borges' *Obra poética 1923–1967.*

258

The difference between the two poems lies in the attempt—in "Benares"—to re-create imaginatively a place unseen. It is striving, in fact, to conquer the limitations of the senses, of the realization—brought about in "Vain Words" by the perception of an encompassing reality—of the self bound in time and space. But in the appeal to fantasy, more clearly limitless than objective reality, the attempt to translate the mind's intimation of extensional continuity into a poem brings about equally the consciousness of the limited self as the manipulator of limited means—of words which, because tied to Borges, coming from him, are caught, as is he, in the net of time and space.

Just as "Benares," the deprecated conjuring of an unknown city, claims a logical place in *Fervor de Buenos Aires,* so does "Forjadura" (The Forging), a poem on the imminence of fervor, of mastery. Here, the attempt itself is the key to the poem and its subject. In comparison with "Vain Words" and "Benares," "The Forging" seems exultant, with the poet as a giver of life:

> **. . . to the sower of words**
> **night is land lying fallow.**

There is good reason for the underlying optimism. While the poem meditates on the ability to give life—Poetry—to words, it is also a love poem, written by a young man. For that young man, no higher praise can be found for the woman he loves than to admit that his love for her allows him to achieve what he has so often sought in vain.

In "Forjadura," in the forging of language, we also notice the seed of another idea—that of the poem as a thing somehow apart from the poet himself, a maverick, unwilling if not unable to express the poet's sense of Poetry. The creator has to contend now with his creation, which differs from himself. In "Jactancia de quietud" (Gladly Still) from *Luna de enfrente,* the idea is clearly expressed.

> **I ask my verse not to contradict me, and that is a great deal.**

At bottom, this is again a preoccupation with the word as a tool by essence unfit to do the job it must. Timebound, spatially circumscribed, words cannot succeed in reproducing that which, by

259

definition, is limitless. At his best, then, the poet manages to do no more than allude. Still, the attempt to do more than simply allude is an urgent necessity and, as such, becomes a central issue in Borges' poetry. In another poem, in a later book, *El otro, el mismo* (The Self and the Other), Borges will try to capture that elusive reality, free from all bounds, by stalking a single object. The success of "The Other Tiger," perhaps Borges' best known poem, may be partially explained as that same single-minded search for just one splendid iota of reality. Because everything else is sacrificed to the quest, the quest itself—the quest for "the other tiger, the one beyond the poem"—becomes crucially problematic. Morris' "And the craft that createth a semblance . . . ," which Borges uses as the epigraph for the poem, thus acquires poignant meaning. In "The Other Tiger," there is an almost desperate attempt to re-create reality, not merely to set down its verbal semblance. The three stanzas invoke three tigers: each is different from the preceding in degree, and each is the cause of the next. The first is the poet's tiger, his imagination at work. The second is born of the knowledge that the first is a false re-creation, and constitutes a search for the "real" tiger; the third tiger, barely mentioned, finally, is the "other" tiger, the real animal which is brought to our collective inner eye as readers, while, paradoxically, its occurrence in the poem again traps it in the world of craft and semblance, in the world of words —a flawless poem about the failure of the poet, himself flawed in his ability to re-create a flawless reality.

Sensing the imperfection of words, and knowing that they are his only tools, the only link between his intimation of a total reality (whether objective or fantastic) and its expression, leads Borges to despair of his own work, and from despairing to disparagement. The awareness of the conflict between an essentially infinite vision and its essentially finite expression involves the awareness of the risks he must take in order to overcome the limitations of his means. Since the conflict stems from the need to reduce the timeless and spatially infinite vision of Poetry to words, Borges is impelled to attempt, in every poem, something he knows beforehand to be impossible—the task of freeing the word from the warp and woof of time and space, the net in which he himself, through pondering his creations, feels caught. What makes the risk enormous is that in every instance Borges, clearly sensing the infinite in the shape of Poetry, is forced to face his own felt mortality, his own lonely finitude.

Not surprisingly, at times he seems almost unwilling to assume creative responsibility. As if wishing to maintain some sort of distance between himself and his creations, with their reminders of mortality, he quotes FitzGerald as a measure of self-effacement in the epigraph of his third book, *Cuaderno San Martín* (San Martín Copybook):

As to an occasional copy of verses, there are few men who have leisure to read, and are possessed of any music in their souls, who are not capable of versifying on some ten or twelve occasions during their natural lives: at a proper conjunction of the stars. There is no harm in taking advantage of such occasions.

The book was published in 1929; by that time, Borges had found his poetic voice in a grave, resonant, baroque song. It dovetailed exactly with his strongly metaphysical themes, which began to undergo a series of complex variations. These variations deal with the ways—ingenious, pathetic, comic, tragic—in which men have tried to use their highest intelligence to avoid the trap of time and space. Beyond the aesthetic pleasure derived from examining these intellectual constructs, Borges feels the nobility of their vision, along with their admixture of vain hope and useless courage. A fine example of this struggle to be rid of limits is found in "The Cyclical Night," from *The Self and the Other*. Here the organ-like words ring every change, in a harmonious fugue which seems stolen from a greater harmony, and indeed refers to it. Here is the City as an elusive symbol of words frozen into stone:

> This, here, is Buenos Aires. Time, which brings
> Either love or money to men, hands on to me
> Only this withered rose, this empty tracery
> Of streets with names recurring from the past
> In my blood.... (*SP, 79*)

And at the end of the poem, the endless hope: the poem, like the city, and rising from its contemplation, seems to be saved from the ravages of time by time itself, repeating, cyclical—like the poem:

261

It returns, the hollow dark of Anaxagoras;
In my human flesh, eternity keeps recurring
And the memory, or plan, of an endless poem beginning:
"They knew it, the fervent pupils of Pythagoras..." (*SP,* 81)

The last verse repeats the first, in an attempt to merge the eternal with the temporal, in an effort to equate Poetry with the poem, and thus to save it.

But these are, after all, only technical representations of the games so dear to Borges, which toy with mankind's "elegant hopes." On a deeper level, the poem itself, as a mass of words, must become a bulwark against ravaging time. For that to happen, the old distinction between the thing and its verbal symbol, between *res* and *signum,* must cease. The distinction is temporal in essence: words are tied to time, to the temporal consciousness of their speaker. Things, on the other hand, being free from the consciousness that inhibits, partake of the Infinite, and so are beyond the words that so imperfectly represent them. Borges is well aware of this lack of adjustment between the two.

In "Matthew XXV : 30," another of the poems—again from *The Self and the Other*—that have come to constitute his "canon," Borges says:

From the unseen horizon
And from the very center of my being,
An infinite voice pronounced these things—
Things, not words. This is my feeble translation,
Time-bound, of what was a single limitless Word:

"Stars, bread, libraries of East and West,
Playing cards, chessboards, galleries, skylights, cellars,
A human body to walk with on the earth,
Fingernails, growing at nighttime and in death,
Shadows for forgetting, mirrors busily multiplying,
Cascades in music, gentlest of all time's shapes,
Borders of Brazil, Uruguay, horses and mornings,
A bronze weight, a copy of the Grettir Saga,
Algebra and fire, the charge at Junín in your blood,
Days more crowded than Balzac, scent of the honeysuckle,
Love and the imminence of love and intolerable remembering,
Dreams like buried treasure, generous luck,
And memory itself, where a glance can make men dizzy—
All this was given to you and with it
The ancient nourishment of heroes—
Treachery, defeat, humiliation.

262

> In vain have oceans been squandered on you, in vain
> The sun, wonderfully seen through Whitman's eyes.
> You have used up the years and they have used up you,
> And still, and still, you have not written the poem." *(SP, 93)*

Several things are to be noticed here. The first is the very title of the poem, referring to the biblical verse "And cast ye the unprofitable servant into outer darkness: there shall be weeping and gnashing of teeth." We will examine this more closely in due course. Another is the conjunction of the two visions of infinity mentioned earlier—that of an objective reality, and fantasy, or subjective reality. Another oddity is the sounding of a voice—the voice implied in the epigraph. And finally, we begin to see why "chaotic catalogues" are so dear to Borges: they are catalogues of *things,* shorn, insofar as possible, from any context which might tie them down to *words.* As such, in fact, they are the least imperfect reflections of a limitless reality. Their very mention provides an intimation of infinity, and a refuge from temporality. In "Poema del cuarto elemento" (Poem of the Fourth Element)—also from *The Self and the Other,* Borges addresses water the way others would a god—namely, as a savior:

> Water, I beseech you. By this vague
> Web of numerical words I speak,
> Remember Borges, your swimmer, your friend.
> Fail not my lips at the end.

These intimations of the Infinite given through the contemplation of things, of objects devoid of their verbal representations as far as possible, posit the question, as we see in "Matthew," of a greater voice than the poet's, "an infinite voice" which is able to transcend the human voice—and its concomitant limitations—against which Borges' poetry struggles. In a sense, the new presence of a greater voice is a form of belief hard won at the end of despair. Time after time in Borges' cosmogony, a voice emerges from long and painful meditation—verbal meditation on his mortality. In "Matthew," this severing of tonalities produces almost shy references to the poet who sees himself as the "unprofitable servant," the translator of another and greater voice. But in his very next poem, "Compass," the pathos of such modesty, such insufficiency,

263

has become secondary to the strong voice of adherence—Borges is now more the advocate, the priest:

> **All things are words of some strange tongue, in thrall**
> **To Someone, Something, who both day and night**
> **Proceeds in endless gibberish to write**
> **The history of the world. . . .** **(SP, 97)**

Here, the sight of an object leads the poet to meditate on the word for it, on its *signum*, and from there to the idea of a Writer, from whom "all things are words." In this context, the word triumphs over temporal and spatial limitations, since it is uttered by a speaker who is beyond them.

Thus the belief that things, when they are the words of a greater voice, provide salvation from the threat of time leads to the larger question, and the unanswerable one: Who is able to utter that word? In "Compass," it is "Someone, something"; not quite the recognition of a theological deity, the statement paves the way for such a recognition's coming about. In no sense, however, is this an approach to religious, or orthodox, faith. Rather it reflects Borges' passionate involvement with words—the beginning of the poet's faith, not that of the priest. It is true that the "infinite voice" of "Matthew" implies the voice of God in the traditional Judeo-Christian sense; but it is the concept of God as a semantic term—as the Word, simply—devoid of its theological attributes.

The poet, then, creates the poem, but not its endurance, since both creator and creation are bound in time; what persists of the poem is Poetry, imposed on the poem by a Greater Voice, in whom are intertwined the attributes of deity (the essence of creative will and power) and the absence of human limitations. Borges, wishing with apparent modesty to be remembered "for a few good lines," is, in fact, wishing to equate himself with the creative godhead, not so much out of pride as out of love for Poetry. For himself, and for his fellow poets, he claims no more than the meager role of amanuensis. In "El otro" (The Other One) he bluntly states that

> **The pityless, nameless god gives**
> **His chosen tool to his chosen few. . . .**
> **His is what remains in the memory**
> **Of man.   Ours the rubble.**

When we explore Borges' road to his Greater Voice, we skirt dangerous ground. Borges' reputation as an ironclad agnostic precedes him and seems incompatible with any idea remotely similar to the orthodox Judeo-Christian belief in God. Still, as has been suggested earlier, Borges' faith in the Word springs from his faith in the power of Poetry as a web of words, and to that must be added his passion for our common Hebraic tradition and its Christian revitalization. In some ways, Borges' approach to his Greater Voice bears close parallels to mysticism, in the sense of union between the soul ("the very center of my being") and the infinite ("the unseen horizon"), so that coming face to face with God is, in the deepest sense, an awareness of self. It is fitting, then, that in his latest published work of poetry, *Elogio de la sombra* (In Praise of Darkness), all these factors should unite in an extraordinary poem, "John I : 14." The biblical title, as in the case of "Matthew," and its reference ("And the Word was made flesh . . .") are telling. All the themes which have appeared dispersed in other poems are presented here in a single, humble, and humbling statement. The strains between creator and creation; the awareness of the eternal —and, with it, of our own sorry temporality—leading to the realization that at best we are not truly creators, but creatures translating as best we can, into our own dimension, a larger harmony of ineffable Spirit; the concrete presence of that Spirit itself, in true poetic Eucharist—all blend to integrate this complex work. Slowly the reader is made aware of the identity of the speaker, who is God Himself:

> **This page will be no less a riddle**
> **than those of My holy books.**
> . . . .
> **I who am the Was, the Is, and the Is To Come**
> **again condescend to the written word,**
> **which is time in succession and no more than an emblem.**[4]

And Borges goes on to describe—again the "chaotic list"—the wonderment of the Word made flesh:

4. This and the following excerpts are from the translation by Norman Thomas di Giovanni published in *The New Yorker,* February 12, 1972, p. 38. Copyright © 1972 by The New Yorker, Inc. Reprinted by permission.

> I knew memory,
> that coin that's never twice the same.
> . . . .
>
> I knew wakefulness, sleep, dreams,
> ignorance, the flesh,
> reason's roundabout labyrinths,
> the friendship of men,
> the blind devotion of dogs.

He also describes the Word's human bewilderment at the variety of his own creation:

> My eyes saw what they had never seen—
> night and its many stars.
> I knew things smooth and gritty, uneven and rough,
> the taste of honey and apple,
> water in the throat of thirst,
> the weight of metal in the hand,
> the human voice, the sound of footsteps on the grass,
> the smell of rain in Galilee,
> the cry of birds on high.

These verses indicate how far Borges has come along his own road leading toward the admission of a Greater Voice in the creation of Poetry. There is a tacit and very noble theory of poetry imbedded in these lines—that the poet does no more than set down, as best he can, the voice of the Spirit. But Borges does it with supreme success, managing to communicate to the reader not simply *what* he believes but *how* he believes. As we have earlier felt and shared his anguish when confronted by the disparity between his vision of infinity and the limited means at his disposal with which to render it faithfully, now we are able to share, also, his calm humility; and this enables us as it does him:

> I have entrusted the writing of these words
> to a common man;
> they will never be what I want to say
> but only their shadow.
> These signs are dropped from My eternity.
> Let someone else write the poem, not he who
> is now its scribe.

A Borges family chronicle

[*Colonel Isidoro Suárez (1799–1846), the author's maternal great-grandfather.*] [My mother's] grandfather was Colonel Isidoro Suárez, who, in 1824, at the age of twenty-four, led a famous charge of Peruvian and Columbian cavalry, which turned the tide of the battle of Junín, in Peru. This was the next to last battle of the South American War of Independence. Although Suárez was a second cousin to Juan Manuel de Rosas, who ruled as dictator in Argentina from 1835 to 1852, he preferred exile and poverty in Montevideo to living under a tyranny in Buenos Aires. His lands were, of course, confiscated, and one of his brothers was executed.

[*Colonel Francisco Borges (1833–1874), the author's paternal grandfather.*] [M]y grandfather was, in the early 1870's, Commander-in-Chief of the northern and western frontiers of the Province of Buenos Aires. . . . In 1874, during one of our civil wars, my grandfather, Colonel Borges, met his death. He was forty-one at the time. In the complicated circumstances surrounding his defeat at the battle of La Verde, he rode out slowly on horseback, wearing a white poncho and followed by ten or twelve of his men, toward the enemy lines, where he was struck by two Remington bullets. This was the first time Remington rifles were used in the Argentine, and it tickles my fancy to think that the firm that shaves me every morning bears the same name as the one that killed my grandfather.

[*Isidoro Acevedo (1828–1905)*, LEFT, *the author's maternal grandfather, with his brother Wenceslao.*] My mother's father, Isidoro Acevedo, though a civilian, took part in the fighting of yet other civil wars in the 1860's and 1880's. So, on both sides of my family, I have military forebears; this may account for my yearning after that epic destiny which my gods denied me, no doubt wisely.

[*Georgie Borges at ten months, his first photograph.*] I was born [in Buenos Aires], in the very heart of that city, in 1899, on Tucumán Street, between Suipacha and Esmeralda, in a small, unassuming house belonging to my maternal grandparents. Like most of the houses of that day, it had a flat roof; a long, arched entranceway, called a *zaguán;* a cistern, where we got our water; and two patios.

[Borges, age three, in his first trousers.] We must have moved out to the suburb of Palermo quite soon, because there I have my first memories of another house with two patios, a garden with a tall windmill pump, and, on the other side of the garden, an empty lot. Palermo at that time . . . was on the shabby northern outskirts of town, and many people, ashamed of saying they lived there, spoke in a dim way of living on the Northside. We lived in one of the few two-story homes on our street; the rest of the neighborhood was made up of low houses and vacant lots. I have often spoken of this area as a slum, but I do not quite mean that in the American sense of the word. In Palermo lived shabby, genteel people as well as more undesirable sorts.

[Jorge Borges and Leonor Acevedo de Borges, the author's parents.] My father . . . worked as a lawyer. He was a philosophical anarchist—a disciple of Spencer—and also a teacher of psychology at the Normal School for Modern Languages, where he gave his course in English. . . . My father's English came from the fact that his mother, Frances Haslam, was born in Staffordshire of Northumbrian stock." I think I inherited from my mother her quality of thinking the best of people and also her strong sense of friendship. . . . For years, until recently, she handled all my secretarial work, answering letters, reading to me, taking down my dictation, and also traveling with me on many occasions both at home and abroad. It was she, though I never gave a thought to it at the time, who quietly and effectively fostered my literary career.

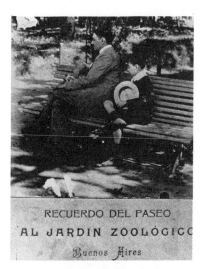

RECUERDO DEL PASEO
AL JARDIN ZOOLÓGICC
Buenos Aires

[*Father and son, age eight or nine.*] I was always very near-sighted and wore glasses, and I was rather frail. As most of my people had been soldiers—even my father's brother had been a naval officer—and I knew I would never be, I felt ashamed, quite early, to be a bookish kind of person and not a man of action.

[*Borges family, with sister Norah, in St. Mark's Square, 1914. Leonor Borges wrote her mother-in-law on the back of the photo: "Though the children look horrible and wish I wouldn't do it, I'm sending you with a kiss this photograph of the family feeding St. Mark's pigeons."*] In 1914, we moved to Europe. . . . The idea of the trip was for my sister and me to go to school in Geneva; we were to live with my maternal grandmother, who traveled with us and eventually died there, while my parents toured the Continent. . . . We were so ignorant of history, however, that we had no idea that the First World War would break out in August.

[*Borges, Norah, and mother in Geneva during the First World War. In Borges' hand on the back: "Mother, Norah and me—(note the wrinkles on my sleeve")*.] We lived in a flat on the southern, or old, side of town. I still know Geneva far better than I know Buenos Aires, which is easily explained by the fact that in Geneva no two streetcorners are alike and one quickly learns the differences. Every day, I walked along that green and icy river, the Rhone, which runs through the very heart of the city, spanned by seven quite different-looking bridges.

[*Norah Borges, 1918 or 1919.*] At home, we spoke Spanish, but my sister's French soon became so good she even dreamed in it. I remember my mother's coming home one day and finding Norah hidden behind a red plush curtain, crying out in fear, *'Une mouche, une mouche!'* It seems she had adopted the French notion that flies are dangerous. 'You come out of there,' my mother told her, somewhat unpatriotically. 'You were born and bred among flies!'

[Sur *group at Victoria Ocampo's house, 1930 or 1931:* BACK ROW, LEFT TO RIGHT, *Eduardo Bullrich, Jorge Luis Borges, Francisco Romero, Eduardo Mallea, Enrique Bullrich, Victoria Ocampo, Ramón Gómez de la Serna;* MIDDLE, SEATED, *Pedro Henríquez Ureña, Norah Borges, María Rosa Oliver, Josefina Stragon, Guillermo de Torre;* FRONT, ON FLOOR, *Oliverio Girondo, Ernest Ansermet.*]

[*The summer home in Adrogué, built for the Borges' in the 1940's.*]
[W]e usually spent our summers out in Adrogué, some ten or fifteen miles to the south of Buenos Aires, where we had a place of our own— a large one-story house with grounds, two summerhouses, a windmill, and a shaggy brown sheepdog. Adrogué was then a lost and undisturbed maze of summer homes surrounded by iron fences with masonry planters of the gateposts, of parks, of streets that radiated out of the many plazas, and of the ubiquitous smell of eucalyptus trees. We continued to visit Adrogué for decades.

[Borges with José Edmundo Clemente, in 1955, at the ceremony naming them, respectively, Director and Assistant Director of the Argentine National Library. Two years before, Clemente had been responsible for bringing Borges' books back to print.] Two very dear friends of mine, Esther Zemborain de Torres and Victoria Ocampo, dreamed up the possibility of my being appointed Director of the National Library. I thought the scheme a wild one, and hoped at most to be given the directorship of some small-town library, preferably to the south of the city. Within the space of a day, a petition was signed by the magazine *Sur* (read Victoria Ocampo), by the reopened S.A.D.E. (read Carlos Alberto Erro), by the Sociedad Argentina de Cultura Inglesa (read Carlos del Campillo), and by the Colegio Libre de Estudios Superiores (read Luis Reissig). This was placed on the desk of the Minister of Education, and eventually I was appointed to the directorship by General Eduardo Lonardi, who was Acting President. A few days earlier, my mother and I had walked to the Library one night to take a look at the building, but, feeling superstitious, I refused to go in. 'Not until I get the job,' I said. That same week, I was called to come to the Library to take over. ¶ My family was present, and I made a speech to the employees, telling them I was actually the Director—the incredible Director. At the same time, José Edmundo Clemente, who a few years before had managed to persuade Emecé to bring out an edition of my works, became the Assistant Director. Of course, I felt very important, but we got no pay for the next three months. I don't think my predecessor, who was a Peronista, was ever officially fired. He just never came around to the Library again. They named me to the job but did not take the trouble to unseat him.

[Borges in Texas, in 1961, with Miguel Enguídanos.] [U]nder the auspices of Edward Larocque Tinker, I was invited as Visiting Professor to the University of Texas. It was my first physical

encounter with America. In a sense, because of my reading, I had always been there, and yet how strange it seemed when in Austin I heard ditch diggers who worked on campus speaking in English, a language I had until then always thought of as being denied that class of people. America, in fact, had taken on such mythic proportions in my mind that I was sincerely amazed to find there such commonplace things as weeds, mud, puddles, dirt roads, flies, and stray dogs. Though at times we fell into homesickness, I know now that my mother—who accompanied me—and I grew to love Texas.

[*With his mother in London, 1963.*] In 1963, thanks to Neil MacKay of the British Consul in Buenos Aires, I was able to visit England and Scotland. There, too, again in my mother's company, I made my pilgrimages: to London, so teeming with literary memories; to Lichfield and Dr. Johnson; to Manchester and De Quincey; to Rye and Henry James; to the Lake Country; to Edinburgh. I visited my grandmother's birthplace in Hanley, one of the Five Towns—Arnold Bennett country. Scotland and Yorkshire I think of as among the loveliest places on earth.

[*On the shores of the Dead Sea, April 21, 1971. Two days earlier, Borges had received the Fifth Biennial Jerusalem Prize.*] Since my Genevan days, I had always been interested in Jewish culture, thinking of it as an integral element of our so-called Western civilization, and during the Israeli-Arab war of a few years back I found myself taking immediate sides. While the outcome was still uncertain, I wrote a poem on the battle. A week after, I wrote another on the victory.

Borges and Stevens: a note on post-Symbolist writing
ROBERT ALTER

> *An argentine abstraction approaching form*
> *And suddenly denying itself away.*
> —*Wallace Stevens, "Reality Is an Activity*
> *of the Most August Imagination"*

The affinity between Borges and a number of other important writers who have flourished in the middle period of our century suggests that one possibly useful way of viewing many of the chief trends in this "post-modern" literature is as varying facets of an anti-symbolist movement. Symbols, we are often reminded, enjoy a peculiar prominence—first in the poetry, then in the fiction, of a good many countries during the latter part of the nineteenth century and the early decades of our own century. In some cases, this new insistent presence of symbols in imaginative works was the direct result of the authors' association with a conscious movement that called itself Symbolist; in other cases, the influence of the actual movement was oblique, perhaps nothing more than the proverbially mysterious workings of the *Zeitgeist*.

Now, when a symbol moves toward a state of quasi-autonomy in a piece of fiction or a poem, manifestly strange things begin to happen to it as a vehicle of meaning. In a traditional realistic novel —say, *Madame Bovary* or *Middlemarch*—the use of symbolic motif is supportive and secondary to the human actions and

275

characters portrayed, and so the semantic range of the symbols is reasonably clear. The clouds of "bluish distances" that surround Emma Bovary—imagistically associated with her light-blue parasol, her dark blue eyes, the blue vortices spinning inside her head—tell us something fairly definite about Emma's sensibility and her aspirations, and are thus an apt instrument for the extension of character and the elaboration of formal unity in the novel. The same is true of the recurrent images of spidery mustiness and labyrinthine darkness that George Eliot associates in her novel with Casaubon: they convey to us, perhaps subliminally, what we need to know and feel about Casaubon's mind and character and his physical being. (How different this handling of the labyrinth and the Minotaur from Borges' repeated use of that same mythic image!) But when we encounter the symbolic presence of the sea —to cite a central example—in symbolist fictions like Conrad's *Nostromo,* Mann's *Death in Venice,* Joyce's *Ulysses,* Virginia Woolf's *To the Lighthouse,* Agnon's *Betrothed,* the symbol, now in the foreground, becomes so potently semantic that discursive reason can no longer encompass it: the sea is at once the source of life and form and the image of their dissolution, the pulsating surge of Eros and the corrosive wash of indifferent death. Symbolist fictions and poems conjure up an imaginative world fraught with meaning, but when a concrete entity can mean almost everything, it also threatens to mean nothing.

It has often been observed, with abundant allusion to the famous Baudelaire poem, that the Symbolist mode of writing depends ultimately on a system, or at least a sense, of correspondences—correspondences among the disparate parts of external nature, between man and nature, among the discrete senses, perhaps also between present and past. There are obviously all sorts of forces in the intellectual history of the last forty years that have made this originally mystic notion of correspondences less and less credible, but there is also an internal, literary reason for the erosion of correspondences. If, ultimately, everything corresponds to everything else—if, for example, Molly Bloom is at once Calypso and Penelope, all-embracing Gea-Tellus and a bitch-goddess, Aphrodite and the Virgin Mary—then a writer may become acutely conscious of the possibility that all symbols are finally arbitrary, all connections between things (which is to say, all meanings) mere constructs of the imagination. After a novelist like Kafka, or for that matter Melville, has created a set of symbols so bewilderingly portentous that they literally defy exegesis, the next logical step may be a literature explicitly designed to deny exegesis.

What I mean to suggest is that after the peak achievements of the classic modern writers in the 1920's, symbolism does not quietly fade into some other mode of writing; rather, many serious writers consciously attempt a sharp literary self-definition by articulating in their work some form of antithesis to symbolism. On a level of sheer reactive energy, this impulse expresses itself first in the manifestoes against meaning of the literary sectarians like the Dadaists, the Surrealists, and their latter-day imitators. With a more self-conscious, if often sterile, art, in the last fifteen years the process has been most evident in the French New Novel. (The beasts in the jungle of Robbe-Grillet's *Jealousy,* screaming portentously, meaning absolutely nothing, provide a neat paradigm for the enunciated denial of symbolism in fiction.) The reaction against symbolism is equally present, in two opposite ways, in the grey, denuded figures of Beckett's world, who insist on being nothing but their gritty selves, and in the iridescent play of Nabokov's inventions, teasing us about meanings while leading us back to the generative activity of art itself. But the tension between symbolism's seductive allure and the transparent factitiousness of symbols has been made most repeatedly a central subject in the work of two very different writers—Wallace Stevens and Jorge Luis Borges.

Stevens, of course, was preoccupied throughout his career with the threat of disjuncture between the mind and the world. Again and again his poems follow out the frustrating or enigmatic ways in which the thing itself eludes the imagination, or, on the contrary, scarcely seems to exist until it is realized or embodied by the imagination. Borges, it hardly need be said, has been continually concerned, both in his poetry and in his prose, with these same ontological puzzles, and in his short stories he has devised his own special mode of anti-symbolist fiction to give form to the process of puzzlement. Stevens provides not only an interesting parallel to Borges but also a useful gloss on the Argentine writer, because his peculiar combination of lyric compression and analytic discursiveness directly illuminates an imaginative model that is implicit in much of Borges' fiction. The anti-symbolist attitude toward meaning is strikingly embodied in one of Stevens' early poems, "Metaphors of a Magnifico," and I would like to offer some comment on it, with reference to Borges:

> **Twenty men crossing a bridge,**
> **Into a village,**
> **Are twenty men crossing twenty bridges,**
> **Into twenty villages,**
> **Or one man**
> **Crossing a single bridge into a village.**
>
> **This is old song**
> **That will not declare itself ...**
>
> **Twenty men crossing a bridge,**
> **Into a village,**
> **Are**
> **Twenty men crossing a bridge**
> **Into a village.**
>
> **That will not declare itself**
> **Yet is certain as meaning ...**
>
> **The boots of the men clump**
> **On the boards of the bridge.**
> **The first white wall of the village**
> **Rises through fruit-trees.**
> **Of what was it I was thinking?**
> **So the meaning escapes.**
> **The first white wall of the village ...**
> **The fruit-trees ...**

The escape of meaning becomes the subject—or rather, there is no longer a subject but instead a process, in which the reader is deeply implicated, of experiencing the escape of a subject. The literary statement itself—and surely this could be said for the most brilliant of Borges' fictions—becomes a "song / That will not declare itself," which nevertheless, stirringly, sings. The twenty soldiers, as in the refrain of an old ballad, march rhythmically, and repeatedly, over the wooden bridge, somehow evocative—but evocative of what, the observer is unable to determine. Their image· has the certainty of meaning, the *feel* of meaning, but not its content. If the utmost logic of metaphor is the substitution of one thing for another, the very possibility of metaphor raises questions about the laws of identity. Are the twenty men really one, is the one bridge really twenty, or are they simply what they seem, intimating more only through the incantatory magic of reiteration? The ostensibly "objective" solidity of the presence of this scene is further unsettled four lines before the end, when our attention is drawn to the consciousness of a bewildered "I" observing the scene, trying to piece it together into some pattern of significance, distracted from that effort by the rhythmically insistent evocativeness of the scene itself. The "I" who loses the train of his thought is presumably the Magnifico of the title, perhaps the commander of the twenty men. By extension, of course, he is a surrogate for the poet, who has made a poem about not quite making a poem; and the reader, surprised at the end by that "I," finds himself implicated in the poet's viewpoint in a way he would not be in a more traditional poetic vehicle—wanting to put together soldiers and bridge and fruit-trees and wall into a unity that always escapes.

Borges, of course, has often used an analogous strategy at the beginning or end of his fictions in splicing the world of the artifice with the world of the author through the obtrusion of a quizzical, commenting "I." It may be worth observing, moreover, that his stories are also often built around images that look invitingly metaphorical while withholding all possibility of a particular metaphorical interpretation. Borges himself has made the point explicitly at the end of one of his most recent pieces, "Pedro Salvadores." This story, set in the lifetime of Borges' grandfather, is the account of a man who hid in a dark cellar for nine years to escape the troops of an Argentine dictator. What did he think of and feel, wonders the narrator; what did he dream in that unchanging gloom? "At first, he may have been a man hunted down, a man in danger of his life; later (we will never know for certain), an animal at peace in its burrow or a sort of dim god" (*A,* 189). The sheer dramatic fascination of what people can think and undergo, or what juxtaposed images can look like, demands interpretation; but the impenetrability of the external object, of the life of another, of time past, makes interpretation a presumption. "As with so many things," Borges concludes his story, "the fate of Pedro Salvadores strikes us as a symbol of something we are about to understand, but never quite do" (*A*, 189). Like the first white wall of the village and the fruit-trees, Borges' Pedro Salvadores, his Warrior and Captive, his Homeric Immortal, his Garden of Forking Paths and Library of Babel tease us into symbolic speculation and leave definite symbolization unattainable.

If the symbolist mode of literature conveys a sense of the unlimited powers of the imagination—that is, of the image-making faculty of the mind—the kind of writing practiced in different ways by Borges and Stevens makes us aware simultaneously of the power of the imagination and of its limits. Much of Borges' fiction seems to push the practice of symbolist fiction beyond its logical extreme, and by so doing to demonstrate how the symbol, which means so much, is ultimately subversive of meaning. Reflecting on the Zahir, the magical coin that is literally, and terribly, unforgettable, Borges contemplates the idea that "the visible world is implicit in every phenomenon" (*L*, 163). But if all things are in each thing, the presence of each thing, fully perceived, becomes like the face of God—intolerable. In story after story, Borges offers images of focused infinity, objects and contrivances that seem to mean everything and necessarily mean nothing, therefore making the mind boggle, inducing a sense of ontological vertigo. The world is full of uncanny resemblances, but if, as Stevens observes in *The Necessary Angel,* "both in nature and in metaphor identity is the vanishing point of resemblance," then for Borges the converse is equally and disturbingly true—resemblance is the vanishing point of identity, and all substance becomes cosmic quicksand. One thinks of the labyrinths, the ingenious varieties of infinite regresses and mirrors upon mirrors, the recurrence of doubles and circularity, the arcane objects like the memory-absorbing Zahir, the Aleph that encompasses all space in a little sphere, the dizzying spots of the jaguar imagined by their observer as God's script of all things. The mind, in its very power to conceive these things, seems all-powerful, but in conceiving that which it cannot possibly comprehend, it also reveals its own impotence. The focuses of infinity dwarf the mind, annihilate individuality, and for all that remain mere mental constructs. The mind can create entire worlds like Tlön and Uqbar, which rival the palpability of the "real" world, yet cannot escape their own fictive nature. In much the same way, Stevens' young man contemplating a pineapple ("Someone Puts Together a Pineapple") seems to bridge the gap of Cartesian dualism by projecting idea into extension—the underlying notion in Borges' "Tlön"—but the achievement remains a precarious piece of real-seeming illusionism effected by a self-englobed mind:

> **He sees it in this tangent of himself.**
> **And in this tangent it becomes a thing**
> **Of weight, on which the weightless rests: from which**
>
> **The ephemeras of the tangent swarm, the chance**
> **Concourse of planetary originals,**
> **Yet, as it seems, of human residence.**

There is a strong dialectic movement in the sense of ontology that informs the work of Stevens and of Borges. Without both sides of the dialectic, their musings about the sheer constructive power of the mind would lack the suggestive force they in fact possess. For the Symbolists, as has been noted, a correspondence is given between the imagination (if not the whole mind) and the world, even though what the imagination grasps of the world may be threatening or unsettling. These two post-Symbolists, on the other hand, are equally aware of how the imagination tends to construct its own world arbitrarily and of how the world, or at least the object, insists stubbornly on its own intrinsic existence, apart from any fashion in which the mind can try to re-invent it, or from any net of words and symbols the imagination can weave to catch it. (In his essays, Stevens takes a somewhat more confident view of the imagination, but his theoretical statements in this respect do not entirely jibe with his own poetic practice.) If one impulse in both Borges and Stevens points toward the sterile ingenuities of solipsism, the expression of

281

that impulse is usually justified because of their awareness that solipsism is in fact a matter of sterile ingenuity—that it is, indeed, one of the perennial perils in the workings of the human mind.

Borges and Stevens are great imaginists whose exercise of imagination—in Borges' case, often fantastication—is directed by a fine skepticism not only about the world of brute matter but also about the imagination itself. Borges would surely subscribe to the quizzical observation Stevens makes on himself as a writer in one of his last poems, "As You Leave the Room": "I wonder, have I lived a skeleton's life, / As a disbeliever in reality, / A countryman of all the bones of the world?" This is, moreover, by no means an eleventh-hour conversion of Stevens the imaginist but one pole of his art from its very beginning. In another statement that has exact Borgesian parallels, this time from an early poem ("The Comedian as the Letter C"), he notes succinctly: "The words of things entangle and confuse. / The plum survives its poems." That essential plum, Stevens goes on to say, may be transmogrified into an artifice of beauty, "colored by ground / Obliquities of those who pass beneath, / Harlequined and mazily dewed and mauved," but these transient projections of the mind upon it do not touch what it is: "it survives in its own form, / Beyond these changes, good, fat, guzzly fruit." The soldiers crossing the bridge are indeed soldiers crossing a bridge. It is only the imagination that fails—perhaps because of the intrinsic limitations of language and imagination—to engage them directly, or to make something of them. Pedro Salvadores, in the unending dark of his underground retreat, is indubitably, pertinaciously *there,* but the imagination falters in trying to make a symbol out of him—as he seems to require—and can only conjecture at the reality of what he underwent.

Readers of Borges' stories may tend to think of him primarily as an inventor of fantasies, for he seems to have used prose more typically as a medium in which he could deploy characters, magical objects, situations, and whole worlds as dramatic elaborations of hypotheses about reality that are contrary to those cherished by common sense. The fictional medium in this way becomes a solvent in which solid notions about time, space, density of matter, identity,

282

causation, thought and extension, memory and experience are temporarily dissolved into fluid in which fascinating new patterns appear. I suspect that poetry, on the other hand, is more characteristically thought of by Borges as a means for attempting to grasp what may still be called reality, the reality that exists independent of the mind's attempts to shape it. In "A Yellow Rose," a brief, haunting reflection on the nature of poetry, Borges evokes the deathbed scene of the Italian Renaissance poet Giambattista Marino. A woman brings a yellow rose in a glass to the bedside of the dying poet, who then murmurs his own elaborate and famous lines on the rose.

Then the revelation came to him. Marino *saw* the rose as Adam first saw it in Paradise, and he felt that it lived in an eternity of its own and not in his words, and that we may mention or allude to a thing but not express it, and that the tall proud volumes casting a golden haze there in a corner of the room were not (as his vanity dreamed) a mirror of the world, but only one more thing added to the world. (*SP*, 258)

This ultimate wisdom accorded the dying poet is another way of viewing the end of symbolism. If the plum eternally survives its poems, if the poem cannot, by its nature, mirror the object but can only rival it crudely or cast trick lights across its surface, the poem surely cannot pretend to make the object a vehicle of meaning for something beyond itself. The very act of symbolization, in fact, is a confession of failure on the part of the poet; when the object in its own terms eludes him, he tries to arrogate it to himself by fixing it at a nexus of signification in his own structure of words. Such an act, of course, however elegantly or persuasively performed, is not an apprehension of the object but its violation.

Borges memorably evokes this permanent predicament of the poet confronted with reality in "The Other Tiger," one of the great anti-Symbolist poems of our century. The poem begins with a powerfully concrete conjuration of the tiger gliding in murderous innocence behind a screen of bamboo stalks in its wordless, timeless world along the Ganges. The poet, however, has only words to use, and he is very much in the world of time—the date of composition, August 3, 1959, is actually mentioned in the text. He therefore realizes that the very act of giving the tiger a name is a falsification, turning the wild creature into "a fiction, not a living beast." The poem, then, like Stevens' less spectacular "Metaphors of a Magnifico," is about the failure of poetry. It brilliantly illustrates the kind of literature that can be created out of the most lucid recognition of literature's inherent limits, joined with a passionate attachment to the literary impulse. If it does not "engage" reality, as more traditional modes of literature were assumed to do, it does approach reality asymptotically, and, in so doing, it illuminates not only the nature of the creative process but something of the palpable presence of reality as well. The two directions of illumination are especially clear in the opening lines of the poem's middle section, which I quote here in Norman Thomas di Giovanni's eloquent translation:

> **It strikes me now as evening fills my soul**
> **That the tiger addressed in my poem**
> **Is a shadowy beast, a tiger of symbols**
> **And scraps picked up at random out of books,**
> **A string of labored tropes that have no life,**
> **And not the fated tiger, the deadly jewel**
> **That under sun or stars or changing moon**
> **Goes on in Bengal or Sumatra fulfilling**
> **Its rounds of love and indolence and death.**   (*SP*, 129)

Writers like Borges and Stevens, who perceive so sharply the limits of language and the necessary falsification of symbols, may well turn to the sheer order-making magic of words and of the mind —Borges delighting in the mental processes that spin the kingdom of Uqbar and the world of Tlön out of nothing; Stevens affirming his singer by the sea who "was the single artificer of the world in which she sang," and who gave the sea "whatever self it had." What prevents them from being merely poets of the imagination's narcissism is that both remain avid of that ungraspable reality to which the mind responds. Borges goes on in his poem to imagine the pursuit of what is, by implication, an infinite regress of tigers, always hoping to come closer to the real one. Stevens could dream (in "Angels Surrounded by Paysans") of an epiphany in which the distortive veil of human concepts and human language would for a moment fall from the face of reality:

284

> Yet I am the necessary angel of earth,
> Since, in my sight, you see the earth again,
>
> Cleared of its stiff and stubborn, man-locked set,
> And, in my hearing, you hear its tragic drone
>
> Rise liquidly in liquid lingerings,
> Like watery words awash; like meanings said
>
> By repetitions of half-meanings.

The repetition of half-meanings brings us back full circle to "Metaphors of a Magnifico" and to "Pedro Salvadores." Perhaps there is even a sense in which this kind of writing, by the full dramatization of its own necessary inadequacy, a strategy at once ingenuous and arch, gives us a glimpse of reality beyond the separating grid of words. In the poet's very confession that he has betrayed the wild tiger into a symbol, we may participate in something of his tense perception of the real creature with "bony frame / Under the splendid quivering cover of skin." A literature created out of the ebbing of symbolism, simultaneously delighting in and doubting the imagination, is bound to be above all a literature of paradoxes; and the poem that is a dream of the tiger's escape may, paradoxically, have caught him after all.

Borges and Hawthorne
JOHN WRIGHT

Borges' fascination with the mind and writings of Nathaniel Hawthorne is due, in part, to his discovery of Hawthorne's inclination
to those ironic, participational, and self-referring modes of fiction
to which more and more modern writers have turned and of which
Borges is now the undoubted and astonishing master. The impression some may have that he reads Hawthorne in his own image
is only half true. Hawthorne's ideas about art and the artist and
the still little-understood *designs* of his short stories make it abundantly evident that Borges' projection corresponds strikingly with
the figure on which it rests. He was the first to see that Hawthorne
belongs to a broadly symbolist tradition of literary invention: a
literature of ambiguity, irony, and paradox strongly inclined to
allegory and parable—to introverted and labyrinthine designs
which are almost perfectly opaque to minds expecting representations of life or expressive communications from works of art.
Borges provides numerous hints for a history of this relatively
esoteric or occult tradition; some of the most important of them
appear when he describes the journals in which Hawthorne's
artistic inclinations were recorded:

286

I shall mention two more sketches [from Hawthorne's notebooks]...; their theme, not unknown to Pirandello or André Gide, is the coincidence or the confusion of the aesthetic plane and the common plane, of art and reality. The first one: "Two persons to be expecting some occurrence, and watching for the two principal actors in it, and to find that the occurrence is even then passing, and that they themselves are the two actors." The other is more complex: "A person to be writing a tale, and to find that it shapes itself against his intentions; that the characters act otherwise than he thought; that unforeseen events occur; and a catastrophe comes which he strives in vain to avert. It might shadow forth his own fate—he having made himself one of the personages." These games, these momentary confluences of the imaginative world and the real world—the world we pretend is real when we read—are, or seem to us, modern. Their origin, their ancient origin, is perhaps to be found in that part of the *Iliad* in which Helen of Troy weaves into her tapestry the battles and the disasters of the Trojan War even then in progress. Virgil must have been impressed by that passage, for the *Aeneid* relates that Aeneas, hero of the Trojan War, arrived at the port of Carthage and saw scenes from the war sculptured on the marble of the temple and, among the many images of warriors, he saw his own likeness. Hawthorne liked those contacts of the imaginary and the real, those reflections and duplications of art; and in the sketches I have mentioned we observe that he leaned toward the pantheistic notion that one man is the others, that one man is all men. (*OI*, 52)

"Nathaniel Hawthorne" is significantly framed by "Partial Enchantments of the *Quixote*" and "A Note on Walt Whitman," essays which reflect the strange effects produced by literature in which the real and imaginary are fused. The *Quixote* essay ends with a tentative (and nonetheless programmatic) speculation on the cause of our disquiet in perceiving self-referring fictions: "if the characters in a story can be readers or spectators [of their own situations], then we, their readers and spectators, can be fictitious" (*OI*, 46).

In "A Note on Walt Whitman," Borges observes that "Whitman derives a personal relationship with each future reader. He identifies himself with the reader, and converses with Whitman ('Salut au Monde!,' 3)":

"What do you hear, Walt Whitman?" (*OI*, 72)

The identification fuses the world of the reader with that of the work, and aims at communion through displacement of "the real world—the world we pretend is real when we read . . ." (*OI*, 52).

Hawthorne's art, like Whitman's and Cervantes'—and like Borges' as well—tends to refer to itself, to depict, often secretively, the process of its own making and its being read, fusing the real and imaginary. It is this aesthetic complex which provides the key to Borges' singular perception of Hawthorne—and not his aversion, as some disparaging remarks might suggest, to what he assumes was Hawthorne's unfortunate attempt "to make art a function of the conscience" (*OI, 60*). Conscience and the imagery of ethical consciousness play the same role in Hawthorne's fiction that learned reflection and philosophic speculation do in Borges' writing. In each case their main concern is with metamorphoses of consciousness. Neither is a mimetic artist in the usual sense; their fictions approximate meditation and approach the condition of poetry. Both are anatomists operating on the thresholds of personal and cultural awareness. Borges has treated the republic of letters (under the form of Gutenberg Galaxy, as things have comically turned out) as Hawthorne treated Puritan New England culture. Their narrators are often historians manqués who project the imagery of zealous and defeated consciousness upon an audience meant to collaborate in the discovery that the mind is as much a theater as a faculty, and that life and art are but two halves of one sphere (*OI, 9*). For both, the problems of belief, of institutions and propriety, and of identity are the raw materials of an art distinctively engaged with the dispositions of its audience. For this reason they do not prolong the particular into the specific, but proceed in the opposite direction, by ironic displacement of customary voices and legendary realities to evoke parables of awareness and those enigmas of comprehension and interpretation for which the dialectic of author, work, and audience is a vast metaphor.

Hawthorne's allegory has always been a puzzle. Henry James saw it as an unfortunate by-product of awkward metaphysical moods. In these moods, he wrote, "Hawthorne . . . is nothing if not allegorical, and allegory, to my sense, is quite one of the lighter exercises of the imagination." [1] Borges, apparently regarding James's remark as one of the lighter exercises of criticism, indicates a partial solution to the problem of Hawthorne's allegory. He entertains the traditional puzzle and dismisses it with spacious elegance: "Two tasks confront us: first, to ascertain whether the

1. Henry James, *Hawthorne* (Ithaca, 1963), p. 49.

288

allegorical genre is, in fact, illicit; second, to ascertain whether Nathaniel Hawthorne's works belong to that category" (*OI,* 49). He mentions Croce's attack on allegory and Chesterton's prior defense of it to show that the task of discrediting resolves itself into a fruitless opposition between arbitrary definition and metaphysical mystery. Croce's argument (the arbitrary definition) unravels: allegory is bad because the meaning obtrudes itself, flattening any aesthetic texture. Chesterton's defense is interesting for its attempt at "negative" proof: do we, the criticizers and readers, really believe we can accurately name the " 'tints [in the soul] more bewildering, more numberless, and more nameless than the colours of an autumn forest?' " (*OI,* 50). "I don't know whether Chesterton's thesis is valid," Borges concludes; "I do know that the less an allegory can be reduced to a plan, to a cold set of abstractions, the better it is." With the puzzle about genre thereby dismissed, Borges admits to some adventitious allegorical follies in Hawthorne's work, and quickly transfers attention from the sordid subject to the symbolism in Hawthorne's "world of dream."

Borges' view of the main tendency of Hawthorne's "oneiric" symbolism appears near the end of his essay, when he speaks of the fissure image in *The Marble Faun:*

It is a multiple symbol, a symbol that is capable of many, perhaps incompatible, values. Such values can be offensive to reason, to logical understanding, but not to dreams, which have their singular and secret algebra, and in whose ambiguous realm one thing may be many. Hawthorne's world is the world of dreams. (*OI,* 62)

This is the only mention he makes of Hawthorne's ambiguities, and it is significant that he has in mind here the thematic ambiguity of image and metaphor rather than Hawthorne's more prominent and puzzling ambiguities of structure, situation, and narrative attitude. He sees in Hawthorne's art a flow of symbolism from the reservoir of the world of dreams, and has responded to what he calls its "germinal vision":

In Hawthorne the germinal vision was always true; what is false, what is ultimately false, are the moralities he added in the last paragraph or the characters he conceived, or assembled, in order to represent that vision. (*OI,* 60)

The disproportion Borges finds between the source of Hawthorne's art and its embodiment on the page, and his curiously conventional disparagement—perhaps his misapprehension—of the latter, is apt to conceal much of the kinship of their fictions. If carefully interpreted, however, Borges' idea of Hawthorne's "germinal vision" can point the way to a deeper perception of what they share. He calls the curiously modern story "Wakefield" a "brief and ominous parable" (*OI*, 56), parable being one of the forms of allegory. The character Wakefield undergoes an archetypal experience of withdrawal and return to society against so empty a background and with so little significance either in the withdrawal or in the return that Borges calls it a "nightmare" which "prefigures Franz Kafka." He quotes Hawthorne's moral, inviting the reader to generalize the experience of Wakefield and see how Everyman, " 'by stepping aside for a moment' " from ordinary experience, " 'exposes himself to a fearful risk of losing his place for ever. Like Wakefield, he may become, as it were, the Outcast of the Universe' " (*OI*, 56). As Borges interprets this story, Hawthorne's visionary germ was a shadow figure, the twin or double of Everyman. An "Outcast of the Universe" is already No Man—the same No Man figure, in fact, that haunts Borges' fiction. He has grasped Hawthorne's fascination with the enigma of identity, personal and authorial alike, and has read "Wakefield" as a parable depicting the slow unconscious processes of loss (or gain) of No Man's (or Everyman's) name, place, and power of action. In "The Immortal," "The Circular Ruins," and "Borges and Myself," Borges has written of this No Man figure from a point of view more nearly within the character. (Ultimately the circularity of the immortal narrator's mind turns out to be indistinguishable from that of the mysterious text and finally of the story itself; the story thus becomes an instance of its own theme.)

Borges' idea that Hawthorne's "germinal vision was always true" is paradoxical and leads to an awkward and significant conclusion: that Hawthorne's fiction is not the allegory it often appears to be, but a special kind of symbolist literature whose outer form is in some way typically worthless or corrupt and whose inner form is perhaps intrinsically inexpressible. This is closer to the truth, I think, than might readily appear. The framework of a Hawthorne story is often little more than a screen for his art—a screen on which the reader is invited to project his own moral or aesthetic character. Hawthorne's richest work has the larger compass of eliciting and shaping the reader's awareness of the transaction between him, the work, and the author. Borges' sense of this is evident at the start of his essay, when he mentions Joseph Addison's opinion that "When the soul dreams . . . it is the theatre, the actors, and the audience" (*OI,* 47). If, by extension, we regard a story as a script for the soul's dreams, the figure of the artist will appear, as it were, in the form of director, now in the wings, now in the audience, or again in mufti on stage. And this is exactly how we perceive the author's positions when we read through Hawthorne's and Borges' fictions.

When we look at the design of some of Hawthorne's tales it will be clear that one of the reasons they most resemble, and yet are not, allegory is that he begins with situations which reflect his own emotional and moral ambivalence—we might call them incipient paradoxes of natural and moral consciousness—and then proceeds (like Borges) to treat this material with perspectival shifts. The result is an art of process, in a sense a kinetic art of open form, radically opposed to the kind of verisimilitude and autonomous unity required by the closure of Aristotelean poetics. Hawthorne's use of the rhetoric both of allegorical narration and of representation is one means, an ironic one, of bringing the reader to a relation of complicity with the text. Borges' own method of placing problematic texts and dubious explication in already ambiguous situations within the frame of his fictions (in some cases they are coextensive with the boundaries of that fiction) is precisely parallel to Hawthorne's method of allegorizing pseudo-legendary materials and projecting his fictions from a variety of eccentric or biased (often Puritan) points of view. While he seems to point the way to it, Borges curiously neglects this side of Hawthorne's art—the very side from which his own works suggest he may have learned most.

Ironic treatment of the theme of fatal and futile artistic realization pervades Hawthorne's tales of human art, and even the metaphor of works of art as hapless, abortive progeny is common. His "Feathertop" appears to be a moralized legend, but as usual its moral is opaque, veiling a comic parable of artistic uselessness. Hawthorne suggests as a parallel for Feathertop's reception in town the actual reading of his story. And, to use the phrase Borges notes, he approaches "making himself one of the characters" in the form of Mother Rigby, "one of the most potent witches in New England." Her fate, and Feathertop's, does "shadow forth" Hawthorne's own ("for years [and years] one of the obscurest men of letters in America").

The old witch starts out one morning to make a scarecrow to put in "the middle of her corn patch," but meanwhile she becomes fond of it and decides to give it a similitude of life, and sends it off to town to play a trick on old acquaintances. The narrator, who pretends he is retelling a legend, observes the animation process:

In obedience to Mother Rigby's word and extending its arm as if to reach her outstretched hand, the figure made a step forward—a kind of hitch and jerk, however, rather than a step—then tottered and almost lost its balance. What could the witch expect? It was nothing, after all, but a scarecrow stuck upon two sticks. But the strong-willed old beldam scowled, and beckoned, and flung the energy of her purpose so forcibly at the poor combination of rotten wood, and musty straw, and ragged garments, that it was compelled to show itself a man, in spite of the reality of things. So it stepped into the bar of sunshine. There it stood—poor devil of a contrivance that it was!—with only the thinnest vesture of human similitude about it, through which was evident the stiff, rickety, incongruous, faded, tattered, good-for-nothing patchwork of its substance, ready to sink in a heap upon the floor, as conscious of its own unworthiness to be erect. Shall I confess the truth? At its present point of vivification, the scarecrow reminds me of some of the lukewarm and abortive characters, composed of heterogeneous materials, used for the thousandth time, and never worth using, with which romance writers (and myself, no doubt, among the rest) have so overpeopled the world of fiction.[2]

The duplication (to use Borges' term) between Feathertop and the story "Feathertop" is characteristically elegant and unemphatic. "Feathertop: A Moralized Legend" is one of Hawthorne's abortive artistic progeny or simulacra. If the reader happens to count tales,

2. Nathaniel Hawthorne, *The Complete Works of Nathaniel Hawthorne,* 13 vols. (Cambridge, Mass., 1883), II, 260. Hereafter cited as *Works.*

he finds that it stands thirteenth among the twenty-six pieces in *Mosses from an Old Manse*—right in the center, that is, of the enlarged edition of the corn patch which contains such other memorable "vegetable progeny" as "Rappaccini's Daughter," whose heroine is sister to a plant.

Like Hawthorne, Borges has been repeatedly drawn to the metaphor of the artist as necromantic dreamer, and his dreamers' works of art share a similar fate. "The Circular Ruins," "The Golem," and "The Aleph" contain regressions which ultimately include the narrators' own end: ". . . Fire was the only one who knew his son was a phantom. . . . He feared that his son might wonder at this strange privilege and in some way discover his condition as a mere appearance" (*A*, 61). When the artist-dreamer of "The Circular Ruins" finally realizes his own unreal condition, it appears with the same irreal embarrassment that Borges divines in Hawthorne's life and work: "In relief, in humiliation, in terror, he understood that he, too, was an appearance, that someone else was dreaming him" (*A*, 62). A significantly related passage in Hawthorne's journal of 1840 has been quoted by Henry James and, more selectively, by Borges:

And now I begin to understand why I was imprisoned so many years in this lonely chamber, and why I could never break through the viewless bolts and bars; for if I had sooner made my escape into the world, I should have grown hard and rough, and been covered with earthly dust, and my heart might have become callous by rude encounters with the multitude. . . . But living in solitude till the fullness of time was come, I still kept the dew of my youth and the freshness of my heart. . . . I used to think that I could imagine all passions, all feelings, and states of the heart and mind; but how little did I know? . . . *Indeed, we are but shadows:* we are not endowed with real life, and all that seems most real about us is but the thinnest substance of a dream—till the heart be touched. That creates us—then we begin to be—thereby we are beings of reality and inheritors of eternity.[3]

This passage perhaps reflects the heart of Hawthorne's dream—as John Keats's now famous account of soul-making is said to reflect his; Hawthorne's writings everywhere suggest that ours cannot be more than a dream caught in a "dim sphere of half-development," to quote the narrator of "The Birthmark." It is important that we

3. *Hawthorne*, p. 42. The passage cited by Borges (*OI*, 63) is in italics.

have no better idea of Hawthorne's ethic or theology than we do of Shakespeare's. He clearly wondered whether art—his own particularly—was a medium by which the heart could be touched. Borges is right to suggest that Hawthorne's mind was naturally "intuitive," "oneiric"; the dialectical power of Hawthorne's mind is a power or disposition not for affirmation nor for inference in the logical sense, but for the construction of conditions of inference in the sense familiar to readers of Borges' fiction. Like Borges, though at a far less propitious time, Hawthorne tried to make art a function of consciousness, of insight into the grounds for what people and readers are apt to think, feel, and do in given situations—not of conscience or instruction in what they should do or should have done.

Often Hawthorne's narrators seem authorized spokesmen for the morality his audience expected from a responsible artist; but they are also, and essentially, characters who tell stories, as Borges' narrators do, from particular and often subtly eccentric points of view. The reader must learn to distinguish between the stories they tell and the larger compositions in which his narrators and his readers, too, play a part. The relationship between the narrator, his tale, and the reader comprises the material of another story or drama of imagination. The dreamlike quality readers experience from the fictions of Hawthorne (and Kafka) is so palpable not simply because the story moves like a dream or employs the imagery of dreams, but because the reader's responses are anticipated in a variety of ways and the reader senses (more or less) that he is playing some undefined role in the composition of the fiction that develops as he reads the story. The effect is one of inclusion and interiority, as opposed to the more usual fictional modes of exclusion and exteriority in relation to the reader's consciousness.

In "The Artist of the Beautiful," "poor" Owen Warland's miraculous butterfly emerges from a jewel box on which the story of its author's struggles is engraved (compare Borges' "The Garden of Forking Paths"). Throughout the quiet oddity of this ironic tale, which contains the sentimental story of the hopeless artist, there are recurring hints of the absurd redundancy of attempting to endow an emblem of the soul with life. Hawthorne knew that the legendary *psyche* meant both "soul" and "butterfly" in Greek and that his narrator's sententious conclusion had no more depth than the pun:

And as for Owen Warland, he looked placidly at what seemed the ruin of his life's labor, and which was yet no ruin. He had caught a far other butterfly than this. When the artist rose high enough to achieve the beautiful, the symbol by which he made it perceptible to mortal senses became of little value in his eyes while his spirit possessed itself in the enjoyment of the reality.[4]

The reality of what? The moral does, as Borges would say, seem to falsify the story until we recognize that the design is an ironic projection. A pivotal pun upstages the narrator, who is an apologist for aesthetic transcendentalism, and explodes his sentimental representation. "The Artist of the Beautiful" is itself a "mechanical butterfly," as Hawthorne indirectly informs us through his "Translator's Preface" to "Rappaccini's Daughter," where the alternative title is given as *"Le Papillon Mechanique."*

The "Translator's Preface" is important not only for the deliberate interrelation between the tale it prefaces and "The Artist of the Beautiful," but also for the more elaborate, more rounded framing effect it provides in the form of an apologia for what is probably Hawthorne's best story. Hawthorne might well be amused to learn that his famous tale of a woman nurtured on poisons is commonly reprinted without its "Preface"; it is here that the "translator" tells us that "Rappaccini's Daughter" is one of the productions of M. de l'Aubépine, whose writings

might have won him greater reputation but for an inveterate love of allegory, which is apt to invest his plots and characters with the aspect of scenery and people in the clouds, and to steal away the human warmth out of his conceptions.[5]

This "translator" defers to the reader to rescue the tale from "nonsense" by regarding it from "precisely the proper point of view." Of course, the story which follows is not the wooden allegory we were warned of. The translator, the preface, and M. de l'Aubépine,

4. *Works,* II, 535–36.
5. *Works,* II, 105.

all comprise Hawthorne's frame for a story which then takes on the aspect of a gently sarcastic allegory on the reading of itself. Beatrice, the heroine, was nurtured on poisons; she is the butterfly in the box, the emblem of the story's soul, which has been tampered with, injected with impurities, made noxious, yet "worthiest to be worshiped" by the author. The role of her suitor, Giovanni Guasconti, corresponds to that of the eager, and unfortunately naive, reader. Signor Baglioni, Guasconti's avuncular protector, clearly plays the mediating role so familiar in Hawthorne's tales of art: the mentor of "ordinary experience." Finally, the infamous Rappaccini, like M. de l'Aubépine, is the creator of the hapless living allegory on the futility of art—the beautiful Beatrice.

What is strikingly Borgesian about this design is the way the work refers to itself as a text by incorporating analogues for our reading *of* the work *in* the work. The reader thus encounters a mirror of his activity as a reader. This is precisely the "theme" mentioned by Borges as "not unknown to Pirandello or André Gide"—"the coincidence or confusion of the aesthetic plane and the common plane, of art and reality" (*OI,* 52). In "Tlön, Uqbar, Orbis Tertius," Borges employs the same self-referring mode of composition in developing a parable on the evolution of human culture.

"Tlön . . ." is a many-sided "mirror of engimas" of human learning. It looks like a partly satiric, mock-utopian science-fiction story, and within certain limits that is what it is: a sardonic, learned tale, told ostensibly by Borges, of the discovery of a plot to usurp the familiar world. Borges arranges this impression by mentioning one of his friends at the start:

Bioy Casares had had dinner with me that evening and we became lengthily engaged in a vast polemic concerning the composition of a novel in the first person, whose narrator would omit or disfigure the facts and indulge in various contradictions which would permit a few readers—very few readers—to perceive an atrocious or banal reality. (*L,* 3)

Many readers doubtless sense that their scheme bears in some way on the design of "Tlön, Uqbar, Orbis Tertius," but how it may apply is not so readily apparent. True, its narrator seems to run into inconsistencies and contradictions, as in his appalled discovery, near the end, of "small, very heavy cones (made of a metal which is not of this world) [which] are images of the divinity in certain regions of Tlön"; he continues, saying that "Tlön is surely a labyrinth, but it is a labyrinth devised by man, a labyrinth destined to be deciphered by men" (*L*, 17–18). The unearthly metals are inconsistent—that much is clear. But what atrocious or banal reality do they invoke? If they are "destined to be deciphered," what stratum of commonplaces can underlie the manifest fiction—the discovery of a labyrinthine plot to take over the world? The parallel implied between Tlön, the narrator's subject, and "Tlön . . . ," the Borges story, is a good starting point, for it marks the very fusion of art and reality which Borges notes in Hawthorne's journals.

Shortly after describing "the first intrusion of this fantastic world into the world of reality," the narrator of "Tlön . . ." says, "the rest is in the memory (if not in the hopes or fears) of all my readers" (*L*, 16–17). The story, in other words, depicts relations between an enigmatic text, a shadowy authorial corporation (ironically "duplicated" or reflected in the Borges-Bioy project), and a clamorous legion of readers. In fact, the reader of "Tlön . . ." is reading texts about texts, and he is called upon to judge matters of authenticity and consistency while the context for his judgment hovers uncertainly between the narrator's report and the document (the enigmatic encyclopedia) presented at second hand. Gradually the sense may develop of a still larger and unwritten text for which the entire narrator's story is a vehicle.

There are, I think, three interlocking designs: the essay by the narrator which seems to be the whole story at first; the implicit story of the narrator as victim *or* agent of the "plot"; and the "story" "Tlön, Uqbar, Orbis Tertius," which contains the others and in which the reader's judgments on the narrator's reliability play a larger "unwritten" part. We can relate these stories as levels of design in the following way. First, one ostensibly reads as a story a fictional essay—an account of the narrator's progress with a certain project. The essay's intelligibility is subverted by a contradiction in the facts. A second level emerges when this narrative is seen

297

not as the subject but as the object of the narrator's project(ion), in which case the whole fiction appears as an ironic projection—a kind of dramatic monologue whose subject is the zealous and defeated consciousness of the narrator. But the problem of inconsistency and distortion reappears in the fact that the narrator neglects to consider for his readers the obvious question raised by the existence of the cones; if they are made of unearthly materials, they must contradict his tenacious conjecture that Tlön is "a labyrinth devised by men, a labyrinth destined to be deciphered by men" (*L, 18*). He maintains his theory of human agency by ignoring the real significance of his "find." This ambiguity limits the second of the levels of the whole design.

Once we have recognized how the narrator's predicament has itself been contrived, it also becomes clear that we cannot determine whether he is a Tlönist agent or the hapless victim—*either* of the secret society whose machinations he thinks he has discovered, *or* of a higher power in whose service the society itself has been fabricated into *either* fictitious *or* actual historical existence. But in any case, the reader, like the narrator (but aided, as the narrator has not been, by the clue of the narrator's and Bioy's plan for a novel), has already begun to participate in determining the design and significance of the story. He must come to see the narrator as an object through which a still larger design is projected; that design is a special form of self-referring fiction, the *regressus ad infinitum*. On this third level, "Tlön" emerges as a labyrinthine and collaborative fiction about the process of discovering the design of a labyrinthine and collaborative fiction. It is designed to involve readers (inside and outside the story, across its threshold in a sense) with discovering the apparently singular design of the labyrinthine fiction, which is in fact only one term of an infinitely repeating series of fictions designed to be discovered as things-designed-to-be-discovered. "Atrocious" as the design of this repeating series may appear to some, Borges, in his authorial mercy, has set a limit to it or, rather, to the appropriateness of responding to it.

Like "The Artist of the Beautiful," the whole artifice in Borges' story turns on a "banal" pun whose discovery releases the mind from the labyrinth of ratiocination and sentimental involvement with the story, and carries it on toward awareness of the displaced creative consciousness hinted at in "Borges and Myself" and traced in "Nathaniel Hawthorne." Borges has indicated that "Tlön" was invented to sound like the English "to learn." † Borges' English homonym, set as it is in the title of a story originally written in Spanish, thus serves as an emblem of the self-illustrating character of the whole design. The conventional story does dissolve between its atrocious regress and the banality of its self-betraying pun.

Another story where Borges and Bioy Casares act as audience for a strange revelation is even more directly related to Hawthorne. "The Man on the Threshold" uses the nightmare vision of Kafka's tales and parables to conclude a narrative which recapitulates and extends the essential design of Hawthorne's now famous tale "My Kinsman, Major Molineux." The most obvious similarity between these two stories is the situation of a young man vainly searching for someone in a foreign city which is secretly opposing his search. More significant is the fact that both narratives skillfully conceal from the reader the circumstances behind the young man's delay and so create a parallelism between character and reader in the final recognition of the wild ceremony just across the threshold. That "The Man on the Threshold" treats the art of fiction and involves some form of a fusion of art and life may be immediately evident to some readers familiar with Borges (though, as usual, how and why this is done is probably less clear). If we can see how Hawthorne has fused subject and method in his story, the manner and scope of Borges' extension and refinement of it can be made evident.

"My Kinsman, Major Molineux" is the story of a young rustic's first visit to a city where he expects to find an eminent kinsman and through him to rise in the world. He is variously thwarted and beguiled by the town's night people, who eventually persuade

† I seriously question this interpretation of what Borges intended merely as an aid to *pronouncing* the word. N. T. DI G.

him to wait at a certain spot for Major Molineux. When his noble old kinsman finally makes his appearance in an agony of "tar and feather dignity," the young nephew's "long evening of ambiguity and weariness" leads him through recognition to a "species of mental inebriety" from which he emits a shout of laughter which is the loudest laughter of the whole reviling multitude.

For a long while, this story seemed only an engaging and clever anecdote of Colonial America. Robin seemed little more than a stock rustic—the kind of naif needed to carry off a trick narrative whose circumstances are concealed until, with a show of victory for Yankee fellowship and fraternity over monarchy, the amusement is finished. Then, about twenty-five years ago, doubtless with help from the discovery of Franz Kafka in America, Robin's story began to emerge from the general obscurity and anachronism accruing to Hawthorne as a tale of initiation and a kind of miniature trial of the national character. It was allowed that Robin was unfortunate, but still educable and serviceable as an apprentice for urban democracy. About a decade ago, criticism deepened the story: archetypes were observed—Oedipal and Christian materials—from which belief spread that Hawthorne had risen to myth by locally incarnating a representative of common humanity who inadvertently or unconsciously joins in reviling the noble representative of father, king, and even deity. "My Kinsman, Major Molineux" is all of the above and yet essentially something else: a meditative parable of the very processes of interpretation its allusions and ambiguities have generated. Its allusions to the passage to the underworld and to Christ's revilement before the multitude are now familiar. Beyond these, and more indicative of the playful detachment of Hawthorne's constructivist and projective methods in this story, one finds devices of ironic allusion which share with Borges' fictional subleties the virtue of scarcely disturbing the surface of the narrative.

A veritable stream of comically pointed visual imagery, optical descriptions of Robin's attempts to see or make things out, suggests that Hawthorne may have been familiar with the career of William Molyneux (1656–1698), [a seventeenth-century British scientist, friend of John Locke, and stimulus to Bishop Berkeley's *A New Theory of Vision*]. Molyneux removed cataracts to determine whether a man born blind and then made to see (compare Locke's theory of education) would be able to relate the visible to the tangible cube. Thematically and structurally, "My Kinsman . . ." reads like a witty eighteenth-century application of the Molyneux question to the moral sphere. Hawthorne may also have been influenced in his design by the then popular stories of rustics visiting the town theater, mistaking the play for a real situation, and even jumping to the stage to help the actors, only to find the action dissolving. He fashioned the situation of his rustic naif, unable to read the urban labyrinth and caught up in the action of a kind of *Festspiel* or morality play, by deliberate use of the methods, scenery, and even the theory of drama; Robin's "shrewd" blindness is dramatized comically, as is the awesome, dreamlike vision of his meeting with his kinsman. In accordance with Aristotle's famous recipe, Hawthorne makes recognition and reversal occur together, and at that moment gives his narrator the master words for tragic catharsis: "They stared at each other in silence, and Robin's knees shook, and his hair bristled, with a mixture of pity and terror." [6] I think this peripety leads us back to what Borges would call the "germinal vision" of the story. Hawthorne did not allude to Aristotle only to surround his homespun narrative with an incandescence of literary irony, but rather because he was fascinated by the threshold of consciousness, where reality and illusion interpenetrate in that moment of recognition. Robin's frustration with the ambiguities of the urban labyrinth becomes radical helplessness before the strange language, costumes, and make-up of the vigilantes. Caught up in a ritual drama entailing the expulsion of the king's representative, he becomes for a moment an actor; by betraying his kinship with the socially expelled member, Robin ritualizes and sanctifies the brotherhood of democrats aborning. In short, the frenzied, ceremonial reality which supervenes on Robin's evening of ambiguity and weariness is a work of art itself (a play), and Robin, who has been a person in a town, becomes a character in a

6. *Works,* III, 639.

drama which is on its revolutionary way to conferring an historical identity on the city—the same generic city, it might be noted, where dropouts like Wakefield become No Men.

Borges' remarks on the passages in Hawthorne's journals which illustrate his fascination with "the coincidence of the aesthetic plane and the common plane, of art and reality" (*OI*, 52), are particularly relevant to "My Kinsman, Major Molineux." He notes the theme "not unknown to Pirandello or André Gide" (*OI*, 52):

"Two persons to be expecting some occurrence, and watching for the two principal actors in it, and to find the occurrence is even then passing, and that they themselves are the two actors." (*OI*, 52)

Without Borges' fiction and his essay on Hawthorne, it is possible that "My Kinsman, Major Molineux" would not have been recognized as a variation on this theme or as a variant, as well, of the ancient device of the story within a story. The elements are there, but they are handled loosely, as something about which Hawthorne was thinking intuitively (Borges would say), rather than as the deliberate center of a dialectical design (which is the way Borges handles them in "The Man on the Threshold"). Part, at least, of Hawthorne's deliberate design appears when we consider the analogy between Robin's situation and that of the reader. Robin is transported from a trying and ambiguous ordinary reality into a ritualized history play. The story's allusiveness, its alternation of concealment and revelation, and its ambiguously muted anticlimax force the reader who senses its undercurrents to attempt to find a principle, or at least a belief, beneath a design that has most of the marks of a moral fable. Just as Robin's already unsure "optics" are dazzled a moment before his revelation by "a dense multitude of torches . . . concealing by their glare whatever object they illuminated," so the reader's insight is obscured.

In "The Wall and the Books," Borges makes an observation about our relation to art which operates as a principle in his essay on Hawthorne: "that imminence of a revelation that is not yet produced is, perhaps, the aesthetic reality" (*OI*, 5). "My Kinsman, Major Molineux" seems to have been designed as just such a threshold of paradoxical revelation, whose torches "concealed by their glare whatever object they illuminated." Hawthorne's reader completes the ambiguous story in his own image, and by reenacting its essential design, unites art and life and the past and present—just as Borges' criticism suggests and just as one of his finest stories shows.

The main narrative of "The Man on the Threshold" resembles a dramatic monologue in the manner of Robert Browning (whom Borges also lists, along with Hawthorne, among the precursors of Franz Kafka). In Kafka's writings, as in his forebears', the perspective of the narrator is commonly a threshold where attention to any one thing admits many others systematically. This, again, is part of the reason for Borges' linking Hawthorne's art to the relationship between dreams and theatrical performances (*OI*, 47). The narrator in "The Man on the Threshold" is in the position of a Robin Molineux retelling years later the strange circumstances of his meeting with his kinsman. Borges' recapitulation of Hawthorne's design involves the same basic situation, the same narrative device of doubling the concealment so that protagonist and reader simultaneously see, or fail to see, the light. Borges, however, draws the device of the story-within-a-story into the center of his fiction. The superb result of this refinement is an astonishingly direct and perfect parable of "aesthetic reality." A short account of the narrative will make it clear how the parable emerges through his larger design of a story about a story about a story.

The introductory paragraph mentions a strange knife and a certain Christopher Dewey of the British Council, who once told Borges and Bioy Casares about an episode from his youthful experiences in India. Borges calls on Allah to help keep his own account of Dewey's narrative "faithful," and observes that the tale has "a certain ancient simplicity that it would be a pity to lose—something perhaps straight out of the *Arabian Nights*" (*A*, 129). Dewey proceeds to tell of the circumstances of his search for a judge whom he names David Alexander Glencairn, who had mysteriously disappeared in the Muslim city he ruthlessly brought to heel. His search was at first fruitless: "I felt, almost at once, the invisible presence of a conspiracy to keep Glencairn's fate hidden.

There's not a soul in this city (I suspected) who is not in on the secret and who is not sworn to keep it" (*A*, 131). "Some of those meticulous liars I went so far as to knock down," he explains, for misleading and confusing the search. (His responses to the network of concealment he is trapped in take on unmistakably the characteristics of Robin's search for a similarly unpopular governor.) Finally he is directed to a house by "an envelope containing a slip of paper on which there was an address." There, "some kind of Muslim ceremony was being held," at the end of a "succession of unpaved inner courtyards." "At my feet, motionless as an object, an old, old man squatted on the threshold." Shortly upon talking to this ancient figure, Dewey concluded, that "This man might give me news of the Mutiny or of Akbar (I thought) but not of Glencairn. What he told me confirmed this suspicion" (*A*, 131–32). Within Dewey's story, then, the apparently uncomprehending old man tells the strange story of how an earlier colonial administrator had disappeared and been tried by his many victims or their "orphans and widows," and how he had been judged and executed; and as the old man's recollections come to an end, crowds begin to stream from the house, where, we then learn, the same judgment has just been completed upon Glencairn.

"The Man on the Threshold" seems at first an urbane narrative of East-West misunderstanding; and yet the fretwork of empire is touched by mysterious coincidence to unveil a more patient rhythm of justice in the universe. If one reflects on the matter of what the old man knew as he told his tale, the ostensible grand theme seems little more than a threshold on which the reader is encouraged to linger if he will. Ambiguities then appear in Dewey's narrative too. He has said "What he told me confirmed" the suspicion that one might get from him news of Akbar but not of Glencairn. (The style of surmise clearly resembles Robin's.) Dewey is emphatic about the response to his first questions.

The old man did not understand me (perhaps he did not hear me), and I had to explain that Glencairn was a judge and that I was looking for him. I felt, on speaking these words, the pointlessness of questioning this old man for whom the present was hardly more than a dim rumor. (*A*, 132)

The parenthesis emphasizes what Dewey seems to believe about the old man years later. Has he only concealed his suspicion for the sake of the story?

There is a temptation at this point to see Dewey either as a specimen of neocolonial blindness or as a trick storyteller. To choose either is to short-circuit Borges' design, much in the way that "My Kinsman, Major Molineux" has been spoiled with psychology, morality, and myth. Perhaps the axis of Borges' design can best be approached through his own typically curious remarks on the story. A candid and modestly misleading statement about its origins, which seem, he notes, different to him at different times, is followed by an apologetic and perhaps misleading comment on its form and design:

> I'm sorry to say that "The Man on the Threshold" is also a bit of a trick story and a game with time. What is told as having happened years and years earlier is actually taking place at that moment. The teller, of course, as he patiently spins his yarn, is really hindering the officer from breaking in and stopping the trial and execution. (A, 275)

Other remarks by Borges on "Ibn Hakkan al-Bokhari, Dead in His Labyrinth" hint at the connection between the execution of a story and a crime or a judgment—a relation explored years earlier, in a sketch called "The Haunted Mind," by Nathaniel Hawthorne. In his note to "Death and the Compass," Borges associates the reader with the "all-too-subtle detective," Lönnrot—for both of whom a "false track" is provided (A, 269). When Borges refers to the old man as the teller of his "trick" story and neglects the symmetrical form of the narrative by which he and Bioy Casares were, like the officer, hindered and entertained, he extends Dewey's reticence.

That is, I think, what he means by "a game with time"—an artifice whose locus in the past is always equally or in the same way a situation in the present between a story, its teller, and its audience. Logically, such a scheme exemplifies very well the magical identification of two (seemingly) different times which Borges uses to refute the idea of time as an ironclad order of succession and contemporaneity (OI, 176). Aesthetically it is, per-

305

haps, a perfect illustration of the work which fuses art and reality by incorporating its audience. When Dewey repeats the old Indian's device in telling his own old narrative, the actual or present situation is that of a storyteller who in fact knew about Glencairn, pretending in his narrative that he did not know, that there was no chance of finding him, and that he had given up instead to listen for a little while to the recollections of an old man. Borges and Bioy Casares thus expected to hear something of the old man and old India—just as Dewey had. At the point where the two stories converge—that is, when Dewey says he beheld the executioner and found Glencairn's body in the stables out back—Borges and Bioy Casares repeat the aesthetic revelation Dewey had transmitted to them. Borges' own faithful retelling of the narrative—beyond all human interest (that is, his show of retelling it as a story he had heard rather than as a story he invented)—repeats this experience of the convergence of past and present, the real and the imaginary. For as the Borges story of the Dewey narrative ends, the reader repeats the experience of the individual who is led to believe the story is about some circumstance in the past, when in fact it is just now happening to him.

In his "New Refutation of Time," Borges mentions the idealism of George Berkeley and Leibnitz's principle of (the identity of) indiscernibles as sources of his argument (*OI*, 173). He may have noticed that Berkeley's *"esse* is *percipi"* is related to Leibnitz's idea of the Monad as an unextended unit of force which exists somewhat in the manner of an audience for a god whose creation is an infinite sentence. Because the audience is part of the "story" itself, "The Man on the Threshold" is analogous to the Leibnitzean Monad, which develops its attributes "purely from within according to a preestablished series of continuous changes." [7] Borges' tentative definition of "aesthetic reality" agrees perfectly with Berkeley's immaterialist axiom: revelations are made, not given. Once the story is perceived as incorporating our perception of it, what seems remote, detached, and perhaps suspect emerges as an intimate, passionate, and perhaps inescapable communion. The logical and

7. Frederick Copleston, *A History of Philosophy* (New York, 1963), IV, 298.

aesthetic form of this ceremony across the threshold remains quite indifferent to the circumstances of its potentially limitless and, if we agree with Borges' time paradox, inherently timeless reenactment; as indifferent as geometry and the alphabet are to their application, or to the uses to which one may put the "strange dagger with a triangular blade and a hilt in the shape of an H" (*A,* 129) which occasions Dewey's story. That dagger is perhaps the fittest emblem for Borges' design. A triangle, after all, is expressive of the formal relations between author, story, and audience, and a handle in the shape of an H would be a fitting tribute to the author of "My Kinsman, Major Molineux."

There is, of course, much more to say about the frame or threshold of "The Man on the Threshold," and it would be well to go on to relate its Kafkaesque conclusion to Giovanni Guasconti's forced entry into Rappaccini's ceremonial and fatal sanctuary, and to go back then to Hawthorne's Borgesian "Preface." But it is perhaps enough for the present to suggest that Borges' observation, relative to Hawthorne and Kafka, that "every great writer creates his precursors" because their achievement "modifies and refines our reading" of them, applies in no less striking a way to Borges' relation to Nathaniel Hawthorne. Borges' special awareness of the paradoxical relations of art and reality, and of the literary traditions in which this consciousness has been preserved, has enabled him to understand anomalous characteristics of Hawthorne's art and, what is more important, to create masterpieces of his own in whose light Hawthorne's achievement will at last be visible. In creating Hawthorne as one of his precursors, Borges makes it possible to read Hawthorne anew and, who knows, to find perhaps that his fine old art so modifies and refines our reading of Borges that we will have to place Borges among the precursors of Hawthorne as well.

Notes on Borges
and American literature
ALEXANDER COLEMAN

Alfred Kazin has recently reminded us that Borges may well have
existed before in this country, a transmigratory soul variously in-
habiting the towns of Salem, Concord, and New York at different
times and with differing cosmic unease. Let us suppose Borges an
americano back then, at a time when the balances between God,
Nature, and Man were still delicate, still debated, and soon to spin
off into such splendid affirmations and denials as Emerson's
Essays, Melville's *Moby-Dick,* and Thoreau's *Walden.* Kazin
rightly projects Borges back to our nineteenth-century authors,
because they themselves are so indelibly defined in Borges' sensibility, still there in spite of his distance from them:

... there is something about his intellectual solitude, and the form that his essay-
tales take, that reminds me of 19th-century Americans having to make up their
own literature from the ground up.

So let me talk about my strange fancy that Borges really grew up with Poe, Emerson, Melville, Thoreau. He strikes me as a man who literally had to make up a
world he could live in; he has gone far enough to please his imagination. One has
the sense, confronting his shut-in state, of some immense need that *is* satisfiable,
of some primary personal effort at renewal—through the word alone—that one

308

associates with poets, fantasists, alchemists before the age of the novel and realism.[1]

Here in America, literature as construction "from the ground up," writing in which authorial intrusion constantly affirms the imaginary dominion and control over space and time—if I read Kazin correctly, the text might be further spun out to embrace an awareness, in the nineteenth century, that meaning derives from an immense impulse of the will to order, although the substance of the order had long since disappeared from what were our formerly theological imaginations.[2] And so, like Hawthorne, Melville, and Emerson, Borges' texts register metaphysical auras without being at all religious; they modify and confirm one another because they are all part of different categories of the same projection—a projection of the mind, totally. "The man of thought wins by generalizing," says Donoghue, "by abstraction, by resisting the 'usurpation of particulars.' " The very idea of such a man, exemplar of our so-called genteel tradition, reminds us of the various achievements of Emerson, Santayana, and Stevens. In turn we are forced to think of Borges as belonging to this tradition, partly because the tenuous relationship between the aforementioned writers and the societies of which they ostensibly formed a part is so basic to Borges' deliberately imprecise vision of Argentina and Buenos Aires, "ineffably far-flung, a multitude, yet strangely empty of everything except place-names, anecdotes, and a few friends." [3] As non-binding proof of "the old-fashioned American ability to make one's own God out of the fancies of the human brain," [4] here are the final stanzas from a poem whose theme and development would have delighted Emerson, and which Borges has unknowingly approximated many times in his own poetry:

> Here, now, we forget each other and ourselves.
> We feel the obscurity of an order, a whole,
> A knowledge, that which arranged the rendezvous.

1. Alfred Kazin, "Meeting Borges," *The New York Times Book Review* (May 2, 1971), p. 5.
2. Denis Donoghue, *Connoisseurs of Chaos* (London, 1956), p. 14 ff.
3. Kazin, p. 22.
4. *Ibid.,* p. 5.

Within its vital boundary, in the mind.
We say God and the imagination are one ...
How high that highest candle lights the dark.

Out of this same light, out of the central mind,
We make a dwelling in the evening air,
In which being there together is enough.

We owe this final, definitive expression to Wallace Stevens.[5]
Stevens' and Borges' powers of thought conquer the easy polarities
between order and chaos, but it is a conquest in which Nature has
been summarily ruled out as mediator. Theirs is a victory, of
course, but at the expense of emotion and cognizance of the
possibility of a sexual sensibility. As Borges hinted when he
laconically complained of the "absence of life"[6] in the work of
Henry James, we must be aware of the consequences of the mind-
as-being, and recognize that it is only in the light of Borges'
metaphorical and imaginative dominion over matter[7] that we can
understand how he in turn reads our classic literature of the nineteenth century.

How, in fact, does Borges read us? Needless to say, American
authors have at times had even more impact on him than the more
celebrated tutorials of De Quincey, Sir Thomas Browne, Shaw,
Chesterton, or Wells. There are abundant testimonies to this
influence throughout his work, sometimes in fragmentary mention
or quotation, but other times in significant introductions, poems,
or whole essays on Emerson,[8] Hawthorne,[9] Whitman,[10] and Mel-

5. "Final Soliloquy of the Interior Paramour," in *The Collected Poems of Wallace Stevens* (New York, 1955), p. 524.
6. Jorge Luis Borges in collaboration with Esther Zemborain de Torres, *Introducción a la literatura norteamericana* (Buenos Aires, 1967), p. 40.
7. Kazin, p. 5: "Borges has built his work—and, I suspect, his life itself—out of
the same dogged effort to make himself a home in his own mind."
8. Introduction to Emerson's *Representative Men* (Buenos Aires, 1949). Borges
had the following to say about Emerson, in a deleted portion of the *Paris Review*
interview (Winter–Spring, 1967) with Ronald Christ and now published as a footnote in Christ's study *The Narrow Act* (New York, 1969), p. 42: "I'm very fond
of Emerson; he was a very great writer. I remember that Nietzsche said that he
could not praise Emerson, because he found that they were so close that it was like
praising himself. But I think Emerson a finer writer and a finer thinker than
Nietzsche, though most people wouldn't say that today."
9. The influence of Hawthorne on Borges is studied elsewhere in this volume
(John Wright, "Borges and Hawthorne").
10. "El otro Whitman," in *Discusión* (1932), and "Note on Walt Whitman," in
Other Inquisitions 1937–1952, pp. 66–72; see also Borges' preface to *Hojas de
hierba* (Buenos Aires, 1969), his translation of selections from *Leaves of Grass*.

ville,[11] to name but a few. But Borges' critical method toward American literature is most evident in a booklet that with justification may be considered a minor entry in Borges' bibliography. I refer to his co-authored *Introducción a la literatura norteamericana*.[12] Even a cursory inspection of this booklet reminds us of the complaint of one of Borges' students at the University of Buenos Aires, who said that his professor chose for class discussion ". . . what is most important for Borges and not what is most important in that literature."[13] No matter how the *Introducción* is taken, it is a most unsatisfactory exposition of a body of literature. What can we say of a manual, however brief, that begins dutifully enough with paragraphs on Cotton Mather, Jonathan Edwards, and Philip Freneau, but then proceeds erratically through the eighteenth and nineteenth centuries, with considerable gaps and summary dismissals, only to end with a penultimate chapter entitled "The Detective Novel, Science Fiction, and the Novel of the Far West" and a final chapter on "The Oral Poetry of the Redskins"? One can easily sympathize with the inquisitive student's irritation. But this apparently erratic survey (it is only sixty-two pages long) demonstrates once again that Borges' responses to literature are actuated only as the books in question allude to his innermost world of symbol. Within the relatively insubstantial limits of the booklet, it is a mine of intuitions and revelations about Borges and how he sees our literature.

Take, for instance, Borges' gloss upon his own translation of a sentence from Jonathan Edwards' sermon "Sinners in the Hands of an Angry God":[14]

Metaphors such as this have generated the suspicion that Edwards was fundamentally a poet, frustrated by theology. . . .

11. Preface to *Bartleby* [sic] (Buenos Aires, 1944).
12. Much of the book seems to be in the form of transcribed classroom notes, and it is quite possible that some of the comments upon contemporary literature, such as the paragraph on Truman Capote's *In Cold Blood,* are the work of his collaborator.
13. Christ, p. 44
14. The sentence is: "The bow of God's wrath is bent, and the arrow made ready on the string, and justice bends the arrow at your heart, and strains the bow, and it is nothing but the mere pleasure of God, and that of an angry God, without any promise or obligation at all, that keeps the arrow one moment from being made drunk with your blood." Jonathan Edwards, *Basic Writings,* ed. O. A. Winslow (New York, 1966), pp. 158–59.

> In books he sought out nothing else but a stimulus for his own activity.... He knew nothing of Berkeley, with whom he agreed in the affirmation that the material universe is no more than an idea in the mind of God, nor did he know of Spinoza, who, as he did, identified God with Nature. In one of his last treatises, he said of God: "He is everything and He is alone." [15]

Again, the enforced company of Spinoza and Berkeley is immensely more important for our knowledge of Borges than for a specific intellectual portrait of Jonathan Edwards. And yet, by denying the relative importance of dogma in Edwards' theological constitution and concomitantly viewing him as a poet, Borges affirms what Perry Miller has suggested of Edwards:

> That he poured his consciousness into the ungrateful molds of theology was an accident of history; what gave vitality to this thinking was not the logic of his polemical tracts but the intensity of his love for a universe that divinity had made and in which divinity was immanent.[16]

In this sense, it is clear that Borges sees in Edwards the essential typologist, a mind of metaphysical capability which seeks "a pattern of repetition, the recurrence of eternal verities, not the caprices of fiat." [17] Typology, to be distinguished from tropism, denies the dualism of subject and object, and argues instead for a fusing of the two in a fleeting moment of perception, as did Berkeley (highly esteemed by Borges) and Edwards, who knew nothing of Berkeley's work. The congruity between Edwards and Berkeley is attractive to Borges, while Edwards' determinism and his essentially conservative theological stance within the gradually weakening structure of Puritanism are of little interest to him. In a recent sonnet entitled "Jonathan Edwards (1703–1758)," Borges gives an even more illuminating proof of his voracious appropriation of symbolism from other American authors. It might be best to quote the whole of this somber little masterpiece:

> Far from the Common, far from the loud
> City and from time, which is change,
> Edwards dreams, eternal now, and comes
> Into the shadow of golden trees. Today
> Is tomorrow and yesterday. Not one

15. Borges, *Introducción* ... , p. 11.
16. Jonathan Edwards, *Images or Shadows of Divine Things,* ed. Perry Miller (New Haven, 1948), p. 38.
17. *Ibid.,* p. 39.

Thing of God's in the motionless world
Fails to exalt him strangely—the gold
Of the evening, or of the moon.
Content, he knows the world is an eternal
Vessel of wrath and that the coveted
Heaven was created for a few
And Hell for almost all. Exactly
In the center of the web there is
Another prisoner, God, the Spider. (SP, 169)

The shadow of predestination and the inevitable doom of the majority within the Calvinist universe are evident, but what draws our attention is Borges' rethinking of the significance of one of Edwards' favorite symbols—the spider. In "Sinners in the Hands of an Angry God," Edwards compared the fate of man to that of a spider held over a flame:

The God that holds you over the pit of hell, much as one holds a spider, or some loathsome insect over the fire, abhors you, and is dreadfully provoked: his wrath towards you burns like a fire; he looks upon you as worthy of nothing else, but to be cast into the fire; he is of purer eyes than to bear to have you in his sight; you are ten thousand times more abominable in his eyes, than the most hateful venomous serpent is in ours.... And there is no other reason to be given, why you have not dropped into hell since you arose in the morning but that God's hand has held you up.[18]

Borges makes a key transposition of the symbol; far from repeating the hierarchy, both spatial and spiritual, of God-Man-Spider, Borges transfigures this hapless human fate in the hands of God into a metaphor of an entrapped and imprisoned God—the Spider, a Being encased, as it were, in the almost invisible filigree of Its own creation.

This is a modest but illuminating example of the literary imposition Borges performs upon other literatures. His examination of American authors subsequent to Edwards will repeat and amplify this erratic, highly personal, and entirely aggressive kind of appropriation. But Borges' affinities to our literature are not really evident until he begins to speak of Hawthorne and Emerson. He is brief and laconic on Freneau, while passing over all political

18. Edwards, *Basic Writings*, p. 159. One might also recall the essay written by Edwards in his eleventh year entitled "Of Insects" (pp. 31–37). For another view of the same sources, see the poem "Mr. Edwards and the Spider" by Robert Lowell, in *Lord Weary's Castle* (New York, 1961), pp. 58–59.

writing of the American Revolution in silence. (There is no mention of Tom Paine or of the authors of the Federalist Papers.) Borges proceeds directly to those authors whose works give some evidence of playful literary mystification or conscious deceit; thus the bizarre treatment of Franklin:

Mystifications pleased Franklin, as they did Poe. In 1773, the British government wished to impose a tax on its colonies; Franklin published in a London newspaper an apocryphal edict from the King of Prussia, demanding an identical tax from England, since that island had been colonized in the fifth century by Germanic tribes.[19]

In the same manner, the schematic obfuscation in Irving's *History of New York,* attributed to a "pedantic and imaginary Dutch chronicler, Dietrich [sic] Knickerbocker," [20] appeals to Borges. But these comments are only preliminaries to Borges' central concerns in American literature. As the balance of his survey indicates, and as the abundant commentary by Borges on our nineteenth-century authors proves, his passionate readings begin with Poe, Melville, Hawthorne, and Emerson—each for different motives, but each reading corresponding to a Borgesian "tic" already present in his work. His American readings are visible as early as 1925, as his truculent review of Guillermo de Torre's *Literaturas europeas de vanguardia* tells us in no uncertain terms. Here is a key paragraph:

...I set down ...an observation confirmed by the reading [of this book]: the irrefutable influence that Americans have and exercise upon European literature. Illustrious are the names of Laforgue and Browning and the more distant Góngora, but there is something provincial in them, very much of one country, of one imprisoning date, compared to names of such breadth as Walt Whitman, Emerson, and even Edgar Allan Poe.[21]

These terms would give pause to a European—Laforgue, Browning, and Góngora imprisoned within their chronology in time and space? It is as if Borges were saying that there was nothing timeless or abstract about them. Of course, the paragraph is unjust, but it is a good indication of where his reading eye was drawn after

19. Borges, *Introducción* ... , pp. 13–14.
20. *Ibid.,* p. 15.
21. *Martín Fierro,* 20 (August 5, 1925).

Ultraism had exhausted the literary preferences acquired in Europe during and after the First World War.

In this sense, Poe is a prime mover in defining Borges' aesthetic of narration, as Ronald Christ has so brilliantly demonstrated in his full-length study of Borges.[22] Poe's contribution to aesthetic form and logical analysis in narration was the invention of the detective story. In his 1932 essay entitled "Narrative Art and Magic," written some three or four years before his first narration of a basically "detective" format, "The Approach to al-Mu'tasim," Borges describes in general terms the plan of Poe's *Narrative of A. Gordon Pym,* and then begins to distinguish, albeit in a rather murky way, two kinds of causation in fiction—"natural" and "magic":

> ... it may rightly be inferred that the main problem of the novel is that of causation. One kind of novel, the slow-moving psychological variety, attempts to frame an intricate chain of motives akin to those of real life. . . . In the adventure novel, cumbersome motivation of this kind is inappropriate; the same may be said for the short story. . . .

> ... magic is not the contradiction of the law of cause and effect but its crown, or nightmare. . . .

> Let me sum up the foregoing. I have pointed out two chains of cause and effect: the natural, which is the incessant result of endless, uncontrollable processes; and the magic, in which—clear and defined—every detail is an omen and a cause. In the novel, I think that the only possible integrity lies in the second. Let us leave the first to psychological fiction, where all things are plausible.[23]

In essence, Borges is arguing for a massive expansion of the detective method, with causation apparent in all details as they are arranged in prediction, execution, and fulfillment. At the center of the plan stands an all-seeing, dehumanized consciousness that is constructed with all the inclusive, cosmic calm of a secondary seer—a Dupin, or, if you wish, a M. Teste, a Tiresias, or even a Lönnrot or Scharlach from Borges' own pantheon. Borges will take over the figure of Dupin for his own purposes, and extend the metaphorical possibilities of this master of ratiocination until he begins to lurk unexpectedly behind many of Borges' characters.

22. *The Narrow Act,* pp. 120–30.
23. See translation in *TriQuarterly 25* (Fall, 1972), pp. 209-15.

Clearly, Dupin has taken his toll; here is a good sample from a book review by Borges of *The New Adventures of Ellery Queen:*

Always infallible in error, Miss Dorothy Sayers prefers the contrasts and amenities of the Watson–Sherlock Holmes *ménage* (almost Panza–Don Quixote, almost Bouvard and Pécuchet, almost Laurel and Hardy) to the decent voluntary impersonality of C. Auguste Dupin,* illustrious ancestor of Holmes and even of Monsieur Teste. The world seems to share this preference. Nonetheless, Bernard Shaw ... declares that [one descends] with delight from the "ingenious automaton" Dupin to the inept adventures of Sherlock Holmes, "prince of duffers and dullards" ... the dictum is humorous, but it underlines (as always in Shaw) a truth. Sherlock is inferior to Auguste, not only because a decipherer of ashes and a hunter of bicycle tracks is inferior to a reasoner, but above all because he is not an "ingenious automaton." [24]

* [Note by Borges.] We know nothing even of the face of this investigator who dates from the year 1841; he has no more visible features than infinite night or libraries.

It is precisely the lack of psychological appeal and dialectical play between a pair like Holmes and Watson that appeals to Borges' sense of directive causation within the structure of a narration; this is evidently the beginning of a literary program that would bring to realization such works as "Pierre Menard, Author of the *Quixote*" and "The Garden of Forking Paths." He was interested not in a tension between opposing stereotypes, but in placing one "abstracting" consciousness, like Poe's Dupin, at the narrative center. Borges' friend and collaborator Adolfo Bioy Casares recalls an occasion in 1939 when he, Borges, and Silvina Ocampo meticulously planned a story. Unfortunately, as occurs with many of Borges' plans, the story was never written, but Bioy does recall that the protagonist, in search of manuscripts of a dead writer,

arrived at the castle where the master had lived and finally gained access to his papers. He turned up brilliant drafts, irreparably truncated. At the end of his search he found a list of prohibitions, which we wrote out that evening on the crumpled book jacket and blank pages of a copy of *An Experiment with Time;* here is a transcription of them:

In good writing one must avoid: ...
—Pairs of characters too obviously dissimilar: Quixote and Sancho, Holmes and Watson.
—Novels with a pair of heroes: references that send you back and forth from one character to the other are a nuisance. It may also be argued that this kind of novel writing creates difficulties: if the author ventures an observation concerning one of the characters, he has to make up a similar one about the other, without

24. *Sur,* 70 (July 1940), 61–62.

falling into too dissimilar differences or falling into sloppy coincidences—situations which can hardly be avoided: *Bouvard and Pécuchet*. . . .
—In the telling of a story, self-flattering tricks with time and space. Faulkner, Priestley, Borges, Bioy, etc.[25]

This last self-critique indicates that Bioy and Borges were well aware of the dangers of the strict structuralization that the "detective" method was to induce in their narratives. But Borges is insistent; in a 1939 review of two detective novels, he attacks the idea of a detective novel as such. The argument adduced is essentially this: ". . . all detective novels consist of a very simple problem which can be explained orally to perfection in five minutes, and which the novelist—perversely—draws out for 300 pages. The reasons for this are commercial; they obey no other necessity than to fill out the volume. In such cases, the detective novel ends by being an extended short story." [26]

In Borges' *Introducción* Poe is mentioned principally as the author of the *Philosophy of Composition,* which is given a meticulous résumé; Borges also makes an elementary distinction between Poe's tales of "horror" and tales of "ratiocination." [27] But other texts might be adduced to help us sound Borges' thinking on Poe; there is a spirited defense of Poe as the founder of the detective novel in a review of Roger Caillois' *Le Roman policier,*[28] and an equally loyal affirmation of Poe's "Americanism" in "Una vindicación de Mark Twain," in which Borges reminds us that

it has been declared infinitely that [Poe] was accidental in America, and that he could have easily "occurred" in London or Uppsala. I cannot agree. The terrifying and humorous Poe is not only an American but also a *Yankee:* in the continu-

25. Adolfo Bioy Casares, *La otra aventura* (Buenos Aires, 1969), pp. 145–47. Unpublished translation by Norman Thomas di Giovanni.
26. "Dos novelas policiales," *El Hogar* (April 7, 1939). The phenomenon of Borges contributing book reviews to a magazine dedicated to the tastes of the Argentine homemaker deserves comment. The reviews, dating from October 16, 1936, to July 7, 1939, on an irregular basis, constitute what surely must have been the most incisive book reviewing for a popular audience ever published in Latin America. These single pages, commenting upon at least four books and generally including an introductory "synthetic biography" of a European author, would have continued had it not been for Borges' near-fatal accident recounted in fictional terms in his story "The South." When asked recently why he did not pick up the series later, Borges said simply, "They never called me again, and it was evident that they weren't at all interested." The reviews constitute an as yet unstudied chronicle of Borges' reading in the years prior to the composition of his first stories. There is an incomplete collection at the New York Public Library.
27. Borges, *Introducción . . . ,* pp. 18–20.
28. *Sur,* 91 (April 1942), 56–57.

ous precision and skill of his many plays with darkness, in his secret writings and verses, in the bursts of monstrous charlatanism which remind us of P. T. Barnum. That trait will endure in his descendants: take note of the mystagogical air and sensational typography in which M. Teste delights.[29]

In a review in *El Hogar* of Edward Shanks's *Edgar Allan Poe,* Borges makes a catalogue of "what is left" after all of Poe's denigrators have had their say:

There remains the peculiar ambiance of these stories, as unmistakable as a face or a piece of music. Also, the *Narrative of A. Gordon Pym.* The invention of the detective genre. M. Paul Valéry. All this is enough to justify his renown, in spite of the redundancies and slips which mar every page.

As Borges himself recognizes, there is an intimate relation between the denatured consciousness of a Dupin and such later versions as Teste, Leonardo da Vinci as envisioned by Valéry, and Borges himself and his spiritual children. What Borges has taken over is the very idea of imagining at length the structure and operation of omniscience—a total all-encompassing intelligence. All of Borges' characters are glosses upon this unique totality. The relation between the mind-consciousness of the creator and his characters is the problem here, and once again Poe is central to Borges' self-justification. He clarifies the evident "suppression" or "reduction" of the ego in his work and the resultant hypertrophy of the intellect in commenting upon Poe and Valéry:

... why did Poe want to write a poem, "The Raven," that way? What need was there to write this story of the raven which repeats its name? ... I think that all of this must have satisfied him somehow. If not, he would not have written the poem. Or, what comes to be the same thing, all the logical reconstruction that he carried out was done *pour épater le bourgeois.* Or perhaps because he himself was a profoundly romantic poet and being a great romantic poet he wanted to be something else—to be a kind of Auguste Dupin, a strong and very intelligent detective. Something he was not. He was a very nervous and weak man, a very unfortunate man. *But he wanted to imagine himself as an abstract god of the intellect.* Like Valéry, who doubtless was much less abstract, much less conscious.

Valéry would have loved to be Monsieur Teste. Evidently, he was not M. Teste. No one is M. Teste. We don't even know if Testes are desirable. They would be nothing but monsters—[italics added].[30]

29. *Sur,* 14 (November 1935), 41.
30. Georges Charbonnier, *Entretiens avec Jorge Luis Borges* (Paris, 1967). Unfortunately, I have only the Spanish translation at hand: *El escritor y su obra: Entrevistas de Georges Charbonnier con Jorge Luis Borges* (Mexico, 1967), p. 43. See also the fervent note on Valéry's death, "Valéry as a Symbol" (*OI,* 73–74). There is a "synthetic biography" of Valéry in *El Hogar* (June 25, 1937): "In 1895, Valéry

Borges repeats Emerson's condemnation of Poe ("the jingle man"), and generally reserves his praise for Poe's poetic theory and creation of Dupin rather than his literary practice. His estimation of Emerson, on the other hand, has little of these qualifications and prevarications. Emerson, in fact, is at the heart of Borges' aesthetics, and for reasons that are intimately related to the kind of total consciousness espoused by Poe and later by Valéry. Ronald Christ puts it plainly enough, saying that "The character, the only character, I think, in all of Borges, is the literary Over-Soul," [31] and that both Borges and Emerson, "stressing the transcendental elevation at the expense of the ego, insist that to be is not to be"; [32] through Borges' mind we confront Emerson as an abstract intelligence victimized by his own tendency to abstract and universalize. Borges has always fervently espoused the cyclical theory of history and a resultant reorientation of the individual vis-à-vis the cosmos, and so Emerson is a convenient subject for this exercise in anchoritic consolation:

Our destiny is tragic because we, irreparably individuals, are restricted by time and space. There is nothing, therefore, more gratifying than a belief which eliminates circumstances and declares that each man is all men and that there is no one who is not the universe.[33]

Are we not approaching the Emersonian sense of the Over-Soul? "The mind is one, and the best minds, who love truth for its own sake, think much less of property in truth. They accept it thankfully everywhere, and do not label or stamp it with any man's

---

published his first volume, *Introduction to the Method of Leonardo da Vinci*. In that book, of a symbolic or adivinatory character, Leonardo is a pretext for the exemplary description of a type of creator. Leonardo is a sketch of Edmond Teste, limit or semi-god whom Paul Valéry resembles. That personage—the tranquil and barely visible hero of the brief *Evening with M. Teste*—is perhaps the most extraordinary invention of contemporary letters." As for Valéry on Poe, see "Au sujet d'*Eureka*," *Oeuvres*, ed. Jean Hytier (Paris, 1957), I, 854–67. The opening sentences could not be more auspicious: *"J'avais vingt ans, et je croyais à la puissance de la pensée. Je souffrais étrangement d'être, et de ne pas être. Parfois, je me sentais des forces infinies . . ."* (p. 854). A complete treatment of this topic can be found in Christine M. Crow, " 'Teste parle': The Question of a Potential Artist in Valéry's M. Teste," *Yale French Studies* (Special number on Valéry), 44 (1970), 157–68.

31. Christ, *The Narrow Act*, p. 225.

32. *Ibid*, p. 30.

33. Borges, Introduction to *Representative Men*, p. xiii. Translated by Ronald Christ.

name, for it is theirs long beforehand, and from eternity." [34] Since by now it is a commonplace for Borges to consider himself another mere incident in the universe, the act of writing might well be considered as progressively inferior the more it becomes "expressive" and univocal.

Borges' insight into Emerson confirms the relation between impersonality and the uses of literary history as a conscious, ordered collage of related sensibilities and responses; the opening paragraph of "The Flower of Coleridge" is the most perfect expression of this tendency in Borges:

Around 1938 Paul Valéry wrote that the history of literature should not be the history of the authors and the accidents of their careers or of the career of their works, but rather the history of the Spirit as the producer or consumer of literature. He added that such a history could be written without the mention of a single writer. It was not the first time that the Spirit had made such an observation. In 1844 one of its amanuenses in Concord had noted: "I am very much struck in literature by the appearance that one person wrote all the books; . . . there is such equality and identity both of judgment and point of view in the narrative that it is plainly the work of one all-seeing, all-hearing gentleman" (Emerson, *Essays: Second Series,* "Nominalist and Realist," 1844). (OI, 10)[35]

34. *The Complete Essays and Other Writings of Ralph Waldo Emerson,* ed. Brooks Atkinson (New York, 1950), p. 267. Emerson's essay on Shakespeare in *Representative Men* may well have been the source for Borges' apocryphal biographical sketch of Shakespeare entitled "Everything and Nothing," with its fractionalized sense of self: "The tale runs that before or after death, when he stood face to face with God, he said to Him, 'I, who in vain have been so many men, want to be one man—myself.' The voice of the Lord answered him out of the whirlwind, 'I too have no self; I dreamed the world as you dreamed your work, my Shakespeare, and among the shapes of my dreams are you, who, like me, are many men and no one' " (*SP,* 260).

35. This is, in essence, the most acute manifestation of authorial humility in Borges—a role one can never discount in his work—and it suggests a new literary genre: the "collation." Others far less modest than Borges have profited by this method: Eliot in *The Waste Land,* Juan Goytisolo in *Reivindicación del Conde Don Julián,* Evan S. Connell, Jr., in *Notes from a Bottle Found on the Beach at Carmel,* and even Luciano Berio in his sonic collage *Sinfonía,* whose third segment is based on entire passages drawn from the third movement of Mahler's *Second Symphony.* Berio explains that "the Mahler movement is treated like a container within whose framework a large number of references is proliferated, interrelated, and integrated into the flowing structure of the original work itself. The references [in the integrated section] range from Bach, Schoenberg, Debussy, Ravel, Strauss, Berlioz, Brahms, Berg, Hindemith, Beethoven, Wagner, and Stravinsky to Boulez, Stockhausen, Globokar, Pousseur, Ives, myself, and beyond. I would almost say that this section of *Sinfonía* is *not so much composed as it is assembled* to make possible the mutual transformation of the component parts. . . . The juxtaposition of contrasting elements, in fact, is part of the whole point of this section . . . which can also be considered, if you will, a documentary on an *objet trouvé* recorded in the mind of the listener." From "Notes," by Luciano Berio, accompanying the Columbia MS

In the interview with César Fernández Moreno, Borges was asked about his poem dedicated to Emerson (*SP,* 171), and he responded with a considerable degree of autobiographical passion:

I was thinking of a poem by Emerson entitled "Days," in which he says that the days passed before him like a file of muffled women, and that they offered him everything—the universe—and that he simply accepted a few herbs and a little water, whereupon the days went away and he saw their scorn . . . he is repentant of having lived little, of having contented himself with a few experiences and much literature.[36]

Of course, Borges is describing himself as much as he is referring to Emerson's dilemma, and true to the spirit of "amanuensis" that Borges divines in Emerson, the actual creation of "Days" corresponds exactly to Borges' ideal of creation. Emerson himself recalls that ". . . I have written within a twelve month verses ["Days"] which I do not remember the composition or correction of, and could not write the like to-day, and have only, for proof of their being mine, various external evidences, as the MS. in which I find them."[37] What is obsessive in Borges' view of Emerson—as in his view of Poe and also, to some extent, of Whitman—is the hypertrophy of intellects so far beyond the resources and limitations of the body that they carry on a wholly alien existence. Metaphors of this mental possibility run through the pages of the present essay in the form of Dupin-Teste-Menard-Quain; but as the reverent testimonial poem and his occasional comments show, Emerson is yet another version of the *vates* and *grammaticus*[38] combined in a seminal figure that confounds individual differences and speaks for all men. "[T]he striving for glory, the reverence for and preoccupation with language, the prolix weaving of theories in order to justify the work, the man aware of himself as the embodiment of an epoch"[39]—thus Borges describes Sir Thomas Browne and Ben Jonson, although Emerson, too, comes

---

7268 recording by Leonard Bernstein and the New York Philharmonic (italics added).

36. César Fernández Moreno, *La realidad y los papeles* (Buenos Aires, 1967), p. 606.

37. As quoted in F. O. Matthiessen, *American Renaissance* (New York, 1968), p. 59.

38. See Christ, pp. 142–47.

39. Borges, *Inquisitions* (p. 32), as quoted in Christ, p. 141.

under the rubric of prolixity and a curiously selfless self-importance. As James said of Emerson, "passions, alternations, affairs, adventures had absolutely no part" in his development; his life "stretched itself out in enviable quiet—a quiet in which we hear the jotting of the pencil in the notebook." [40]

Perhaps sharing Emerson's chagrin in the face of the unwelcome barbaric presence of Walt Whitman, Borges is more reserved and even contradictory in his critical judgments of this poet. Part of the problem seems to lie in the ferociously *willed* aspect of Whitman's multiple autobiographical roles in his poetry —a construction of an image that derives, as Emerson was to regret to some degree later, from the final pages of his own essay "The American Scholar": ". . . if the single man plant himself indomitably on his instincts, and there abide, the huge world will come round to him. . . . We will walk on our own feet; we will work with our own hands; we will speak our own minds." [41] This is all very fine as a poetical program for Borges, for he, no less than Whitman, has held a highly acerbic view of "the courtly muses of Europe" whom Emerson felt compelled to malign in "The American Scholar." But Borges' Whitman is not the orgiastic and consciously corporeal *persona* that many of us think of as Whitman; instead Borges emphasizes the multiple *personae,* a kind of universalized self, as the primary dramatic protagonist evident in the "Song of Myself." This composite voice is echoed by Borges in such early works as *Fervor de Buenos Aires* (1923). [42] In 1927, there appeared an announcement [43] of a projected translation by Borges of *Leaves of Grass,* a task apparently never

40. Henry James, "Emerson," *The American Essays* (New York, 1956), p. 52.
41. Emerson, *The Complete Essays . . . ,* p. 63.
42. The whole subject of Whitman in Latin American poetry has yet to be thoroughly explored. For a good example of how powerful an influence he exercised on poets like Pablo Neruda, see "Las personas del poeta," in Emir Rodríguez Monegal, *El viajero inmóvil: Introducción a Pablo Neruda.* (Buenos Aires, 1966), pp. 16–20. Denis Donoghue's handling of the *persona* problem is most deft: "Let x equal the self. Then x equals A plus B plus D plus E, and so on, where each letter stands for a new experience contained and possessed, and the self is the sum of its possessions. This is the law of Whitman's lists. If you say that the self—x—is the sum of its possessions, A, B, C, D, and so on, then the more you add to the right-hand side of the equation, the more you enrich the left, *and you do this without bothering about the 'nature' of the x."* Donoghue, *Connoisseurs of Chaos,* p. 25 (italics added).
43. *Martín Fierro,* 38 (February 26, 1927).

322

realized until quite recently.[44] But if one compares the generous tone of such an essay as "El otro Whitman" (1929) with the summary condemnation recently issued by Borges in conversation with Richard Burgin, we have at least full cognizance of the range of Borges' passionate skepticism with regard to Whitman:

> ... in Whitman everything is wonderful, you know? I don't think that anybody could really believe that everything is wonderful, no? Except in the sense of it being a wonder. Of course, you can do without that particular kind of miracle. No, in the case of Whitman, I think that he thought it was his duty as an American to be happy. And that he had to cheer up his readers. Of course, he wanted to be unlike any other poet, but Whitman worked with a program, I should say; he began with a theory and then he went on to his work. I don't think of him as a spontaneous writer.[45]

Well, this is terribly unjust; Borges dismisses the whole specter of evil and death from Whitman's vision,[46] and dispatches with no comment such contrarily pessimistic masterpieces as *Democratic Vistas*. But no matter, at this stage we hardly expect judiciousness from Borges. But certainly in that 1929 essay Borges had found an objective and tactful tone to describe similar concerns. Speaking then of Whitman's reception among the French, Borges noted that

> The economy of Whitman's verses was so extraordinary to them that they never got to know Whitman. They preferred to classify him: they praised his *license majestueuse*, turning him into the precursor of the many homey inventors of free verse. What's more, they mimicked the weakest aspect of his diction: the complacent geographical, historical and circumstantial enumerations that Whitman strung out in order to fulfill a certain prophecy of Emerson concerning the poet worthy of America.[47]

Thus, says Borges, the Whitmanesque sense of wonder before the universe produced a false image of the poet, that of "an insistent Hugo." Borges, at least in 1929, saw instead of the stereotype a "poet of tremulous and sufficient laconic quality" and a "peculiar poetry of arbitrariness and privation" that contrasts effectively with the commonplaces so often uttered about Whitman. In a later essay, from 1946, Borges notes that Whitman offers the

44. *Hojas de hierba* (Buenos Aires, 1969).
45. Richard Burgin, *Conversations with Jorge Luis Borges* (New York, 1969), p. 141.
46. See Donoghue, pp. 28–29.
47. Borges, "El otro Whitman," *Discusión,* pp. 51–52.

trusting reader "a taste of the fullness of life" (*OI*, 31), recounted by a semi-divine protagonist whose excesses lie in the "doctrinal happiness . . . inexorably imposed upon himself" (*OI*, 144). And so the contradictory readings continue; there is a magnificently orchestrated condemnation of Léon Felipe's unfortunate translation of "Song of Myself," [48] along with a revealing contrast, to which Borges obsessively returns in later commentary, between Whitman's biography, "the insipid chronicle of his day," and the "paradisaical sphere of his poetry" (*OI*, 68). Recently, Borges published a short poem, "Camden 1892," which makes its quiet and painful point amidst a grey, subdued rhetoric:

> **The fragrance of coffee and newspapers.**
> **Sunday and its tedium. This morning,**
> **On the uninvestigated page, that vain**
> **Column of allegorical verses**
> **By a happy colleague. The old man lies**
> **Prostrate, pale, even white in his decent**
> **Room, the room of a poor man. Needlessly**
> **He glances at his face in the exhausted**
> **Mirror. He thinks, without surprise now,**
> ***That face is me.* One fumbling hand touches**
> **The tangled beard, the devastated mouth.**
> **The end is not far off. His voice declares:**
> **I am almost gone. But my verses scan**
> **Life and its splendor. I was Walt Whitman.   (*SP*, 175)**

The same contrast between life and fiction is underlined with even more vehemence in Borges' very recent preface to his own translated selections from *Leaves of Grass:*

> Those who pass from the glare and the vertigo of *Leaves of Grass* to the laborious reading of any of the pious biographies of Whitman always feel disappointed. In those gray and mediocre pages, they seek out the semi-divine vagabond that these verses uncovered for them, and they are astonished not to find him. This, at least, has been my own experience and that of all my friends. One of the aims of this preface is to explain, or try to explain, that disconcerting discord.[49]

Borges then proceeds to analyze the possibilities of the epic genre in America by means of an acute contrast between *Leaves of Grass* and *The Song of Hiawatha.* Longfellow is dismissed as a "good poet who explored libraries and who is not lacking in imagination and a good ear," but Whitman's work, far from the library, is

48. *Sur,* 88 (January 1942), 68–70.
49. Preface to *Hojas de hierba,* p. 27.

described as the "cursed revelation of a man of genius." Borges then imposes upon Whitman—one of his own most insistent themes—the primacy of the "spirit" over the individual, the utter democracy of creation:

In each of the illustrious models that the young Whitman knew and that he called feudal, there is a central character—Achilles, Ulysses, Aeneas, Roland, the Cid, Siegfried, Christ—whose stature is well above that of the others, who are subject to him. Whitman said to himself that this primacy corresponds to a world that has been abolished or that we wish to abolish—that of the aristocracy. My epic cannot be that; it must be plural, it must declare or presuppose the incomparable and absolute equality of all men. . . .

He needed, as did Byron, a hero; but his hero had to be innumerable and ubiquitous, symbol of a populous democracy, like the omnipresent god of the Pantheists. That creature has a two-fold nature; he is the modest journalist Walter Whitman, native of Long Island, a man whom some friend in a hurry might greet in the streets of Manhattan; and he is, at the same time, the other person that the first man wanted to be and was not, a man of adventure and love, indolent, courageous, carefree, a wanderer throughout America. . . . [T]here is almost no page on which the Whitman of his mere biography and the Whitman that he wanted to be and now is are not confounded in the imagination and affections of generations of men.[50]

In effect, just as Borges saw in Valéry the perfect metaphor for an abstract god of the intellect, so he sees in Whitman's ubiquitous roles and "communality" of authorship the essence of the abstract god of the body, ever present, "turbulent, fleshy, sensual, eating, drinking and breeding."

As the projective imagination in Poe, Emerson, and Whitman is at the heart of Borges' admiration for them, there are allegorical projections of longer works, novels and novellas, which greatly appeal to him. Behind the cluster of events in Melville's *Moby-Dick,* for example, there already rests a latent structure of "magical" rather than "natural" causality. Borges sees the whole sweep of allegorical possibilities in *Moby-Dick* without in any way affirming quality or "roundness" of character, as E. M. Forster would have it, in the characters themselves—above all, not in Ahab. The Burgin conversations are a good demonstration of Borges' amplifying, distorting critical sense:

. . . in the case of *Moby-Dick,* I think that I believe in the story rather than in the characters, because the whole story is a symbol, the white whale stands for evil,

50. *Ibid.,* pp. 28–29.

and Captain Ahab stands, I suppose, for the wrong way of doing battle against evil, but I cannot believe in him personally.[51]

This recent opinion matches almost to the letter Borges' opinions on *Moby-Dick,* first voiced in 1944 in a preface to "Bartleby the Scrivener." The opinion is forthright and uncompromising:

In the winter of 1851, Melville published *Moby-Dick,* the infinite novel which gave him his fame. Page after page, the story grows until it usurps the dimensions of the cosmos; at the beginning, the reader might suppose that its theme is the miserable life of whale hunters; farther on, that the theme is the madness of Captain Ahab, desperate to hunt down and to destroy the White Whale; finally, that the Whale and Ahab and the pursuit which fatigues the oceans of the planet are symbols and mirrors of the Universe. . . . [B]ut the symbol of the Whale is less apt to suggest that the cosmos is evil than it is to imply its vastness, its inhumanity, its bestial or enigmatic stupidity.[52]

Borges is so insistent upon the ultimate symbolism of the novel— its overwhelming domination over mere human character—that he makes a grotesque error, a mistake so perfect for Borges' argument that I am only half-convinced that it was unintentional: ". . . the monomania of Ahab perturbs and finally annihilates all the men on the boat. . . ."[53] Not true, of course; Ishmael escapes. It is almost as if Borges were rewriting the work in his mind as he thought about it. The monstrosity of the book has taken over everything in Borges' mind, and he gives to Melville a sentence to underline this deluge of evil: "It is as if Melville had written, 'It is enough that only one man be irrational for other men and the universe to be so.' The history of the world abounds in confirmations of this fear."[54] In this sense, Melville is close to Kafka, but, even more acutely, the author of *Moby-Dick* belongs to the distinguished but occult American tradition of "secret men," from Poe to Lovecraft: "The vast population, tall cities, erroneous and clamorous advertising have all conspired to make the great secret man one of the traditions of America. Edgar Allan Poe was one of them; Melville also."[55]

Borges' sympathy does not rest entirely with these "underground" figures; he is just as apt to come to the defense of a well-

51. Burgin, *Conversations* . . . , p. 62.
52. Preface to *Bartleby* [sic] (Buenos Aires, 1944), p. 9.
53. *Ibid.,* p. 10.
54. *Ibid.,* pp. 10–11.
55. *Ibid.,* p. 12.

known writer whom he believes to have been maligned, misunderstood, or simply victimized by an ordinary stereotype. Such is the carefully argued essay "Una vindicación de Mark Twain" (1935). Ostensibly a commemorative piece on the occasion of the centenary of Mark Twain's birth, the essay immediately proceeds to dispense with all preliminaries in order to rectify two "outrages" committed against Twain's memory:

> One, that of simulating that in his felicitous work the moments of complaint or sarcasm are the fundamental ones; the other, committed by those who reduce him to the symbol of the artist frustrated and mutilated by the arid nineteenth century and a brutal continent. Both errors are rampant in his native land; it is best to denounce them before they propagate themselves here. Their source probably can be found in the book by Van Wyck Brooks, *The Ordeal of Mark Twain*. [56]

Borges then expands his argument into a brief examination of Twain's humoristic techniques, based on novelty, surprise, and exaggeration, all while noting that Twain, at least as we read him now, still carries with him some sense of comedy but often (to quote the phrase of Bernard De Voto) with "the laughter gone out of it." What Borges *does* sense in Twain is his nihilism, "his conception of the stellar universe as a blundering perpetual machine, his continual creation of cynical or blasphemous apothegms, his vehement denial of free will, his affinity with the idea of suicide, his fanatic atheism, his adoration of FitzGerald's versions of Omar. . . ." [57] The whole essay is a model of the "inner" vindication of a writer; in the same vein Borges takes De Voto to task for branding Bret Harte a "literary impostor" only in order to exalt, more understandably if still unjustifiably, the stature of Twain. [58]

It is by now a commonplace in Borgesian criticism to put special emphasis on what might be considered Borges' "arcane" tastes. Chesterton, De Quincey, Stevenson, and H. G. Wells (the latter an overwhelming influence, if the number of Wells's books reviewed in *El Hogar* and elsewhere is any indication) are all motivating forces in his literary ethic, but few other authors of Borges' generation anywhere can still be said to share his taste in literature. Borges'

56. "Una vindicación de Mark Twain," *Sur*, 14 (November 1935), 40.
57. *Ibid.*, pp. 42–43.
58. Preface to Bret Harte, *Bocetos californianos* (Buenos Aires, 1946), p. 9.

fascination with Henry James may or not be a case in point, since he has such a typically perverse view of James's work as a whole. For a start, Borges has no patience whatsoever with James's novels,[59] in his survey commenting only briefly on *The Ambassadors* (has he really read it?), leaving the rest of the major novels unmentioned. He concentrates his critical interest on the short stories, explaining himself this way: "The tales of James are no less dense than the novels but make much more interesting reading."[60] Borges expresses a much less guarded admiration in his preface to James's "The Abasement of the Northmores," in which he recalls the "other" James not generally visible in the novels: "I have perused some Oriental literature and quite a few literatures of the West; I have translated Kafka and Melville, Swedenborg and Bloy; I know of no more strange body of work than that of James."[61] Borges is here most exact in his definition: "I am speaking of a lucid omission of one part of the novel, a gap which permits us to interpret the work in one way or the other, *both ways having been contemplated by the author*"[62] (italics added). This is, of course, Jamesian ambiguity and narrative unreliability synthetically defined; but Borges' enumerated preferences among the tales give us even more precise data to confirm the definition. "The Figure in the Carpet" (1896), mentioned with much enthusiasm by Borges in his pamphlet,[63] is a good example. Hugh Vereker, James's multifaceted novelist in whose work there is a central proposition that can only be glimpsed at the beginning of his career, is the object of a parodistic critical search for this central meaning by a group of critics, who are taken to task by the author himself in terms that remind us of the satiric bibliographical tone first set down by Borges in "Pierre Menard, Author of the *Quixote*":

59. Although Borges states in a footnote to "The Flower of Coleridge" (1945) that "I have not read *The Sense of the Past,* but I am acquainted with the competent analysis of it by Stephen Spender in his book *The Destructive Element,*" he corrected the deficiency six years later by a careful reading and annotation of James's last, large, and unfinished work.

60. Borges, *Introducción . . .* , p. 39.

61. Preface to Henry James, *La humillación de los Northmore* (Buenos Aires, 1945), pp. 10–11.

62. *Ibid.,* pp. 11–12.

63. Borges, *Introducción . . .* , p. 39.

... It stretches, this little trick of mine, from book to book, and everything else, comparatively, plays over the surface of it. The order, the form, the texture of my books will perhaps some day constitute for the initiated a complete representation of it. So it's naturally the thing for the critic to look for.[64]

The burlesque search for a primal plan reminds us once again of the fundamentally similar urge toward totality emanating from so many of Borges' narrators and characters, where each paragraph, each partiality forms a part of that total book once dreamed of by Mallarmé and Valéry; it is thus perfectly just for Kazin to remind us that "For Borges, too, the 'imagination' he constantly celebrates —and works in—is God." [65]

My thanks and gratitude to Ronald Christ, who lent me most of the materials cited in this essay, above all the pages from El Hogar *and the prefaces to the works of Emerson, Melville, Bret Harte, and Henry James. All translations, unless otherwise indicated, are my own.*

64. Henry James, "The Figure in the Carpet," *The Complete Tales of Henry James: 1892–1898,* ed. Leon Edel (New York, 1964), p. 282. Other stories of James's that might be worthy of examination in the light of Borges' allusions to them are "The Jolly Corner," "The Lesson of the Master," "The Tree of Knowledge," "The Great Good Place," "The Private Life." The theme of Borges and James is of the richest significance and deserves intense concentrated treatment.

65. Kazin, p. 5. Borges' reading and translation of contemporary American literature after James has been severely selective. Aside from the brief comments available to the student in the *Introducción . . . ,* one might mention the "synthetic biography" of Edgar Lee Masters in *El Hogar* (December 11, 1936); the short review of Faulkner's *The Wild Palms* in *El Hogar* and Borges' own brilliant translation of the novel (Buenos Aires, 1941); the review of *Absalom, Absalom!* (*El Hogar,* 1937); the "synthetic biography" of T. S. Eliot, along with a translation of the first chorus from "The Rock" in *El Hogar* (June 25, 1937); a "synthetic biography" of S. S. Van Dine in *El Hogar* (June 11, 1937); and Borges' preface to a translation of Ray Bradbury's *The Martian Chronicles* (Buenos Aires, 1955). One must perforce mention also the poetry translations done in collaboration with Adolfo Bioy Casares and published in *Sur,* 113–114 (1944), a double number dedicated to North American literature. Among the poets translated are Robert Penn Warren, John Peale Bishop, Hart Crane, e. e. cummings, Delmore Schwartz, Karl Shapiro, and Wallace Stevens (a complete "Sunday Morning"). Previously, Borges had translated three poems by Langston Hughes and three by Edgar Lee Masters in *Sur,* 3 (1931). As a final example of Borges' catholicity of taste regarding the North American continent, one cannot neglect this succinct review (*El Hogar* [October 30, 1936], p. 35) of a then recently issued book on the Dionne quintuplets: "One of the baffling characteristics of our age is the enthusiasm which, for biological and numerical reasons, the Dionne sisters have provoked on the entire planet. Doctor William Blatz has consecrated to them a vast tome, foreseeably illustrated with enchanting photographs. In the third chapter he affirms that 'Yvonne is easily recognizable by being the eldest, Marie by being the youngest, Annette because everyone confuses her with Yvonne, and Cecile because she is indistinguishable from Emilie.'"

Borges and the new Latin-American novel
JAIME ALAZRAKI

> *Hence the final meaning of Borges' prose—without*
> *which there simply would not be a modern Spanish-*
> *American novel—is to attest that Latin America lacks*
> *a language and, consequently, must create it. To do*
> *so, Borges confounds all genres, rescues all tradi-*
> *tions, kills all bad habits, creates a new order of*
> *exigency and rigor over which there may rise irony,*
> *humor, play—indeed—but also a profound revolution*
> *that matches freedom with imagination, and with both*
> *he constitutes a new Latin-American language which,*
> *by sheer contrast, reveals the lie, the submission*
> *and the deceit of what traditionally was taken for*
> *"language" among us.*
> —Carlos Fuentes, La nueva novela hispanoamericana

At a time when Borges' work is being acknowledged as a driving
force in what has been called "the Borgesian phase" [1] of recent

1. I quote Morris Dickstein, *The New York Times Book Review*, April 26,
1970: "... in the last three years an important segment of American fiction has
entered a new and more unexpected phase, a more deliberately experimental one,
far less likely to issue in best-sellerdom and *succès de scandale*. Call this the Borgesian phase, though Borges has not been the only model for the short, sometimes
dazzlingly short, and multi-layered fiction that is involved. (Interestingly, Borges'
example has served to release the influence of others, including his own master,
Kafka, and even such different writers as Beckett and Robbe-Grillet.)" I should

American fiction, little or nothing has been said about his impact on contemporary Latin-American fiction. One reason for this anomaly is that Spanish-American students and critics take Borges so much for granted that the extent of his influence has been deluged in vague generalities. While Fuentes' statement that "without Borges there simply would not be a modern Latin-American novel" is sweeping enough to supply an epigraph, I believe it is time to move from a notion which is accepted as axiomatic to the specifics of its verification: "technicalities," warns Harry Levin, "help us more than generalities."

In Ernesto Sábato's novel *Sobre héroes y tumbas* (On Heroes and Tombs), two of the characters, Bruno and Martín, walking down a Buenos Aires street, meet a man moving cautiously aided by a cane. "Borges," says one to the other. Bruno engages in a short conversation with Borges, and Sábato reproduces some of Borges' habits of speech. This fictional Borges seems also to be acquainted with Alejandra, one of the novel's axial characters. After this encounter, Bruno and Martín discuss various aspects of Borges' writings and Argentine literature in general. To one's question as to whether Borges, as a writer, is more European than Argentine, the other replies: "What else can he be but an Argentine? He is a typical national by-product. Even his Europeanism is national. A European is not a Europeanist but simply a European."[2] In explaining the non-Argentine traits of Borges' writings as only another true manifestation of Argentine temperament, Sábato paraphrases a belief long held and defended by Borges himself. In his essay "The Argentine Writer and Tradition," Borges maintains that *La urna,* a book of sonnets by Enrique Banchs, is no less Argentine than *Martín Fierro,* which is, by definition, *the* Argentine poem. Borges goes on to explain that in lines like "The sun shines on the slanting roofs / and on the windows. Nightingales / try to say they are in love . . . ," from a poem written in a

---

add that American writers such as John Barth and John Updike have dedicated enthusiastic and lucid essays to Borges' work. See also Tony Tanner's remarks on Borges in his recent book, *City of Words: American Fiction 1950–1970* (London, 1971).

2. Ernesto Sábato, *Sobre héroes y tumbas* (Buenos Aires, 1969), p. 164.

suburb of Buenos Aires, where there are neither slanting roofs nor nightingales, "Argentine architecture and ornithology are of course absent, but we find [in these lines] the Argentine's reticence and constraint. . . ." [3] The conversation between Bruno and Martín, in Sábato's novel, is a critique of Borges' work in the context of Argentine literature. Here Sábato airs opinions on Borges he has previously cast in essay form,[4] mixing his great admiration for the author of *Ficciones* with a relentless aversion to the formal rigor (he calls it "Byzantinism") which has always characterized Borges' prose. Sábato gets his point across through Bruno:

Can you imagine Tolstoy trying to dazzle the reader with an adverb when one of his characters' life or death is at stake? [5]

Yet, not everything in Borges is Byzantine, really. There is something very Argentine in his best pages—a certain nostalgia, a certain metaphysical sadness. . . . Actually, many stupidities are said about what Argentine literature *should* be like. The important thing is that it should be profound. All the rest is derivative. And if it is not profound it will not help to display *gauchos* or *compradritos* [Argentine hoodlums]. The most representative writer in Elizabethan England was Shakespeare. However, many of his plays do not even take place in England.[6]

This attack on Borges is strange on two accounts. First, Sábato accuses Borges of local color when it was Borges himself who fought the decisive battle against local color in Argentina; [7] Borges

3. Borges concludes as follows: "The fact that Banchs, when speaking of his great suffering which overwhelms him, when speaking of this woman who has left him and has left the world empty for him, should have recourse to foreign and conventional images like slanted roofs and nightingales, is significant: significant of Argentine reserve, distrust and reticence, of the difficulty we have in making confessions, in revealing our intimate nature" (*L*, 180).

4. See Sábato's articles "En torno de Borges," *Casa de las Américas* (Havana, 1963), III, No. 17–18, 7–12; "Los dos Borges," *Indice* (Madrid, 1961), XV, No. 150–151, 6–7; "Borges y Borges el argentino y la metafísica," *Vida Universitaria* (Monterrey, Mexico, April 12, 1964), pp. 3–18; and, particularly, "Borges y el destino de nuestra dicción," in his book of essays *El escritor y sus fantasmas* (Buenos Aires, 1964), pp. 245–57.

5. What Sábato does not seem to realize is that Tolstoy (as any other writer) deals with his characters' lives or deaths by means of words, and that in a reality constructed with words (literature), one adverb too many or too few is often decisive. Also, if one takes Sábato's irony at its face value, the importance of one adverb varies in degree according to the genre. In poetry, for example, or in the short story, one word (even an adverb) may sometimes be the key to its success. Finally, as Borges has not written any novel, Sábato's example of Tolstoy is, to say the least, rather imprecise.

6. Sábato, *Sobre héroes y tumbas*, p. 174.

7. On this aspect of his work, see "The Argentine Writer and Tradition," *Labyrinths*, pp. 177–85.

was also the first Argentine writer to achieve genuine universality in spite of the *gauchos* and *compadritos* one finds in his stories. Second, the arguments Sábato uses to remedy a nonexistent evil (since one can safely say that the most representative writer of contemporary Argentina *is* Borges, although many of his stories are set in such places as Tlön, Babylon, the land of the troglodytes, and similar extraterritorial territories) are, oddly enough, of pure Borgesian extraction. Consciously or unconsciously, Sábato is repeating one of the arguments Borges uses in his fight against local color: "I think," Borges writes, "Shakespeare would have been amazed if people had tried to limit him to English themes, and if they had told him that, as an Englishman, he had no right to compose *Hamlet,* whose theme is Scandinavian, or *Macbeth,* whose theme is Scottish" (*L,* 180–81).

Sábato, along with other Latin-American writers, accepts Borges even when attacking him.[8]

The very device of mixing real beings (Borges) with fictional characters (Bruno and Martín) is of unquestionable Borgesian lineage. It could be argued that the reference to Borges in a novel that aims to portray all the features that shape the face of Buenos Aires is only natural, in the same degree that the references to Gardel, Firpo, or Roberto Arlt give expression to some of the myths which are part of that city. Yet the difference between these and other figures mentioned or commented upon throughout the

8. In the case of Sábato, it should be pointed out that he worked with Borges on the editorial board of the magazine *Sur* during the years when Borges published most of his prose writings. Many of his stories and essays appeared in the same magazine, and the least one can assume is that Sábato read them and discussed them thoroughly with friends and colleagues.

Obviously the question of what is Argentine and what is not was a problem that troubled most Argentine writers who, from the twenties on, engaged in a search for alternatives to the regionalist themes that dominated Argentine fiction. Borges was not alone in that quest, but undoubtedly the flourishing of fantastic and detective literature that followed can hardly be explained without bearing in mind Borges' efforts in that direction. Cortázar, another Argentine writer deeply preoccupied by this question, has said of this matter: "Like Borges and a few others, I seem to have understood that the best way to be an Argentine is not to run around broadcasting the fact all the time, especially not in the stentorian tones used by the so-called autochthonous writers. . . . I think there's a deeper way of being an Argentine, which might make itself felt, for instance, in a book where Argentina is never mentioned." L. Harss and B. Dohmann, *Into the Mainstream* (New York, 1967), p. 238.

334

novel, and the allusion to Borges, lies in the fact that the latter is presented not just nominally but as a living presence. The reader sees Borges walking through the streets of Buenos Aires and stopping casually to chat, as no doubt has occurred many times in the life of the town. It is this experience that Sábato probably strove to capture: Borges, the author of a mythical Buenos Aires, now strolling the streets of a real Buenos Aires. A novel that seeks to re-create the very pulse of Buenos Aires cannot afford to miss such a ponderable dimension. The result, however, goes far beyond Sábato's intention. Borges appears in the novel not only as one more reality among the many that cluster under the roofs of the city, but also as a symbol of the impact produced by his work on contemporary Latin-American fiction. Borges' passage through the pages of one of its fairly representative novels becomes a symbol— a *lapsus linguae* through which Latin-American fiction of the last three decades acknowledges its debt to Borges.

Let us now ask the obvious questions: What is the nature of Borges' impact, and what is the extent of his influence? I have already pointed out how the very fact that fictional characters in Sábato's novel intermingle with real ones responds to an imaginative freedom which—although it is already found in Spanish-American fiction since *modernismo* and its first explorations into the realm of the fantastic—only gained momentum with the publication of Borges' first *ficciones* from the forties on. The concept of the fantastic as found in modernist short stories—Lugones being the exception—is one of overrefinement and virtuosity. The point of departure in their stories is the split between the real and the unreal, and also the assumption that the story moves within the limits of the latter, where everything is permissible, however whimsical. This fracture between the real and the unreal ends by producing estrangement: the former seems to be ruled by laws and norms identical to those which govern historical life, while the latter appears to repudiate and break those very laws and norms. In the fantastic stories of the modernists, one finds a flat acceptance of this break, and no bridge is provided to cross from one territory to the other. Thus, these stories are closer to a supernatural and marvelous world—a mixture of Poe and H. G. Wells with the lyricism of a Maeterlinck. Their sole purpose seems to be to re-create our imagination, and the difference between this type of fancy and the fantasy that nourishes a wide area of children's books is only one of degree.[9] Not only does Borges move freely between the literature of the real and the unreal, but he has gone so far as to efface the borderline between the two. The fantastic in his stories springs less from the subject than from the treatment of it. His premise is that "unreality is the necessary condition of art." His *ficciones* are not only a way of freeing imagination but also a form of suggesting a new understanding of the world. Borges seems to be saying that we cannot de-realize the world we have so neatly constructed and that to grasp the reality that lies on the other side of our obedient mirror is a privilege of gods, not a task of men. His treatment of the fantastic therefore differs intrinsically from the stories of marvel and astonishment of his modernist predecessors, and this approach to the fantastic has opened a wide road in Latin-American fiction.

Among those who have followed that road, Julio Cortázar is the most obvious and distinguished example. Although his short stories go their own way, responding to a fictional outlook quite different from Borges', it is clear that Cortázar found the way to fantastic literature under the stimulus of Borges' achievements.[10] Cortázar's poem in prose *Los reyes* (The Kings) was first published in *Los anales de Buenos Aires,* a magazine edited by Borges. Its subject—like Borges' "The House of Asterion"—is a

9. In this regard, Roger Caillois distinguishes between marvelous (*merveilleux*) and fantastic art; while the marvelous encompasses *"les oeuvres d'art créés expressément pour surprendre, pour dérouter le spectateur par l'invention d'un univers imaginaire, féerique, où rien ne se présente nie se passe comme dans le monde réel,"* the fantastic is a more permanent and universal art: *"le fantastique me parut venir, plutôt que du sujet, de la manière de le traiter."* *Au coeur du fantastique* (Paris, 1965), pp. 8–9. For further discussion on the differences between the two concepts, see Roger Caillois' preface to *Anthologie du fantastique* (Paris, 1958), and also his *Images, images . . .* (Paris, 1966).

10. In a recent interview, Cortázar said: *"Borges nous a beaucoup marqués, nous les écrivains de ma génération. Il nous a montré les possibilités inouïes du fantastique. En Argentine, on écrivait plutôt une littérature romantique, réaliste, un peu populaire parfois, le fantastique est né vraiment à haut niveau avec Borges."* C. G. Bjurström, "Entretien avec J. Cortázar," *La quinzaine littéraire,* 100 (August 1970), 16.

re-creation of the myth of the Minotaur. Cortázar's choice of a motif (the labyrinth), already so clearly dominant in Borges' work, is in itself indicative of close affinities. Other examples of this osmotic influence are Cortázar's stories "Las puertas del cielo" (The Gates of Heaven) and particularly "El móvil" (The Motive). The reader immediately associates the latter with Borges' "Street-corner Man." [11] There are no knife fights in Cortázar's stories, but the vindication of the literary worth of low life out on the raw edges of Buenos Aires deepens a trend in Argentine letters which, if not initiated by Borges, was certainly updated and renewed by him from the thirties on. In addition to stories like "Streetcorner Man," "The Dead Man," and "The South," which deal directly with old-time Argentine hoodlums (*compadritos*), Borges published in 1945 an anthology whose title alone is informative— *El compadrito: su destino, sus barrios, su música* (The *Compadrito: His Destiny, His Barrios, His Music*). It was an invitation to write the poem that would do for the *compadrito* what *Martín Fierro* did for the gaucho. It seems unlikely that a poet as Mallarméan as Cortázar was at the time he wrote the narratives of *Bestiario* (Bestiary) would have chosen characters from the *compadrito's* underworld as the protagonists for his stories without the incentive of Borges' early efforts to vindicate the literary potential of this segment of Argentine society.

Other instances of Borges' influential presence in contemporary Spanish-American fiction can easily be singled out. Traces of this presence are found in works far removed from the Borgesian scope of theme and genre. His influence resonates through the novel *One Hundred Years of Solitude* by Gabriel García Márquez, whose story of an imaginary family, the Buendías, in a fictitious community, Macondo, is so skillfully told that it becomes a microcosm of all Latin America—with the legends, myths, history, and magic of a whole continent. While it is true that one of its themes is "the wonder and strangeness of a continent in which *the fantastic*

11. Elsewhere, I have studied these two stories in an attempt to show how the same theme is resolved differently at the levels of structure and style. See "Dos soluciones estilísticas al tema del compadre en Borges y Cortázar," in a forthcoming issue of *Nueva narrativa hispanoamericana*.

is the normative"[12] (a face of Latin America that has nurtured much of Miguel Angel Asturias' novels), it is equally true that the magic of the book stems not from a reality historically chronicled but from a view of life imaginatively and fantastically elaborated. To explain the nature of this alchemy, García Márquez has, in an interview, told the story of a Colombian girl who eloped. To avoid the shame, the family declared that the last time they saw her she was folding linen sheets in the garden, but then she rose to heaven. In the novel, this experience goes through a Borgesian transmutation. ("Funes the Memorious," as the literary sublimation of Borges' own insomnia, and "The South," as the metaphor of an unhappy experience, are obvious examples at hand.) One of the characters—Remedios, *la bella*—is asked to help Fernanda fold her linen sheets in the garden, and when a mild wind begins to blow, Remedios rises with the sheets until she and they vanish into heaven. The naive excuse becomes a literary reality which now functions not as a metaphor nor as an allegory but according to a strength of its own. Imagination blends fantasy and experience into an autonomous world, with loyalties to both.

But where one most distinctly sees the traces of a Borgesian mode that delights in assembling and disassembling narrative components, as if they were pieces of a Chinese box, is in the treatment of one of García Márquez' most puzzling characters—Melquíades. He is a gypsy who spends the last years of his life in Macondo with the Buendías, writing enigmatic books on sheets of parchment which nobody can decipher. After Melquíades' death, his ghost appears to one of the Buendías' descendants, who struggles unsuccessfully to read the parchments. Melquíades tells him that he is willing to convey to him his wisdom but he refuses to translate the manuscripts because "no one must know their meaning until one hundred years have elapsed."[13] And indeed, the mysterious contents of the book are revealed only when the reader reaches the novel's last two pages, which not only conclude the story but also complete the one hundred years predicted by Melquíades.

12. Jean Franco, *An Introduction to Spanish-American Literature* (Oxford, 1969), p. 346.
13. Gabriel García Márquez, *Cien años de soledad* (Buenos Aires, 1967), p. 161.

Only then does the impenetrable language, which turns out to be Sanskrit, yield its meaning to the last offspring of the Buendías. Thus Aureliano reads the parchments, "as if they had been written in Spanish," to discover that they contain the history of the family down to the most trivial details as written by Melquíades one hundred years ahead of time. Fascinated, Aureliano reads what the reader has been reading through the novel from the first page on, finally reaching the very sheet which describes what he is doing at that moment: "he began to decipher the instant that he was living, deciphering it as he lived it, prophesying it to himself in the act of deciphering the last page of the parchments, as if he were looking at himself in a talking mirror." [14] The artifice reminds us of *Don Quixote's* Chapter IX, in which Don Quixote learns that the whole novel has been translated from the Arabic and that Cervantes acquired the manuscript in the Toledo marketplace. In his essay "Partial Enchantments of the *Quixote,*" Borges has surveyed with some exhilaration the most illustrious examples of this artifice. Along with the *Quixote,* he mentions *A Thousand and One Nights,* and particularly night DCII, "magic among the nights, when the Sultan hears his own story from the Sultana's mouth." But the example from which García Márquez seemed to have benefited most is the third one, the *Ramayana.* "In the last book," comments Borges, "Rama's children, not knowing who their father is, seek refuge in a forest, where a hermit teaches them to read. That teacher, strangely enough, is Valmiki; the book they study is the *Ramayana* [epic poem by Valmiki]. Rama orders a sacrifice of horses; Valmiki comes to the ceremony with his pupils. They sing the *Ramayana* to the accompaniment of the lute. Rama hears his own story, recognizes his children, and then rewards the poet" (*OI,* 45). As if the idea of a minor character—Melquíades—writing the story that the novel unfolds, and of a main character—Aureliano—reading it up to the point where both texts overlap, were not close enough to the device used by Valmiki in the great Sanskrit epic of India, García Márquez makes Melquíades write the history of Macondo in Sanskrit—a kind of mischievous wink signaling the remote source. But the existence of a book within a

14. *Ibid.,* p. 350.

book, of a fictional book which already contains what the actual book tells, page after page, reminds us most of all of that Borgesian artifice which suggests that "if the characters in a story can be readers or spectators, then we, their readers or spectators, can be fictitious" (*OI*, 46). Such inversions, by means of which reality and fiction seem to exchange domains, are, of course, one of the constants of Borges' fiction. In his story "Theme of the Traitor and the Hero," for example, Ryan, the great-grandson of Fergus Kilpatrick, engages in writing a biography of the assassinated hero, but he realizes at the end of the tale that he too forms part of the assassins' plot. Like García Márquez' hero in the act of deciphering the last page of the parchments, Ryan discovers that in the plan of the assassins he is but one ingredient more, and that even the book he publishes, dedicated to the hero's glory, was perhaps also foreseen in the assassins' work.

The device of turning characters from other works into characters of his own fiction, so common in Borges' narratives that the reader is inclined to think of Don Quixote ("A Problem"), Auguste Dupin ("Death and the Compass"), Martín Fierro ("The End"), Leopold Bloom ("The Zahir"), Cruz ("The Life of Tadeo Isidoro Cruz"), John H. Watson ("The Approach to al-Mu'taṣim"), the Negro ("The End"), Theseus ("The House of Asterion"), and others as real beings interpolated in a fictitious world, is a device also found in *One Hundred Years of Solitude*. García Márquez himself has spotted for us the guest characters he intermixed with his own fictional beings:

Victor Hughes, a character from Alejo Carpentier's *Explosion in a Cathedral;* **Colonel Lorenzo Gavilán, from Carlos Fuentes'** *The Death of Artemio Cruz.* **There is also another character in my novel who goes to Paris and lives in a hotel on the Rue Dauphine, in the same room where Rocamadur, a character from Julio Cortázar's** *Hopscotch,* **died. I am also convinced that the nun who carries the last of the Aurelianos in a small basket is Mother Patrocinio from Mario Vargas Llosa's** *The Green House.*[15]

When, in García Márquez' novel, Aureliano finally verifies that in the manuscript "Melquíades had not put events in the order of man's conventional time, but had concentrated a century of daily

15. G. Márquez–V. Llosa, *La novela en América Latina: diálogo* (Lima, 1969).

episodes in such a way that *they all coexisted in one instant,"* [16] it is hard not to recall Borges' speculations with time, and particularly the infinite and iridescent Aleph, which Borges introduces with these words: "In that single gigantic instant I saw millions of acts both delightful and awful; not one of them amazed me more than the fact that *all of them occupied the same point* in space, without overlapping or transparency" (*A,* 26; italics added).

Still, these and other analogies [17] are far from sufficient to define the role of Borges' writings as a catalyst for the new Spanish-American literature. They do, however, suggest on the part of the Latin-American writer a great fascination for another Latin-American writer—a rather unusual phenomenon in a literature that has consistently sought its models in foreign letters. The full strength of Borges' impact lies in his having produced for Spanish-American fiction what Rubén Darío produced for its poetry at the turn of the century: namely, the forging of a linguistic instrument, exact, effective, authentic, capable of revealing an undiscovered Latin America. This is not to say that in this quest Borges was alone. Neither was Darío alone in that poetic revolution which brought forth a whole generation of brilliant poets; however, it is generally agreed that it was Darío who not only capitalized on all the achievements and innovations of modernism, but also brought them to their highest accomplishments in his own poetry. Today we accept as a truism that before Darío and the modernists Spanish was a lifeless, inflated language incapable of giving poetic

16. G. Márquez, *op. cit.,* p. 350. Italics added.
17. In one of Octavio Paz's most ambitious poems, "Blanco," I found these verses in which, much as they reflect Paz's own metaphysical preoccupations, no reader of Borges will fail to sense familiar vibrations.

> *El espíritu*
> *Es una invención del cuerpo*
> *El cuerpo*
> *Es una invención del mundo*
> *El mundo*
> *Es una invención del espíritu*

For the unfamiliar reader, I quote the following lines with which Borges closes his essay "Avatars of the Tortoise": "We ... have dreamed the world. We have dreamed it strong, mysterious, visible, ubiquitous in space and secure in time; but we have allowed tenuous, eternal interstices of injustice in its structure so we may know that it is false" (*OI,* 115).

expression to the nuances of modern perception. The poets who came after modernism and who produced the best poetry ever written in Latin America have all acknowledged their indebtedness to Rubén Darío. Poets like Vallejo, Neruda, Borges, and Paz have left some form of testimony of this admiration and recognition. Neruda, for one, has clearly stated: "Many believe that they have nothing to do with Darío, and yet, if they write the way they do it is owing to Rubén's brilliance, which so radically modified the Spanish language." [18] And Paz has written in similar terms:

Spanish poetry had its muscles numbed by dint of solemnity and pathos; with Rubén Darío the language begins to move. Darío's place is central. He is not a living influence but a term of reference: a point of departure or arrival. To be or not to be like him: in both ways Darío is present in the spirit of contemporary poets. He is the founder. He is the origin.[19]

Borges himself has referred to Darío as "a great master and poet," and he has pointed out that Darío created with the Spanish language a kind of music which did not exist before him. Says Borges:

I think that when a great poet passes through the language it matters not if we like or dislike him. Something has happened to the language and that will not be forgotten. We may like or dislike Chaucer but, of course, after *Troilus and Criseyde* and the *Canterbury Tales* the English language is not what it was before. The same thing, I think, might be said of Darío.[20]

Similarly, I believe, contemporary Spanish-American fiction, consciously or unconsciously, willingly or unwillingly, is marked by a prose that did not exist in Spanish before Borges. Shuffling a few words in Paz's statement, one can safely say: "To be or not to be like Borges: in both ways he is present in the spirit of contemporary Spanish-American fiction." A writer like Sábato, who, as we have seen, has branded Borges' writings with facile labels

18. G. Castañeda Aragón, "P. Neruda habla para Colombia," interview published in *Repertorio Americano* (Costa Rica, August 9, 1941). This statement was later elaborated in Neruda's book *Viajes*. There he has written: "Martí has said of Quevedo: 'He penetrated so deeply into what was coming that those who live today speak with his tongue.' Speak with his tongue. . . . What is Martí referring to here? To Quevedo's status as father of the language—a situation similar to Rubén Darío's, whom we will spend half of our lives disowning, to understand later that without him we would not speak our own tongue, that is, that without him we would be still talking a hardened, pasteboard, tasteless language." *Viajes* (Santiago, 1955), pp. 12–13.
19. Octavio Paz, "Rubén Darío," in *Cuadrivio* (Mexico, 1965), pp. 11–65.
20. J. L. Borges, "Leopoldo Lugones," unpublished lecture given at Princeton University, 1967. (The passage is a transcription from the recorded version.)

342

like "evasion" and "Byzantinism," has openly stated through his character Bruno: "What I am sure about is that Borges' prose is the most remarkable being written today in the Spanish language." And writers like García Márquez and Vargas Llosa have made similar statements. At the invitation of a Peruvian university, these two young novelists engaged in a dialogue on the Latin-American novel, in which Borges became the inevitable subject:

> Vargas Llosa: ... I have always had problems in justifying my admiration for Borges.
>
> García Márquez: Ah, I have no problem at all. I have a great admiration for him, I read him every night. I just came from Buenos Aires and the only thing I bought there was Borges' *Complete Works*. I carry them in my suitcase; I am going to read them every day, and he is a writer I detest. ... But, on the other hand, I am fascinated by the violin he uses to express his things. ... I think that Borges' writings are a literature of evasion. Something strange happens to me with Borges: he is one of the authors I read most and have read most and perhaps the one I like least. I read Borges because of his extraordinary capacity for verbal artifice. I mean that he teaches you how to tune up your instrument for saying things.[21]

From García Márquez' controversial view of literature, one can learn about the understated difficulties that the Latin-American writer must face. What becomes particularly clear is that a linguistic vacuum confronts him, the lack of a literary tradition in his own language, forcing him to resort to foreign literatures, mostly in bad translations. Cortázar has pointed out the differences separating the European writer from the Argentine, and presents the case for the Latin American at large:

> European novelists (genius aside) waged a war with weapons sharpened collectively through centuries of intellectual, esthetic, and literary tradition, while we

21. García Márquez–Vargas Llosa, *La novela en América Latina: Diálogo* (Lima, 1969[?]), pp. 36, 40.

Undoubtedly, García Márquez' admiration for Borges' "extraordinary capacity for verbal artifice" has left deep imprints on his own prose. In a recent article on this subject, Suzanne J. Levine traces some possible influences on García Márquez' approach to biography. She mentions Marcel Schwob's *Vies imaginaires* and Borges' *Historia universal de la infamia*. She also points out that there are reasons to believe that Virginia Woolf's *Orlando* had a strong impact on García Márquez' novel, and that in all probability he read *Orlando* in the Spanish translation by Borges, "thus assimilating the style and the art of the English writer through the language of Borges in a translation that, in many cases, is more concise and imaginative than the original itself." (*"Cien años de soledad* y la tradición de la biografía imaginaria," in *Revista Iberoamericana* XXXVI, 72 [July–Sept., 1970], 453–63.)

are forced to create for ourselves a language which may rid us of *Don Ramiro* [22] and other mummies with Hispanic bandages, a language which may rediscover the Spanish that produced Quevedo or Cervantes and that produced for us *Martín Fierro* and *Recuerdos de provincia*. . . .[23]

For Cortázar, then, and for the new novelists in general, the quest in the Latin-American novel is "the unavoidable battle for the conquest of a language." [24] "Radical in facing his own past," wrote Carlos Fuentes, "the new Latin American writer undertakes a revision starting from a self-evident fact—the lack of a language." [25] If the problem of the language represents one of the central preoccupations of today's Latin-American novelists (and it does), one begins to understand their attraction to Borges. Borges was the first (after Sarmiento, one must add) to undertake that revision of the Spanish language which contemporary novelists find indispensable if Latin America is to speak with a voice of its own. This is not to say that there were no prose writers in Latin America. There were, and excellent ones: Sarmiento, Martí, Rodó, Alfonso Reyes, to mention just a few. But their prose was written in the mold of the essay. When a powerful essayist like Martí wrote a novel—*Amistad funesta*—he produced the same overrefined prose, consecrated by modernism, which on the one hand created the seminal "new" poetic language but on the other forced fiction writing into a prose of preciosity whose ideal was "the eternal beauty of art." Modernist novels and stories were written in a prose full of color and melody which became ornate for its own sake; the themes of those narratives were either deluged by the color or deafened by the rhythm of the prose. For the modernists, narration was a pretext—although a beautiful pretext—which allowed the author to create a world of sensory impressions, artistic transpositions, and verbal rhythms where all things were valued for their esthetic potential and their capacity for generating beauty.[26]

22. An Argentine novel, written in 1908 by Enrique Larreta, which typifies the archaic and inflated Spanish that Cortázar deprecates.
23. Julio Cortázar, *La vuelta al día en ochenta mundos* (México, 1967), p. 100.
24. *Ibid.*
25. Carlos Fuentes, *La nueva novela hispanoamericana* (México, 1969), p. 30.
26. Juan Ramón Jiménez, theorist and practitioner of this esthetic, has defined modernism as "a movement towards beauty."

The regionalist novel, which came after modernism, described the exuberances of Spanish America—the pampa, the *llano* (of Venezuela), the jungle—in the luxuriant language inherited from Rubén Darío. Borges represents a double renovation in Latin-American fiction: he abandoned the realistic mode that had traditionally prevailed in the regionalist narratives, and sought in the fantastic a more creative treatment of his themes; and with regard to language, he sought a new concept of style. For the modernists, the color and rhythm of language were the most admired characteristics of good prose. A stylist was, consequently, a writer who handled language with the greatest splendor, who showed the greatest display of verbal wealth and achieved the most talented rhythms. In contrast to this external understanding of style, Borges concentrated on the inner effectiveness of language. "Those who labor under that superstition [of style as an end in itself]," he wrote in 1930, "give no thought to the effectiveness or ineffectiveness of a page, but are merely conscious of a writer's supposed skills: his metaphors, his ear, the circumstances of his punctuation and word order." [27] Borges understands style not as ornamentation but as function. The adjective or adverb which in some way is not a living, functioning cell is a dead and useless body that only obstructs the healthy physiology of the text. In opposition to the verbal profusion of modernism, Borges proposed a definition of style which constitutes a veritable turning point: *"Plena eficiencia y plena invisibilidad serían las dos perfecciones de cualquier estilo."* ("Total effectiveness and total invisibility should be the twin aims of any style." [28]) Here, as early as 1928, Borges had enunciated a theory of style that only two and a half decades later found a similar formulation in so-called "zero degree of writing."

In contemporary French fiction, Roland Barthes' dictum came to define a whole trend against the tradition of stylistic artistry; the intention was to replace estheticist language by a bare, simple, colorless one. "This neutral writing," according to Barthes, "re-

27. Borges, "La supersticiosa ética del lector," in *Discusión* (Buenos Aires, 1957), p. 45.
28. Borges, "Eduardo Wilde," in *El idioma de los argentinos* (Buenos Aires, 1928), p. 158.

discovers the primary condition of classical art: instrumentality. . . . Initiated by Camus' *Outsider,* it achieves a style of absence which is almost an ideal absence of style . . . ; it deliberately forgoes any elegance or ornament; it is the mode of a new situation of the writer, the way a certain silence has of existing." [29] But if Barthes found a felicitous designation for this new outlook of style, the style itself was not only, as Barthes himself acknowledges, "a phenomenon invented by authors like Camus," [30] it was also clearly and keenly defined by Camus himself two years earlier. "If," writes Camus in *The Rebel,* "stylization must necessarily be rather exaggerated, since it sums up the intervention of man and the desire for rectification which the artist brings to his reproduction of reality, it is nevertheless desirable that it should remain *invisible* so that the demand which gives birth to art should be expressed in its most extreme tension. *Great style is invisible* stylization, or rather stylization incarnate." [31] This is identical to Borges' formula of invisibility of style. What is even more surprising than the coincidence, however, is its implication. Camus published his essay in 1951. By then, Borges had already published most of his narrative work; back when he formulated his concept of style, Camus was only fourteen. My point is that if it is true that the tradition of a highly wrought language came to Latin America primarily from France,[32] it is no less true that through Borges Spanish-American novelists rid themselves of estheticism much earlier than the French, who only did so, led by Camus, in the late forties. This is certainly a new phenomenon for a literature like that of Latin America, which has traditionally depended on foreign models.

As a theorist of the new language the Latin-American writer was searching for, Borges did not abound in slogans or manifestoes. Instead, he diligently applied himself to the difficult task of dissecting the deadened language in an effort to establish the causes

29. Roland Barthes, *Writing Degree Zero* (London, 1967), pp. 83–84. (First published in 1953 as *Le degré zéro de l'écriture.*)

30. *Ibid.,* p. 73.

31. Albert Camus, *The Rebel* (New York, 1961), pp. 271–72. Italics added.

32. Although modernism borrowed from many sources, it is generally accepted that it primarily derived from French symbolism and the Parnassian school, bringing from the French much blessing as well as much evil (for *afrancesa-miento* and other ills in Spanish literature, see Unamuno).

of its long disease. One has only to look into his half-dozen books of essays to realize the extent of this undertaking. As early as 1927, Borges saw the wealth of words about which the Royal Spanish Academy boasts as "a necrological spectacle" and "a statistical superstition," since "what counts is not the number of symbols but the number of ideas," and he adds that the Spanish language cannot claim "great thoughts or great feelings, that is to say, great poetry or great philosophy." [33] He further assails the Academy for having "always used the Spanish language for purposes of death, of discouragement, of advice, of remorse, of scruples, of misgivings, or—in too many cases—for puns and plays on words, which in themselves are a form of death." Borges finally offers his own program: "... we would prefer a pliant and hopeful Spanish, which would be in harmony with our landscape and our own ways and our professed faith." [34] In search of this language, Borges resorted to style analysis long before stylistics became a practiced method in Spanish criticism. Disregarding conventions and canons, he treated established writers with the same rigor as he did his contemporaries. In the close examination of a sonnet by Góngora or Quevedo, in the minute analysis of a line from *Martín Fierro,* in the meticulous "inquisitions" into the expressive possibilities and limitations of the adjective and the metaphor, Borges explored and studied the mechanics of a text. He did not hesitate to disparage established work in an effort to destroy the myths that had stiffened literary language. Thus, for example, in distinguished pieces by Ortega, Lugones, or Gabriel Miró he found that the language was euphoniously beautiful but expressively superfluous. Overwhelmed by the exigencies of studying a writer through close examination, Borges has pessimistically concluded that a consistent esthetic is altogether impossible:

If no word is useless, if even a common *milonga* is a whole network of stylistic successes and failures, how can anyone hope to explain that "tide of pomp that beats upon the high shore of this world"—the 1056 quarto pages attributed to Shakespeare? How can we take seriously those who judge these pages en masse, with no method other than a wondrous flow of awestricken praise, and never looking into a single line?" [35]

33. *El idioma de los argentinos* (Buenos Aires, 1928), pp. 170–74.
34. *Ibid.,* pp. 182–83.
35. Borges, "Elementos de preceptiva," *Sur,* III, 7 (April 1933), 161.

Borges was also among the first in Latin America to stimulate and advise the use of colloquial language in a literature where, as Cortázar jests, the writer "wears a stiff collar and climbs the highest mountain whenever he decides to write." Borges defended the legitimacy of colloquial language in literature, thus anticipating the wide use of it in the present Spanish-American novel, where it has become a significant asset. As far back as 1927, Borges posed the question:

What unbridgeable gap lies between the Spanish of the Spaniards and that of the Argentines? I say none, luckily for the mutual understanding of our speech. There is, though, a nuance of difference: a nuance so slight as not to hamper the full circulation of the language, and yet clear enough to make us fully aware of an Argentine consciousness. I am not thinking here of the many thousands of local colloquialisms that Spaniards hardly understand. I think of the different tone of our voice, of the ironic or kindly coloring we give to certain words. . . . We have not varied the intrinsic meaning of words, but we have varied their connotation.[36]

Among the new Latin-American novelists, it is Cortázar who has best echoed Borges' efforts on behalf of a more expressive and living Spanish and has most brilliantly taken over "the battle of language." While acknowledging that he is neither critic nor essayist, Cortázar has created an original and highly successful type of essay entirely appropriate to his search for naturalness, humor, and anti-solemnity in language. An attentive reading of his essays immediately shows that his revision of Spanish in the framework of Argentine letters is a renewal of Borges' earlier undertaking. In one of his central essays on this subject, Cortázar urges "the revision of our literary impossibilities as Borges once did." [37] Cortázar renews the attacks against "the pseudo-style of surface," "the verbose Spain of *tertulias*," "inflated language," and "the lavish adjective"; like Borges, he praises the Spanish of Cervantes and Quevedo and the prose of Sarmiento. And again, like Borges, Cortázar formulates his own concept of style, one "born out of a patient and arduous meditation of our reality and our word," [38] which could well be the complement of Borges' "total effectiveness and total invisibility."

36. Borges, *El idioma de los argentinos*, pp. 178–79.
37. Cortázar, *La vuelta al día en ochenta mundos*, p. 96.
38. *Ibid.*, p. 100.

348

The alternative to an invisible style has come from the Cuban novelist Alejo Carpentier. He holds that "our art has always been baroque," and that "the legitimate style of today's Latin-American novelist is the baroque." [39] Thus Carpentier belabors a point that is hardly acceptable, for when he says "today's Latin-American novelist" he is thinking primarily of himself. In his novels he has adopted an Olympian, baroque style which stands at the opposite extreme of Borges' dictum—a style so *visible* that it ends by distracting the reader and even annoying him. Just as Borges struggles to avoid uncouth, archaic, or astonishing words, Carpentier wrestles to display all the treasures of the dictionary—in fact, he has advocated a return to "the forgotten part of the dictionary." The prose of the new Spanish-American novel has carefully avoided this lavish language. The reason is clear: while the baroque style preached and practiced by Carpentier flaunts a bookishness that alienates the reader, the new novel seeks—conversely—to involve him deeply. What Carpentier's dazzling style creates is an estranging distance between author and reader, while in the new novel the effort is toward producing a "reader-accomplice" who, according to Cortázar's explanation, becomes "a coparticipant and cosufferer of the experience through which the novelist is passing." [40] As for stylistic artistry, the same text points out that to reach this reader "artistic tricks are of no use: the only worthwhile thing is the material in gestation . . . transmitted through words, of course, but the least esthetic words possible." [41] Hence the presence of colloquial and informal language in the new novels. Even in the works of younger novelists like Néstor Sánchez, Manuel Puig, Guillermo Cabrera Infante, or Severo Sarduy (the last two are Cuban), where language seems to become a reality in itself, style is straightforward and masterfully plain rather than ostentatiously baroque. It would be accurate to conclude that the new Latin-American novel, instead of choosing the road of baroque language, has followed Borges' formula of invisibility, which in its latest version reads:

39. Alejo Carpentier, *Tientos y diferencias* (México, 1964), pp. 42–43.
40. Cortázar, *Hopscotch* (New York, 1966), p. 397.
41. *Ibid.*

I lay no claim to any particular theories. Time has led me to the use of certain devices: to shun synonyms, which labor under the disadvantage of suggesting imaginary differences; to shun Hispanisms, Argentinisms, archaisms, and neologisms; to employ common words rather than unusual ones; to work into a story circumstantial details, which readers now insist on; to feign slight uncertainties, for, although reality is exact, memory is not; to narrate events (this I got from Kipling and the Icelandic sagas) as if I did not wholly understand them; to bear in mind that the rules I have just set down need not always be followed, and that in time they will have to be changed. Such devices, or habits, hardly make up a theory of literature. Besides, I am skeptical of aesthetic theories.[42]

If one considers that the prose of his early essays suffered the same ills he intended to cure,[43] it was not Borges' patient laboratory of "inquisitions" into the language that truly set a model for the new novelists, but the prose of his short stories. There Borges has created a language that, to use Cortázar's words, "can invent and can open the door to the game; a language that has produced a style born out of a patient and arduous meditation of our reality and our word." The novelists who came after Borges are now writing a prose different from that written by the author of *Dreamtigers,* but before leaving Borges they had first to come to him. In both ways, he is present in the spirit and the flesh of the contemporary novel.

42. Borges, Preface to *Elogio de la sombra* (In Praise of Darkness) (Buenos Aires, 1969), pp. 9–10. Translated by Norman Thomas di Giovanni in collaboration with the author.

43. One can easily understand Borges' adamant refusal to republish those "forgotten and forgettable" early volumes of essays.

Borges the craftsman
FRANK MACSHANE

Discussions of Borges' metaphysical complexities have made readers forget that he has had to face the same problem every writer faces—what to write about, what material to make use of. This is the fundamental task a writer must confront, for it will influence his style and mold his literary identity.

Borges has written on a wide range of subjects, but in his most recent work he has returned to his point of origin. I refer to the stories in *El Aleph* and in *Doctor Brodie's Report* that come from his experiences as a young man living in the suburb of Palermo on the north side of Buenos Aires. In a long autobiographical essay, Borges described this part of the city as being made up

of low houses and vacant lots. I have often spoken of this area as a slum, but I do not quite mean that in the American sense of the word. In Palermo lived shabby, genteel people as well as more undesirable sorts. There was also a Palermo of hoodlums, called *compadritos*, famed for their knife fights, but this Palermo was only later to capture my imagination, since we did our best—our successful best—to ignore it. (A, 204)

Here is the classic situation of the writer. Borges, the heir of a distinguished line of Argentine patriots, with English blood in his

Adapted from remarks delivered on April 6, 1971, when Borges received an honorary Doctorate of Letters at Columbia University.

veins and military heroes as ancestors, finds himself, through no fault of his own, living in a community on the skids or worse— one where all the crudities of the new world are painfully obvious. In Palermo, Sarmiento's war between civilization and barbarism was fought every day.

For a while Borges kept Palermo out of his literary consciousness. And so almost every young writer shies away from writing about the life that's around him. He thinks it's dull, or embarrassing. Father's a bore, mother a scold, the neighborhood is shabby and tedious. Who would be interested in it? Therefore the young writer often turns to an exotic subject and renders it in an exquisitely complex and obscure fashion.

To a degree, Borges did the same. Although he wrote some stories about Buenos Aires, for the most part he concentrated on literary subjects. "Life and death have been lacking in my life," he has said; he has also referred to himself as being "infested with literature." The results, in his early writing, were predictable. He tried, he said,

to play the sedulous ape to two Spanish baroque seventeenth-century writers, Quevedo and Saavedra Fajardo, who stood in their own stiff, arid, Spanish way for the same kind of writing as Sir Thomas Browne in "Urne-Buriall." I was doing my best to write Latin in Spanish, and the book collapses under the sheer weight of its involutions and sententious judgments. (A, 231)

Then he tried another approach: he filled his work with as many Argentine expressions as he could find and, as he said, "worked in so many local words that many of my countrymen could hardly understand it."

Finally, through some process that is mysterious and inexplicable, although certain evidence of maturity, Borges began to turn his attention to the life of suburban Palermo. After the mazes and the mirrors, the philosophical speculations concerning time and reality that occupied much of his early writing, he came back more and more to his own back yard, describing the process as "going back to sanity, to writing with some attempt at logic and at making things easy for the reader rather than dazzling him with purple passages." What helps make this important for us is that Borges' back yard is our back yard, for it is the modern city. Buenos Aires could be the prototype of the twentieth-century urban center, without history or character, no Inca or Aztec ruins, no Roman forum, no Acropolis. Like Los Angeles, Calcutta, São Paulo or Sydney, it is an urban sprawl pleading for someone to give it expression.

But before he could deal with his own back yard, he had to sweep out the accumulated detritus. Mainly this meant that he had to deflate the romanticism of the gaucho, who was supposed to represent Argentine character. He had to go beyond the cheap reliance on local color that so much gaucho literature depended on. He did this by simple observation: the wide pampas became for him simply an "endless distance" where "the nearest house was a kind of blur on the horizon." As for the gauchos, they were just farmhands.

Once this preliminary work was done, once he revealed things as they were in the country, he was able to do the same thing for the city, and in the process become its spokesman. That is one reason for his universal appeal. His observations are always direct and clear. You need only glance at a few sentences to tell. Here is the opening of *Rosendo's Tale:*

It was about eleven o'clock at night; I had entered the old grocery store–bar (which today is just a plain bar) at the corner of Bolívar and Venezuela. (*A,* 193)

Note the authenticity: he does not say that the bar was in a remote or drab section of the city; no, it is on the corner of Bolívar and Venezuela, which is to say on the corner of Christopher Street and Seventh Avenue, or Broadway and 110th. The world he gives you is a real one: it is not a sham, a bundle of half-digested myths or pieces of local color. Also, note the touch about the bar, which once was also partly a grocery store. This shows the author has been around long enough to know his subject. You can trust him.

With equal economy and competence he introduces a character:

Benjamin Otálora, along about 1891, is a strapping young man of nineteen. He has a low forehead, candid blue eyes, and that country-boy appearance that goes with Basque ancestry. (*A,* 93)

Much of the quality of Argentine life is summarized here in a few words of physical description.

Borges' breakthrough has importance for readers and writers everywhere. He has shown people that they can face up to the experience of their lives. There is nothing to be ashamed of. Recently Borges has written:

> I have given up the surprises inherent in a baroque style as well as the surprises that lead to an unforeseen ending. I have, in short, preferred to satisfy an expectation rather than to provide a startling shock. For many years, I thought it might be given me to achieve a good page by means of variations and novelties; now, having passed seventy, I believe I have found my own voice. (*DBR*, 11)

Borges is a world writer, because he knows all the rules and knows how and when to break them. His literary life has been a long struggle to liberate the word, to give it a new vitality in an age when it is constantly under attack. He is a magician of language, but like all the best tricksters and poets he makes us feel, when the trick is revealed and the poem said, that it was always there, somewhere unexpressed within us. Carlos Fuentes has written of Borges that without his prose there would be no modern novel in South America today. We honor him for that, but also for what he has done for writing and writers all over the world. He is a great conservative who is also experimenting every time he puts pen to paper.

Borges' new prose
CARTER WHEELOCK

In 1966, some ten years after "God's magnificent irony" had given him "books and the night," apparently ending his career as a writer of prose fiction, Jorge Luis Borges published a short story, "The Intruder." His devotees sat up with interest, but many leaned back again because the new story—devoid of brain-rattling sophistry and erudite allusions—was not like the old Borges, whose three dozen gripping "fictions" published up to 1953 had made him the most important living writer in the Spanish language. Since "The Intruder," Borges has written more than a dozen new narratives, most of them collected under the title of one in the series, *Doctor Brodie's Report*. Two of them, along with several other short prose pieces, are interspersed with the poetry of *Elogio de la sombra* (1969). A long story, "The Congress," was published separately in 1971.[1]

1. The prose from *Elogio de la sombra* (In Praise of Darkness) has been translated by Norman Thomas di Giovanni in collaboration with the author and published in English as follows: "Pedro Salvadores," *The New York Review of Books,* Aug. 21, 1969; "His End and His Beginning," *The Antioch Review,* Fall–Winter 1970–1971; "The Anthropologist," "A Prayer," "Legend," and "Episode of

355

This new prose has yet to be fully appraised. My effort here can be only a superficial beginning, and we must start by remembering the old Borges.

The former Borges

Toward the end of the 1930's Borges turned from poetizing Buenos Aires and fictionalizing the hoodlums of the city's outlying slums (as in "Streetcorner man," 1933) and took to playing literary games with time, infinity, destiny, and the nature of reality. He was well equipped for it, being multilingual and having spent most of his forty years as an eclectic reader, absorbing everything from Burns's *The Saga of Billy the Kid* to Berkeley and the Panchatantra. His life, he has said, has been devoted less to living than to reading. In the following ten or so years he produced three small collections of compact fiction (the first two are now combined as *Ficciones* [1944; enlarged 1956]; the third is *The Aleph* [1949; enlarged 1952]). These stories, suggestive of highbrow detective fiction and of Symbolist poetic theory applied to prose, are utterly lacking in social consciousness or moral implication; unemotional, sexless, and uncontemporary, they wave no banners and press no points. They allude to everything and recommend nothing.

For the most part, these highly intellectual creations of the 1940's are clinical, cosmic tales peopled with almost faceless characters who are not really people but archetypal miniatures that move about in a purely cerebral universe. They often act like mythical beings in primitive cosmologies, or like dream figures: two men can be one, they can be dead but alive, and they can be only half real; they can pass in and out of mortal life ("The Immortal"), stare at magic coins until they go mad ("The Zahir"), behold the universe under the cellar stairs ("The Aleph"), live a year in a moment ("The Secret Miracle"), or dream other people into being ("The Circular Ruins"). Borges' people live in ignorance

---

the Enemy" (collected under the title "Anxieties"), *The New Yorker,* Feb. 20, 1971. *In Praise of Darkness* will be published in book form by E. P. Dutton in 1973. "The Congress" appeared in translation by di Giovanni and Borges in *The New Yorker,* Nov. 6, 1971.

of the secret laws, or the secret will, which guide their destinies, and their actions are not finally their own. Borges surrounds them with the dicta of metaphysical philosophers who make all things logical, and their behavior is told in deftly ambiguous language. The reader finds himself acclaiming with emotion what he doesn't quite grasp and perhaps doesn't believe. He is floated into a kind of esthetic hysteria, feeling spoofed but also sublimated. Although Borges insists that he does not push a philosophical viewpoint (or any other), his underlying skepticism, or idealism, comes through.

Far from being verbose in proportion to their intricacy, these earlier stories are written in a wondrously frugal and exact style— richly suggestive, poetic, and full of ironic humor, baroque artifice, and rhetorical sleight of hand. Prominent symbols—mirrors, labyrinths, tigers, towers, knives—are repeated with unabashed regularity (Borges calls himself monotonous), and the repetition of other images or secondary symbols suggests an esoteric pattern with a meaning: circles, coins, pyramids, horses, swamps, cards.

But again, no messianism intrudes into Borges' work. The ideas of men are arbitrary formulations with infinite alternatives. Certitude is intellectual death; therefore, for Borges, even his basic philosophy is a conjecture. Speculation is the law of intellectual life. Out of this view come the irony and humor of Borges' prose. He mocks knowledge by displaying it lavishly, finally turning it against itself. But his jibes are gentle, because he relishes all ideas for their esthetic value.

Every strange figment of thought implies a whole new structure of reality, a realm in which the errant idea would not be strange at all. By piling up these pieces of heretical "fact," Borges overpowers us with the illusion that we almost understand that realm and that if we did we would know everything. The creation of this illusion of near-understanding seems, on the surface, to be the whole esthetic motive of Borges' older fiction. By attacking our conception of reality and implying another—a secret order in our chaos—he stalks the "esthetic occurrence" in an Olympian arena. In a short essay, "The Wall and the Books" (*Other Inquisitions,* [1952]), he tentatively defined the esthetic event or fact (*el hecho*

357

estético) as "the imminence of a revelation, which never comes." But to say that Borges fabricates esthetic situations is a fundamental error; for he has not believed, apparently since the early 1920's when he split with Ultraism, that the esthetic is man-made.

Much light is thrown on Borges' fiction by his essays, his short prose thoughts, and his poems, where he often centers his attention on literature and philosophy, but where he just as often focuses upon a natural, historical, or literary event that strikes the sensitive intellect as marvelous because of what it implies (that is, what it does not reveal) of time, destiny, or reality. For example, a gaucho murdered by his son does not know that perhaps he died only to repeat Caesar's death along with the words "And thou, my son"; or when a man dies, an infinite number of things in his memory die with him and leave the world poorer, as when the last man died who had seen Woden's rites or the living Christ. These are not intellectual fabrications of an esthetic illusion but simple wonder at the mystery and suggestiveness of real facts. When Borges adds metaphysical half-explanations, the little miracle he is pointing to is only heightened. When he marvels at the strange spiritual likeness between Omar and FitzGerald, there are inevitable overtones of circular time, reincarnation, and Platonic form, or of the primordial metonymy that makes two men one if they share merely a characteristic. When Borges writes that Shakespeare is nobody because he so long pretended on the stage to be other men, he conjures the old theological platitude that God, being everything, is not any one thing, therefore is no thing—nothing. Such logic is a trick of language—both intellectually palliative and spiritually cathartic. Such deliberate speciousness is rare in fiction, and its proliferation in Borges' prose has moved critics to treat it as an esthetic principle. Most readers of the old Borges, if pressed for a quick characterization of his typical stories, would call them dramatizations of intellectual propositions. This makes Borges a coiner of abstruse parables or fables, an allegorist; he is frequently defined as a writer who allegorizes heretical ideas, and more often than not there is the implication that he is some kind of truth-seeker who uses literature as a megaphone for his anxieties or his agnostic faith. Borges knows this. In his new fiction he seems to be telling us that his strange literature of the past is not an intellectual destruction of reality but an esthetic affirmation of it.

The new Borges

The excellence of "The Intruder" appears to have been somewhat overlooked because many were disappointed that Borges' first story in many years was not of the old vintage. Borges punctured any hope that he would return to the "type" by telling an interviewer in 1967 that he was fed up with "labyrinths and mirrors and tigers and all that." [2] In the future he would write "straightforward" stories, somewhat after the manner of Kipling's early tales, with "little vocabulary" and "without tricks." [3] What caused this change? Anyone who reads such recent stories as "Doctor Brodie's Report," "Guayaquil," or "The Gospel According to Mark" soon realizes that near-blindness has hardly impaired Borges' ability to produce organized intricacy in precise and frugal language. No, the real cause was visible as early as 1962, when James Irby noted that Borges regarded his older fictions as baroque and vain.[4] Even before taking up fiction, Borges had abandoned (with Ultraism) the idea that literature can show us the essences of things or that art is any kind of key to metaphysical knowledge. He had abandoned faith in the reality of the "revelations" that can come out of new metaphors, contrived paradoxes, or juxtaposed antinomies. Now he has abandoned Ultraism's essentially baroque style; but he continues to espouse the idea that literature should "show us our own face," by which he means that it should show us *its* face, for to him the world and literature are the same

2. See César Fernández Moreno, "Harto de los laberintos," *Mundo Nuevo,* 18 (Dec. 1967), 25, 29; a translation of it, by John Murchison, is in *Encounter* (Apr. 1969).

3. Richard Burgin, *Conversations with Jorge Luis Borges* (New York, 1969), pp. 130–31.

4. James E. Irby, "Encuentro con Borges," *Universidad de México,* XVI, 10 (June 1962), 8. Borges speaks as if he had written all his stories while believing that literature is only an exercise: "I used to believe that literature was technique and nothing else, but I no longer think that. The best writers do not have contrivances; or at least, their contrivances are secret" (trans. mine). In Borges' work, obviously, technique and artifice are only facets of a much grander execution.

thing: "If art is perfect, the world is superfluous." [5] The "imminence of a revelation" is perhaps the ultimate knowable reality, and men do not create it. They comprise it, behold it, and try to transmute it into language. This idea precludes any esthetic theory —that is, any rule or formula for producing an imminent revelation.

Borges writes in the preface to *In Praise of Darkness* that he is not the possessor of an esthetic; and in the preface to *Doctor Brodie's Report* he seems to disclaim the attribution to him, by others, of an "esthetic of the intelligence": [6]

The art of writing is mysterious; the opinions we hold are ephemeral, and I prefer the Platonic idea of the Muse to that of Poe, who reasoned, or feigned to reason, that the writing of a poem is an act of the intelligence. (*DBR*, 10) [7]

In the same preface, in answer to those critics who have deplored his lack of artistic concern for national and social issues, he says:

I want to make it quite clear that I am not, nor have I ever been, what used to be called a preacher of parables or a fabulist and is now known as a committed writer. I do not aspire to be Aesop. My stories, like those of the Thousand and One Nights, try to be entertaining or moving but not persuasive. (*DBR*, 9–10)

This may also be understood as Borges' justification for deserting those metaphysical fictions which have been taken as essentially allegorical, for Borges is well aware of the bad connotations of "allegory." He has called allegory "an error," although he admits to allegorizing. (In the foreword to the second part of *Ficciones* he calls "The Sect of the Phoenix" an allegory.) Apparently he does not mind being called an allegorist if only the implication of didacticism is removed. Stripped of its moralism, allegory becomes a valid and powerful esthetic device, a long metaphor rich in suggestion. In a recent interview Borges characterized himself as a former parabolist turned storyteller; speak-

5. Burgin, p. 80.
6. An "esthetic of the intelligence" is attributed to Borges by Enrique Anderson Imbert in his *Historia de la literatura hispanoamericana* (Mexico, 1964), II, 268. I repeat the attribution in my *The Mythmaker* (Austin, 1969), p. 4.
7. In quoting from Borges, unless otherwise indicated, I use the translations made by di Giovanni and Borges. I am indebted to Mr. di Giovanni for supplying translations which had not been published when I was writing.

ing of the new stories he would write (those of *Doctor Brodie's Report*), he said: "They will not be like my former work, parables or pretexts for writing essays. I want to be a storyteller, a narrator of real stories, without tricks." [8]

In "The Approach to al-Mu'tasim" (*Ficciones*), Borges says of the fictitious novel he is "reviewing" that the version of 1932 was somewhat symbolic, but that the 1934 version "declines into allegory" (*A*, 50). In the foreword to Robert Lima's translation of Ana María Barrenechea's work on Borges (*Borges the Labyrinth Maker* [New York, 1965], p. viii), Borges acknowledges his occasional recourse to allegory: "My best writings are of things that were striving to come to life through me, and not simply allegories where the thought comes before the sign." In other words, Borges strives for a true symbolism but thinks that he, too, may occasionally "decline into allegory."

New narratives

Borges' new manner is indeed more straightforward. Much of the stylistic complexity has disappeared, leaving his themes and plots more conspicuous. In these narratives the plots—the *fabulae*, tales as tales—are in my opinion superior to those of *Ficciones* and *El Aleph*, not because they are less fantastic but because truth itself is fantastic and these new tales, for the most part, are closer to it than are the stories about the equivocal verities of our mental life. In the eleven stories of *Doctor Brodie's Report* we do not get lost in limitless libraries or go wandering around inside the mind of the Minotaur. We go back, mainly, to the straggling outskirts, or *arrabales*, of Buenos Aires and to the pampa. These are the suburbs and plains as they were, or could have been, at the close of the nineteenth century or the early years of the twentieth, when *compadritos* (Argentine hoodlums, or gang toughs, with a lot of the classical gaucho in them) would hang around the saloons deciding who was the toughest, often by fighting with knives. Thus Borges continues to show his lifelong fascination

---

8. Yulan M. Washburn, quoting *La Nación* (Buenos Aires) of Dec. 15, 1969, in "Artists and Authors," *Hispania*, 53, 2 (May 1970), 328. Trans. mine.

with the cult of physical courage, which is present in "The Intruder" and commands at least five other *Brodie* stories.[9]

These narratives about blustering *compadres* are among the eight in *Brodie* that are based on some type of interpersonal rivalry. Of the ruffians of the *arrabal* the most conspicuous is Rosendo Juárez ("Rosendo's Tale")—not because he is the toughest but because he is the same Rosendo Juárez who turned coward (apparently) in "Streetcorner Man," a story Borges wrote as far back as 1933. In the new story, Rosendo explains to Borges that his refusal to fight when challenged was due to disillusionment and disgust with his style of life. The most pathetic of the duelers are the gauchos Manuel Cardoso and Carmen Silveira of "The End of the Duel." These are two longtime rivals who have often faced each other knife in hand but have avoided killing each other because their rivalry gives meaning to their "poor and monotonous lives" (*DBR*, 46). Drafted into the army, they fight side by side, without speaking, until they are finally captured by the enemy. A sadistic captain, knowing their rivalry, orders that they die in competition. Their throats cut, they run a race to see who can go farthest before collapsing.

Borges plays many variations on the rivalry theme. "The Intruder" gives us a rivalry caused by a woman and transcended by a murderous brotherly love. The Nilsen brothers, a pair of illiterate Saturday-night brawlers, pick up and share a country wench, sell her to a brothel to quiet their growing jealousy, and later retrieve her when each of them begins going to the brothel on the sly. Unable to save their comradeship and affection with the girl between them, the older brother kills her. When the younger is told, the two embrace, almost in tears.[10]

9. The best commentary, to my knowledge, on this cult of courage is a piece written by Borges himself in 1952, later slightly altered and inserted into the 1955 edition of *Evaristo Carriego* (1930) under the heading "El culto del coraje" as a subchapter of "Historia del tango." Translated by di Giovanni and Borges under its original title "The Challenge," it appeared in *The New Yorker* of May 23, 1970, and is included in *The Aleph and Other Stories*.

10. In December 1969, Borges told me that by making the protagonists of this story brothers he hoped to avoid a homosexual connotation. See also his commentary on the story in *The Aleph and Other Stories*, pp. 278–79.

In "Juan Muraña" the personal conflict is more fanciful; it is hardly a rivalry, but it involves a tough whose knife was feared. Muraña, long dead, is a bloody legend, and his widow, sister, and nephew are about to be dispossessed by their landlord Luchessi. Muraña's widow, Aunt Florentina, is a bit daft; she keeps assuring the others that her beloved husband will not let the gringo throw them out. Luchessi is butchered one night in his doorway by an unknown knifer. Later, Aunt Florentina shows her nephew her beloved husband—the notorious knife of Juan Muraña.

In "Juan Muraña" the fanciful equation of a man with his knife is explicable as Florentina's mental aberration or as a symbol of Muraña's continuing influence. But in "The Meeting," Borges goes straight to the fantastic—to a mystical, metonymical equation of men with their instruments. Two men—not *compadres* but civilized upper-class Argentines—get tipsy at a stag party and quarrel over a card game. As if driven by something beyond themselves, they do the unthinkable. They go to a display cabinet, take out two knives made famous by a pair of rivals long dead, and fight. Neither knows anything about knife fighting, but they fight like experts. One is killed; the other is incredulous and ashamed. In a kind of postscript, Borges suggests that it was not the men who fought, but the knives; the men were instruments of an ancient enmity inherent in the weapons.

But of all these tales of the mythic outskirts of the city, "The Unworthy Friend" is perhaps the most ambiguous and intriguing. Don Santiago Fischbein (whose real name is Jacobo) tells his story to Borges. He was a Jewish boy and a confessed coward in a neighborhood where the physical courage of the *compadre* was admired. He was terribly eager to be accepted thereabouts, but also to be accepted as an Argentine and a good citizen. He fell in with a gang of hooligans headed by one Francisco Ferrari, not because he had what it took to run with that crowd but because he adulated the leader, who lured him in. Ferrari planned to break into a textile factory one night and assigned Fischbein to keep watch outside. But before the time came, Fischbein went to the police and told all, causing Ferrari's death.

After reading "The Unworthy Friend," one does not know who betrayed whom, who is really judged unworthy, and unworthy of what. In one way this story reverses the plot of "The South" (*Ficciones*), whose nameless old gaucho appears to correspond to the old man of "The Unworthy Friend," Eliseo Amaro, the only gang member who is named. Fischbein's betrayal of Ferrari is prefigured in his verbal denial, at one point, that he knows Ferrari (he feels unworthy of knowing him); this vaguely suggests Peter's denial of Jesus. (Borges' interest in Christ's betrayal is shown in "Three Versions of Judas" [*Ficciones*] and other places, and in his new fiction it is most prominent in "The Gospel According to Mark.")

The possible reasons why Fischbein betrayed Ferrari are numerous. He wanted to prove himself a good Argentine; his hero had tried to corrupt and use him; he lost respect for his idol when he saw him pushed around by the police; he saw him as a punk, the way Rosendo Juárez saw himself; he had to justify his own cowardice by causing his hero's courage to destroy him. The ostensible reason is psychological; men often betray those of whom they feel unworthy.[11] The most probable explanation of the treachery is purely Borgesian: the inscrutable cosmos somehow required it; it repeated the Great Betrayal. Ferrari is a subverted Christ figure. Adored by his followers and persecuted by the authorities, he is first denied, then sold out, then killed.

Why is Peter suggested, however remotely, along with Christ's real betrayer, Judas? I think it is because the betrayal has somehow saved the traitor. The key to this lies in the reasoning of the strange Gutre, or Guthrie, family of "The Gospel According to Mark." Father, son, and daughter, all illiterate, work on a ranch being visited by the protagonist, a medical student named Baltasar

11. Late in 1970 Borges and di Giovanni wrote a special Afterword for the English version of *Doctor Brodie's Report*, in which Borges reveals that "The Unworthy Friend" was inspired by a personal experience. As a young man Borges was offered the friendship of a companion he idolized, and he thrust it aside thinking he did not deserve it. He also reveals that the protagonist of "The Elder Lady" was his great-aunt, and that the terrible duel of "The End of the Duel" actually took place in Uruguay a century ago.

Espinosa. Isolated with this rather stupid trio when the ranch is surrounded by floodwaters, Espinosa passes the time in the evenings by reading them the Gospel of St. Mark. Ordinarily unresponsive to the student, they listen with deep interest; when he treats their pet lamb for an injury, he wins their devotion. The rains destroy part of the roof of the tool shed attached to the house, and, according to the Gutres, this accounts for the hammering that goes on while Espinosa sleeps and dreams of the building of the Ark. One night the girl, a virgin, comes to his room naked and has intercourse with him without embracing or kissing him. The next day the father asks him whether even those who crucified Jesus were saved from hell, and Espinosa, whose theology is vague, says yes. After lunch Espinosa leaves his room to find the Gutres kneeling and asking his blessing; then they curse him and spit on him and push him to the door of the wrecked tool shed, from the timbers of which they have built a cross.

The transference of identity from Christ to Espinosa (whose name suggests Baruch Spinoza and also the word "thorny," like a crown of thorns) is plausible, given the superstitious mentalities of the Gutres. But the matter lies deeper. The idea of being saved by killing one's redeemer is a reversal of the idea of being killed *by* him, Job-like, as in "The House of Asterion" (*El Aleph*), where the Minotaur is "redeemed" by Theseus. While Borges equates salvation with death in that case, he makes it equivalent to life in this one, where the Gutres appropriate the virtues of their sacrificial victim through the symbolic ritual of cannibalism. Fischbein's cowardice, likewise, is somehow mitigated by the death of his superior, his "redeemer." In the story of the Gutres there are suggestions of correspondences between the death of Christ and the human sacrifices of primitive peoples. Just as the Gutre girl gave herself to Espinosa without the enthusiasm of love, as if in obeisance, the Aztecs (for example) chose sacrificial victims whom they coddled for a time, giving them luxury and women, before killing them. In a higher sense of the word, Jesus was "coddled" for a while, as during the triumphal entry into

Jerusalem. The Gutres petted Espinosa, who, like Jesus, was thirty-three years old, a healer, bearded, and noted for oratory and goodness.

The cannibalism in these two stories is finally of an abstruse and philosophical kind, echoing the interplay of order and chaos that characterizes much of Borges' older work. Let me illustrate. The Gutres, who remind me of the oxlike Troglodytes of "The Immortal" (*El Aleph*), are of part-Scotch ancestry and are a mixture, Borges tells us, of Calvinist fanaticism and the superstition of the pampa Indian. Let us say they have a fixed and limited world-view. In words that paraphrase a reference in his confessional essay "The Maker" (*Dreamtigers*) and that allude to the Odyssey of Homer, Borges compares the Gutres to a lost ship searching the seas for a beloved island. The Odyssey and the Crucifixion are called the two histories which men, down through the ages, have repeated. On the symbolic level they are contrasted: the voyage of men lost in chaos, seeking a center, versus the exaltation through death (dissolution) of a supreme centrality on Golgotha. The medical student's mentality is contrasted with that of the Gutres; he is a freethinker who has no overriding or centered viewpoint, and no need for one. He likes to gamble, but not to win or to argue; he has "an open intelligence" and an "almost unlimited goodness." Unlike the world-view of the Gutres, then, his fluid and easy outlook seems magnanimous and noble. The Gutres, the lost ship, are searching for a secure idea, but Espinosa is not looking for anything. The Gutres see the Gospel as a conveyor of terribly important truth, but Espinosa reads it for its esthetic value. The Gutres seek order and meaning, but Espinosa is happy with a kind of agnostic equivocality, and, paradoxically, he is more ordered, more saved, than they. The narrow and fanatical Gutres believe that the sacrifice of their new pet, this other lamb, will redeem them.

How will it redeem them? We have to look back at Borges' older "system." Borges has made both salvation and hell equivalent to intellectual obsession (the inability to forget), as in "The Zahir" (*El Aleph*) where the narrator cannot forget a coin and goes happily, painlessly mad; or as in "Deutsches Requiem" (*El Aleph*) where the poet David Jerusalem is driven insane by an unnamed obsession inculcated by his tormentor, Otto zur Linde, who observes that any common thing, if not forgettable, is the germ of a possible hell; or as in "The House of Asterion" (*El Aleph*), where the Minotaur, bewildered by a house-universe that has too many galleries and doors, is "saved" by the world-simplifying sword that takes his life. In the story of the Gutres, as in Christian dogma, the death of the "Christ" is the vicarious death (redemption) of lost men; "Christ" becomes for the Gutres the holy obsession, the beloved island. Paradoxically, he represents not a limited, obsessive world-view, but its erasure.

"The Gospel According to Mark" is not one of the stories of rivalry. I want to go back to that type in order to mention "The Duel" and "Guayaquil." The first is a kind of parallel story to "The End of the Duel," mentioned earlier; the rivalry depicted is one that enriches the lives of the competitors. Two society women, Clara Glencairn and Marta Pizarro, compete in a friendly way in the field of painting. Painting is here analogous to literature, and I think we can infer that Borges is contrasting his own work—imaginative, ambiguous—both with the almost unintelligible literature of the vanguardist and with the clear-cut, rational literature of the *engagé* writer who tries to mirror the world and push a message. The story is humorous and satirical; in the artist Clara Glencairn we can perhaps see a caricature of Borges himself as he is seen, or thinks he is seen, by some Argentine men of letters who, on the one hand, have criticized his work for its universalism and aloof unconcern with national issues and, on the other hand, do not include him among the really "far out." [12] Clara tried to be an abstract artist—a vanguardist—but that school rejected her work. She smiled and went on. Eventually she won a prize because some judges could not decide between two other artists, one of them too conventional and the other too "modern."

12. This does not preclude, of course, Borges' direct satire of society ladies and artists. I am assured by his collaborator, di Giovanni, that some of the personages in this story are real people.

Her friend and rival was the "straight" artist Marta Pizarro, a painter of portraits and patios with a nineteenth-century look. The two women painted against and for each other, and when Clara died, Marta's life lost its meaning. She painted Clara's portrait and laid her brushes aside for good. In that delicate duel, says Borges, there were neither defeats nor victories.

"Guayaquil" consists largely in the dialogue of two historians who are thrust into momentary rivalry. The narrator is a scholar whose specialty is the Independence movement and the life of the Argentine hero General San Martín. His adversary is a German Jew from Prague who has fled Hitler's tyranny, one Eduardo Zimmerman. Zimmerman is not a specialist in South American history but has proven himself adept at cleansing the biased histories of others (he has written on the Carthaginian Jews, who formerly were known only through the accounts of their enemies, the Romans). The two men are contending for the privilege of being officially chosen to go to another country to copy, appraise, and publish a newly discovered letter presumably written by Bolívar, which could clear up a famous historical mystery: what was said between San Martín and Bolívar, when they met in Guayaquil, which caused the former to retire from revolutionary activity and leave the destiny of the continent in Bolívar's hands. By conventional standards the narrator is better qualified to appraise the letter (a specialist, he is also the proud scion of revolutionary heroes), but he surrenders the privilege to Zimmerman after the two scholars converse. On leaving, Zimmerman divines that the narrator has conceded the honor because he intimately willed to do so. Still showing his penchant for alluding to philosophers, Borges weaves into the story a mention of Schopenhauer's "law" that no human action is involuntary; this serves a central purpose in the structure of the tale, which is about will and implies that volition—commitment—causes bad literature. I will comment on this story later in connection with Borges' esthetic ideas.

"The Elder Lady" shows Borges' ability to write in a charming and delicate way, with nostalgia for the glories of Argentine history and with both sympathy and satire of the *criollo* sensibility.

The story is about the hundredth birthday of the last person who can claim to be the daughter of a revolutionary hero. The bustle and excitement of her anniversary celebration, which her countrymen turn into a celebration of national history and which she probably does not comprehend because she lives in the distracted world of the senile, hastens her end. She has long partaken of the glory of her famous father, hero of the battle of Cerro Alto; now she is somehow the last victim of that battle, for its celebration brings on her death.

Among the more ingenious of Borges' earlier stories are those in which he enumerates the irrational characteristics of some fantastic thing, apparently allegorizing an unnamed common reality. In "The Lottery in Babylon" (*Ficciones*), for example, he describes a "vertiginous country" where citizens are governed by pure chance, taking part in a lottery that awards them fame or ignominy, riches or poverty, life or death, on a day-to-day basis. Interpretation is up to the reader, and in this case the story seems to suggest the fortuitous and unstable nature of what men call reality. In "The Sect of the Phoenix" (*Ficciones*) Borges rounds up the random characteristics of a secret rite which is never identified but could be any number of things.[13] In the new fiction, the title story of *Doctor Brodie's Report* is of this enigmatic type. It is an outrageous description of an incredible tribe called the Mlch, or Yahoos (the latter is the name of the degenerate humans in *Gulliver's Travels*). As a narrative device, Borges lays before us the incomplete manuscript of a Scottish Protestant missionary, David Brodie, who lived among the Yahoos. It reminds us of many things: Gulliver, a story by H. G. Wells, Pío Baroja's *Paradox Rey,* and other accounts of bizarre peoples. But mostly it reminds us of the old Borges, particularly of his description of the mind of Ireneo Funes ("Funes the Memorious," *Ficciones*), who could not forget details and was unable to form abstractions, "to think Platonically"; or it suggests the imaginary planet Tlön ("Tlön, Uqbar, Orbis Tertius," *Ficciones*), which is made of purely

13. Borges has told Ronald Christ that the secret ritual was the sex act. See Christ's *The Narrow Act* (New York, 1969), p. 190, n.

ideal—i.e., mental—elements. The Yahoos suffer the opposite of Funes' affliction; they have a language of pure abstractions and cannot remember details. They cannot combine phenomena except of a homogeneous, Platonic type. Unlike the people of Tlön, who can concoct anything at will, the Yahoos cannot fabricate at all. In the story of Tlön, the imaginary planet begins to concretize —to impose itself materially on the planet Earth; in the Yahoos of "Doctor Brodie's Report" we may see the grotesque end-result of that imposition. The Yahoos cannot count above four, can hardly speak, and appear to have no discrimination of time. In a limited way, they can predict the events of the immediate future (these appear to be only extrapolations). They remember almost nothing, and if they do remember an event they cannot say whether it happened to them or their fathers, or whether they dreamed it. They live in the present, they eat in secret or close their eyes while eating, they execute their fellows for fun, and if one of them is a poet (if he puts a few words together unintelligibly, but with moving effect) he is considered a god and anyone may kill him. Their king is blinded, mutilated, gelded, and kept in a cavern, except in war, when he is taken to the battle front and waved like a banner. Instead of declining into allegory, Borges' prose now tends to sharpen into satire, or even to move toward the intensive case of the modern novel, where the parable intersects with cultural anthropology, and whose characters obscure and overwhelm the symbols they encounter.

The unchanging Borges

Borges' characters are still chessmen, however, and both character and action are subservient to situations of a chessboard kind. His settings are still indifferent; the *compadritos* could almost as easily be Chicago gangsters or western gunmen. Despite his return to the *arrabales,* Borges is not a portrayer of local color and customs; as somebody must have said before, his Buenos Aires is a situation, not a city. Many of his themes are still highbrow, esthetic, "irrelevant." References to systems of ideas, famous and arcane, are no longer profuse, but they have not vanished; we

370

still find Spinoza, Euclid, Schopenhauer, the Kabbalah, Carlyle, Lugones, Carriego, Henry James, Hudson, and others. Still, these allusions seem to serve less purpose than formerly and to be more often literary than philosophical. Familiar Borgesian language crops up only here and there; in "The Intruder" we find "contentious alcohol" (*alcohol pendenciero*), a phrase he has used since the 1930's. Missing now are those very frequent words with which Borges used to point to the vast or infinite, such as "dizzying" (*vertiginoso;* this word used to do double duty, suggesting also the rise to an esthetic moment). Borges seldom plays with time and infinity, and instead turns to destiny, cosmic irony, and chance. Regrettably, we find no rich poetic images that suggest impossible intuitions like the plight of man before the chaotic universe: veiled men uttering blasphemous conjectures in the twilight ("The Lottery in Babylon") or old men hiding themselves in the latrines, with some metal disks in a prohibited dicebox, weakly imitating the divine disorder ("The Library of Babel," *Ficciones*).

Borges' language is still superbly laconic. It is less connotative, and conceits and etymological uses of words are no longer plentiful. Fantastic ideas still appeal to him, as we see in "The Meeting" and in "Juan Muraña," but they are no longer intended to rattle or astonish us; instead, they appeal to our esthetic sensibilities. There appears to be no significance, beyond Borges' personal whim, to the fact that the new stories are laden with Scotsmen (Brodie, Clara Glencairn, Glencoe, the Gutres), Germans (Zimmerman), and other North Europeans (the Nelsons or Nilsens of "The Intruder"). The prominence of red hair is consistent with all of these nationalities; all red things have symbolic meaning, I think, in Borges' work, and there may be a hidden significance here.[14]

14. I am indebted to Norman Thomas di Giovanni for this information: Borges made some of his characters Scotch "so they could have red hair"; Borges greatly admires the Scots. When he was writing "The Duel," di Giovanni suggested to Borges that he not use the name Glencairn, since it is also the name of a character in "The Man on the Threshold" (*The Aleph*). But Borges insisted, because he thought the name fine-sounding. Believing in many intimate intercon-

As before, Borges continues to throw in generalizations that are external to the narrative: "Carlyle says that men need heroes to worship" ("The Unworthy Friend"). Their effect is to give intellectual justification to a character's action, obviating a realistic or contextual explanation. This economy is fundamental to Borges' narration. He often inserts his own opinions; he tells us that the aged protagonist of "The Elder Lady" was gradually "growing dimmer and dimmer," and he justifies the metaphor by adding, "Common metaphors are the best because they are the only true ones" (*DBR*, 92); and to explain Clara Glencairn's reason for taking up abstract instead of traditional art, he generalizes that "all esthetic revolutions put forth a temptation toward the irresponsible and the far too easy" (*DBR*, 37). These asides almost always have the value of esthetic commentary. In "Guayaquil," for example, Borges remarks: "The successiveness of language ... tends to exaggerate what we are saying" (*DBR*, 102). This is given as a warning to the reader that Zimmerman's enumerated traits are "visual trivia," apparently not as important as the conclusion that he had lived an arduous life.

Borges has tallied, in the preface to *In Praise of Darkness,* a handful of his *"astucias"*—his stylistic and structural devices. The tabulation omits the majority of the subtleties that scholars have abstracted from his older works, and is obviously a declaration of present, not necessarily former, practice. Time, he says, has taught him to avoid synonyms, Hispanisms, Argentinisms, archaisms, and neologisms; to prefer habitual to astonishing words; to insert circumstantial details, "which the reader now demands"; to feign small uncertainties; to tell things as if he did not fully understand them; and to remember that former norms

---

nections in Borges' work, I suspect a deeper reason. David Glencairn of "Threshold" imposed peace upon two warring religious sects; Clara Glencairn is a kind of compromise between two opposing groups of painters; Alexander Glencoe of "The Congress" is a powerful figure who coordinates the activities of many men and at one point intervenes between two fighting gauchos. This function of transcendence may, of course, be incidental or accidental. In G. K. Chesterton's poem "Glencoe," there are lines that fit the Glencoe of Borges' story, such as "Sterile though they be and void of rule / You know my shapeless crags have loved the stars" (*The Collected Poems of G. K. Chesterton,* New York, 1945, p. 117).

are not obligations. In the preface to *Doctor Brodie's Report* he says he has renounced "the surprises inherent in a baroque style" (*DBR*, 11). He does not call his new, "straightforward" stories simple: "I do not dare state that they are simple; there isn't anywhere on earth a single page or single word that is, since each thing implies the universe, whose most obvious trait is complexity" (*DBR*, 9).

Two of the devices he mentions are conspicuous because they preserve in Borges' new fiction an essential property of the old: namely, feigning small uncertainties and telling a story as if he did not fully understand it. Borges' chessmen—his people "seen through the wrong end of a telescope" (James Irby)—are not so much characters as props. Their faces are wiped off by Borges' aloof posture. He masks the activity of writing under the pretense of listening: "People say (but this is unlikely) that the story was first told by Eduardo" ("The Intruder," *DBR*, 63); "... Carlos Reyles ... told me the story ... out in Adrogué" ("The End of the Duel," *DBR*, 45); "here is the story, with all the inevitable variations brought about by time" ("The Meeting," *DBR*, 71). An occasional disclaimer, like "probably," keeps this objectivity in front of the reader: "... she was unable to keep hidden a certain preference, probably for the younger man" ("The Intruder," *DBR*, 66). The only new story in which he does not keep his distance is "Guayaquil," where he writes as the protagonist; but it is also in this story that he speaks of the necessity of objectifying and states the principle clearly: "I shall with all probity recount what happened, and this may enable me to understand it. Furthermore, to confess to a thing is to leave off being an actor in it and to become an onlooker—to become somebody who has seen it and tells it and is no longer the doer" (*DBR*, 99). In contrast to the narrator of "Guayaquil," who is so involved that he purports to understand only dimly what has happened, his rival historian, Zimmerman, is noteworthy for his objective detachment from events and opinions; we feel that Zimmerman understands everything—even the things he cannot express but can only allude to.

373

Borges' objectivity, his blurring of faces, is directly related to his esthetic. I have suggested [15] that in his older fiction Borges carries his reader to a mythic awareness, an esthetic moment of near-revelation, and at the same time alludes to that moment symbolically through images of dizziness: vertigo, fever, alcohol, inebriation, exaltation, delirium. These images are part of a whole system of secondary symbolism (i.e., below the level of such overt symbols as mirrors and labyrinths) through which Borges used to create, in each narrative, a background drama—a play of allusions in which the overt action of the story is duplicated by symbolic forms as if these were the enlarged shadows of the characters. In Borges' system there are symbols of order and being (blood, tower, light, coin, tree, tiger, sword), symbols of chaos or nonbeing (circles, ashes, mud, dust, swamps, plains, night, water, wall), and symbols of purely ideal being and of world dissolution, made largely of combinations and interplays of the images of order and chaos. They comprise an archetypal, almost Olympian representation of the activity of the human consciousness as it creates, destroys, and re-creates reality. In this shadowy undulation there is a moment between the chaos of nonbeing (mere perception of meaningless things) and the lucidity of full being (complete, meaningful abstraction) when the consciousness hovers on the brink of a higher revelation. That revelation never comes; instead, what occurs is a kind of short-circuit resulting in "language," the abstraction of a bathetic reality small enough to be expressed. But that hovering instant when some kind of supernal truth seems imminent is the "vertiginous" moment to which Borges refers as the esthetic event.

We find far less evidence of this background drama of symbols in Borges' new fiction. Avowing his disbelief in esthetic *theories,* which he says are only occasional stimuli or instruments, Borges speaks continually of the esthetic *occurrence* or *fact,* "the imminence of a revelation." He built it allusively or allegorically into the fabric of such stories as "The End" (*Ficciones*); now it stares

15. *The Mythmaker,* pp. 13–14.

at us ingenuously from many of his new ones, and the forewords to the books he has published since 1960 are conspicuously concerned with the central point—the esthetic fact is not a collection of words on paper, but an experience: "A volume in itself is not an esthetic reality, but a physical object among others; the esthetic event can occur only when it is written or when it is read" (preface to *In Praise of Darkness;* translation mine).

Borges has shown that he is willing to judge literature good or bad using the *hecho estético* as a criterion. In the preface to his *Personal Anthology* (1961) he points to Croce's pronouncement that art is expression. To that idea, or to its deformation, he says, we owe some of the worst literature. He quotes verses from Valéry about a fruit whose form perishes in the mouth, giving delight by perishing, and other lines from Tennyson in which a boat fades into the distance and "vanishes into light." He doubts that anyone will finally include such verses among the best, saying that they represent a "mental process." We should infer that they carry an image or idea to its completion and that this is esthetically wrong. Borges adds: "At times, I too have sought expression; I know now that my gods grant me no more than allusion or mention" (translation mine). His comments do not finally cohere unless we understand that his "gods" are his ideas about how literature should be made. By opposing expression to suggestion he contrasts a finished mental process with one that is open-ended and indefinite, hovering over an unformulated idea. He seems to believe that allusion is not at all intellectual, hence the emphasis on event, on fact.

Borges likes the fruit image from Valéry. In another preface (to his *Obra poética,* [1964]), he says he applies to poetry what Berkeley applied to reality: "The taste of the apple . . . lies in the contact of the fruit with the palate, not in the fruit itself. . . . What is essential is the esthetic act, the thrill, the almost physical emotion that comes with each reading." The bad writer, for Borges, is the one who *eats the fruit for us,* finishing the idea before we can savor its insinuations—or worse, letting his foregone conclusion shape the composition. Croce's "expression" is the complete verbal capture of a clear idea or feeling—the short-circuit that evaporates the pregnant myth. Borges points out in an essay on Nathaniel Hawthorne (*Other Inquisitions*) that Hawthorne's moralisms do not usually ruin his work, if only because they come in the last paragraph and because he did not fashion his characters to prove his conclusions. An "expressive" writer, an Aesop, builds a narrative that yields a simile between two realities (with the intention of giving one the color of the other), or between his fictitious events and the moral point or social theory he is trying to illustrate, while Borges himself wants only to distract his reader. Some quality held in common between two or more things links them secretly, and this is not something contrived by Borges but perceived by him. That perception, imparted to us, brings the momentary illusion that the chaotic world is somehow simplified or illuminated, and we are lifted toward a new insight or comprehension—which never solidifies.

Borges' esthetic idea is worked into his new fiction in at least two ways. In some stories he presents esthetically loaded situations, a "missing apex" type of suggestion which leaves the mystery incomplete. Usually this involves irony or paradox, and inevitably it raises the question of the character of God or of Destiny: an ironic competition between two dying rivals who had refused to kill each other in life; the redemptive crucifixion of an unbelieving, unsuspecting, unwilling "Christ"; a brother love that is no less admirable in itself (and perhaps is even more so) for having expressed itself in murder. The second way is that of the abstruse "allegory" (I now use the term inexactly, for lack of another) in which the esthetic event is pointed to by allusion as an objective idea. Only one of Borges' new stories is clearly of this kind, although others may be more subtly so; before turning to "Guayaquil," it will be helpful to look first at obvious allusions to the *hecho estético* in the short prose of *In Praise of Darkness*.

Borges uses, more often now, stories he has heard. Long ago he heard the one called "Pedro Salvadores," which is not really a story but a historical episode to which Borges adds his comments and shows his own esthetic reaction. Salvadores was an Argentine who, as an opponent of the dictator Juan Manuel de Rosas (deposed in 1852), was forced to hide in his cellar for nine years.[16] This, plus the details, is his whole story. In the same way that Camus wondered, in *The Myth of Sisyphus,* what Sisyphus thought as he carried his eternal rock, Borges wonders at those nine years of dark isolation. (Internal elements lift the episode to a universal plane, and there is reason to suspect a parallel with Borges' blindness and his intellectual history). He conjectures about Salvadores' feelings, actions, thoughts, and very being— with no possibility of corroborating his intuitions. "As with so many things, the fate of Pedro Salvadores," he concludes, "strikes us as a symbol of something we are about to understand, but never quite do" (*A,* 189).

Very like that episode is the one called "The Anthropologist." Borges says he heard the story in Texas and he gives it to us without comment. Fred Murdock, a student of indigenous languages, goes into the desert to live with an Indian tribe and to discover the secrets behind its esoteric rites. After a long time he returns to the university and informs his disappointed professor that he has learned the secret but cannot tell it—not because of a vow or the deficiencies of language; in fact, he could enunciate it a hundred ways. But the secret is less valuable than the steps that lead to it, and "Those steps have to be taken, not told."

"The Anthropologist" is brief and deceptively simple; it is not a story about an anthropologist but about a young man in chaos, uncommitted, who tried to reduce the world to a facet of itself, hoping to find in it the centripetal vortex of vision that would explain or justify the whole. It is the same story as "The Library of Babel" (*Ficciones*) in which the inmates of the library go blind looking for the compendious book. It is the story of a frustration, like "Averroes' Search" (*El Aleph*), where Averroes is

16. There are many nines in Borges' older stories, to which these historical nines can be added: Borges worked nine years in the municipal library of Buenos Aires (1937–1946); Perón was dictator of Argentina for nine years (1946–1955). In most of its occurrences, Borges seems to use the number to symbolize the completion of a time cycle or to indicate perfection or fulfillment.

compared to the frustrated god "mentioned by Burton . . . [who] tried to create a bull and created a buffalo instead" (*L,* 155). It is the story told in Borges' poem "The Golem," where a rabbi tries to create a man and can only create a clumsy doll. Here we see vestiges of an allusive imagery that is much more evident in Borges' older work; it is not mere coincidence that the student dreamed of mustangs (in the Spanish, it is bison). He went into the desert to find a revelation and found only language. As he implies, the search was more valuable than the result, and the search has to be experienced, not told. The esthetic experience is in the contact of the fruit with the palate, not in the digestion of it.

Borges believes—I think it is clear—that the tales men tell and retell, the ones that comprise our myths, are all of the open kind. They respect and embody an esthetic of the unconsummated, rehearsing the cosmic mystery. All our science, philosophy, and explanations of the universe are buffaloes.

In a tiny poetic essay, "The Unending Gift," an artist promises Borges a painting but dies without sending it. If it had come, it would be a thing among things; but now it is limitless and unceasing, capable of any form or color. It somehow exists and will live and grow like music. "In a promise," Borges concludes, "there is something that does not die."

"Guayaquil" and *el hecho estético*

"Guayaquil," which I summarized earlier, is the story of a scholar who renounces intellectual fulfillment in order to preserve esthetic life. He sees more value in a myth than in an explanation, more virtue in an unformulated idea than in the language that purports to convey truth. The narrator of the story and his rival historian, Dr. Zimmerman, are contending for the privilege of appraising the newly found letter of Bolívar which will give Bolívar's answer to the renowned question of what happened in the interview with San Martín. We must remember that San Martín, after talking with Bolívar, withdrew from the revolutionary struggle; we might say that he, too, quit before his drama was done. Bolívar led his country's fortunes until his death, leaving his indelible stamp on the revolution and its aftermath. Transferred from the historical plane to the literary, San Martín's story is unconsummated and esthetic; but Bolívar's finished career (a completed "mental process") makes bad "literature." The conversation of the revolutionary heroes is somehow duplicated in that of the historians, who observe that it was no doubt Bolívar's will, not words, that determined the outcome at Guayaquil. The narrator finally concedes to Zimmerman the honor of publishing the letter in order not to repeat the action—the will—of Bolívar. To repeat Bolívar's error would be to turn an esthetically attractive historical event—a living myth—into mere short-circuiting language. The reason is this: there is mystery in the San Martín incident, and Zimmerman believes the letter cannot really clear it up because it gives only Bolívar's version, perhaps written in self-justification. If Zimmerman interprets the letter for the public, he will preserve the mythic ambiguity by weighing Bolívar's words in the proper perspective. But the biased narrator feels that if he publishes a commentary, the effect will be deadly; he is the descendant of revolutionists, very much involved in history and partial to San Martín, and his conjectural position on the matter is well known (although we are not told what it is). The public will link him with the letter, and the myth (the suggestive indeterminacy) will be destroyed by some miserable "explanation" which the public will suppose has been made by his conclusions on the subject. "The public at large," Zimmerman remarks, "will never bother to look into these subtleties" (*DBR*, 105). If the narrator imposes his will, he will act, as Borges expressed a similar urge in *Dreamtigers*, from "no other law than fulfillment," and the result will be "the immediate indifference that ensues" ("The Maker").[17]

To show Zimmerman that he has understood, the narrator recites two parables in which we can see a tension between simple correspondence and the esthetic fact. In the first parable, two kings play chess on a hilltop while their armies clash. One loses

17. These words translated thus by Mildred Boyer (*DT*, 22), are translated by di Giovanni and Borges as "no other law than to enjoy things and forget them" (*A*, 155). The original Spanish is: *"sin otra ley que la fruición y la indiferencia inmediata."*

the game and his army loses the battle; the chess game was a mere duplication of the larger reality. In the second, two famous bards have a contest of song. The first sings from dawn until dusk and hands the harp to the other. The latter merely lays it aside and stands up, and the first confesses his defeat. We can take the second parable to mean that the best song remains unsung—limitless, unending, like a promise. The narrator makes statements at the beginning and end of "Guayaquil" which can be understood to mean that he will not destroy the esthetic indefiniteness surrounding San Martín's talk with the Liberator. At the beginning: "Now I shall not journey to the Estado Occidental [Western State]; now I shall not set eyes on snow-capped Higuerota mirrored in the water of the Golfo Plácido; now I shall not decipher Bolívar's manuscripts . . ." (*DBR,* 99). At the end the narrator, a man whose life has been dedicated to nailing down the definitive truths that explain history, seems to confess his conversion to an esthetic of the indefinite: "I have the feeling that I shall give up any future writing" (*DBR,* 107). Borges fashioned the opening lines of this story from Conrad's *Nostromo.*

In the original Spanish, "manuscripts" is *letra,* which means handwriting or letter. *Letra* is one of Borges' old symbols for clear conception, visible reality, or abstraction, as in "The Secret Miracle" (*Ficciones*), where God is a tiny letter on a map. Among other symbols of ordered or abstract reality in Borges' older stories are mountains and other kinds of upward projections. The things the narrator of "Guayaquil" says he will not do are all symbolic, it seems, of the production of intelligible reality through expressive language; he will not see a mountain duplicated, behold a "letter," or write his definitive conclusions. As for the "western country," it seems enough to say that "western" is the opposite of "eastern" with its implication of mystery. This, too, is consistent with Borges' old symbolism, in which all things eastern and yellow suggest the chaotic, mythic, and esthetic.

Borges is still building into his fiction the occasional guide-images or omens that facilitate interpretations but certainly do not corroborate them. For example, when Zimmerman enters the narrator's house, he pauses to look at a patio tiled in black and white (an old image in Borges' work), prefiguring the parable of the chess game and perhaps suggesting that the events to follow will be a kind of duplication. Indeed, during the conversation it seemed to the two scholars "that we were already two other people"; their encounter occurs at twilight, which in Borges' familiar work is a frequent symbol of change or suspension of reality. When the first bard sings, he sings from morning twilight to evening; his song is a daylight song, a finished and patent thing, superseded by the unsung music that belongs to the dreaming hours as day recedes. And at one point Zimmerman remarks: " 'Everything is strange in Prague, or, if you prefer, nothing is strange. Anything may happen there. In London, on certain evenings, I have had the same feeling' " (*DBR*, 106). Zimmerman is from Prague, the native city of Kafka, and of the ambitious rabbi of "The Golem," who tried to create a man but produced only a monster. Also in "Guayaquil" is a reference to *Der Golem*, a novel by Gustav Meyrink of Prague. In conversation Borges has said that the creation of the golem is "a parable of the nature of art." [18]

One other important symbol deserves mention: blood. In Borges' older work, it is associated with fullness of being—with completeness, domination, victory, or will. The will in question in "Guayaquil" is not Zimmerman's, imposed upon the narrator; it is, rather, the narrator's, suppressed for a cause. Zimmerman observes that the narrator carries Argentine history in his blood, implying that he would treat Bolívar's letter with willful prejudgment. The narrator tells us that Zimmerman's words were "the expression of a will that made of the future something as irrevocable as the past" (*DBR*, 104), but we must understand that Zimmerman's "expression" delineated the undesirable willfulness of the narrator, which the latter willfully subdued.

This interpretation of "Guayaquil" suggests taking another look at such stories as "The Gospel According to Mark"; instead of comparing the mentalities of Espinosa and the Gutres in terms of

18. Burgin, *Conversations,* p. 75.

order and chaos—or, to use a term from Borges, order and *adventure* ("The Duel")—we might infer a contrast between the open, uncommitted, mythic-minded writer (Espinosa) and the closed-minded, compromised, or committed writers (the Gutres) who are guided by their determination (their "Calvinist fanaticism") to get a point across, to find their "beloved island." The work of such writers is predetermined; its meaning is as irrevocable as the preconceptions of the authors.

If we can judge by "The Maker," even his blindness is to Borges analogous to the abandonment of Aesopism, somewhere in his past, and to his espousal of the idea that literature should be written "blind"—for its own sake, not for an intellectual or practical purpose. Most of his stories are punctiliously contrived allusions to the idea of art for art's sake; in that sense they comprise art about art.

Ethics

With the appearance of *In Praise of Darkness* (as Borges notes in the preface) two new themes are added to his work: old age and ethics. What he calls ethics goes beyond and embraces much of his philosophy and its esthetic foundations.

"Fragments of an Apocryphal Gospel" could be called poetry or prose; it is a collection of numbered apothegms and injunctions modeled in part on the Beatitudes. They alter many of the sayings of Jesus and other moral or theological axioms, often contradicting them or seeming to. They reflect a point of view which denies heaven and hell, reduces men to predestined beings who are ignorant of their destiny, rejects the idea of morality for the sake of reward, believes in pursuing justice for its own sake, and looks with kindly, humanistic eyes at the human species. These dicta strongly imply a pessimism overcome by courage—not stoicism, which suggests a dogged refusal to be affected, but blind, Tillichian faith, which has only rigor to justify it. Borges' ethic, as he seems to declare in "A Prayer" (discussed below), consists in a devotion to lucid reason and just action.

In his "Fragments" Borges is satirical, warm, wise, heretical, moralistic, sly, and often majestic. "Blessed are they who know," he says, "that suffering is not a crown of glory," and "Wretched are they that mourn, for they have fallen into the craven habit of tears." He has no use for the poor in spirit, who expect heaven to be better than earth, nor for those who comfort themselves with feelings of guilt; and the actions of men, he says, deserve neither heaven nor hell. You can't judge a tree by its fruit nor a man by his works; they can both be better or worse than they look. "Give that which is holy unto the dogs, cast your pearls before swine: for what matters is giving." To one who strikes you on the cheek you may turn the other, provided you are not moved by fear. To do good for your enemy is to give him justice; but to love him is a task for angels, not men. Happy are the lovers and the loved, and those who can do without love, and those who forgive others and themselves, and "Happy are the happy."

The latter pronouncement has an esthetic motive, expressed in "The Unworthy Friend": "The only thing without mystery is happiness, because happiness is an end in itself" (*DBR*, 29). And there are other esthetic admonitions: "Swear not, for an oath may be only an emphasis." The moral and the esthetic are combined in: "Forgetting is the only vengeance and the only forgiveness." This idea is the theme of another new prose piece, "Legend," in which Cain asks Abel to forgive him. But Abel has forgotten who killed whom. Cain sees that Abel has truly forgiven, and says he will try to forget too. "Yes," Abel agrees, "as long as there's remorse, there's guilt." This idea is expressed also in "The Unworthy Friend."

"A Prayer" is perhaps the frankest and most intimate thing Borges has ever written and in my opinion the most magnificent. He begins by acknowledging that a personal prayer demands an almost superhuman sincerity. It is obvious, he says, that he cannot ask for anything. To ask that he not go blind (he is not entirely sightless) would be to ask for the suspension of cause and effect, and "Nobody is worthy of such a miracle." Neither can he ask pardon for his errors; forgiveness is an act of others, which purifies the offended, not the offender, and only Borges can save

Borges. He can only give what he himself does not have: courage, hope, the urge to learn. He wants to be remembered less as a poet than as a friend; let someone recite a line from Dunbar or Frost and remember that he first heard it from Borges' lips. Faithful to his "gods" to the end, he combines the esthetic and the moral in a final observation: "The laws of the universe are unknown to us, but we are somehow sure that to reason clearly and to act righteously is to help those laws, which will never be revealed to us." When he dies, he wants to die wholly, "with this companion, my body."

The uncertain darkness of death and of blindness is the theme of *In Praise of Darkness*. In a piece called "His End and His Beginning," the two are united in superb metaphorical prose that subsumes all forms of transition into the unknown. Having died, and suffering the agony of being dead, Borges accepts death and it becomes heaven; blind, he accepts blindness and it becomes the beginning of an adventurous life in a new world. He praises his darkness, and in that praise there is a victory, as limitless as a promise, over all men's darkness. And somehow Borges extols the darkness of his own skepticism, his agnostic unknowingness, which is his philosophy; he translates it positively into an esthetic of conjectural expectancy. Borges' mind ranges over reality as the Vikings ranged over the world, plundering not for plunder but for adventure.

Reading this book, we are convinced of the sincerity of his apocryphal fragments, one of which says: "Let a candle be lighted though no man see it; God will see it."

"The Congress"

Not every story written by Borges in his heyday was a good one; "The Shape of the Sword" (*Ficciones*) has something fake about it. His story "The Congress," finished late in 1970 and published in 1971, does not "come off" on the first reading. Borges has said that he toyed with the plot for twenty years. Because of its long gestation alone, it is extremely important to the study of Borges' work. One gets the feeling that if it could be caught from the right

384

angle and given a good shake, it would fall into the right pattern, shedding light on all Borges' major fiction. To be appreciated, I think, this long story has to be accepted as allegory and as exemplary technique, and even as Borges' deliberate circumvention of his own esthetic. In this story, the esthetic event, the sacred *hecho estético* which Borges upholds as the superior alternative to intellectual effort and "expressive" language, is itself, by implication, as meaningless as those other fruitless approaches to reality: philosophy and history.

The name of the story derives from the effort of one Alejandro Glencoe, a rich Uruguayan rancher living in Buenos Aires, to call together a "Congress of the World which would represent all men of all nations." This body would convene four years after the start of preparations. "Planning an assembly to represent all men was like fixing the exact number of Platonic types—a puzzle which had taxed the imagination of thinkers for centuries." One of the fifteen or twenty planners suggests that "don Alejandro Glencoe might represent not only cattlemen but also Uruguayans, and also humanity's great forerunners, and also men with red beards, and also those who are seated in armchairs." Glencoe finances the project, which consists largely in collecting books—at first encyclopedias, then the great books of the centuries, then random account books and Ph.D. theses. The narrator, Alejandro Ferri, visits Glencoe's ranch and sees him transformed into "the stern chief of a clan" of gauchos; later, Ferri is sent to London to find a suitable language for the Congress to use, and in that city he has a love affair with a girl named Beatrice, while Glencoe's nephew, Fermín Eguren, on the same mission in Paris, plays with prostitutes. Ferri goes back to Buenos Aires, where Glencoe, precisely at the end of the four-year period of preparation, has concluded that the Congress is impossible, for it embraces an irreducible world: "The Congress of the World began with the first moment of the world and it will go on when we are dust. . . . The Congress is Job on the ash heap and Christ on the Cross. The Congress is that worthless boy who squanders my substance on whores." At his order the group burns the collected books, and one member remarks: "Every few centuries, the Library of Alexandria must be burned down." Then, acting as if they had been cleansed of an evil and were on a somewhat languid holiday, the members of the Congress anticlimactically tour the city to "see the Congress."

The effort to classify all the world's men under a few abstract headings suggests the search for a syncretic philosophy, or for a literature that reduces chaotic reality to a recurring set of relations. One feels that if the Congress convened someplace, the world would be vacated. The members are relieved to discover that their efforts are futile, and as the books burn one remarks, "I wanted to do evil and I have done good." The story implies the spiritual or esthetic benefit of liberating men periodically from their structured certitude and restoring to them a perception of reality as an anarchy of things-in-themselves. Philosophically, this is a return to myth, to rebirth, to orgy; literarily, it suggests a return to uncontrived, straightforward storytelling about things as they are, unstructured and unmoralized. The book burning is reminiscent of the fire that swept the circular ruins in the story of that name (*Ficciones*) and the one that destroyed the dogmatists of "The Theologians" (*El Aleph*).

"The Congress" is complex, laden with familiar Borgesian images, symbolic names, and suggestions of identities: two Alejandros and an Alexandrian library. Again there is an allusion to the esthetic event: Ferri's amorous sojourn in London (like Prague, a dizzying sort of place, here called a red labyrinth) with a girl named Beatrice, like Dante's esthetic ideal finally unattainable (she refuses to marry Ferri). This episode comes just before what we may call the esthetic frustration or the loss of the impending revelation—in this case the end of hope for the fulfillment of the Congressional dream.

In all the episodes of "The Congress" the nearness of revelation, intellectual, linguistic, and esthetic, always leads to the same disillusion—a final return to reality as a mythic disorder incapable of being organized or interpreted with finality. The intellectual attempt to order the universe is the Congress itself; truth-in-art,

386

by analogy, is not found in the classicist's attempt to reduce the world to abstract forms. The engaged writer's pursuit of art through direct, expressive language, used for a mission and therefore subordinate in its own right, is satirized in Eguren's visits to prostitutes; he "enjoys and forgets" like the protagonist of "The Maker," who acts from "no other law than fulfillment," with "the immediate indifference that ensues." Borges treats Fermín Eguren, whose first name suggests vermin and who has a very low forehead, with humorous disdain. (He is also of Basque ancestry, which Borges derides. A low forehead and Basque origin are qualities also assigned to Benjamín Otálora of "The Dead Man.") Ferri shows his superiority over Eguren in one episode; confronted by a ruffian with a knife, Eguren quails, but Ferri reaches inside his coat, as if to draw a knife, and faces the hoodlum down. Ferri and Eguren are in the company of a writer much admired by Ferri; he is the author of a fine work whose title, *The Marble Pillars,* strongly suggests the classical. The author, Fernández Irala, also symbolizes the Congress; he is perhaps its staunchest member. Considering the satirical nature of the whole story, there is possibly an intentional correspondence between Borges' literature of suggestion (his unproduced revelation) and Ferri's bluster with a hidden knife that is not really there.

Why does "The Congress" give the impression that it is not one of Borges' better stories? Its failure, if I can call it that, may be owing precisely to its accomplishment. It seems deliberately, successfully compendious, reflecting all the facets of a background idea which, I believe, has inspired the major part of Borges' fictional literature about literature. It closes the book. Though it is not a plain-language story with a clear meaning, it represents what Borges despises: a completed "mental process." Instead of symbolic allusion, it constitutes symbolic expression. There is a finished progression, by three implied routes, from chaos to near-order and back to chaos. Although this progression is depicted incidentally in some of his other stories, in "The Congress" it seems to be the whole purpose. The satirical denial of the esthetic event prevents the sacred event from seeming to be diffused into

387

the structure of the story, embodied as a reality behind the symbols. For this reason I suggest that Borges is aware of the story's "failure."

It is hard to believe, moreover, that Borges, the supreme literary technician, could be ignorant of having violated his own techniques by overdoing them. In the episodes at the ranch, in London, and on the street where the hoodlum appears, as well as in the description of the Congress members, there is too much realistic detail to be consistent with an essentially fantastic plot. There is too much half-esoteric commentary of an autobiographical type, which yields clues to Borges' literary theories only after study and speculation. I venture to say that the story is not intended to be read but to be studied. Not only is "The Congress" heavy with hints and allusions and loaded with symbolic attributes (names, red beards, places), but it is slowed by superfluous actions (two knife episodes, the overlong love affair), and weighted with seemingly irrelevant descriptions (of the gauchos at the ranch, for example), so that it becomes ponderous. I said earlier that Borges' stories are floating tales; this one is too dense to float. I also suspect that "The Congress," being satirical, is full of intended humor that is too private, at least for an English-speaking reader.

This story is an overexpression which, purposely or not, stultifies its own inner insinuation that the esthetic phenomenon is a meaningless illusion. Borges' satire of himself and his esthetic is not convincing because it begs to be refuted. At the end, the Congressmen are not really joyful, as they appear; they are only disillusioned and released from struggle. The story seems to deny the value of that struggle—man's pursuit of the impossible. It denies the positive element in Borges' skepticism. The members of the disbanded Congress, who do not want to speak to each other again, cannot help reminding us of the disillusioned, bored and speechless Troglodytes of "The Immortal" (*El Aleph*).

The former Borges would have ended the story with an insinuation of positive conviction that the book burning was inevitable and right; but here he leaves us with the feeling that it is inescapably wrong. In "The House of Asterion" (*El Aleph*), where the

388

miserable Minotaur is happy when Theseus comes to kill him, we are somehow happy for him because his bewilderment is dissolved in fatal meaning. But with the destruction of the books and the end of the Congress, Theseus has in some way faltered, and the Minotaur goes wandering on toward a meaningless end somewhere in his confusing labyrinth—a labyrinth whose anarchical variability no longer offers possibility and adventure. Again, this may be exactly what Borges has intended; at the beginning of the story Ferri explains that he is going on seventy-one (Borges' age); he came to Buenos Aires in 1899 (Borges' birth year), and a symptom of his age is that adventure no longer appeals to him: "... novelties—maybe because I feel they hold nothing essentially new, and are really no more than timid variations—neither interest nor distract me." None of the infinite attributes of the universe, therefore, is a possible essence; no fortuitous position of the kaleidoscope can reveal anything; in the vast Library of Clementinum there is no tiny letter that is God, and we must not seek it in art, or philosophy, or language.

Perhaps the return to the nominalistic heterogeneity of things-in-themselves is only the symbol for Borges' decision to tell simple stories for their own sake. There is reason to wonder if he can do it consistently.

Borges' translations

Borges' new inclination toward the simple and straightforward has been carried into English, not only in the translations of his new fiction but also in the recasting of stories written years ago. This is undoubtedly better than trying to produce in English the complicated linguistic effects of the Spanish originals. For example, as Norman Thomas di Giovanni, Borges' collaborator in translation, has noted, the special effect produced by writing Spanish while thinking in English, using English word order, cannot be duplicated in English even by reversing the process. But it would be absurd not to admit that something is lost, as it always is in translation. Judging from what I have seen (which does not include translations of some of the most cryptic and ambiguous of the old stories),

389

I would say that di Giovanni's and Borges' translations are by far the best yet, particularly from the standpoint of their enjoyability to the average reader. Scholars will find them in some respects problematical.

By undertaking to translate Borges' works, Borges and di Giovanni have created a situation as ambiguous and subtle as one of Borges' tales. The case is reminiscent of "Pierre Menard, Author of the *Quixote*" (*Ficciones*), where Menard sets out to write *Don Quixote* in the exact language of Cervantes' original, by being the kind of man who would write, in the present century, what another man wrote centuries ago under different circumstances. With regard at least to Borges' older work, we cannot escape the fact that the translations are being made twenty years or more after the stories were composed, with all that this implies: slips of memory, changes in theory, the urge to improve the story, the influence of intervening criticism and the public's reactions, and the hand of a recent co-translator. Critics who are given to integrating an author's life and opinions with his work will lean heavily on the belief that Borges remains Borges across the years, and on his and di Giovanni's insistence upon being faithful to what Borges intended when he wrote. Others, who consider that a work is a work, to be isolated and beheld in itself—*res ipsa loquitur*—are likely to see the English versions as a body of fresh literature which neither affects nor depends upon the Spanish originals.

The independence of the English versions (I am still speaking of the old stories) will be strengthened to the degree with which critics judge them to be unfaithful to the originals, or even discrepant with more literal translations. The old fiction is full of involutions and nuances heavily dependent on a particular vocabulary, often shockingly ill-fitting, ambiguous, or otherwise strange. This puzzling prose has been in the public's hands for many years; Borges' fame is largely built on it, and much criticism has been based on its implications. According to Borges' own theory (very like Valéry's), he is now only one of his readers, and any clarification of strange language that he and di Giovanni might make must constitute in some degree a re-creation or an interpretation. In numerous interviews Borges has said—despite his incredible memory—that he has forgotten why he included an incident in a story, used a color, or wrote a certain word, and some of these forgotten things are of critical importance. Di Giovanni has been diligent in ferreting out the original reasons for the use of unusual language and equally diligent in making it rational. Borges wrote his early stories for a limited, somewhat erudite, and very Argentine readership, at a time when he was little known or appreciated; he and di Giovanni translate under the spur of fame and for a much larger and less intellectual readership that is largely ignorant of the context and tradition of Argentine literature.

In view of these special factors, I am not disturbed over the loss of such celebrated phrases as "unanimous night" (*unánime noche*), which has been rationalized into "encompassing night" in "The Circular Ruins." The change smacks of decoding poetry, and there is a loss of flavor; but it also points, without doubt, to what Borges now calls baroque trickery and indicates what in his opinion is not essential in his earlier work. A more radical deviation occurs when "enormous hallucination" (*enorme alucinación*) is changed to "populous vision." This phrase, also from "The Circular Ruins," refers to the college of imaginary students from which the magician tried to abstract one in order to insert him into reality. The antecedent of "enormous hallucination" is unclear in the original but can be inferred; the epithet suggests not that the students were numerous and imaginary (we already know that) but that the magician's very method was wrong. "Populous vision" makes the antecedent clear but loses all other implications, along with the insinuation of a second level of meaning.

Some of Borges' most conspicuous trademarks, such as his repetitious use of words like "notorious" and "attribute," seem to be suppressed in the translations. In the preface to *Doctor Brodie's Report* we find the words "most notorious attribute" (*más notorio atributo*) interpreted "most obvious trait." Given the frequent implication of evil that attaches to Borges' use of *"notorio,"* particularly when it refers to the universe, "most obvious trait" loses or ignores the valuative tenor of the original phrase. Again, in "The Dead Man," the phrase which tells us that Bandeira's horse, saddle, and mistress are his *"atributos o adjetivos"* (a significant evocation of a substance-attribute or noun-adjective simile) is weakened to "attributes or trappings." The possibly metaphysical intention of the original is far less apparent in the English.

As another random example of the apparent decision of the translators not to carry certain insinuations into English, the name of the knife-wielding hoodlum of "The Congress" can be cited. This character's name is utterly unimportant to the story, but in his typical way Borges takes the trouble to give it: "Tapia or Paredes or something of the kind." The reader who does not know Spanish is unaware that both *tapia* and *pared* mean "wall," an image common enough in Borges' older fiction to raise an immediate question about its possible symbolism here.

One thing is obvious. The author-made translations now being published are most readable. They are smoother, in general, than the Spanish version; this diminishes the cerebral, deliberate quality conveyed by the more abrupt Spanish narrations, in which the uneven stops and starts give each word and phrase an intentionality and a singular authority. Conjunctions now smooth the path and relax the reader where semicolons used to jar him; transitions are made where there were only juxtaposed ideas. While such changes in the fluidity of language and idea can be attributed to di Giovanni's sense of clarity and polish, they also testify to Borges' abandonment of what he calls, in the preface to *Doctor Brodie's Report,* "the surprises inherent in a baroque style" (*DBR,* 11).

Norah Borges on her brother: an unpublished interview by Victoria Ocampo

Norah Borges: Georgie was born on August 24, 1899, in the old house of our maternal grandfather, Isidoro Acevedo, on Tucumán Street. The house had one patio, paved with black and white marble, containing a large jasmine. In the second patio was a well and an Arabian jasmine.

Victoria Ocampo: Norah, what are your first childhood memories in which your brother appears?

N.B.: I always see Georgie beside me. He is seated on a tricycle that has a horse's head. He plays with big marbles of all colors. He chases butterflies around the garden with a green net. He has a musical top, a magic lantern, and some of those water-filled tubes used in Carnival, something like today's water pistols.

V.O.: What games did you play when you were children, and where?

N.B.: All our games took place under an immense palm tree that was filled with the singing of birds, or on the long wooden stairway, with its wonderful smell of pine. There was one time when we liked playing Jules Verne's "Trip to the Moon," shutting ourselves inside a red folding screen. We thought we were inside a rocket, traveling through space. We had a stereoscope that we loved, with views of Venice. When Halley's comet passed through the sky over our garden, Georgie waited for it on the balcony every afternoon with opera glasses.

V.O.: Did both of you read the same books?

N.B.: Until the age of ten we had Miss Tink, who taught us English and reading. We didn't go to school. Georgie learned quickly and I lagged behind. First there were fairy tales, the stories of Canon Schmidt, *The Arabian Nights*. I was always rereading the same stories: "Genoveva de Brabante" and "Rosa de Tanenburgo." Georgie went through his wild-animal period; I still see him sprawled on the rug, drawing striped Bengal tigers. Then his dinosaur period, and then the time when he repeated the opening pages of *Don Quixote*.

V.O.: Did you have friends in common?

N.B.: Our cousin Álvaro Melián Lafinur came to the house every night. In the library, with my father, they read aloud Prescott's *Conquest of Peru* and the novels of Eça de Queiroz. Álvaro played the guitar and sang verses from Bécquer and from the Uruguayan Elías Regules. When he sang "La canción del pirata" (*By the light of the pale, pale moon / In a pirate ship I was born . . .*), with a wonderful, unforgettable voice, Georgie wept with emotion. The same as when my mother sang at the piano "Quand l'amour meurt." During our whole childhood we went every year to the summer home of the Haedos, somewhere to the north of Montevideo. We used to watch with so much joy when the trunks were being packed. The steamer, *The Aeolus*, had a figurehead at the prow. We loved the little cookies in the shape of letters that we had with breakfast while we looked at the Cerro through the porthole! And that summer place! It had a tower with lozenge-shaped colored-glass windows; a summer house in the garden, where an older cousin read *The Mystery of the Yellow Room* and *The Perfume of the Lady in Black;* a rickety wooden lookout tower, painted green, that peeped into the tall branches of a eucalyptus; a swimming pool whose tiles had blue figures and was covered by a jasmine vine. We spent our last summer there with our cousin Esther, wearing black eye masks and searching the garden for a ghost that we actually saw reflected in a closet mirror, so scared that it would come after us that we hid in the farthest corners of the coach house or behind the swings.

V.O.: When did Georgie begin to write, as far as you remember?

N.B.: I don't remember exactly when Georgie wrote his first work, a little story called "The Fatal Visor." He must have been less than ten.

V.O.: When did he start having sweethearts or falling in love with girls?

N.B.: It must have been when we returned from Europe and he began writing poetry.

V.O.: Were you two very religious?

N.B.: Yes. We couldn't go to bed in peace until we said the Lord's Prayer.

V.O.: In which things did you differ and in which did you agree?

N.B.: Georgie was incapable of telling a lie; he felt everything passionately. When I began reading *Jean-Christophe*, it reminded me of Georgie. When we traveled through Europe, I see us in a train looking at the landscape, my father reciting Keats's poems and Georgie saying lines from Swinburne or Verlaine.

V.O.: What did the two of you do in Adrogué during those summers so well remembered by your brother?

N.B.: We strolled by the summer houses; in the air there was a perfume of burned twigs mixed with the odor of jasmine. In the house at Adrogué where we once spent a whole winter, my mother read us our first novels: *The House on the Marsh, The Hound of the Baskervilles,* and José Mármol's *Amalia.* When we returned from Europe we rediscovered Adrogué. The statues in the niches, the masonry planters, the colored-glass panes, the round and smooth columns of the galleries, the palm trees, the magnolias. All those things dazzled us. At the Hotel Las Delicias there was a fountain with nymphs and tritons, a drawing room with a painted ceiling, bedrooms with mosquito netting, a maze in the park, vines with tiny black grapes, patios with palm trees, and balconies with marble balustrades. It was a source of inspiration for his poems and my pictures.

V.O.: Was Georgie interested in your painting and painting in general?

N.B.: Yes, we were much alike in our love for those slightly melancholy gardens and old houses of Buenos Aires. I painted what Georgie mused and wrote.

V.O.: Were you interested in what he wrote?

N.B.: Yes, I loved that plastic and almost sketched quality he had when he described all that was peculiar to our country.

translated by Norman Thomas di Giovanni and Eduardo Paz Leston

Borges at N.Y.U.
EDITED BY RONALD CHRIST

On April 8, 1971, at the invitation of Professor Alexander Coleman, Borges came to the Washington Square campus of New York University, accompanied by Norman Thomas di Giovanni, to appear briefly before a group of students and answer their questions about his work. The questions had been submitted beforehand, and near the beginning of the program di Giovanni called me to the platform to help him sort and perhaps invent a few questions, so I was in a good position to tape Borges' replies. What follows is a transcript of that tape.

But a few words of clarification might be useful, and some explanations are necessary. The occasion, like many another academic affair, was not especially brilliant—either because the students avoided Borges (who he is and what he has written) or because they asked after matters already well known. (In preparing their questions the students had more often than not questioned their own responses to Borges' work or reviewed what they knew about him, rather than inquiring into Borges' intentions, methods, or pleasures.) Those questions implied a monologue, really, on the part of the students; but Borges is an old hand at monologues and so he was, perhaps, more than usually willing to enter playfully into the pseudo-dialogue.

At any rate, what the occasion lacked in profundity it made up for in range of expression. More than most other question-and-answer sessions (including interviews), this one presents Borges in a lively and characterizing performance. On the one hand he answers a question about the figures in his work with a straightforward seriousness and accuracy that are rare in his oral comments on his own writing; on the other he coyly dodges an inquiry into the escapist nature of his fiction. Then, too, he acts out his timidity and ironic remove from what he has done, only minutes before he tearfully stutters a response to an *engagé* questioner from the floor. In short, what you may get from a reading of these remarks is a sense of person rather than a set of facts useful for critical evaluation. Some of those facts are here, all right, but the real attraction is the style of their exhibition.

But if you are going to realize that attraction, you will have to treat the following pages not as transcript but as script. You will have to play the strenuous formality in Borges' put-ons and take-offs, the measured authority of his slight misquotation of Rossetti; the genial mockery in his use of Johnson's "Sir"; you will have to supply the glimmers of irritation in his voice, his constant search for the iamb of any thought, the tenacity of his diversionary humor—all of which I have foregone emphasizing with complicated punctuation or awkward stage directions. Most of all, however, you will have to imagine the laughter echoing from platform to auditorium and back, because, from the very first moments, Borges won his audience with fooling and held them, sometimes against their own interests, with his humor.

In addition to all that laughter, some unimportant things are missing. I have edited the other speakers' remarks, condensed the questions, and in some few instances deleted the unintelligible or inconsequential while, as a general rule, I have omitted the merely repetitious. What follows, though, is essentially what was said, and the participants required no small bravery or humility to lend themselves to this *phono-verité*. Borges himself summarized their attitude when he replied to my request for permission to record what he had said. "Publish away!" he laughed.

Since Borges needs no introduction, as Alexander Coleman indicated in his, we start with the end of Coleman's opening remarks:

Coleman: . . . and therefore dithyrambs and poems of praise in wild meters simply cannot be used in praise of Borges. Borges hardly needs any praise. But I would like to introduce to you Norman Thomas di Giovanni, to Borges' right—
Borges: Fancy *needing* praise! You gush all over!
Coleman: —who, with Borges, is in charge of the complete re-edition of Borges' work in English. Now, Borges, I think the only thing I can do is just tell you what sort of inquisitorial army you're facing.
Borges: Yes.
Coleman: It looks like around two hundred people.
Borges: Oh, *really!* Well, I have to face them, eh? In fact, I'm doing it.
Coleman: Let me tell you who they are. Fifty or sixty of them are students who just began Spanish last September, and they will be finishing their year by reading five of your pieces, beginning with "Borges y yo"—
Borges: Oh, *really!*
Coleman: —and then ending with "La intrusa." Okay?
Borges: Yes. Good. I'm very fond of "La intrusa."

Coleman: But I don't think there are any enemies here.

Borges: No.

Coleman: There may be a Maoist lurking under a seat, but I don't think he's appeared yet.

Borges: What! Only one?

Coleman: Now, the only other classification—

Borges: I thought China had a larger population.

Coleman: It's true China has a large population, but somehow the distances reduce the possibilities of immigration.

Borges: Yes.

Coleman: The only other possibilities I can describe to you are the twenty maniacs—

Borges: Only twenty?

Coleman: Yes, only twenty, who are at least theoretically under my charge. They have been doing nothing for the last semester but reading the works of Jorge Luis Borges.

Borges: Well, I'm awfully sorry. But I'm not to blame, eh?

Coleman: No, no, hardly. But that's all I can say about this *aglomeración.*

Borges: That sounds pretty impressive, eh?

Coleman: I think Norman is sifting out the questions.

di Giovanni: I can't find any literary questions. They're all about imperialism, about Latin America—

Borges: I'm not an authority on Latin America.

di Giovanni: "Borges, what is your role in the Vietnam war?"

Borges: Well, I think I got killed off last year, no? ... Are they all like that?

Coleman: Well, Norman, you have "real" questions to ask of Borges?

Borges: Do you?

di Giovanni: I can't find one interesting one.

Borges: Well, you shouldn't say that, eh?

di Giovanni: Why not?

Coleman: Can I start? You can use me as a straight man if you wish. It's okay.

Borges: Yes. Well, go ahead.

Coleman: I was wondering if behind any of your stories, after you had written them, you felt you had emitted a moral judgment. Do you feel that one might argue the impossible by arguing for a moral purpose in literature?

Borges: I can only speak about myself. I don't think I have any moral purpose when I write. When I write, I'm trying to set down some kind of tale, not some kind of fable, but if the reader wants to read something moral into the text, that's all to the good. When I'm writing a story, I'm not thinking in terms, let's say, of political or ethical opinions: I'm merely trying to be true, let's say, to the plot, to the dream, perhaps. Of course, if my writing is any good, then I suppose many purposes should be creeping in; but that's up to them, not to me. I'm merely trying to be sincere to the plot, to the dream. And as to my political opinions, I have them,

398

but I don't let them interfere, I don't let them tamper with my literature.
Coleman: But you're asking the reader to take part in the reading of the story almost as much as you have in the writing of it.
Borges: The reader, of course, is allowed his freedom, as I'm allowed mine. If people find more in a story than what I intended to put in there, well, that's all to the good, because I think any story or any poem should have more in it than what was intended by the writer; because, if not, it would be a very poor one. I think that's all I have to say. —But when I'm writing a story or a poem, I'm concerned about that story and about that poem, and I try to forget my convictions, my opinions, even my personal feelings. To be honest only. It's a kind of willful . . . well, willful dreaming, I should say, in writing a story; but I let myself go. At least I do my best.
di Giovanni: May I read a question?
Borges: And I'll try to find an answer.
di Giovanni: I don't think you need answer this.
Borges: Well, why not?
di Giovanni: Because this is the most incredible question. "Last year you refused to come to the United States of America because of the war in Vietnam—"
Borges: Did I?
di Giovanni: "—and other government policies. What changes in America allowed you to reconsider and come now to speak?"
Borges: I don't know. What changes made me reconsider a decision I never took? —All this is fancy work.
Coleman: I tell you what's happened. Borges, you've been confused with Carlos Fuentes.
Borges: Or with Charlie Chaplin, if you want. Or with King Charles I. Or any other Charles.
Coleman: May I ask you a question about Valéry? In looking at "Pierre Menard" and even at "Funes," I was wondering if not only *Monsieur Teste* but also the first pages of the *Introduction to the Method of Leonardo da Vinci* might have somehow goaded you to the elaboration of a monstrous mind, such as Monsieur Teste—a man who's not very human, you have to admit.
Borges: He's not very human and he's not very intelligent, either. No, I'm sorry to say that I haven't been goaded on in my writing by Valéry. Valéry is hardly to blame for my writing. I'm to blame. And as to Funes, I don't think of him as being intelligent. On the contrary, he was simply a gigantic memory, and as such incapable of intelligence, because in order to think you have to, well, let's say, make certain mistakes, you have to forget, you have to connect, and he couldn't do that. He said his memory was full of mere facts and naturally those hindered him from thinking.
di Giovanni: I've got a few questions. "What is the relevance of character in your work?"
Borges: This is a hard nut to crack, because I'm afraid there are no characters in my work. I'm afraid *I'm* the only character; or rather, I should say,

a kind of wishful thinking. For example, my forefathers were military men —I'm not much of a military man myself, as such—I'm merely a librarian —so I suppose there's some wishful thinking in what I write. But as to characters, I don't think I have evolved a single character. I think I'm always thinking in terms of myself, of my limitations, and of the possible lives I should have lived and haven't.

di Giovanni: How about your new stories? Those aren't about yourself, are they?

Borges: . . . No. The problem is that I've quite forgotten all about them. I never think about my own work; I prefer remembering other writers. And I'm a very poor hand when it comes to being asked questions about my own work since I do my best, my successful best, to forget it once it's written.

Coleman: But you know, the most wonderful thing is that you really *do* forget your stories.

Borges: Yes.

Coleman: You can find thousands of students who can remind you of details and you've honestly forgotten them—for good reasons in some cases and in others not.

Borges: Well, I suppose the real reason is that I want to write new ones. If I'm to be recalling my old ones, how can I go on? I'd be hampered by that.

di Giovanni: That comes up so many times when we're translating. Sometimes he'll come upon a sentence and say, "Hey, that's pretty good, isn't it?" as though it were somebody else's, and sometimes he says, "We've got to make that better."

Coleman: Ronald Christ has written about the remarkable translation you gave *"unánime noche,"* which has puzzled many a commentator, and now in English—

Borges: Well, to tell you the truth, it has puzzled *me!* I wrote it down because I thought it had a fine sound, hadn't been used before. But I wonder what it really means, if it means anything.

Coleman: —in English it comes out "encompassing night"—

Borges: That's far better.

Coleman: —which is lovely.

Borges: Of course. I'm very sorry I wrote *"unánime."* But there is no word for "encompassing" in Spanish.

di Giovanni: A mere rough draft.

Borges: A mere rough draft, yes. I was doing my best in a Romance language, say.

di Giovanni: Here's a question: "What do you think of space?" Not NASA, I suppose.

Borges: I tend to be always thinking of time, not of space. When I hear the words "time" and "space" used together, I feel as Nietzsche felt when he heard people talking about Goethe and Schiller—a kind of blasphemy. I think that the central riddle, the central problem of metaphysics—let us call it thinking—is time, not space. Space is one of the many things to be found inside of time—as you find, for example, color or shapes or sizes or feelings. But I think the real problem, the problem we have to grapple with, and of course the problem whose solution we'll never find, is the problem of time, of successive time, and, therein, the problem of personal identity, which is but a part of the problem of time.

Coleman: Do you like the South? It is very much the preferred geographic space in your writing.

Borges: Yes, it is; but this has a quite simple explanation. I think of myself as being a man of Buenos Aires. When I think of Buenos Aires, I'm not thinking of that awful, large, shabby, sprawling city. I'm thinking also of the Province of Buenos Aires. The North is full of agriculture and so on, while to the west and to the south—of course, the word *"oeste"* is rather an uncouth word, while the word *"sur"* is a fine word—there you come across the large, open spaces; there, if we're very lucky, we may get a gaucho or so. And so I think of the South in terms of the past of my country. That is to say, when the country was a country of horsemen and large, empty *estancias.*

Coleman: Just think what the South means to us.

Borges: Oh, it means something very important. It means the Deep South. I know. Yes, I can feel that kind of south also.

di Giovanni: "Do you ever feel that you can travel through time or that events recurring exactly create an impression of time travel?"

Borges: Of course, the most obvious answer would be that we're traveling in time all the time, just as we're doing now. But as to the idea of things coming back, I wonder if that isn't a mere laziness of the imagination. I think that we should expect at least some novelty or novelties, perhaps, in the same cyclic pattern.

Coleman: But you have felt the sense of *déjà vu;* it's not absent from your own work.

Borges: Well, it's not absent from my own life, but I'm not looking for it. It has been given me, several times.

Coleman: Is there the possibility, twenty years hence, of occupying the same space and conditions you did twenty years ago at the exact same moment?

Borges: Yes. But if things were exactly the same I wouldn't be aware of it. Let's suppose that it has happened. We're now living in nineteen hundred and . . . and ninety-two. Now, of course, I can't remember it because if I could remember it, if I could recall it, there would be a difference. But if the moment is exactly the same, I can't be expected to remember it. Of course, we all know about that feeling. I'm very fond of a quite forgotten poet, Rossetti, who expressed all that when he said—

> **I have been here before,**
> **But when or how I cannot tell.**
> **I know the grass beyond the door,**
> **The sweet, keen smell,**
> **The sighing wind, the lights around the shore**

—in a poem called "Sudden Light" about the *déjà vu*. I think there's also a passage in Dickens' *David Copperfield* about it, so he must have got the same feeling. But I think that the theory was really worked out logically by David Hume in a book called, I think, *Treatise Concerning Natural Religion,* or some such title. Then it was rediscovered by Nietzsche; and, well, many people have gone over that. Sir Thomas Browne also.

Coleman: I remember "Feeling in Death" from your "New Refutation of Time."

Borges: Exactly. That was back when I got that feeling. That was years and years ago, on the Northside of Buenos Aires.

Coleman: It's just magnificent.

Borges: Yes, I know. One of my best pieces of writing, yes?

Coleman: I think so.

Borges: Well, it was when I wrote it, but still that was ever so long ago.

Coleman: There seems to be a topic that connects with this one.

di Giovanni: "Could you please tell us of your own feelings about death? Do they agree with the statement in one of your stories that refers to death as 'the oblivion that awaits us all'?"

Borges: I think of death as oblivion. I am hungering and thirsting after oblivion. I do not want to be remembered; and—this is most important— I am tired of being myself. In fact, I am tired of being an ego, an "I"; and I suppose that when I'm dust and ashes, then I'll be nothing. I'm looking forward to that prospect. But of course I won't be able to enjoy it because I won't be there.

Coleman: You don't want any repeats in the future life?

Borges: No. I don't want to be threatened by personal immortality of any kind. I only think of an afterlife as a kind of awful possibility, but I think we should rather speak of it as a kind of awful *im*possibility.

di Giovanni: "Does God play an important part in your mystic themes?"

Borges: Well, if you, Sir, are thinking of a personal God, the answer is decidedly no. If you think of God as an ethical purpose, as an intellectual purpose, as what Matthew Arnold called "the something not ourselves that makes for righteousness," in that case I believe in God. Perhaps there is a moral purpose or intellectual purpose to the universe; however, I know nothing about that. I know that I am attempting in my own tiny way to further that purpose by writing quite unimportant short stories.

di Giovanni: "If you were to write in English, would your work have a different impact?"

Borges: Yes, it would, because it would have the full strength of the English language behind it. But I respect English too much to attempt the writing of English. Although I have done most of my reading in English.

di Giovanni: "You've often talked about the 'verbal music of English' and its effect on you. What exactly is that 'verbal music'?"

Borges: When I wrote that down, I wasn't thinking of myself as a writer, but as a reader. I think that English *has* a word music of its own; and it springs, of course, from the fact that it is not merely a Germanic tongue but also a Romance language. To quote the most obvious of all examples, it might make all the difference in the world were I to use, in a poem written in English—but I don't write poems in English—the word "Holy Ghost" or "Holy Spirit," because those words have the same logical meaning and quite a different, let's say, spiritual or literary connotation. You see, the word "ghost" is a fine and a dark word, while the word "spirit" has something light and shining about it. Yet those words are supposed to be synonyms. Of course, far more is the case with such words as "royal" and "kingly" or "brotherly" and "fraternal" or "folk" and "people," and so on. If you read your Bible, you are finding that continual shifting, that rich music, of the Saxon and of the Latin element.

Coleman: I remember an etymology you gave of the Spengler title.

Borges: Der Untergang des Abendlandes. That would be "The Down Going of the Evening Lands," which is far better than *The Decline of the West.* In the German you are made to feel *Untergang* = "under" and "going down." By the way, the word "gangster" comes from the same root, because people thought of those men as walking together. Then there's the same thing in the Scots: *gang* is "to go." *Abendland* is a beautiful word, but it's only used, I think, for literary purposes. I don't think any German would speak of *Abendland* or *Morgenland.* But in Old English I found quite a fine word for the morning—the *morgentid,* "morningtime," or "morningtide." Tennyson translated it as "But when first the great sunstar of morningtide," where he is hinting at a metaphor, where the idea is not only of "tide" in the sense of time, but also the idea of the day as breaking forth in a kind of tide. And then "sunstar"—that's a fine word. In the Saxon we have something perhaps stronger, but different. In the Saxon text of the "Battle of Brunanburh" we read something like "The sun, that famous star"—which is quite fine in its own way.

di Giovanni: "Do you think that the presence of Ortega y Gasset had an intellectual influence in Argentina?"

Borges: Well, I suppose he did, but not for me. I merely had some five minutes' talk with him, and, I think, well—period, full stop.

di Giovanni: "How do you feel about your name's having become an adjective—Borgesian—like other adjectives: Kafkaesque, Dickensian?"

Borges: I think that all those words are impartially ugly, I should say, and I should avoid them. Still, I'm not to blame for that kind of thing.

di Giovanni: "What is mythology to the writer?"

Borges: . . . I am trying to think, and I'm hardly accustomed to that operation. But I think—you see, here I am trying to think *again*—whether he knows it or not, every writer is attempting a mythology. I mean, if we are to live at all, then our work is to become a kind of myth, as even, for example, in the case of Dr. Watson and Sherlock Holmes, Boswell and Johnson. I suppose that every writer creates, even if he doesn't intend to, a small but worldwide mythology of his own. Every writer lives in some

403

kind of inside world; that should be his mythology. But I don't think a writer should take any pains about that, or worry about it. If he's a good writer, that kind of thing is bound to happen.

Coleman: Do you think the worst writers are the ones who end their life in *costumbrismo* or local color or anecdote?

Borges: I dare say you're right, Sir. And you're very brave, because I've always thought the same thing but I've never dared to say so. Here you're saying it before a number of people.

Coleman: But I'm supposed to be the straight man in all this.

Borges: . . . I quite agree with you.

Coleman: I always thought so, reading you, because you escape the vices that have plagued so many different kinds of literature.

Borges: I *think* I escaped them because I began by committing them. According to the Gnostics, you can't get rid of a sin until you've committed it. You're a possible murderer until you have murdered somebody. After the murder, then you're purified and—

Coleman: —you're a saint.

Borges: Yes, yes, maybe you're a saint. So we should try, as Luther had it, *pecca fortiter*, no? Sin strongly. And then in the end you'll be a saint.

di Giovanni: "Could you explain your idea of literary inspiration and shed light on the existing unity between author and work?"

Borges: I can only say that when I am writing, I feel I am being led somewhere by something. I can't go beyond that. I don't think I should talk in terms of the Muse or the Holy Ghost or the subconscious. I know that when I am writing, I am merely a tool, but as to the real name of the tool, I know nothing whatever. So that would be inspiration. But I think that there's another part of the question that I have utterly forgotten. How does it run?

di Giovanni: ". . . and shed light on the existing unity between author and work."

Borges: Well, I fail to see the link between the two parts of the question. I'm being very, very dull, no? After a heavy lunch and so on.

di Giovanni: Well, try this one: "What is the cause-effect relationship in your world of labyrinths?"

Borges: That should be an easy one. I am continually feeling perplexity. I feel, of course, all the common emotions of mankind, but perplexity would be the chief—or, as Chesterton had it, *wonder*. And of course the most obvious symbol of perplexity, the obvious token of amazement, is a maze. So you find only too many mazes in my work, but I'll do my best to get rid of them if I can—to find other symbols—because I'm already a bit tired of my pet symbols.

di Giovanni: "Mallarmé said a poet sculpts his tomb. Would you agree?"

Borges: . . . I wonder what Mallarmé meant by that? And then I might agree or disagree.

di Giovanni: Maybe that means the same thing you wrote in the last paragraph of *El hacedor*.

404

Borges: But what on earth *did* I say in my last paragraph? That's another big mystery!

di Giovanni: About all the elements you write about in your lifetime, and then in the end you find that they trace your own face.

Borges: That's possibly the quotation, but I wonder whether my own face is a tomb? At least I hope it isn't.

di Giovanni: So much for Mallarmé. "Your stories are filled with murders, defenestrations"—what's that?

Borges: That means being thrown out of the window. There are no windows here, so there is no danger.

di Giovanni: Your stories are?

Borges: I don't know. I have never—

Coleman: You have never defenestrated anyone.

Borges: No, not to my knowledge. In any case, I have forgotten it. Well, my stories are full of defenestrations—why not? It's a fine word.

di Giovanni: ". . . and very little sex. How do you feel about humanity?"

Borges: The answer is obvious. I have been worried all my life by falling in love, sex, and that kind of thing.

di Giovanni: Falling out of windows?

Borges: Not yet, but it may happen at any moment. And as to murder, I wonder. I don't think there are many murders. I rather think in terms of men getting themselves killed, but not of men killing other men. I rather think in, let's say, ethical terms. And even in such stories as "La intrusa"— which you will read in due time, as I am told—there is a murder, but I have purposely left out the way it was committed, because I don't go in for being blood-and-thundery. In fact, I rather dislike that kind of thing. We know that "A" killed "B," but we are not told how he did it, and in fact I don't know because I am not too curious about my own creatures. As to love, I think I have written any amount of poems on the subject—not of stories. Perhaps I have written too much. I accuse myself of thinking all the time of some woman or other.

di Giovanni: "Do you see mysticism as a way out of the maze?"

Borges: For all I know, mysticism is the only way; but my gods, whoever they may be, have not allowed me that particular way. So that, as mysticism is denied me, I have to go in for being an amateur student of metaphysics, being a reader of Schopenhauer, of Hume, of Bradley; but except for that one strange experience I had that my friend has remembered ["Feeling in Death"], really I can say very little about mysticism personally, though of course I have studied, I have read my *Varieties of Religious Experience,* and I have done much reading in the mystics, especially Swedenborg, also Blake.

di Giovanni: "Some Argentine writers accuse you of being too abstract and too little of an Argentine. Do you feel at one with your country?"

Borges: Only too much so. At this moment I am not crying for the Carolines, as the song has it, but I'm thinking back on Buenos Aires. I know that Buenos Aires is perhaps the ugliest city on earth; I know it's far too

405

straggling, too uneven, too shabby, too shabby-genteel also, and yet I love it. Perhaps I am too much of an Argentine. But I should be excused for this since I also think of myself as a citizen of Austin, a citizen of Cambridge, Massachusetts, a citizen of Geneva, a citizen of Montevideo, a citizen of Edinburgh, and at this moment, of course, as a citizen of the capital city of the world—New York.

di Giovanni: Do you think that behind the question there's this—that it's impossible to be abstract *and* an Argentine? Is it written somewhere that you can't be both things?

Borges: Well, perhaps it is written somewhere; it's laid up in heaven! But why not be an Argentine and also go in for abstractions? For example, I was a good student of algebra and that doesn't make me less of an Argentine. Also, what does it mean to be an Argentine? It means to be the inheritor of what might be called "Western culture." (And of course if we can get anything from the East, we should grab as much of it as we can.) So that I don't think being Argentine is necessarily a limitation, except in the sense that belonging to some country, some land, is a limitation. Those things can't be helped. I was born in Buenos Aires, so were my people before me, and I may be allowed to be an Argentine, I suppose. In fact, I am—what can I do about it?

di Giovanni: "If you could spend an afternoon in your garden with the beings and beasts from your *Book of Imaginary Beings*—"

Borges: I'd be frightened to death!

di Giovanni: "—or with the beasts from T. H. White's *Bestiary* or with real animals, which would you choose?"

Borges: The answer is easy: I would choose something else.

di Giovanni: "What ever happened to the translation of Whitman's 'Song of Myself' that you undertook many years ago?"

Borges: I'm sorry to say I undertook it, being quite unworthy of the task, and I'm sorry to say it found its way into print. I translated the "Song of Myself" and the "Children of Adam" and then some pieces chosen at random, and they were published in Buenos Aires in a far too expensive edition.

Coleman: Did you take up the translation of Faulkner because you felt it had to be done, or someone asked you, or—

di Giovanni: Or you needed the money?

Borges: At first it was merely hack work. I was asked to do it, and I needed the money. As I went on, I felt I was doing right, and I did my best to do full justice to Faulkner. Of course, once the translation came out in Buenos Aires, people said that I had been betraying Faulkner because they said the sentences were far too long and too involved. Then I had to remind them that perhaps long and involved sentences might be found in the text. Translators are always blamed, no? Texts are always perfect.

di Giovanni: How many translations of Faulkner, Virginia Woolf, and other American writers—

406

Borges: Virginia Woolf is hardly an American writer.

di Giovanni: —and other writers *in English* were done by Leonor Acevedo de Borges?

Borges: Yes, she did the translations, but I *signed* them!

di Giovanni: Did you really do them, or did your mother help you with them? Or did she do them and you polish them?

Borges: No, I think the truth—and I owe you the truth—is that I did some of them and that she polished them.

Coleman: Borges, can I ask you—

Borges: Of course you can!

Coleman: I was just going to ask about your seemingly real attraction to Melville and Hawthorne. I think the nineteenth century in North America attracts you more than the twentieth?

Borges: Oh, far more. No question about it.

Coleman: Could you speak of your interest in Hawthorne as is shown in your lecture in in, I guess it's *Other Inquisitions?*

Borges: I guess it is. As a matter of fact, I was quite a small boy when I read Edgar Allan Poe, and it was many years after that I came to Hawthorne, and I saw that in spite—at least I divined it or I had it—that despite the fact that Hawthorne was thinking along moral lines all the time (most of his stories were intended to be fables or allegories) and Poe wasn't, I think there is a kinship between them—a kinship in the style— but here I'm speaking as a mere foreigner and I may be making any amount of mistakes. Besides, I discovered a story—"discovered" is too ambitious a word—a story by Hawthorne called "Wakefield," and that story is one of the most remarkable stories I've ever read. There I found one of the many forerunners of Kafka, and, strange to say, he wrote that one quite different story when he was a young man. Then he went on to write such books as *The Scarlet Letter, Twice-told Tales,* and so on.

But in the case of nineteenth- and twentieth-century American literature, I don't think we should set one against the other. What I know is this fact: that at least two or perhaps three of America's nineteenth-century writers have had an influence all over the world. I'm speaking, of course, of Poe. Poe was the begetter of Baudelaire, was the begetter of the Symbolists, of Valéry, and so on. Then, of course, I'm thinking in terms of Walt Whitman, and I'm not sure that there are any contemporary American writers who have that kind of interest.

Coleman: You seem to read Henry James in a very dark manner.

Borges: In a very dark manner? Well, he *wrote* in a very dark manner.

Coleman: Most people here in the United States don't look on him as a dark writer.

Borges: Well, I suppose I'm very dull, but I find him dark. I don't only find him dark but also very mazy and very intricate. I find him as intricate, for example, as Frost. When you read Frost and take him at his face value, he seems a quite simple kind of poet. But he's deceptively simple. When I

407

think of Henry James, I'm not thinking of his novels—I think they are rather boring—but of his short stories, and in those stories I think you get labyrinths and mazes, endlessly. But I haven't invented a fancy Henry James for myself.

Coleman: The tales are given short shrift here.

Borges: Well, they shouldn't be, if I may be allowed to make that remark.

di Giovanni: "Would you object if your work in its totality were to be classified as escapist, anti-realist, and neocolonial?"

Borges: No, I shouldn't object. I don't object to *anything* people say about my work, even if they find it good; but if they point out something derogatory to me, I fully agree with them, of course—being a modest man.

di Giovanni: Part two: "If so, is there any aspect of Argentine reality that you have not treated as a mere vehicle for metaphysical 'tripping'?" (I don't think he knows what "tripping" means.)

Borges: "Tripping"? Yes, I know what that means.

Coleman: Viaje en el espacio.

di Giovanni: No, not in this sense you don't.

Borges: Thinking of the light fantastic, too?

Coleman: It's an imaginary voyage induced by drugs.

Borges: In that case I know nothing whatever about it—drugs. Here is my glass of *water* before me. But I may be allowed to say something that may smack of vanity—I *am* a part of Argentine reality.

di Giovanni: "Many of your earlier works reflect the books you read, but your recent works don't—at least not to the same extent. What are the books or authors that interest you now?"

Borges: I lost my sight, for reading and writing purposes, way back in 1955 —the year of the revolution. Since then I've had little time for my contemporaries, so I may have done some rereading or very little reading. And my time is busy. In the morning I work at my own stuff in the National Library; every afternoon I work with my friend Norman Thomas di Giovanni on translating and, I hope, bettering my stuff in English; and at night I may meet a few friends—I'm meeting one at a time because I don't think I know more than six or seven people in Buenos Aires. So all this kind of experience—having to answer questions—is quite new to me. Those things don't happen to me in Buenos Aires, for nobody would stay for an answer, and that's all I can say.

Coleman: When you dictate a story, is it different from when you actually wrote it down?

Borges: The answer to this particular question was revealed to me—was given unto me, may I say biblically—by Norman Thomas di Giovanni last night. He told me—and I think he was telling me the truth—that the simplification that came to me through the fact of living in a colorless world (the only color I can make out is yellow; all the others are much the same) also stands for a simplification in my vision of the world in a metaphysical sense, and in my style also. Even as when nighttime comes

408

and things are simplified, so when night fell on my eyes, things were also simplified for me. As I want to know what I'm writing, as I want to be gazing at what I'm writing, I couldn't very well go in for elaborate, baroque writing; I couldn't go on aping Sir Thomas Browne, for example, or even De Quincey's amazing sentences; and so I fell back on simplicity, and, naturally, not only in style, but I fell back on quite simple, straightforward plots such as in "La intrusa."

di Giovanni: Of course, I was also thinking of the most physical sense of all, having seen Borges' early manuscripts, which were written in the most minuscule possible hand and were keyed in with various kinds of symbols, interpolations, additions, contradictions, and which it would now be physically impossible for him to dictate or to do himself. In other words, he was forced—

Borges: No, no secretary would stand that kind of thing.

di Giovanni: The kind of secretary he has now is very amusing.

Borges: Yes, she is. I feel I have found the right person, because I feel I am quite alone when I am with her. For example, if I dictate a sentence to her and then say "semicolon" or "period," she writes those words down. I tried dictating to my mother, but she was always saying, "No, that's the wrong rhythm," or "That's the wrong word," or "You shouldn't write that." While with my secretary, who shall be nameless here, and to whom I am duly grateful, I feel quite at home. I feel quite at ease, quite alone with myself.

Coleman: You've spoken about how you were stuck at one point in "La intrusa."

Borges: Yes, and my mother gave me the words. "La intrusa" is a rather nasty story about hoodlums, and my mother hated it thoroughly. I was dictating it to her, and she said: "God, what an awful story! Promise me this is the last time you'll try your hand at this kind of stuff." I said yes, dutifully, knowing I was lying all the time. But there was a moment when something quite important had to be said by one of the characters, and then I stopped. My mother said, "Well, what has happened to you?" And I said, "I don't know what the man said." She said: "I know quite well what he said," and then she gave me the key word I was looking for. Now, of course, she denies the anecdote, saying it was made up by myself because she is thoroughly ashamed of the story.

Coleman: How does the line go? *"A trabajar, hermano"?*

Borges: That's it. A man has to tell his brother that he has killed the woman they are both in love with. He has done that out of friendship, because he thinks that the friendship is far more important than the woman or than any woman. Now the man had to blurt that out to his brother, and I would have committed the capital sin of saying, "I killed her," and that would have spoiled the whole story; but my mother found—being a *criolla,* coming from old Argentine and Uruguayan stock—she found the right word. She made him say: "Now, to work, brother. I killed her this morning." And then they go on to bury her. I have to thank her for that gift—well, for many gifts.

Coleman: We're coming to the end—

di Giovanni: I think we have more time—

Coleman: No, we're being thrown out at four-thirty.

di Giovanni: Out the window.

Borges: We're being defenestrated. . . . I'm quite enjoying all this. . . . I wonder where the Chinaman is, eh? He hasn't shown up yet.

Coleman: Oh, the Maoist. I can see him. In fact, I'm looking at him right now.

Man from audience: A Maoist is convenient; a Castroite is convenient.

Coleman: I'm sure we have other adversaries of your literary principles, but they're being very courteous.

Borges: Well, I suppose they're as timid as I am, and I can beat anyone at timidity. That, of course, is a form of boasting also.

Coleman: Norman, do you have one more question?

di Giovanni: "Could you write a story about revolution and still view it in metaphysical terms?"

Borges: As a matter of fact, I am going to write a story about a revolution, about our revolution in 1955, and it won't be metaphysical. I have a plot. That plot has been haunting me since—since 1955. When I get back to Buenos Aires, I'll set it down, and it will be, I think, my finest story, because it is a story of friendship, and friendship is perhaps the best thing to be had in my country. The story will be called, as a matter of fact, "Los amigos"—"The Friends." That's all I'm allowed to reveal now.

Man from audience: May a Maoist ask a question? How do you define revolution? I've heard of the revolution of 1955, but as far as I am concerned it would not be a revolution at all—

Borges: Wasn't it? They threw Perón out!

Man: However you might want to characterize—

Borges: It *was* a revolution. I have known people—

Man: A social revolution? What changes were there, really?

Borges: Well, there was a big change. Now we have gentlemen governing us, and then we had hoodlums. I think, ethically, that should be enough.

Man: They are the same *military* gentlemen.

Borges: No. They are not.

Man: You've had a series—nine, I think, in the last three years.

Borges: No. But if you think of military men, you should think of the military men we have in the Argentine. They are quite mild and quite harmless and well meaning. But Perón was a hoodlum, a rascal. Well, I . . . I . . . I . . . I . . . I . . . I . . . I can hardly mention his name because I think . . . I think his . . . his name is obscene, somehow. Perhaps because my sister was in prison, my mother was in prison, my nephew was in prison, I was . . . I was being followed by a detective; and still more because I have known people who were tortured to death. And even during Perón's regime no man dared to say that he was a *peronista* because people would have laughed at him.

410

They made it very clear that if they were *peronistas,* it was because it suited their convenience, because he was filling their pockets. And I had to live all through that time, and in fact I should know something about it.

di Giovanni: Borges, would you like to say something about your newest story?

Borges: "El Congreso" is a story that has been haunting me for the last thirty or forty years. I thought I should be worthy of that plot, but as time went on I felt that I had no such hope. I was always telling it to my friends, and then one of my friends said: "Well, the story is already there. Why don't you write it down?" And so I did. It is a story about a mystical experience. (The Congress is not the Argentine Congress, of course.) The story is about a mystical experience I never had, but maybe before I die I'll be allowed to have it. I can say no more—the story hasn't been published as yet. It may be, for all I know, my best story or my justification as a storyteller.

411

Index:
homage to Borges
JOHN HOLLANDER

Bourbaki, Nicholas, 219.

Chinese Boxes, *see* "Mirrored Mirrors."

Conus gloria maris, 346.

Dreams, 2, 4, 6, 8, 10, 12; of dreaming, 3, 5, 7, 9, 11; the White King's dream of Alice, 67.

Deneb, 42; believed to be something else, 43, 53, 63, 73; tale of, 83; irregularities in the spectrum of, 84.

"Dr. Jekyll" (pseud.), 68; his descendents in South America, 69.

"Enigma Variations" (Elgar), 333.

Examples in philosophy, 7, 5, 12; dictionary of, 371.

Fermat's "last theorem," 222 (margin).

Fibonacci, Leonardo, 13, 21, 34, 55, 89, 144, 233, 377.

France (baldness of the present king of), 146.

Frege's "Venus," 147.

Godel, Kurt, xix.

Holy of Holies, 175; contents listed, 176ff.

I, i.

James, M. R., 333.

Jews, the, 88n., and the Borges question, 144.

Marmape (Goodman's), 351.

Mathews, Harry, 222.

McFleery, I. I., 214; the pomma, 214n.

Milverton, Charles Augustus, *see* "The Adventure of Charles Augustus Milverton."

Moran, Col. Sebastian, 312.

Necronomicon, 179n.

"Nightsoil, Mustapha" (pseud.), 180.

Norman, ii–xviii.

One Million Random Digits (Published by Rand Corporation), 3, 9, 7, 5, 8.

Paradoxes, *passim;* Burali-Forti's, 354; Epimenides', 354; Niemand's, 354; Rollo's, 354; Russell's, 354; Weyl's, 354; pseudo-paradox of Minsky, 355.

Portugal, Fritz, i.

Portugal, John (*see* Portugal, Fritz).

Psalm #47 (Shakespeare's hand in translation of), 47.

Quaker Oats Package regression, *see* "Mirrored Mirrors."

Reliquaries, 22, 238.

Reminiscence, 48, 167.

Checklist of the principal works of Jorge Luis Borges
COMPILED BY
NORMAN THOMAS DI GIOVANNI

1. Spanish first editions

Fervor de Buenos Aires
(Privately printed, 1923)

Inquisiciones
(Proa, 1925)

Luna de enfrente
(Proa, 1925)

El tamaño de mi esperanza
(Proa, 1926)

El idioma de los argentinos
(Gleizer, 1928)

Cuaderno San Martín
(Proa, 1929)

Evaristo Carriego
(Gleizer, 1930)

Discusión
(Gleizer, 1932)

Las kenningar
(Colombo, 1933)

Historia universal de la infamia
(Tor, 1935)

Historia de la eternidad
(Viau y Zona, 1936)

El jardín de senderos que se bifurcan
(Sur, 1942)

Seis problemas para don Isidro Parod
with Adolfo Bioy Casares
(Sur, 1942)

Poemas [1922–1943]
(Losada, 1943)

Ficciones
(Sur, 1944)

Dos fantasías memorables
with Adolfo Bioy Casares
(Oportet & Haereses, 1946)

Un modelo para la muerte
with Adolfo Bioy Casares
(Oportet & Haereses, 1946)
Nueva refutación del tiempo
(Oportet & Haereses, 1947)

El Aleph
(Losada, 1949)

Aspectos de la literatura gauchesca
(Número, 1950)

Antiguas literaturas germánicas
with Delia Ingenieros
(Fondo de Cultura Económica,
1951)

La muerte y la brújula
(Emecé, 1951)

Otras inquisiciones 1937–1952
(Sur, 1952)

El lenguaje de Buenos Aires
with José Edmundo Clemente
(Peña, Del Giudice, 1953)

El "Martín Fierro"
with Margarita Guerrero
(Columba, 1953)

Poemas 1923–1953
(Emecé, 1954)

Los orilleros
El paraíso de los creyentes
with Adolfo Bioy Casares
(Losada, 1955)

La hermana de Eloísa
with Luisa Mercedes Levinson
(ENE, 1955)

Leopoldo Lugones
with Betina Edelberg
(Troquel, 1955)

Manual de zoología fantástica
with Margarita Guerrero
(Fondo de Cultura Económica,
1957)

Poemas 1923–1958
(Emecé, 1958)

La poesía gauchesca
(Centro de Estudios Brasileiros,
1960)

El hacedor
(Emecé, 1960)

Antología personal
(Sur, 1961)

Obra poética 1923–1964
(Emecé, 1964)

Introducción a la literatura inglesa
with María Esther Vázquez
(Columba, 1965)

Literaturas germánicas medievales
with María Esther Vázquez
(Falbo, 1965)

Para las seis cuerdas
(Emecé, 1965)

Obra poética 1923–1966
(Emecé, 1966)

Obra poética 1923–1967
(Emecé, 1967)

Crónicas de Bustos Domecq
with Adolfo Bioy Casares
(Losada, 1967)

Introducción a la literatura
norteamericana
with Esther Zemborain de Torres
(Columba, 1967)

El libro de los seres imaginarios
with Margarita Guerrero
(Kier, 1968)

Cuentos
(Centro Editor, 1968)

Nueva antología personal
(Emecé, 1968)

Elogio de la sombra
(Emecé, 1969)

Fervor de Buenos Aires
(Emecé, 1969)

Luna de enfrente y Cuaderno
San Martín
(Emecé, 1969)

El otro, el mismo
(Emecé, 1969)

El informe de Brodie
(Emecé, 1970)

El Congreso
(El Archibrazo, 1971)

El oro de los tigres
(Emecé, 1972)

2. English translations

Labyrinths
(New Directions, 1962)

Ficciones
(Grove Press, 1962)

Dreamtigers
(University of Texas Press, 1964)

Other Inquisitions 1937–1952
(University of Texas Press, 1965)

A Personal Anthology
(Grove Press, 1967)

The Book of Imaginary Beings
with Margarita Guerrero
(E. P. Dutton, 1969)

The Aleph and Other Stories
1933–1969
(E. P. Dutton, 1970)

Extraordinary Tales
with Adolfo Bioy Casares
(Herder and Herder, 1971)

An Introduction to American
Literature
with Esther Zemborain de Torres
(University of Kentucky Press,
1971)

Doctor Brodie's Report
(E. P. Dutton, 1972)

Selected Poems 1923–1967
(Delacorte, 1972)

A Universal History of Infamy
(E. P. Dutton, 1972)

On Borges in English

Borges the Labyrinth Maker
by Ana María Barrenechea
(New York University Press, 1965)

The Cyclical Night
by L. A. Murillo
(Harvard University Press, 1968)

The Narrow Act: Borges' Art of
Allusion
by Ronald Christ
(New York University Press, 1969)

Conversations with Jorge Luis
Borges
by Richard Burgin
(Holt, Rinehart and Winston, 1969)

The Mythmaker
by Carter Wheelock
(University of Texas Press, 1969)

Jorge Luis Borges
by Martin Stabb
(Twayne, 1970)

Jorge Luis Borges
by Jaime Alazraki
(Columbia University Press, 1971)

The Cardinal Points of Borges
*edited by Lowell Dunham and Ivar
Ivask*
(University of Oklahoma Press,
1971)

Contributors

MARY KINZIE has studied comparative literature in Ohio, Chicago, Berlin, and currently at Johns Hopkins University. She has been associated with *TriQuarterly* since 1966. **NORMAN THOMAS DI GIOVANNI** is Borges' principal English-language translator. He recently left Buenos Aires after a stay of three and a half years and now resides in England, where he is at work on the sixth and seventh of the ten volumes of Borges' prose and verse to be published by E. P. Dutton. He is also the co-editor of the forthcoming *Borges on Writing*. **ADOLFO BIOY CASARES** is the distinguished Argentine novelist and short story writer. Two of his novels, *Diario de la guerra del cerdo* and *Sueño de los héroes,* and two short story collections, *Historias fantásticas* and *Historias de amor,* will be published shortly in English translation. His *The Invention of Morel and Other Stories* appeared here in 1965. He has also written several works in collaboration with Borges. **CARTER WHEELOCK** is the author of *The Mythmaker: A Study of Motif and Symbol in the Short Stories of Jorge Luis Borges,* published in 1969 by University of Texas Press. **HUMBERTO M. RASI,** born and raised in Buenos Aires, became acquainted with Borges in the fifties while attending the lectures he gave on English and American writers. He is currently chairman of the Modern Language Department at Andrews University in Michigan. **ALASTAIR REID** has published three volumes of poetry and numerous books for children. His volume of new and selected poems is scheduled to appear next year. He is currently poet-in-residence at St. Andrews University in Scotland. **ANTHONY KERRIGAN** was conceived in Panama, born in Massachusetts, and reared in Cuba. He is presently at work on a ten volume edition of *The Selected Works of Miguel de Unamuno* for Princeton University Press and the Bollingen Foundation. He has published two volumes of verse, edited two collections of work by Borges, and published the first translations of Borges in 1952. **BEN BELITT** has translated Borges, Neruda, Lorca, and many others. His fourth and most recent volume of verse is *Nowhere but Light.* **JAIME ALAZRAKI** is professor of Spanish literature at the University of California, San Diego. He has published two books on Borges (*La prosa narrativa de Jorge Luis Borges* and *Jorge Luis Borges*), and one on Neruda (*Poética y poesía de Pablo Neruda*). He studied the Kabbalah at the Hebrew University in Jerusalem, and heard the last lectures given there by

Martin Buber. **FRANK MACSHANE** heads the writing program at Columbia University, and is the author of a biography of Ford Madox Ford. **EMIR RODRÍGUEZ MONEGAL** teaches contemporary Latin American literature at Yale. He is the author of two books on Borges, *El juicio de los parricidas* and *Borges par lui même,* and is currently at work on a literary biography of Borges to be published by E. P. Dutton in 1973. **RICHARD HOWARD** is the translator of a dozen sonnets in the *Selected Poems of Jorge Luis Borges,* as well as the author of four volumes of poetry, the third of which, *Untitled Subjects,* won the Pulitzer Prize for 1970. **R. H. W. DILLARD** teaches at Hollins College in Virginia. He is the author of three books of poems, *The Day I Stopped Dreaming About Barbara Steele, News of the Nile,* and *After Borges.* **JOHN C. MURCHISON** teaches at the University of British Columbia. In 1967-1968 he was Borges' personal secretary while both were at Harvard. **JOHN WRIGHT** teaches at the University of Michigan. He recently produced a relief-etched facsimile of William Blake's illuminated relief etchings for *Songs of Innocence and Experience.* **ALEXANDER COLEMAN** teaches at New York University. **NÉSTOR IBARRA,** an old friend of Borges, is an Argentine who has been living in Paris for years. Borges calls him "my French translator." **RONALD CHRIST** teaches English at Livingston College, Rutgers University, and is the editor of *Review '72,* an English-language journal devoted to Latin American literature. **JOHN HOLLANDER**'s latest book of poems is *Night Mirror.* Two more of his books are scheduled to appear this fall under the titles *City & Country Matters* (Godine) and *The Immense Parade on Supererogation Day & What Happened to It* (Atheneum). **ROBERT ALTER** teaches at the University of California at Berkeley. His *Defenses of the Imagination,* a collection of essays on modern literature, will be published next year. **E. RUBINSTEIN** is an associate professor at Richmond College, CUNY. **KENNETH FIELDS** is the author of a book of poems, *The Other Walker,* which was published last fall. He teaches at Stanford University, where he is writing a book on the poetry of Yvor Winters. **VICTORIA OCAMPO** was the editor of the Argentine magazine *Sur,* which, for a number of years, was Borges' main publisher. In Buenos Aires, Argentina, **JORGE LUIS BORGES** learned Zeno's paradoxes and the magic and music of language from his father.